Søren Kierkegaard's Journals and Papers

SØREN KIERKEGAARD'S JOURNALS AND PAPERS

Volume 7, Index and Composite Collation

EDITED AND TRANSLATED BY

Howard V. Hong and Edna H. Hong

ASSISTED BY GREGOR MALANTSCHUK

INDEX PREPARED BY

Nathaniel J. Hong and Charles M. Barker

INDIANA UNIVERSITY PRESS

BLOOMINGTON AND LONDON

This book has been brought to publication with the assistance of a grant from Carlsberg Fondet.

Library of Congress Cataloging in Publication Data
(Revised)

Kierkegaard, Søren Aabye, 1813-1855.
 Søren Kierkegaard's journals and papers.

  Translation of portions of the 20 volume Danish work published 1909-48 under title: Papirer.
  Includes bibliographies.
  1. Philosophy—Collected works. I. Hong, Howard Vincent, 1912- ed. II. Hong, Edna (Hatlestad) 1913- ed. III. Malantschuk, Gregor.
B4372.E5H66 1967 198'.9 67-13025
ISBN 0-253-18246-8 (vol. 7) 1 2 3 4 5 82 81 80 79 78
    0-253-18239-5 (complete set, vols. 1-7)

Preface

The present volume contains an Index and a Composite Collation for *Søren Kierkegaard's Journals and Papers,* volumes 1-6. Its purpose is to permit readers to locate writings on a given theme in the present English edition and to provide a means of reference to corresponding entries in the original Danish edition: *Søren Kierkegaards Papirer,* edited by P. A. Heiberg, V. Kuhr, and E. Torsting, I-XI³ (20 vols.) (Copenhagen: Gyldendal, 1909-1948); 2nd edition, I-XI³ and supplementary volumes XII-XIII, edited by Niels Thulstrup (Copenhagen: Gyldendal, 1968-1970). This work is referred to herein as *Papirer.*

Entries in volumes 1-4 of the *Journals and Papers* are organized by topical sections, alphabetically arranged, while volumes 5-6 contain autobiographical entries, chronologically arranged. Volumes 5-6 also include some of Kierkegaard's letters, translated from *Breve og Akstykker vedrørende Søren Kierkegaard*, I-II, edited by Niels Thulstrup (Copenhagen: Munksgaard, 1953). This work is referred to herein as *Breve.*

Acknowledgement is gratefully given to the National Endowment for the Humanities and to the St. Olaf College Humanities Research Fund for financial support in the preparation of the Index. N. J. Cappelørn, editor of the Index to *Søren Kierkegaards Papirer*, has given good counsel and assistance. N. J. H. and C. M. B. have done a quietly heroic work. *Tak.*

Kierkegaard Library   H. V. H.
St. Olaf College   E. H. H.
Northfield, Minnesota

v

Søren Kierkegaard's Journals and Papers

Index

Plan of the Index

Rubrics printed in small capitals (ABSURD) refer to the alphabetically arranged topical sections in *Søren Kierkegaard's Journals and Papers (J.P.)*, volumes 1-4. For the central group of entries on a theme for which there is a topical section, see the appropriate volume of *J.P.* Entry numbers given in the index cite references to that subject *in addition* to those in the topical sections.

Rubrics in regular type (Aarhus) are subjects not represented by topical sections.

Entries pertaining to Søren Kierkegaard are marked (S.K.): Childhood (S.K.), Engagement (S.K.), Family (S.K.).

Each entry is designated by two numbers: 5452 (III A 52). The first is the serial number in *J.P.*; the second, in parentheses, is the corresponding reference to the Danish *Papirer*. In successive citations of the same volume and section of the *Papirer*, the volume and section designations are omitted: 6308 (x^1 A 39), 6347 (118). References to letters from the *Breve* are marked L.: 6702 (L. 162).

Serial numbers appear in *J.P.*, 1-6, as follows:

Volume 1, A-E	1-1093
Volume 2, F-K	1094-2303
Volume 3, L-R	2304-3828
Volume 4, S-Z	3829-5050
Volume 5, Autobiographical	5051-6140
Volume 6, Autobiographical	6141-6969

Index

Aarhus. 5452 (III A 52), 5453 (53), 5466 (71), 5472 (79).

Abaris. 1774 (IV A 21).

Abelard, Peter. 2722 (x^3 A 594), 5596 (IV C 43), 5609 (IV A 31), 5703 (177).

Abgarus. 288 (II A 276), 5351 (270).

Ability. 975 (x^1 A 430), 990 (x^3 A 248).

Abraham. 11 (x^6 B 80), 12 (81), 298 (II A 569), 374 (VIII^1 A 629), 1081 (x^2 A 180), 2222 (x^4 A 572), 2223 (x^5 A 132), 2672 (x^4 A 454), 3020 (338), 3130 (x^2 A 594), 3269 (II A 790), 3380 (538), 3714 (x^4 A 357), 4003 (II A 446), 4641 (x^2 A 129), 4665 (x^3 A 774), 4806 (XI^1 A 329), 5394 (II A 490), 5485 (III C 4), 5641 (IV A 77), 6598 (x^6 B 68), 6791 (x^4 A 458).

Abraham and Isaac. 298 (II A 569), 908 (IV B 67), 1109 (76), 2223 (x^5 A 132), 3020 (x^4 A 338), 3189 (II C 8), 3714 (x^4 A 357), 5640 (IV A 76).

Abraham of St. Clara. 1538 (XI^2 A 5), 2000 (VIII^1 A 201), 2229 (IX A 470), 3741 (VIII^1 A 211), 3787 (203), 4307 (x^3 A 425), 5062 (II A 12), 5917 (VII^1 A 41), 6024 (VIII^1 A 204), 6027 (212), 6028 (VIII^2 C 2:1-61), 6044 (VIII^1 A 252).

Absolute. 485 (IX A 284), 486 (292), 487 (297), 488 (300), 492 (394), 504 (x^1 A 72), 659 (IX A 127), 1376 (305), 1578 (II A 454), 1606 (v B 41), 1612 (VIII ^{1} A 14), 1877 (x^3 A 409), 2017 (x^1 A 463), 2534 (x^4 A 25), 3613 (x^3 A 193), 3710 (x^2 A 624), 4449 (IX A 194), 4680 (x^4 A 456), 6323 (x^1 A 72), 6528 (x^2 A 184).

Absolute relationship. 844 (x^2 A 617), 1376 (IX A 305).

ABSTRACT, ABSTRACTION. 629 (VI A 115), 705 (v A 68), 1309 (II A 237), 1328 (IV A 102), 1347 (VII^1 A 139), 1348 (143), 1587 (III A 1), 1606 (v B 441), 1904 (x^4 A 354), 1967 (I A 337), 2166 (x^3 A 275), 2172 (XI^1 A 25), 2324 (x^2 A 235), 3301 (v B 14, pp. 73-76), 3757 (x^3 A 560), 3815 (I A 294), 4955 (I A 164), 5181 (I A 328), 6410 (x^1 A 377).

ABSURD. 575 (x^3 A 760), 1123 (VIII^1 A 649), 1124 (661), 1125 (672), 1348 (VII^1 A 143), 1642 (IX A 196), 2096 (XI^1 A 268), 2287 (VI B 42), 2532 (x^4 A 7), 2591 (IV A 78), 2803 (x^2 A 529), 3707 (x^1 A 66), 3710 (x^2 A 624), 4782 (549), 6373 (x^1 A 187), 6598 (x^6 B 68).

Acceptance. 1160 (v A 83).

Accidental. 3652 (IV C 71), 5522 (III A 167).

Accommodation. 223 (IX A 475), 329 (x^1 A 201), 409 (XI^2 A 349), 497 (x^1 A 217), 510 (x^2 A 37), 554 (XI^1 A 324), 557 (349), 561 (XI^2 A 102), 567 (VII^1 A 162), 608 (VIII^1 A 354), 612 (x^2 A 57), 613 (397), 614 (XI^2 A 80), 647 (VIII^1 A 564), 946 (223), 1081 (x^2 A 180), 1084 (x^3 A 27), 1478 (269), 1541 (I A 340), 1786 (x^3 A 312), 1882 (552), 2089 (430), 2221 (293), 2510 (x^2 A 334), 2563 (XI^1 A 37), 2665 (462), 2711 (x^3 A 175), 2994 (XI^{2}A 146), 3013 (IX A 273), 3246 (I A 98), 3602 (XI^1 A 364), 4341 (x^4 A 226), 4901 (613), 4904 (x^5 A 40), 6172 (IX A 83), 6415 (x^1 A 406), 6688 (x^3 A 550).

Accountability. 854 (I A 254).

"The Accounting." 6388 (x^1 A 266), 6407 (351), 6737 (x^4 A 85).

Acknowledgment. 3886 (XI^2 A 59).

Acorn analogy. 6880 (XI^1 A 206).

A-cosmism. 2712 (x^3 A 558).

ACTION.
—Action of the Apostles. 169 (x¹ A 432), 2961 (x⁴ A 100).
—Christian action. 212 (x³ A 60), 675 (x² A 19), 1099 (III A 36), 1142 (x⁴ A 114), 1324 (III A 101), 1489 (x⁵ A 8), 1818 (xI² A 201), 1868 (x³ A 277), 1869 (283), 1873 (331), 1902 (x⁴ A 349), 1931 (xI¹ A 338), 1940 (xI² A 434), 2118 (vIII² B 91:13), 2119 (vIII¹ A 511), 2423 (x¹ A 489), 2509 (x² A 263), 2542 (x⁴ A 451), 2870 (x³ A 32), 2874 (169), 2894 (x⁵ A 15), 3023 (xI¹ A 339), 3349 (x³ A 482), 3506 (246), 3672 (IX A 474), 4185 (x³ A 346), 4917 (xI² A 204), 4933 (x³ A 470), 5041 (x⁴ A 306), 5067 (I C 34), 5100 (I A 75), 6212 (IX A 179), 6326 (x¹ A 77), 6580 (x² A 413), 6645 (x³ A 189), 6755 (x⁴ A 231), 6780 (383), 6801 (545), 6806 (566).
—Communication of action. 637 (vII¹ A 123), 646 (vIII¹ A 554), 665 (IX A 439), 668 (x¹ A 185), 815 (IX A 289), 6302 (x¹ A 15), 6821 (x⁴ A 651).
—Ethical and ethical-religious action. 774 (IV A 72), 896 (IV C 96), 902 (IV A 112), 912 (V A 72), 1064 (x⁴ A 62), 1243 (IV C 56), 1685 (II A 81), 1830 (x⁴ A 479), 2534 (x⁴ A 25), 2894 (x⁵ A 15), 2911 (xI¹ A 395), 3021 (x⁴ A 403), 3465 (V A 12), 3693 (x⁴ A 289), 3705 (IX A 365), 3707 (x¹ A 66), 3711 (x² A 636), 3793 (IV A 156), 3871 (xI² A 362), 3879 (xI¹ A 178), 3952 (x³ A 707), 4383 (xI² A 33), 4438 (vII² B 266:26), 4470 (x⁴ A 160), 4491 (xI² A 73), 4765 (x⁴ A 138), 4813 (xI² A 76), 4839 (IV C 125), 4914 (xI¹ A 568), 5116 (I B 2), 5897 (vII¹ A 110), 6342 (x¹ A 111), 6395 (320), 6412 (385).
Activism. 469 (vIII¹ A 357), 1037 (vI A 139), 3621 (xI¹ A 213).
"The Activity of a Traveling Esthetician." 6282 (IX A 432).
Actors. 149 (V A 97), 156 (vII¹ A 51), 3145 (x³ A 93), 4965 (x² A 143), 4970 (x³ A 561).
Actuality (see also REALITY). 37 (III A 3), 149 (V A 97), 199 (vI B 54:12), 258 (IV C 47), 508 (x¹ A 558), 511 (x² A 141), 823

(x⁴ A 580), 826 (xI¹ A 394), 859 (II A 165), 934 (vII¹ A 138), 940 (vIII¹ A 143), 973 (x¹ A 395), 1047 (vIII¹ A 226), 1048 (234), 1051 (IX A 154), 1054 (382), 1059 (x² A 439), 1201 (III A 215), 1245 (IV C 62), 1444 (xI² A 53), 1445 (98), 1462 (x⁴ A 582), 1587 (III A 1), 1606 (V B 41), 1828 (x³ A 616), 1832 (xI¹ A 288), 2309 (II A 155), 2310 (156), 2311 (157), 2312 (158), 2359 (xI² A 103), 2500 (x¹ A 595), 3345 (x² A 114), 3346 (202), 3347 (x³ A 16), 3348 (290), 3349 (482), 3350 (x⁵ A 143), 3839 (x⁴ A 264), 4056 (xI² A 106), 4326 (x¹ A 417), 4797 (x¹ A 581), 4829 (IV C 113), 5049 (xI² A 50), 5535 (III A 179), 5575 (IV A 197), 5891 (vII¹ A 104), 6536 (x² A 205), 6846 (xI² A 296).
Adam. 26 (I A 149), 35 (II A 383), 51 (V B 53:15), 102 (x² A 22), 282 (II A 197), 698 (xI¹ A 362), 1034 (vI A 65), 1190 (II A 31), 1541 (I A 340), 2269 (II A 526), 2806 (I A 31), 3003 (xI¹ A 185), 3363 (II A 69), 3801 (I A 140), 3993 (II A 117), 3998 (90), 4411 (358), 5003 (xI¹ A 281), 5092 (I A 72).
Adresseavisen. 5647 (IV A 88).
Adherent. 1854 (x¹ A 631), 5949 (vII¹ A 184), 6102 (vIII¹ A 507), 6415 (x¹ A 406), 6592 (x² A 544).
Adiaphora. 866 (II A 306).
Adler, Adolph P. (see also "Book on Adler"). 234 (vIII² B 13, pp. 61-63), 1348 (vII¹ A 143), 1611 (153), 2020 (x⁶ B 52:1), 2846 (vII² B 256:20), 3026 (vIII² B 15), 3088 (vII² B 256:9-10), 3202 (235, pp. 113-114), 3203 (257:12, p. 288 and note), 3204 (IX B 5:2y), 4437 (vII² B 256:19), 4438 (266:26), 5549 (III B 130), 5679 (L. 83), 5935 (vII² B 236-270), 5936 (242), 5939 (vII¹ A 150), 5940 (154), 5944 (158), 5968 (vII² B 235, pp. 5-230), 5969 (270), 6014 (vIII¹ A 164), 6044 (252), 6049 (264), 6079 (440), 6114 (562), 6220 (IX A 189), 6334 (x¹ A 90), 6346 (116), 6387 (263).
Admiration. 635 (vI B 129), 810 (V A 35), 813 (vIII¹ A 270), 814 (530), 823 (x⁴ A 580), 961 (IX A 314), 963 (372), 974 (x¹ A 412), 1848 (IX A 101), 1895 (x⁴ A 148), 1900 (321), 2760 (x⁴ A 531), 4430

(VI A 123), 4454 (X¹ A 134), 4704 (XI¹ A 8), 4711 (357), 4849 (VII¹ A 32), 4888 (XI¹ A 508).

Admission. 174 (X³ A 187), 536 (X⁴ A 581), 1415 (X³ A 658), 1440 (XI¹ A 381), 1617 (X⁴ A 385), 1796 (80), 1803 (XI¹ A 194), 1849 (IX A 323), 1885 (X³ A 666), 1901 (X⁴ A 340), 1904 (354), 1961 (91), 2038 (104), 2081 (XI² A 135), 2121 (X¹ A 564), 2301 (X⁴ A 247), 2437 (482), 2530 (X³ A 533), 2559 (X⁴ A 446), 2685 (XI² A 427), 2710 (X² A 464), 2725 (XI¹ A 187), 2870 (X³ A 32), 2881 (541), 2902 (XI¹ A 73), 2907 (155), 2971 (234), 3135 (IX A 201), 3212 (XI² A 325), 3317 (X⁵ A 113), 3335 (X³ A 580), 3497 (X² A 581), 3579 (X⁴ A 614), 3585 (XI¹ A 202), 3617 (XI² A 305), 3663 (XI¹ A 33), 3688 (X⁴ A 128), 3729 (X³ A 608), 3731 (X⁴ A 30), 3831 (120), 4183 (X² A 643), 4241 (356), 4339 (X³ A 705), 4363 (XI² A 378), 4469 (X⁴ A 125), 4479 (X⁵ A 95), 4495 (XI¹ A 63), 4499 (348), 4519 (X¹ A 429), 4524 (X⁴ A 639), 4532 (XI³ B 47), 4681 (X⁴ A 481), 4764 (137), 4909 (XI¹ A 351), 4930 (IX A 351), 4951 (X³ A 617), 6070 (VIII¹ A 388), 6103 (508), 6188 (IX A 134), 6344 (X¹ A 113), 6391 (281), 6503 (X² A 75), 6529 (191), 6645 (X³ A 189), 6665 (389), 6684 (487), 6685 (519), 6688 (550), 6699 (599), 6723 (X⁴ A 9), 6727 (33), 6761 (296), 6774 (358), 6776 (367), 6780 (383), 6795 (511), 6802 (554), 6822 (661), 6832 (X⁵ A 43), 6843 (146), 6853 (XI¹ A 1), 6854 (XI³ B 15), 6862 (XI¹ A 72), 6911 (551), 6922 (XI² A 40), 6943 (XI³ B 53), 6946 (56), 6947 (57).

Adoration. 1929 (XI¹ A 158).

Adulthood. 266 (II A 41), 1669 (I A 125).

Adversity (see also COLLISION; Conflict). 1046 (VIII¹ A 127), 1610 (VI B 98:45), 1657 (X³ A 360), 2196 (VIII¹ A 322), 4783 (X¹ A 550), 6016 (VIII¹ A 171).

Aelianus, Cladius. 4289 (X⁴ A 490).

Aeschylus. 5571 (III A 209).

Aesop. 2374 (X¹ A 371).

Aetius. 1430 (X⁴ A 567).

Affectation. 933 (VII¹ A 89).

Aftenbladet. 6098 (VIII¹ A 496).

Age. 804 (III A 95), 1797 (X⁴ A 146), 4414

(II A 500), 6521 (X² A 157), 6638 (X⁶ B 163), 6811 (X⁴ A 592).

Age, the. 471 (VIII¹ A 435), 2636 (418).

Agerskov, Christian. 6339 (X¹ A 104).

Agnes and the Merman. 5668 (IV A 113).

Agorakritos from Paros. 2396 (IV A 195).

Agricola, M. 5580 (IV C 9).

Agrippa, Cornelius. 5699 (IV A 170).

Ahasuerus. 3941 (X² A 350).

Ahlefeldt, Elias C. 5473 (III A 80).

Aladdin. 973 (X¹ A 393), 4928 (II A 451), 5509 (III A 149), 5628 (IV A 215).

Alberg, Conradine C. 5483 (Letter 29).

Albertus Magnus. 5595 (IV C 42), 5700 (IV A 174).

Alcedo ispida. 1023 (II A 612).

Alcibiades. 2444 (XI¹ A 356), 4250 (IV A 203), 4262 (V B 4:3), 4263 (23:1), 4300 (XI¹ A 428), 4302 (448), 5613 (IV A 43).

Ale-Norse. 5740 (V A 58), 5819 (VI A 73), 5832 (VI B 235).

Alexander. 270 (IX A 395), 1404 (X² A 591), 3537 (XI² A 27), 4219 (X⁴ A 575).

Alexandrians. 1154 (XI² A 380).

Algebraic. 1606 (V B 41), 6137 (VIII¹ A 652).

Alien. 4650 (X³ A 114).

Alienation. 3639 (X² A 156), 5493 (III A 97), 6263 (IX A 321).

Alkamenes from Athens. 2396 (IV A 195).

Allegory. 3807 (I A 214), 3816 (306), 4781 (X² A 548).

Aloneness. 1973 (II A 643), 1979 (400), 1985 (III A 236), 4613 (VIII¹ A 582).

Also. 4914 (XI¹ A 568).

Ambrose. 2609 (X² A 566), 4210 (X⁴ A 155), 4669 (156).

Ameipsias. 4258 (IV A 211).

America. 2906 (XI¹ A 154).

Amor. 3978 (IV A 28), 4381 (X² A 462).

Analogy. 162 (VIII¹ A 122), 1258 (X² A 159), 1399 (241).

Anaxagoras. 5921 (VII¹ A 44).

ANCIENTS, THE (see also Classical; GREEKS).

Anders (see Christensen, Anders).

Andersen, Hans Christian. 5077 (I C 46), 5211 (II A 42), 5339 (768), 5348 (781), 5668 (IV A 113), 5988 (VIII¹ A 44), 6360 (X¹ A 146).

Andersen, Jens. 5108 (I A 71).
Andresen, Jacob A. 5465 (III A 69).
Angels. 830 (XI² A 331), 1693 (II A 105), 2070 (XI¹ A 455), 4509 (X⁴ A 438), 5646 (IV A 87), 6969 (XI² A 439).
Anger. 3905 (X¹ A 493), 6022 (VIII¹ A 197).
Animals. 33 (II A 743), 802 (III A 219), 1367 (IX A 75), 1940 (XI² A 434), 2337 (222).
Annunciation. 2672 (X⁴ A 454).
Anonymity. 137 (II A 412), 154 (VII¹ A 12), 366 (XI¹ A 483), 2051 (82), 2152 (VIII¹ A 540), 2153 (IX A 200), 2164 (X² A 314), 2650 (X¹ A 16), 2932 (VIII¹ A 656), 3219 (XI¹ A 51), 3224 (XI² A 107), 3728 (X³ A 326), 4078 (II A 703), 5374 (II A 389), 6074 (VIII¹ A 407).
ANSELM. 532 (X⁴ A 212), 1423 (211), 3615 (210).
Anthony, St. 2175 (II A 304).
Anthropocentricity. 2685 (XI² A 427).
ANTHROPOLOGY.
—Christian anthropology. 334 (X¹ A 279), 390 (X² A 453), 419 (I A 172), 489 (IX A 329), 536 (X⁴ A 581), 554 (XI¹ A 324), 570 (IX A 472), 588 (264), 1237 (II A 752), 1261 (X² A 428), 1383 (X¹ A 59), 1463 (I A 37), 1473 (X² A 219), 1767 (XI² A 189), 1802 (XI¹ A 130), 1943 (X⁴ A 471), 2022 (X² A 457), 2066 (XI¹ A 384), 2333 (XI² A 37), 2384 (II A 462), 2437 (X⁴ A 482), 2467 (IX A 11), 2682 (XI² A 326), 3031 (IX A 322), 3032 (427), 4023 (X¹ A 637), 4183 (X² A 643), 4349 (XI¹ A 363), 4483 (475), 4485 (481), 4712 (377), 4885 (352), 4909 (351), 6076 (VIII¹ A 415), 6469 (X¹ A 644), 6881 (XI¹ A 209), 6882 (210).
—Philosophy of man. 92 (II A 191), 97 (V B 53:23), 684 (X¹ A 51), 749 (VIII² B 168:6), 795 (I A 150), 850 (141), 896 (IV C 96), 903 (IV A 131), 913 (V B 148:38), 914 (207:3), 936 (VII¹ A 172), 992 (X³ A 715), 1005 (XI¹ A 528), 1014 (VIII¹ A 665), 1015 (IX A 44), 1022 (II A 610), 1052 (IX A 358), 1053 (359), 1073 (V B 213:2), 1114 (V C 13:4), 1123 (VIII¹ A 649), 1164 (41), 1176 (XI¹ A 522), 1241 (IV C 39), 1243 (56), 1405 (X² A 644), 1614 (426), 1683 (II A 79), 1777 (IX A 423), 1810 (XI¹ A 432), 1818 (XI² A 201),

1825 (XI³ B 199), 1940 (XI² A 434), 1944 (I A 151), 2006 (IX A 91), 2010 (356), 2067 (XI¹ A 384), 2079 (XI² A 124), 2082 (149), 2203 (X⁵ A 183), 2274 (III A 5), 2323 (VIII¹ A 110), 2337 (XI² A 222), 2353 (VI A 33), 2907 (XI¹ A 55), 2944 (IX A 490), 2973 (XI¹ A 287), 2980 (512), 2986 (XI² A 88), 3214 (VII¹ A 10), 3261 (II C 55), 3558 (X¹ A 666), 3582 (X⁶ B 55), 3587 (XI¹ A 450), 3588 (467), 3834 (XI¹ A 271), 3896 (VII¹ A 47), 4227 (X⁶ B 93), 4231 (XI¹ A 330), 4295 (X⁵ A 133), 4341 (X⁴ A 226), 4400 (II A 163), 4453 (X¹ A 50), 5307 (II A 712), 5792 (VI B 18), 6075 (VIII¹ A 414), 6158 (IX A 55), 6392 (X¹ A 289).
Anthropomorphism. 76 (X² A 491), 280 (II A 133), 857 (150), 858 (151), 1348 (VII¹ A 143), 2561 (X⁵ A 47), 3102 (XI² A 212).
Anti-Christ. 4742 (X⁴ A 312).
Anti-Climacus.
—Practice in Christianity. 677 (X² A 367), 679 (X³ A 624), 1891 (750), 2958 (656), 3685 (545), 4483 (XI¹ A 475), 4727 (XI² A 82), 6686 (X³ A 526), 6687 (530), 6699 (599), 6914 (XI¹ A 475).
—Pseudonym. 10 (X⁶ B 79), 695 (X³ A 653), 6142 (IX A 9), 6350 (X¹ A 121), 6431 (510), 6433 (517), 6439 (530), 6442 (536), 6445 (546), 6446 (548), 6450 (557), 6461 (593), 6462 (594), 6464 (615), 6501 (X² A 66), 6511 (106), 6515 (126), 6517 (147), 6519 (148), 6521 (157), 6526 (177), 6528 (184), 6530 (192), 6532 (195), 6578 (393), 6656 (X³ A 265), 6671 (415), 6690 (555), 6713 (769), 6762 (X⁴ A 299), 6797 (513), 6810 (587), 6518 (X⁵ B 206), 6600 (X⁶ B 77), 6601 (82), 6770 (4:3), 6786 (145), 6434 (L. 213).
—The Sickness unto Death. 102 (X² A 22), 1531 (500), 3567 (X¹ A 679), 4029 (X² A 429), 4030 (436), 4549 (231), 6535 (204), 6689 (X³ A 551).
Antigone. 5546 (III C 37), 5569 (III A 207), 5669 (IV A 114).
Antiquity. 852 (I A 221), 995 (X⁴ A 176), 4118 (VIII¹ A 123), 4119 (134).
Antisthenes. 5600 (IV C 83).
ANXIETY. 44 (IV B 173), 265 (II A 12), 341

(x¹ A 503), 505 (472), 636 (vii¹ A 91), 918 (vi A 35), 1145 (x⁴ A 455), 1167 (viii¹ A 537), 1248 (v B 55:26), 1260 (x² A 243), 1294 (viii¹ A 395), 1327 (iii A 131), 1401 (x² A 493), 1481 (x³ A 410), 1489 (x⁵ A 8), 1510 (viii¹ A 333), 2066 (xi¹ A 384), 2140 (x³ A 672), 3557 (v B 53:9), 3628 (vii¹ A 130), 4023 (x¹ A 637), 4366 (viii¹ A 48), 4367 (93), 4370 (ix A 333), 4374 (x¹ A 477), 5146 (i A 179), 5383 (ii A 420), 5519 (iii A 164), 5588 (iv c 10), 5622 (iv A 65), 5730 (v B 53:26), 5732 (v A 34), 5743 (71), 6274 (ix A 411).

Apathy. 5251 (ii A 637).

Aphorisms. 766 (ii A 709), 2770 (x² A 5), 3190 (ii A 396), 3558 (x¹ A 666), 5186 (i A 333), 5631 (iv A 221), 6398 (x¹ A 325), 6787 (x⁶ B 253), 6788 (254).

Apollonius. 144 (iv c 109), 3289 (iv A 19).

Apologetics. 186 (x¹ A 188), 340 (x¹ A 447), 474 (ix A 2), 502 (x¹ A 443), 503 (467), 760 (x³ A 575), 1144 (x⁴ A 422), 1915 (x⁴ A 626), 3030 (ix A 253), 3842 (x⁴ A 279), 3862 (280), 6708 (x³ A 663).

Apologist. 2662 (x⁴ A 108).

APOSTLE. 169 (x¹ A 432), 352 (x² A 422), 949 (viii¹ A 312), 1062 (x³ A 725), 1293 (vii² B 261:8), 1415 (x³ A 658), 1440 (xi¹ A 381), 1693 (ii A 105), 1901 (x⁴ A 340), 1913 (521), 1914 (556), 1922 (x⁵ A 88), 2057 (xi¹ A 190), 2556 (xi² A 266), 2653 (x¹ A 333), 2724 (xi¹ A 186), 2961 (x⁴ A 100), 3088 (vii² B 256:9), 3213 (xi³ B 175), 3531 (x⁵ A 117), 3703 (viii² B 16:8), 3861 (x⁴ A 110), 3865 (xi¹ A 461), 3899 (x¹ A 65), 4313 (x⁴ A 555), 4617 (ix A 17), 4658 (x³ A 382), 4738 (x⁴ A 86), 4900 (x⁴ A 569), 4971 (x³ A 570), 5646 (iv A 87), 6049 (viii¹ A 264), 6220 (ix A 189), 6407 (x¹ A 351), 6532 (x² A 195), 6727 (x⁴ A 33), 6903 (xi¹ A 460), 6918 (xi² A 21), 6921 (36), 6924 (45).

—The Twelve Apostles. 182 (viii¹ A 225), 237 (x² A 194), 581 (i A 108), 689 (i A 50), 1410 (x³ A 373), 1785 (x³ A 268), 2056 (xi¹ A 189), 2092 (x² A 578), 2854 (i A 26), 2897 (x⁵ A 78), 2901 (xi¹ A 26), 2907 (155), 2908 (157), 3042 (xi¹ A 482), 3346 (x² A 202), 3522 (x⁴ A 330), 3680 (x³ A 232), 4695 (x⁴ A 670), 4939

(538), 5088 (i A 59), 5945 (vii¹ A 160), 6951 (xi² A 377).

Appearance (phenomenon). 3099 (xi² A 51).

Applause. 2741 (vii¹ A 38), 5649 (iv A 90).

Appropriation. 449 (ii A 577), 1497 (xi² A 284), 1858 (x² A 255), 2046 (x⁵ A 121), 4549 (x² A 231), 5646 (iv A 87), 5792 (vi B 18).

Approximation. 2287 (vi B 42), 5790 (16).

A priori. 252 (i A 316), 865 (ii A 303), 2257 (301), 2275 (iii A 9).

Aptitude. 5650 (iv A 91).

Apuleius. 4381 (x⁴ A 462).

Aquinas, Thomas. 1906 (x⁴ A 369), 5543 (Letter 55).

Arabia. 5503 (iii A 142).

Archimedean point. 117 (i A 8), 2089 (x³ A 430), 3426 (ix A 115), 5092 (i A 72), 5099 (68), 5100 (75), 5378 (ii A 406), 5410 (548), 5468 (iii A 73), 5740 (v A 58), 6519 (x² A 148).

Archimedes. 1235 (ii A 281), 2665 (xi¹ A 462), 3988 (xi² A 143), 5099 (i A 68), 5740 (v A 58).

Aridity. 739 (ii A 484).

Aristides. 6856 (xi¹ A 6).

Aristippus. 3328 (x² A 608), 4278 (598), 6036 (viii¹ A 228).

Aristocracy. 3221 (xi¹ A 341), 4113 (vii¹ A 163), 4114 (212), 5941 (155), 5979 (viii¹ A 23), 6085 (452).

Aristocrat. 2058 (xi¹ A 260), 4119 (viii¹ A 134), 5961 (vii¹ A 221), 6074 (viii¹ A 407), 6270 (ix A 381), 6628 (x³ A 142).

Aristophanes. 154 (vii¹ A 12), 1088 (x⁴ A 590), 2814 (vii¹ A 194), 4256 (iv A 209), 4257 (210), 5192 (i c 124), 6284 (ix A 432), 6392 (x¹ A 289), 6602 (x² A 605).

ARISTOTLE. 7 (x² A 354), 143 (iv c 104), 144 (109), 627 (vi A 17), 628 (19), 702 (5), 824 (x⁴ A 633), 892 (iv c 16), 893 (17), 1057 (x² A 328), 1148 (x⁴ A 635), 1182 (ii A 29), 1332 (iv A 157), 1597 (iv c 65), 1941 (v A 75), 2281 (iv c 23), 2353 (vi A 33), 2365 (iv c 31), 2373 (x¹ A 363), 2441 (x⁵ A 34), 2590 (iv c 28), 2617 (xi¹ A 150), 2624 (xi² A 154), 2783 (x³ A 508), 3219 (xi¹ A 51), 3284 (iii A 107), 3292 (iv c 25), 3300 (v A 98), 3652 (iv c 71), 3784 (19), 3892 (26), 3988 (xi²

A 143), 4104 (IV A 9), 4107 (VI A 1), 4252 (IV A 205), 4254 (207), 4309 (x⁴ A 466), 4341 (226), 4418 (IV A 10), 4826 (IV C 110), 4832 (116), 4835 (119), 4839 (125), 5571 (III A 209), 5576 (IV A 8), 5589 (IV C 15), 5590 (18), 5591 (22), 5592 (24), 5598 (45), 5600 (83), 5602 (98), 5606 (124), 5611 (IV A 36), 5618 (63), 5712 (V A 100), 5742 (V C 11), 5779 (VI C 2), 5780 (3), 5781 (4), 5782 (5), 5786 (VI A 146), 5977 (VIII² C 1), 6037 (VIII¹ A 229), 6794 (x⁴ A 488).

Armed Neutrality. 1781 (x¹ A 646), 1958 (IX A 260), 1962 (x⁴ A 553), 2357 (VIII¹ A 681), 3733 (x⁴ A 117), 5341 (II A 770), 6239 (IX A 229), 6325 (x¹ A 74), 6329 (84), 6337 (95), 6416 (422), 6421 (450), 6487 (678), 6649 (x³ A 204), 6739 (x⁴ A 101).

Arnauld, Anton. 3037 (x³ A 622), 3109 (609).

Arndt, Johann. 1404 (x² A 591), 1949 (IX A 391), 2864 (384), 3431 (426), 3446 (x² A 496), 3463 (XI¹ A 11), 3771 (x⁵ A 53), 4026 (x² A 400), 4926 (x³ A 83), 5920 (VII¹ A 43), 6264 (IX A 338).

Arnim, Ludwig A. v. 3553 (II A 558), 3554 (559), 3783 (III A 85), 5159 (I C 101), 5215 (II A 51), 5221 (70), 5482 (L. 27).

ART. 508 (x¹ A 558), 619 (II A 624), 637 (VII¹ A 123), 646 (VIII¹ A 554), 653 (VIII² B 85), 663 (IX A 240), 678 (x² A 466), 755 (III A 92), 761 (IX A 114), 784 (II A 6), 797 (791), 800 (III A 12), 804 (95), 809 (IV C 106), 810 (V A 35), 811 (VI A 25), 815 (IX A 289), 817 (x¹ A 502), 818 (523), 819 (x² A 137), 820 (392), 821 (x³ A 151), 825 (x⁶ B 233), 827 (XI¹ A 570), 973 (x¹ A 393), 1027 (III A 62), 1051 (IX A 54), 1177 (I A 88), 1178 (104), 1179 (I C 58), 1180 (I A 227), 1400 (x² A 443), 1458 (V A 57), 1562 (XI¹ A 501), 1624 (II A 729), 1625 (I A 148), 1627 (242), 1698 (II A 114), 1757 (IX A 399), 1761 (x¹ A 148), 1942 (VIII¹ A 643), 2253 (II A 698), 2322 (V B 115:2), 2570 (XI² A 54), 2788 (I A 291), 2860 (VII¹ A 83), 2907 (XI¹ A 155), 2911 (395), 2924 (VIII¹ A 132), 3305 (VI A 113), 3325 (159), 3512 (x³ A 479), 3535 (XI¹ A 477), 3558 (x¹ A 666), 3559 (x³ A 52), 3610 (x² A 446), 3796 (I A

130), 3805 (200), 4168 (x² A 240), 4353 (XI¹ A 538), 4553 (x² A 336), 4594 (VIII¹ A 32), 5134 (I C 87), 5199 (123), 5206 (II A 21), 5240 (116), 5351 (270), 5361 (312), 5592 (IV C 24), 6227 (IX A 213), 6360 (x¹ A 146), 6491 (x² A 15), 6511 (106), 6521 (157), 6647 (x³ A 191), 6665 (389), 6716 (780), 6717 (782).

Art and life. 808 (IV C 105).

ARTIST. 676 (x² A 146), 1782 (474), 3305 (VI A 133).

ARTISTIC, THE. 487 (IX A 297), 1932 (XI¹ A 391), 2911 (395).

Artistic distance. 2359 (XI² A 103).

Ascension. 622 (V A 18), 1835 (V B 237), 2735 (II A 87).

ASCETICISM. 14 (x³ A 342), 597 (521), 676 (x² A 146), 899 (IV A 92), 1090 (x⁴ A 652), 1199 (172), 1399 (x² A 291), 1408 (x³ A 264), 1860 (x² A 326), 1866 (x³ A 272), 1893 (766), 1915 (x⁴ A 556), 2123 (x³ A 156), 2484 (x¹ A 213), 2513 (x² A 558), 2518 (x³ A 153), 2542 (x⁴ A 451), 2550 (XI¹ A 193), 2608 (x² A 181), 2612 (x³ A 419), 2712 (588), 2755 (216), 2760 (x⁴ A 531), 2762 (XI¹ A 134), 3182 (532), 3487 (x² A 95), 3497 (581), 3877 (XI¹ A 144), 3881 (181), 3883 (537), 4057 (XI² A 161), 4710 (XI¹ A 350), 4730 (XI² A 396), 6592 (x² A 544), 6647 (x³ A 191), 6696 (190), 6812 (x⁴ A 603), 6843 (x⁵ A 146), 6911 (XI¹ A 551), 6966 (XI² A 436).

Association. 2047 (XI¹ A 16), 2063 (368), 2064 (369), 2065 (370), 2074 (518), 2919 (387), 2968 (16), 4069 (I A 304), 4176 (x² A 479), 4186 (x³ A 529), 4231 (XI¹ A 330), 4335 (x³ A 493), 4887 (XI¹ A 438), 5044 (248), 5046 (257).

Association of ideas. 5294 (II A 688).

Astronomy. 2286 (VI B 40:5), 4106 (V A 77), 4386 (I A 121).

Atheism. 3606 (V B 40:11).

Athenæum. 6829 (x⁶ C 6), 6861 (XI¹ A 71).

Athenæus. 5602 (IV C 98).

Atlas. 4351 (XI¹ A 498).

Atomism. 3815 (I A 294).

Atonement (*see also* Reconciliation). 304 (VIII¹ A 83), 693 (x¹ A 132), 902 (IV A 112), 983 (x² A 208), 1223 (x³ A 573), 1305 (I A 30), 1329 (IV A 104), 1347 (VII¹ A 139), 1348 (143), 1423 (x⁴ A 211),

1469 (x¹ A 507), 1471 (x² A 189), 1473 (219), 1877 (x³ A 409), 1909 (x⁴ A 491), 1911 (499), 1919 (x⁵ A 44), 1921 (87), 1936 (xɪ¹ A 573), 2139 (x² A 203), 2461 (vɪɪ¹ A 192), 2651 (x¹ A 119), 2792 (vɪɪɪ² B 133:5), 3044 (xɪ² A 163), 3078 (ɪv A 116), 3093 (x² A 501), 3261 (ɪɪ c 55), 3637 (x¹ A 462), 4011 (vɪɪɪ¹ A 284), 4013 (497), 4016 (ɪx A 341), 4366 (vɪɪɪ¹ A 48), 5634 (ɪv A 234), 5991 (vɪɪɪ¹ A 49), 6092 (472), 6110 (558), 6210 (ɪx A 176), 6494 (x² A 39).

Aubain, St. 2105 (x⁵ A 162).

Auction. 128 (ɪ A 245), 6964 (xɪ¹ A 411).

Audit, auditing. 3865 (xɪ¹ A 461), 6168 (ɪx A 72), 6224 (208), 6754 (x⁴ A 288), 6919 (xɪ² A 31), 6912 (36), 6943 (xɪ³ B 53).

Augsburg Confession. 600 (x⁴ A 246), 1216 (vɪɪɪ¹ A 675), 2459 (ɪɪ A 434), 4035 (x² A 473).

AUGUSTINE. 29 (ɪ A 101), 191 (xɪ¹ A 436), 1154 (xɪ² A 380), 1193 (x² A 564), 1197 (x⁴ A 170), 1199 (172), 1210 (vɪɪɪ¹ A 459), 1268 (x⁴ A 175), 1269 (177), 2400 (ɪv B 148), 2551 (xɪ¹ A 297), 2580 (ɪɪ A 375), 2584 (471), 2759 (x⁴ A 374), 3614 (162), 3642 (174), 3667 (ɪx A 121), 3864 (x⁵ A 134), 4047 (x⁴ A 173), 4299 (xɪ¹ A 371), 4470 (x⁴ A 160), 4670 (158), 4877 (161).

Augustinianism. 1565 (ɪ A 225).

Augustus. 2750 (vɪɪɪ¹ A 403), 4064 (ɪ A 180), 4419 (ɪv A 18), 4500 (xɪ¹ A 534).

AUTHORITY. 174 (x³ A 187), 181 (xɪ² A 328), 207 (vɪɪɪ¹ A 20), 234 (vɪɪɪ² B 13:61-63), 635 (vɪ B 129), 764 (x² A 271), 1112 (v A 32), 1199 (x⁴ A 172), 1258 (x² A 159), 1785 (x³ A 268), 1793 (670), 1904 (x⁴ A 354), 2204 (384), 2283 (ɪv c 99), 2512 (x² A 448), 2886 (x⁴ A 122), 2888 (260), 2921 (xɪ² A 403), 2929 (vɪɪɪ¹ A 461), 3016 (x³ A 383), 3088 (vɪɪ² B 256:9-10), 3218 (x² A 312), 3703 (vɪɪɪ² B 16:8), 3861 (x⁴ A 110), 4893 (x¹ A 625), 4922 (xɪ¹ A 296), 5703 (ɪv A 177), 6307 (x¹ A 37), 6447 (551), 6503 (x² A 75), 6614 (x³ A 67), 6746 (x⁵ A 166), 6924 (xɪ² A 45), 6943 (xɪ³ B 53).

Authority and Revelation. 5968 (vɪɪ² B 235, pp. 5-230), 5969 (270).

Authors' author. 160 (vɪɪɪ¹ A 53), 6547 (x² A 242).

Authorship. 493 (ɪx A 414), 670 (x¹ A 235), 5865 (vɪɪ¹ B 83), 6094 (vɪɪɪ¹ B 186), 6157 (ɪx A 54), 6205 (171), 6216 (185), 6248 (265), 6254 (288), 6268 (375), 6283 (448), 6308 (x¹ A 39), 6347 (118), 6357 (139), 6360 (146), 6388 (266), 6391 (281), 6396 (322), 6416 (422), 6431 (510), 6461 (593), 6467 (640), 6520 (x² A 150), 6522 (158), 6523 (163), 6525 (174), 6561 (281), 6580 (413), 6647 (x³ A 191), 6652 (239), 6654 (258), 6698 (591), 6737 (x⁴ A 85), 6770 (x⁶ B 4:3), 6786 (145, pp. 202-203), 6817 (x⁴ A 628), 6818 (629), 6842 (x⁶ B 232, pp. 371- 378), 3872 (xɪ¹ A 136).

Authorship, aim of. 6152 (ɪx A 42).

Autumn. 2833-2835 (ɪv A 89-91), 2840-2845 (vɪɪ¹ B 205-210), 5269 (ɪɪ A 185).

Averages. 1072 (ɪv c 75).

Awakened, the. 535 (x⁴ A 516).

Awakening. 6096 (vɪɪɪ¹ A 486), 6344 (x¹ A 113), 6347 (118), 6367 (162), 6387 (263), 6436 (520), 6450 (557), 6461 (593).

Awareness. 1367 (ɪx A 75), 2442 (x⁵ A 50), 3957 (x⁴ A 523), 4153 (ɪx A 445), 4764 (x⁴ A 137), 5979 (vɪɪɪ¹ A 23), 5987 (42), 6070 (388), 6108 (549), 6205 (ɪx A 171), 6512 (x² A 109), 6533 (196), 6577 (375), 6578 (393), 6592 (544), 6647 (x³ A 191), 6680 (450), 6712 (742).

Baader, Franz v. 420 (ɪ A 174), 1190 (ɪɪ A 31), 3990 (ɪ c 31), 4863 (x¹ A 448), 5066 (ɪ c 27-33), 5200 (ɪɪ A 7), 6460 (x¹ A 588).

Bacon, Francis. 3298 (v A 31), 4883 (xɪ¹ A 57).

Baden, Torkel. 5926 (vɪɪ¹ A 55).

Badminton. 4201 (x⁴ A 51).

Baggesen, Jens I. 1581 (ɪɪ A 808), 3803 (ɪ A 155), 3816 (306), 4355 (xɪ² A 41), 5125 (ɪ c 78), 5134 (87), 5208 (ɪɪ A 35), 5481 (L. 23), 5749 (v A 91).

Ballads. 132 (ɪɪ A 636), 5136 (ɪ A 147), 5204 (ɪɪ A 585).

Balle's *Lærebog.* 6294 (L. 195).

Balloting (*see* Voting).

Banknote. 5725 (v A 3), 5738 (52).

Baptism. 273 (ɪ A 28), 368 (xɪ² A 25), 426

(II A 628), 452 (V A 10), 494 (IX A 461), 537 (x⁴ A 616), 540 (658), 543 (x⁵ A 114), 602 (XI¹ A 546), 1174 (x³ A 506), 1494 (x⁵ A 103), 1655 (x² A 452), 3086 (VI B 98:82), 4344 (x⁴ A 617), 4656 (x³ A 281).

Barfod, Poul F. 5832 (VI B 235), 5909 (VII¹ A 124).

Barrabas. 612 (x² A 57), 2930 (VIII¹ A 471), 2931 (477), 5367 (II A 346).

Bashfulness. 78 (x³ A 501), 6333 (x¹ A 89).

Basil. 399 (x⁴ A 147), 531 (149), 1494 (x⁵ A 103), 2667 (XI² A 68).

Bath cure. 6043 (VIII¹ A 250).

Bauer, Bruno. 1233 (II A 74), 2211 (71), 3605 (96), 3998 (90), 5222 (92), 5355 (II C 62).

Baur, Ferdinand C. 4243 (II A 186), 5363 (II C 32).

Bayer, Karl. 4110 (VII¹ A 20), 5883 (23).

Bayle, Pierre. 40 (IV C 32), 41 (33), 2363 (IV A 29), 3073 (IV C 29), 4249 (IV A 202).

Beaumarchais, Sophie. 5808 (VI A 44).

Beauty. 797 (II A 791), 799 (III A 10), 885 (135), 932 (VII¹ A 73), 4576 (I A 115), 4846 (IV C 95), 5368 (II A 347), 5510 (III A 150), 5591 (IV C 22), 5606 (124).

Becoming (see also CHANGE). 593 (x¹ A 552), 1057 (x² A 328), 1635 (IV C 35), 2011 (IX A 450), 2045 (x⁵ A 97), 2345 (V c1), 2450 (XI² A 8), 3294 (IV A 54), 3716 (x⁴ A 528), 3852 (x² A 416), 3853 (417), 4319 (VII¹ C 1), 4322 (4), 4363 (XI² A 378), 4933 (x³ A 470), 5712 (V A 100).

Before God. 6146 (IX A 25).

Beginning. 193 (II C 37), 768 (V A 70), 912 (72), 1136 (x² A 371), 2292 (VII¹ A 34), 3306 (VI A 145), 4916 (XI² A 60).

BEING. 263 (x² A 324), 1057 (328), 1578 (II A 454), 1598 (IV A 66), 1599 (67), 1602 (79), 1603 (81), 2011 (IX A 450), 2103 (XI¹ A 500), 3852 (x² A 416), 3853 (417), 3959 (II A 797), 4316 (IV C 69), 4918 (XI² A 205), 5798 (VI c1).

Being-in-and-for-itself. 536 (x⁴ A 581), 1449 (XI² A 133), 4902 (x⁴ A 636), 6679 (x³ A 448).

Benevolence. 1516 (x⁴ A 269).

Bentham, Jeremy. 3641 (x⁴ A 74).

Beranger, Pierre Jean de. 5136 (I A 147).

Berlin. 5506 (III A 146), 5512 (155), 5513 (L. 49), 5538 (III A 180), 5541 (190), 5542 (L. 54), 5543 (L. 55), 5544 (L. 56), 5548 (L. 62), 5549 (III B 130), 5550 (132), 5551 (L. 68), 5552 (L. 69), 5654 (IV A 101), 5655 (L. 80), 5679 (L. 83), 5807 (VI A 42), 5924 (VII¹ A 129), 5978 (VIII¹ A 18), 6013 (163), 6032 (219), 6035 (227), 6041 (246), 6043 (250), 6472 (x⁵ A 149).

Berlingske Tidende. 5884 (VII¹ A 26), 6564 (x² A 302), 6874 (XI¹ A 142).

BERNARD OF CLAIRVAUX. 1517 (x⁴ A 278), 1930 (XI¹ A 306), 2722 (x³ A 594), 2899 (x⁵ A 135), 4295 (133), 5015 (x³ A 589), 6703 (636).

Betrayal. 586 (II A 522).

BIBLE (see also NEW TESTAMENT; Old Testament). 99 (VII¹ A 248), 101 (x¹ A 353), 182 (VIII¹ A 225), 297 (II A 473), 342 (x¹ A 587), 418 (I A 97), 458 (VII¹ A 239), 459 (243), 463 (VIII¹ A 157), 574 (x³ A 755), 578 (I A 56), 581 (108), 1025 (II A 725), 1144 (x⁴ A 422), 1408 (x³ A 264), 1439 (XI¹ A 359), 1637 (V B 64), 1785 (x³ A 268), 1960 (659), 2225 (XI¹ A 151), 2325 (x⁴ A 197), 2327 (199), 2328 (313), 2358 (x¹ A 361), 2425 (635), 2478 (32), 2501 (630), 2552 (XI¹ A 298), 2653 (x¹ A 333), 2854 (I A 26), 2859 (VI A 111), 2865 (x¹ A 221), 2876 (x³ A 233), 2877 (328), 2884 (590), 2888 (x⁴ A 260), 2890 (428), 2903 (XI¹ A 107), 2905 (138), 2911 (395), 3012 (VIII¹ A 69), 3021 (x⁴ A 403), 3704 (IX A 248), 3851 (II A 242), 4781 (x² A 548), 4782 (549), 5089 (I A 60), 5334 (II C 3), 5419 (36), 5436 (10), 5697 (IV A 162), 5788 (VI B 14), 6688 (x³ A 550).

—Favorite text (S.K.) (see Favorite Bible text).

Biblical texts, Old Testament.
—Deuteronomy. 2486 (x¹ A 303).
—Ecclesiastes. 52 (V B 55:4), 1988 (235), 3786 (VII¹ B 147), 4485 (XI¹ A 481), 5383 (II A 420), 6096 (VIII¹ A 486), 6152 (IX A 42).
—Esther. 3941 (x² A 350).
—Exodus. 2212 (II A 354), 5343 (772).
—Genesis. 1306 (II A 73), 5423 (567).
—Isaiah. 1346 (VII¹ A 81), 4352 (XI¹ A 524).
—Job. 1386 (x¹ A 196), 5993 (VIII¹ A 68).

—Judith. 3822 (III A 197).
—Proverbs. 6038 (VIII¹ A 232), 6190 (IX A 137).
—Psalms. 52 (V B 55:4), 1429 (X⁴ A 485), 2497 (X¹ A 474), 4616 (VIII¹ A 633), 5362 (II A 319), 5419 (II C 36), 5436 (10), 6213 (IX A 180), 6745 (X⁴ A 195).
—I Samuel. 5385 (II A 422).
—II Samuel. 1404 (X² A 591).
Biblical texts, New Testament.
—Acts. 410 (I A 4), 2300 (X¹ A 577), 2857 (II A 368), 5057 (I C 11-12), 5436 (II C 10).
—Colossians. 5069 (I C 36), 5070 (37).
—I Corinthians. 2525 (X³ A 302), 3197 (X² A 41), 3807 (I A 214), 3916 (IV C 1), 3936 (X² A 50), 4328 (65), 4520 (X³ A 684), 4521 (685), 5059 (I C 16), 5089 (I A 60), 5205 (II A 20), 5361 (312), 5961 (VII¹ A 221), 6494 (X² A 39).
—II Corinthians. 1705 (II A 147), 4644 (X² A 246), 6029 (VIII¹ A 217), 6323 (X¹ A 72), 6553 (X² A 273).
—Ephesians. 2414 (VIII¹ A 521), 2535 (X⁴ A 54), 2856 (II A 149), 3191 (III C 23), 5060 (I C 17), 5068 (35).
—Galatians. 272 (X² A 320), 349 (170), 2207 (I A 48), 3191 (III C 23), 3199 (X³ A 467).
—Hebrews. 144 (IV C 109), 4745 (II A 366), 5369 (361), 5371 (373), 5375 (395), 5376 (397), 5918 (VII¹ A 42).
—James. 976 (X¹ A 457), 2507 (X² A 244), 6769 (X⁴ A 323), 6800 (X⁴ A 540), 6965 (XI³ B 291:4).
—John. 74 (X² A 407), 311 (VIII¹ A 371), 325 (IX A 368), 479 (20), 677 (X¹ A 480), 940 (VIII¹ A 143), 1652 (IX A 337), 2268 (II A 525), 2673 (X⁴ A 520), 2713 (II C 5), 2857 (II A 368), 2863 (IX A 355), 2866 (X¹ A 287), 3421 (VIII¹ A 532), 3608 (X¹ A 481), 3920 (VIII¹ A 266), 3924 (386), 3998 (II A 90), 4911 (XI¹ A 516), 5060 (I C 17), 5313 (II A 730), 5425 (574).
—Luke. 59 (VII¹ A 206), 74 (X² A 407), 279 (II A 97), 326 (IX A 440), 364 (XI¹ A 45), 816 (X¹ A 248), 837 (VIII¹ A 56), 1127 (IX A 319), 1317 (II A 408), 1833 (324), 1861 (X² A 347), 2717 (VIII¹ A 65), 2868 (X¹ A 482), 3663 (XI¹ A 33), 3776 (116), 3837 (X² A 51), 3900 (X¹ A 255), 3917 (VIII¹ A

260), 3924 (386), 3957 (X⁴ A 523), 4407 (II A 321), 4408 (339), 4973 (X⁴ A 178), 5055 (I C 7), 5060 (17), 5328 (II A 232), 5548 (L. 62), 5961 (VII¹ A 221), 5976 (VIII¹ A 16), 6270 (IX A 381), 6494 (X² A 39), 6495 (40), 6831 (X⁵ A 33).
—Mark. 369 (XI² A 95), 2001 (VIII¹ A 262), 2273 (II A 550), 2725 (XI¹ A 187), 4906 (7), 5055 (I C 7), 5463 (III A 66), 5961 (VII¹ A 221), 6152 (IX A 42).
—Matthew. 74 (X² A 407), 345 (73), 387 (58), 764 (271), 2508 (245), 2523 (221), 2649 (IX B 63:13), 2685 (XI² A 427), 2794 (I A 168), 2864 (IX A 384), 2893 (X⁴ A 607), 2913 (XI¹ A 571), 3420 (VIII² B 107), 3480 (X¹ A 19), 3936 (X² A 50), 3937 (51), 4055 (XI¹ A 562), 4577 (II A 761), 4648 (X² A 513), 4738 (X⁴ A 86), 4961 (VIII² C 3:5), 4973 (X⁴ A 178), 4985 (XI¹ A 563), 5055 (I C 7), 5060 (17), 5480 (Letter 21), 5961 (VII¹ A 221), 6116 (VIII¹ A 570), 6130 (637), 6552 (X² A 261), 6831 (X⁵ A 33).
—I Peter. 5992 (VIII¹ A 61), 6494 (X² A 39).
—Philippians. 2383 (II A 370), 3645 (X² A 296), 3915 (III C 1), 5069 (I C 36), 5542 (L. 54), 6146 (IX A 25), 6359 (X¹ A 143).
—Revelation. 204 (II A 287), 3936 (X² A 50).
—Romans. 51 (V B 53:15), 2509 (X² A 263), 3190 (II C 8), 3191 (23), 3916 (IV C 1), 3993 (II A 117), 3994 (63), 4033 (X² A 467), 4352 (XI¹ A 524), 5060 (I C 17), 5223 (II A 98), 5435 (II C 9), 5455 (III A 55), 5480 (L. 21), 5548 (L. 62), 6146 (IX A 25).
—I Thessalonians. 816 (X¹ A 248), 5069 (I C 36), 5960 (VII¹ A 220).
—II Thessalonians. 2495 (X¹ A 420), 5069 (I C 36).
—I Timothy. 2606 (X¹ A 445), 3913 (II A 1), 6096 (VIII¹ A 486).
—Titus. 5060 (I C 17), 6877 (XI¹ A 153).
Binzer, August D. v. 1226 (X⁴ A 73), 1227 (77), 1228 (81), 4819 (66).
Biographer. 6870 (XI¹ A 131).
Biography. 4968 (X³ A 15), 6907 (XI¹ A 497).
Birchedahl, Schøller P. V. 6322 (X¹ A 71).
Bird of prey analogy. 5336 (II A 760).
Birds. 169 (X¹ A 432), 1280 (II A 23), 1364

(VIII¹ A 573), 1942 (643), 3372 (II A 320), 3701 (VI A 51), 4791 (186), 5092 (I A 72), 5440 (III A 18), 5501 (133), 5761 (VI B 222), 5842 (VI A 119), 5847 (131), 6061 (VIII¹ A 347), 6369 (L. 262).

Birth. 38 (III A 25), 280 (II A 133), 283 (594), 729 (XI² A 199), 730 (200).

Birthday (S. K.). 5723 (V B 148:25), 5999 (VIII¹ A 100), 6394 (X¹ A 309), 6612 (X³ A 30).

Bitterness. 358 (X⁴ A 506).

Blicher, Steen S. 1702 (II A 140), 3797 (I A 131), 5338 (II A 259).

Blosius, Ludovicius. 381 (X¹ A 7), 2413 (VIII¹ A 437), 4017 (IX A 429), 6084 (VIII¹ A 437).

Boccaccio, Giovanni. 5994 (VIII¹ A 71).

Bode, Georg H. 4840 (V A 80).

Boehme, Jacob. 884 (III A 125), 5010 (VIII¹ A 105).

Boesen, Carl U. 5451 (III A 51), 5457 (57).

Boesen, Emil. 5335 (II A 243), 5513, (L. 49), 5542 (L. 54), 5548 (L. 62), 5551 (L. 68), 5552 (L. 69), 5655 (L. 80), 5665 (L. 82), 5711 (L. 101), 6303 (X¹ A 23), 6472 (X⁵ A 149), 6537 (L. 239).

Boethius, Anicius M. T. S. 1245 (IV C 62), 3549 (40), 4833 (117).

Bohringer, Friedrich. 21 (XI² A 302), 399 (X⁴ A 147), 531 (149), 532 (212), 542 (X⁵ A 98), 616 (XI² A 341), 1196 (X⁴ A 145), 1197 (170), 198 (171), 1199 (172), 1269 (177), 1483 (134), 1894 (131), 2080 (XI² A 125), 2617 (XI¹ A 150), 2667 (XI² A 68), 2899 (X⁵ A 135), 3162 (X⁴ A 121), 3212 (XI² A 325), 3615 (X⁴ A 210), 3642 (174), 4046 (133), 4047 (173), 4210 (155), 4295 (X⁵ A 133), 4470 (X⁴ A 160), 4670 (158), 4671 (169), 4765 (138), 4766 (139), 4767 (140), 4768 (141), 4769 (142), 4770 (143), 4771 (144), 6741 (154).

Boiesen, Frederik E. 1014 (VIII¹ A 665).

Boileau, Despreaux Nicolas. 5625 (IV A 69).

Bonartes, Thomas. 5580 (IV C 9).

Bonaventura, St. 5595 (IV C 42).

"Book of the Judge, The." 6380 (X¹ A 239).

"Book on Adler, The." 5968 (VII² B 235 pp. 5-230), 5969 (270), 6014 (VIII¹ A 164), 6049 (264), 6079 (440), 6114 (562), 6334 (X¹ A 90).

Books. 131 (II A 46), 148 (IV A 173), 155 (VII¹ A 13), 770 (I A 146), 782 (II A 4), 793 (X³ A 729), 2157 (IX A 378), 2767 (VII¹ A 77), 3855 (II A 122), 4548 (X² A 145), 5204 (II A 585), 5216 (54), 5297 (693), 5615 (IV A 53), 5958 (VII¹ A 218), 6008 (VIII¹ A 135), 6827 (X⁶ C 4), 6829 (6), 6830 (7).

Boredom. 799 (III A 10).

Borgerdyds School. 5727 (L. 107).

Bossuet, Jacques B. 5609 (IV A 31).

Bourgeois, BOURGEOIS MENTALITY, PHIL-ISTINISM. 236 (X¹ A 135), 995 (X⁴ A 176), 1056 (X¹ A 650), 1688 (II A 627), 2752 (IX A 403), 3632 (XI¹ A 267), 4095 (II A 467), 6354 (X¹ A 131).

Bournonville, Auguste. 732 (IV A 94).

Brammer, Gerhard P. 4058 (XI² A 319).

Brazil. 5092 (I A 72).

Bread riots. 6017 (VIII¹ A 172).

Breathing. 3432 (IX A 462).

Bremer, Frederikke. 707 (X¹ A 658), 6475 (X⁶ B 105), 6493 (X² A 25), 6636 (X⁶ B 137), 6916 (XI² A 11).

Brentano, Clemens. 3551 (II A 32), 3889 (I A 337), 5160 (I C 102), 5215 (II A 51), 5482 (L. 27).

Bride. 587 (III C 15), 3778 (XI¹ A 283), 6316 (X¹ A 54).

Bridge of Sighs. 5234 (II A 611).

Brorson, Hans A. 800 (III A 12), 6129 (VIII¹ A 634), 6245 (IX A 255), 6315 (X¹ A 53), 6316 (54), 6575 (X² A 372), 6711 (X³ A 730).

Bruno, Giordano. 1221 (X² A 516), 1357 (VIII¹ A 148), 2634 (240), 3048 (118).

Bulwer, Edward G. 153 (VI A 118).

Bürger, Gottfried A. 2306 (I A 261), 4657 (X³ A 305), 4822 (I A 25), 4824 (209), 6472 (X⁵ A 149).

Busching, Johann G. G. 2581 (II A 429).

Busy-ness. 1037 (VI A 139), 1076 (VII¹ A 173).

Byron, George Gordon. 1872 (X³ A 314), 5160 (I C 102), 5844 (VI A 128).

Bærentzen, Emilius. 5542 (L. 54).

Caesar. 3537 (XI² A 27), 4219 (X⁴ A 575), 5483 (L. 29).

Cafe. 5656 (IV A 105).

Calculation. 815 (IX A 289).

Caligula, Gaius Caesar. 738 (II A 409), 4065 (I A 246).

CALL, CALLING (*see also* VOCATION). 227 (I C 40), 236 (x¹ A 135), 255 (IX A 32), 320 (16), 470 (VIII¹ A 365), 695 (x³ A 653), 855 (II A 13), 936 (VII¹ A 172), 1293 (VII² B 261:8), 1420 (x³ A 781), 1882 (552), 2271 (II A 528), 2541 (x⁴ A 394), 2711 (x³ A 175), 2793 (x² A 341), 3146 (x³ A 120), 3158 (606), 3487 (x² A 95), 3547 (I A 295), 3569 (x² A 637), 3579 (x⁴ A 614), 3915 (III C 1), 4395 (I A 321), 4597 (VIII¹ A 113), 5961 (VII¹ A 221), 5962 (222), 6497 (x² A 45), 6577 (375).

Calvin, John. 1190 (II A 31), 1704 (146), 2328 (x⁴ A 313), 2538 (325), 3575 (398), 3760 (316), 4742 (312), 6756 (233).

Campanella, Tommaso. 3312 (VIII¹ A 166).

Cana. 346 (x² A 85), 2611 (x³ A 316).

Cane. 1950 (x¹ A 372).

Cannibalism. 176 (x⁴ A 537), 6879 (XI¹ A 177).

Cannot. 3767 (x⁵ A 4).

Canon law. 5813 (VI A 55), 5817 (59).

Capacity. 1007 (XI² A 381).

Capital punishment. 4206 (x⁴ A 83).

Cardanus, Hieronymus. 2188 (VIII¹ A 97), 5580 (IV C 9), 5611 (IV A 36), 5612 (37).

Care, concern. 229 (III A 87), 356 (x³ A 655), 1102 (III A 127), 1103 (128), 2126 (x³ A 356), 2134 (XI¹ A 21), 2422 (487), 4862 (410).

Carlèn, Emilie. 2410 (VIII¹ A 196).

Carpocratians. 5227 (II A 599).

Carriere, Moritz. 3012 (VIII¹ A 69), 3310 (70), 3312 (166), 5994 (71).

Carstensen, George J. B. 6624 (x³ A 99).

Cartouche, Louis P. 5073 (I A 14).

Carus, Carl G. 2809 (VII¹ A 186), 2818 (198), 5950 (VII¹ C 5).

Caspar Hauser. 5186 (I A 333).

Castle. 3308 (VII¹ A 82), 4774 (II A 110), 5384 (421).

Casuistry. 2256 (II A 271).

CATEGORY. 260 (IV C 80), 622 (V A 18), 630 (VI A 147), 953 (VIII¹ A 389), 1042 (VII¹ A 80), 1044 (216), 1596 (IV C 64), 1597 (65), 1598 (66), 1599 (67), 1600 (68),

1906 (x⁴ A 369), 2002 (VIII¹ A 286), 2004 (482), 2087 (II A 47), 2498 (x¹ A 526), 3098 (VIII¹ A 11), 5377 (II A 398), 5572 (IV C 2), 5787 (VI B 13), 5977 (VIII² C 1), 5978 (VIII¹ A 18).

CATHOLICISM. 83 (XI¹ A 358), 164 (IX A 110), 419 (I A 172), 431 (II A 249), 614 (XI² A 80), 825 (x⁶ B 233), 1463 (I A 37), 1681 (II A 75), 1698 (114), 1904 (x⁴ A 354), 1912 (500), 1913 (521), 1917 (x⁵ A 9), 1923 (139), 1976 (II A 223), 2381 (25), 2458 (289), 2539 (x⁴ A 371), 2543 (XI² A 301), 2547 (XI¹ A 77), 2622 (XI² A 150), 2727 (x³ A 676), 2854 (I A 26), 3153 (III A 267), 3182 (XI¹ A 532), 3617 (XI² A 305), 3619 (XI¹ A 106), 3722 (II A 76), 3993 (117), 4003 (446), 4061 (I A 93), 4070 (307), 4398 (I C 126), 4504 (XI² A 410), 4814 (123), 5181 (I A 328).

Catholics. 252 (I A 316), 273 (28), 1698 (II A 114).

CAUSE. 183 (VIII¹ A 416), 224 (IX A 483), 460 (VIII¹ A 102), 577 (x⁴ A 49), 610 (IX A 21), 668 (x¹ A 185), 687 (x⁴ A 34), 947 (VIII¹ A 236), 1333 (IV A 190), 1422 (x⁴ A 132), 1432 (640), 1447 (XI² A 130), 1449 (133), 1770 (I A 196), 1775 (VIII¹ A 54), 1776 (IX A 202), 2027 (x³ A 324), 2094 (764), 2571 (XI² A 55), 2992 (116), 3219 (XI¹ A 51), 3613 (x³ A 193), 3898 (IX A 373), 4602 (VIII¹ A 259), 4692 (x⁴ A 630), 4696 (x⁵ A 11), 4897 (x⁴ A 468), 5598 (IV C 45).

Celibacy. 1847 (IX A 82), 2578 (II A 244), 2602 (IX A 246), 2612 (x³ A 419), 2621 (XI¹ A 313), 2976 (372).

Cellini, Benvenuto. 1068 (II A 58).

CERTAINTY. 197 (IV C 100), 434 (II A 252), 632 (VI B 38), 774 (IV A 72), 1116 (VI A 148), 1148 (x⁴ A 635), 1452 (XI² A 175), 2302 (x⁴ A 310), 2820 (VII¹ A 200), 3108 x³ A 546), 3364 (II A 201), 3709 (x² A 614), 4941 (XI¹ A 453), 4942 (458), 5145 (I A 173).

Cervantes, Saavedra de. 188 (x² A 396), 771 (VIII¹ A 59), 1562 (XI¹ A 501), 1762 (x² A 32), 3902 (x⁴ A 412).

Chains. 5256 (II A 647).

Chamisso, Adelbert v. 2988 (XI² A 90), 5160 (I C 102).

CHANGE, COMING INTO EXISTENCE (*see*

also Becoming; Motion). 420 (I A 174), 1379 (IX A 374), 1594 (IV C 59), 1603 (81), 2013 (IX B 63:8), 2130 (x⁴ A 26), 2396 (IV A 195), 2534 (x⁴ A 25), 2721 (x³ A 532), 2958 (x³ A 656), 4197 (x⁴ A 40), 5601 (IV C 97), 5977 (VIII² C 1).

Changeling. 5254 (II A 642).

Chapels. 3521 (x⁴ A 317).

Character. 15 (x⁴ A 71), 1001 (571), 1183 (II A 50), 1462 (x⁴ A 582), 1676 (I A 239), 2712 (x³ A 588), 2785 (I A 240), 2788 (291), 2963 (x⁴ A 107), 2994 (XI² A 146), 3022 (x⁵ A 12), 3166 (x⁴ A 502), 3728 (x³ A 326), 4353 (XI¹ A 538), 4475 (x⁴ A 430), 4813 (XI² A 76), 4881 (x⁴ A 609), 4991 (x¹ A 436).

Charity. 1768 (XI² A 190), 2434 (x³ A 739).

Chateaubriand, François René de. 681 (x³ A 648), 4150 (IX A 309), 5366 (II A 341).

Chess. 5388 (II A 435).

CHILDHOOD. 1123 (VIII¹ A 649), 1171 (x¹ A 468), 1669 (I A 125), 4067 (I A 288), 4398 (I C 126), 4597 (II A 761), 5254 (642), 5290 (683), 5331 (238), 5427 (802), 6169 (IX A 73), 6420 (x¹ A 441).

Childhood (S.K.). 3098 (XI¹ A 299), 5284 (II A 205), 5331 (238), 5412 (557), 5662 (IV B 141), 5690 (IV A 144), 6298 (x¹ A 8), 6339 (101), 6355 (137), 6379 (234).

Child-judge. 1162 (VII¹ A 58), 4127 (VIII¹ A 531), 5484 (III B 2), 6498 (x² A 48).

Childlike. 1384 (x¹ A 60), 1448 (XI² A 131), 1873 (x³ A 331).

CHILDREN. 1156 (III C 17), 1158 (V A 4), 1159 (60), 1165 (VIII¹ A 58), 2188 (97), 3970 (XI² A 202), 5145 (I A 173), 6909 (XI² A 510).

—Christ, Christianity and. 370 (XI² A 164), 548 (XI¹ A 123), 549 (124), 1448 (XI² A 131), 2619 (XI¹ A 253), 2804 (x⁴ A 519), 5007 (XI² A 192), 6612 (x³ A 30).

—Upbringing of. 91 (II A 18), 509 (x¹ A 649), 519 (x³ A 134), 545 (XI¹ A 39), 566 (VII¹ a 161), 647 (VIII¹ A 564), 782 (II A 4), 785 (III A 231), 841 (VIII¹ A 543), 863 (II A 671), 936 (VII¹ A 172), 939 (VIII¹ A 62), 1161 (VI A 24), 1162 (VII¹ A 58), 1163 (VIII¹ A 25), 1166 (499), 1167 (537), 1169 (616), 1171 (x¹ A 468), 1173 (x² A 454), 1215 (VIII¹ A 663), 1273 (x⁵ A 13), 1366 (IX A 34), 1815 (x¹ A 540), 1835 (V B 237), 1875 (x³ A 378), 2132 (x⁵ A 51), 2627 (XI² A 176), 2630 (241), 2895 (x⁵ A 48), 3211 (XI² A 187), 3407 (VII¹ A 136), 4009 (VI A 105), 4161 (x¹ A 369), 4422 (IV A 52), 4445 (VIII¹ A 208), 4449 (IX A 194), 4453 (x¹ A 50), 5035 (x² A 203), 5678 (IV A 132), 5691 (147), 5953 (VII² B 213), 6155 (IX A 50), 6262 (312), 6294 (Letter 195), 6411 (x¹ A 381), 6425 (488), 6798 (x⁴ A 539).

Children's Crusade. 2701 (I A 281).

Chiliasm. 4066 (I A 285), 5332 (II A 240).

China. 3301 (V B 14), 4123 (VIII¹ A 280).

Chinese painting. 5264 (II A 670).

Chivalry. 5131 (I C 85).

Chladni figure. 4966 (x² A 557), 5393 (II A 482), 5923 (VII¹ A 53).

Choice. 308 (VIII¹ A 344), 522 (x³ A 209), 868 (II A 430), 1256 (IX A 109), 1257 (x¹ A 26), 1261 (x² A 428), 1263 (518), 1269 (x⁴ A 177), 1356 (VIII¹ A 111), 4537 (VI B 19:1-10), 5636 (IV A 246).

Cholera. 2073 (XI¹ A 506).

Cholera analogy. 6932 (XI² A 206).

CHRIST.

—Friend. 1285 (x³ A 200), 3037 (622), 6281 (IX A 428).

—God-Man, Paradox (see also PARA- DOX). 71 (x² A 78), 82 (XI¹ A 236), 170 x² A 380), 236 (x¹ A 135), 270 (IX A 395), 457 (VII¹ A 144), 460 (VIII¹ A 102), 509 (x¹ A 649), 697 (XI¹ A 59), 797 (II A 791), 1100 (39), 1545 (215), 1673 (I A 190), 1690 (II A 102), 1801 (XI¹ A 43), 1851 (x¹ A 179), 2498 (526), 2723 (x⁵ A 130), 3028 (VIII¹ a 585), 3042 (XI¹ A 482), 3076 (IV A 62), 3218 (x² A 312), 3230 (VIII¹ A 370), 4040 (x³ A 181), 4183 (x² A 643), 4214 (x⁴ A 209), 4738 (86), 6238 (IX A 227).

—Life of Christ, suffering. 118 (I A 33), 164 (IX A 110), 189 (x³ A 540), 208 (VIII¹ A 50), 215 (x⁴ A 437), 229 (III A 87), 256 (XI² A 330), 400 (x⁴ A 200), 412 (I A 27), 586 (II A 522), 607 (VIII¹ A 307), 690 (x⁴ A 644), 1641 (IX A 160), 1645 (x⁴ A 208), 1647 (XI¹ A 388), 2017 (x¹ A 463), 2110 (III C 25), 2217 (IX A 424), 2231 (XI¹ A 132), 2421 (x¹ A 444), 2430 (x² A 247), 2431 (262), 2611 (x³ A 316), 2645 (IX A 435), 2662 (x⁴ A 108), 2690 (IX A 366),

2868 (x¹ A 482), 2875 (x³ A 214), 2887 (x⁴ A 157), 2930 (VIII¹ A 471), 2931 (477), 2932 (656), 3105 (x³ A 542), 3191 (III C 23), 3352 (VIII¹ A 510), 3354 (IX A 140), 3548 (II A 399), 3585 (XI¹ A 202), 3672 (IX A 474), 3900 (x¹ A 255), 3934 (x² A 26), 4360 (XI² A 279), 4578 (II A 332), 4602 (VIII¹ A 259), 4604 (275), 4610 (579), 4612 (581), 4618 (IX A 162), 4619 (270), 4633 (x¹ A 405), 4645 (x² A 257), 4651 (x³ A 118), 4994 (554), 5022 (x⁴ A 524), 5071 (I A 41), 5308 (II A 714), 5310 (720), 5419 (II C 36), 6254 (IX A 288), 6324 (x¹ A 73), 6368 (163), 6371 (169), 6389 (272), 6529 (x² A 191), 6635 (x³ A 164), 6644 (183), 6648 (194), 6920 (XI² A 32).

—Prototype [*Forbilledet*] (*see also* IMITATION; Prototype). 692 (IX A 153), 693 (x¹ A 132), 694 (x² A 253), 963 (IX A 372), 1793 (x³ A 670), 2072 (XI¹ A 490), 2438 (x⁴ A 589), 2503 (x² A 30), 2666 (XI¹ A 511), 3188 (XI³ B 197), 3455 (x³ A 317), 3620 (XI¹ A 119), 3903 (285), 4454 (x¹ A 134).

—Savior. 496 (x¹ A 190), 587 (III C 15), 934 (VII¹ A 138), 1034 (VI A 65), 1220 (x¹ A 12), 1223 (x³ A 573), 1329 (IV A 104), 1359 (VIII¹ A 356), 1391 (x¹ A 605), 1469 (507), 1652 (IX A 337), 1686 (II A 84), 1835 (V B 237), 1971 (II A 187), 2027 (x³ A 324), 2054 (XI¹ A 168), 2300 (x¹ A 577), 2397 (IV B 144), 2442 (x⁵ A 50), 2472 (IX A 377), 2641 (141), 2651 (x¹ A 119), 2927 (VIII¹ A 297), 3829 (x³ A 654), 3833 (XI¹ A 159), 4021 (x¹ A 433), 4042 (x³ A 341), 4154 (IX A 499), 4368 (331), 6435 (x¹ A 519), 6494 (x² A 39), 6686 (x³ A 526).

—Teacher. 540 (x⁴ A 658), 591 (x¹ A 271), 601 (x⁴ A 594), 677 (x² A 367), 820 (392), 897 (IV A 73), 1514 (x² A 206), 1780 (x¹ A 435), 2066 (XI¹ A 384), 2652 (x¹ A 220), 2719 (VII¹ A 428), 2753 (IX A 404), 4006 (IV A 189), 4038 (x³ A 180), 4224 (XI¹ A 18), 4270 (VIII¹ A 490), 4274 (x² A 67), 4455 (x¹ A 383), 4462 (x³ A 394), 4685 (x⁴ A 578), 4804 (XI¹ A 3), 4897 (x⁴ A 468), 6445 (x¹ A 546), 6783 (x⁴ A 395), 6955 (XI² A 406).

CHRISTENDOM. 186 (x¹ A 188), 201 (x² A 377), 353 (x³ A 257), 359 (x⁴ A 507), 367 (XI² A 15), 370 (164), 485 (IX A 284), 487 (297), 500 (x¹ A 427), 510 (x² A 37), 516 (460), 520 (x³ A 172), 526 (733), 534 (x⁴ A 470), 542 (x⁵ A 98), 568 (VII¹ A 470), 572 (x² A 305), 581 (I A 108), 588 (IX A 264), 592 (x¹ A 537), 616 (XI² A 341), 661 (IX A 232), 663 (240), 723 (x³ A 250), 1001 (x⁴ A 571), 1061 (x³ A 150), 1087 (x⁴ A 518), 1148 (635), 1149 (XI¹ A 192), 1174 (x³ A 506), 1385 (x¹ A 64), 1435 (x⁵ A 116), 1438 (XI¹ A 188), 1500 (XI² A 100), 1519 (224), 1644 (x¹ A 415), 1649 (XI² A 234), 1650 (235), 1762 (x² A 32), 1767 (XI² A 189), 1781 (x¹ A 646), 1813 (XI¹ A 515), 1818 (XI² A 201), 1882 (x³ A 552), 1891 (750), 1932 (XI¹ A 391), 1933 (396), 1952 (x⁴ A 440), 2004 (VII¹ A 482), 2015 (x¹ A 218), 2021 (x⁵ B 244), 2036 (x⁴ A 29), 2054 (XI¹ A 168), 2068 (421), 2121 (x¹ A 564), 2125 (x³ A 334), 2127 (357), 2129 (x⁴ A 21), 2330 (XI¹ A 205), 2332 (520), 2333 (XI² A 37), 2435 (x³ A 741), 2448 (XI¹ A 414), 2450 (XI² A 8), 2455 (426), 2484 (x¹ A 213), 2601 (IX A 245), 2602 (246), 2662 (x⁴ A 108), 2667 (XI² A 68), 2730 (x⁵ A 122), 2731 (XI¹ A 345), 2803 (x² A 529), 2908 (XI¹ A 157), 2910 (392), 2914 (XI² A 174), 2918 386), 2920 (395), 2996 (155), 3006 (215), 3018 (x³ A 496), 3028 (VII¹ A 585), 3043 (XI¹ A 585), 3099 (XI² A 51), 3101 (81), 3102 (212), 3124 (327), 3170 (x⁵ A 10), 3188 (XI³ B 197), 3196 (x¹ A 451), 3209 (XI¹ A 552), 3213 (XI³ B 175), 3238 (XI¹ A 375), 3334 (x³ A 574), 3336 (XI¹ A 156), 3350 (x⁵ A 143), 3538 (XI² A 71), 3620 (XI¹ A 199), 3621 (213), 3744 (VII¹ A 572), 3878 (XI¹ A 165), 3881 (181), 4043 (x³ A 376), 4053 (x² A 13), 4296 (XI¹ A 15), 4309 (x⁴ A 466), 4490 (XI² A 42), 4499 (XI¹ A 348), 4505 (XI² A 416), 4524 (x⁴ A 639), 4530 (XI¹ A 398), 4670 (x⁴ A 158), 4681 (481), 4717 (XI¹ A 493), 4726 (XI² A 72), 4799 (x³ A 286), 4816 (XI² A 382), 4817 (x⁴ A 10), 4892 (XI¹ A 418), 4902 (x⁴ A 636), 4904 (x⁵ A 40), 5022 (x⁴ A 524), 5043 (654), 6141 (IX A 8), 6167 (71), 6205 (171), 6223 (205), 6227 (213), 6228 (214), 6236 (225), 6237 (226), 6243 (243), 6272 (393), 6308 (x¹ A 39), 6317 (56), 6356 (138), 6371 (169), 6445 (546), 6448 (553),

6451 (567), 6463 (598), 6466 (617), 6475 (x⁶ B 105), 6499 (x² A 56), 6521 (157), 6571 (345), 6688 (x³ A 550), 6761 (x⁴ A 296), 6780 (383), 6849 (xI² A 314), 6868 (xI¹ A 128), 6872 (136), 6911 (551), 6928 (xI² A 79), 6929 (101), 6931 (134), 6932 (206), 6946 (xI³ B 56), 6947 (57), 6949 (xI² A 371), 6953 (383), 6958 (399).

Christensen, Anders Westergaard. 5453 (III A 53), 5466 (71), 6134 (VIII¹ A 648), 6489 (x² A 10), 6629 (x³ A 144).

Christensen, Peter Wilhelm. 5688 (IV A 141).

"Christian art of speaking." 5779 (VI C 2).

Christian Discourses. 638 (VIII¹ A 6), 648 (VIII² B 79), 760 (VIII¹ A 492), 1844 (587), 4131 (598), 6068 (VIII² B 116), 6069 (118), 6096 (VIII¹ A 486), 6101 (504), 6107 (548), 6110 (558), 6111 (559), 6112 (560), 6113 (561), 6118 (576), 6120 (589), 6121 (590), 6124 (596), 6125 (602), 6268 (IX A 375), 6278 (498), 6346 (x¹ A 116), 6356 (138), 6795 (x⁴ A 511).

Christian dogma (*see* Dogma).

Christian VIII. 1169 (VIII¹ A 616), 4180 (x² A 498), 5403 (II A 520), 6042 (VII¹ A 249), 6309 (x¹ A 41), 6310 (42), 6311 (43), 6341 (110), 6344 (113), 6591 (x² A 534), 6625 (x³ A 112), 6730 (x⁴ A 52).

Christian ethics (*see* Ethics: Christian ethics).

Christian Fathers (*see* Church Fathers).

Christian nation. 4168 (x² A 240), 6070 (VIII¹ A 388).

CHRISTIANITY.
—Absolute religion. 46 (V A 16), 191 (xI¹ A 436), 192 (xI² A 404), 427 (II A 184), 447 (499), 498 (x¹ A 301), 1336 (V A 42), 4489 (xI¹ A 29).

—Christian doctrine (*see also* Church; Doctrine). 227 (I C 40), 228 (II A 581), 251 (x⁴ A 473), 254 (VI A 9), 272 (x² A 320), 278 (II A 93), 348 (447), 576 (x³ A 765), 577 (x⁴ A 49), 588 (IX A 264), 612 (x² A 57), 699 (I A 324), 991 (x³ A 714), 1635 (IV C 35), 1682 (II A 78), 1704 (146), 1710 (596), 2867 (x¹ A 288), 2874 (x³ A 169), 3029 (IX A 244), 3086 (VI B 98:82), 3285 (III C 32), 4544 (VIII¹ A

535), 4794 (147).

—Christian suffering (*see also* SUFFERING). 84 (xI¹ A 385), 85 (386), 108 (x⁴ A 387), 171 (II A 795), 174 (x³ A 187), 178 (x⁵ A 99), 201 (377), 206 (IV A 143), 237 (x² A 194), 347 (86), 568 (VIII¹ A 470), 607 (307), 611 (IX A 56), 725 (x³ A 710), 731 (xI² A 422), 780 (x⁴ A 234), 789 (x² A 455), 932 (VIII¹ A 73), 1167 (537), 1474 (x² A 233), 1482 (x³ A 784), 1484 (x⁴ A 230), 1496 (x⁵ A 109), 3039 (II A 789), 3117 (VIII¹ A 367), 3498 (x³ A 48), 3674 (x² A 545), 3680 (x³ A 232), 3749 (166), 3751 (306), 3756 (457), 3777 (xI¹ A 143), 3827 (x⁴ A 223), 4867 (x² A 635), 4906 (xI¹ A 7), 5032 (545).

—Christianity, to be a Christian. 864 (II A 759), 934 (VII¹ A 138), 949 (VIII¹ A 312), 965 (IX A 418), 981 (x² A 178), 984 (224), 999 (x⁴ A 549), 1006 (x² A 113), 1020 (II A 235), 1052 (IX A 358), 1053 (359), 1066 (xI ¹ A 353), 1075 (x⁵ A 76), 1078 (VIII¹ A 202), 1085 (x³ A 464), 1101 (III A 216), 1131 (x¹ A 395), 1137 (x² A 184), 1143 (x⁴ A 123), 1144 (422), 1152 (xI² A 115), 1174 (x³ A 506), 1176 (xI¹ A 522), 1200 (II A 326), 1206 (VII¹ A 167), 1207 (VIII¹ A 114), 1277 (xI² A 261), 1350 (VIII¹ A 24), 1399 (x¹ A 241), 1408 (x³ A 264), 1409 (359), 1475 (x² A 239), 1478 (x³ A 269), 1480 (353), 1501 (xI² A 182), 1663 (II A 566), 1729 (III B 11), 1768 (xI² A 190), 1781 (x¹ A 646), 1787 (x³ A 347), 1798 (x⁴ A 282), 1803 (xI ¹ A 194), 1807 (402), 1810 (II A 758), 1813 (xI¹ A 515), 1841 (VIII¹ A 432), 1843 (536), 1845 (IX A 7), 1847 (82), 1853 (x¹ A 455), 1857 (x² A 47), 1860 (326), 1864 (x³ A 171), 1865 (207), 1875 (378), 1880 (454), 1882 (552), 1895 (x⁴ A 148), 1908 (459), 1911 (499), 1914 (556), 1915 (626), 1925 (xI¹ A 22), 1926 (27), 1932 (391), 1940 (xI² A 434), 1971 (II A 187), 1997 (VIII¹ A 9), 1998 (125), 2004 (482), 2007 (IX A 286), 2026 (x³ A 116), 2028 (339), 2045 (x⁵ A 97), 2046 (121), 2052 (xI¹ A 96), 2053 (148), 2056 (189), 2057 (190), 2072 (490), 2080 (xI² A 125), 2083 (254), 2335 (129), 2383 (II A 370), 2384 (462), 2400 (IV B 148), 2421 (x¹ A 444), 2428 (x² A 63), 2449 (xI¹ A 459), 2455 (xI² A 426), 2600 (IX A 237), 2608 (x² A 181), 2609 (566), 2654 (x¹ A 382), 2687

(XI¹ A 435), 2711 (X³ A 175), 2731 (XI¹ A 345), 2853 (X⁴ A 483), 2875 (X³ A 214), 2904 (XI¹ A 110), 2907 (155), 2909 (316), 2920 (XI² A 395), 2976 (372), 2987 (89), 3023 (399), 3030 (IX A 253), 3031 (322), 3039 (XI¹ A 360), 3042 (482), 3044 (XI² A 163), 3062 (X⁴ A 442), 3065 (XI¹ A 195), 3097 (X⁵ A 142), 3099 (XI² A 51), 3153 (X³ A 267), 3201 (X⁴ A 541), 3211 (XI² A 187), 3337 (XI¹ A 161), 3352 (VIII¹ A 510), 3356 (X² A 154), 3479 (X¹ A 6), 3538 (XI² A 71), 3620 (XI¹ A 199), 3647 (X⁴ A 258), 3663 (XI¹ A 33), 3664 (XI² A 65), 3685 (X³ A 545), 3915 (III C 1), 4004 (III A 118), 4032 (X² A 465), 4091 (II A 323), 4209 (X⁴ A 126), 4240 (XI² A 352), 4280 (X³ A 315), 4349 (XI¹ A 363), 4363 (XI² A 378), 4365 (VIII¹ A 47), 4366 (48), 4376 (X² A 182), 4379 (X⁴ A 411), 4398 (I C 126), 4456 (X² A 80), 4472 (X⁴ A 251), 4478 (X⁵ A 82), 4486 (XI¹ A 564), 4524 (X⁴ A 639), 4543 (VIII¹ A 313), 4564 (X⁴ A 346), 4569 (XI¹ A 201), 4738 (X⁴ A 86), 4800 (X³ A 320), 4852 (IX A 4), 4869 (X³ A 85), 4902 (X⁴ A 636), 4905 (X⁵ A 118), 4911 (XI¹ A 516), 4917 (XI² A 204), 4943 (XI¹ A 502), 4958 (II A 452), 4969 (X³ A 301), 5031 (XI¹ A 519), 5049 (XI² A 50), 5280 (II A 202), 6356 (X¹ A 138), 6649 (X³ A 204), 6682 (472), 6868 (XI¹ A 128), 6969 (XI² A 439).

—Christianity in Christendom. 164 (IX A 100), 184 (VIII¹ A 436), 186 (X¹ A 188), 236 (135), 256 (XI² A 330), 353 (X³ A 257), 572 (X² A 305), 614 (XI² A 80), 639 (VIII¹ A 243), 660 (IX A 198), 671 (X¹ A 345), 675 (X² A 19), 689 (I A 50), 696 (XI¹ A 38), 697 (59), 723 (X³ A 250), 778 (VIII¹ A 7), 825 (X⁶ A 233), 826 (XI¹ A 394), 830 (XI² A 331), 941 (VIII¹ A 144), 979 (X² A 23), 987 (546), 988 (X³ A 66), 1003 (XI¹ A 252), 1087 (X⁴ A 518), 1129 (X¹ A 367), 1132 (554), 1192 (VII² B 187), 1259 (X² A 160), 1396 (X² A 186), 1415 (X³ A 658), 1435 (X⁵ A 116), 1438 (XI¹ A 188), 1510 (VIII¹ A 333), 1539 (I A 100), 1644 (X¹ A 415), 1649 (XI² A 234), 1650 (235), 1766 (183), 1818 (201), 1830 (X³ A 616), 1870 (294), 1931 (XI¹ A 338), 1933 (396), 1934 (492), 2015 (X¹ A 218), 2022 (X² A 457), 2068 (XI¹ A 421), 2074 (518), 2079 (XI² A 124), 2081 (135),

2126 (X³ A 356), 2127 (357), 2134 (XI¹ A 21), 2187 (VIII¹ A 90), 2204 (X⁴ A 384), 2229 (IX A 470), 2330 (XI¹ A 205), 2331 (361), 2332 (520), 2333 (XI² A 37), 2334 (128), 2379 (39), 2437 (X⁴ A 482), 2439 (642), 2492 (X¹ A 376), 2575 (XI² A 152), 2618 (XI¹ A 169), 2619 (253), 2620 (295), 2630 (XI² A 241), 2662 (X⁴ A 108), 2667 (XI² A 68), 2679 (91), 2685 (427), 2724 (XI¹ A 186), 2751 (IX A 362), 2759 (X⁴ A 374), 2760 (531), 2773 (XI² A 363), 2803 (X² A 529), 2804 (X⁴ A 519), 2809 (XI¹ A 157), 2895 (X⁵ A 48), 2918 (XI² A 386), 2940 (IX A 146), 2975 (XI¹ A 346), 2992 (XI² A 116), 3007 (220), 3013 (IX A 273), 3018 (X³ A 496), 3024 (XI¹ A 523), 3074 (X¹ A 396), 3148 (X³ A 176), 3160 (698), 3209 (XI¹ A 552), 3210 (XI² A 38), 3212 (325), 3342 (IX A 239), 3361 (XI¹ A 367), 3487 (X² A 95), 3831 (X⁴ A 120), 3884 (XI² A 20), 3890 (II A 464), 4107 (VI A 1), 4141 (VIII¹ A 618), 4173 (X² A 394), 4191 (X³ A 679), 4220 (X⁵ A 115), 4221 (136), 4232 (XI¹ A 366), 4241 (XI² A 356), 4309 (X⁴ A 466), 4347 (XI¹ A 34), 4352 (524), 4471 (X⁴ A 255), 4490 (XI² A 42), 4493 (232), 4502 (112), 4529 (XI¹ A 397), 4531 (431), 4549 (X² A 231), 4565 (X⁴ A 379), 4570 (XI¹ A 380), 4572 (XI² A 196), 4799 (X³ A 286), 4820 (X⁴ A 70), 4821 (328), 4904 (X⁵ A 40), 4998 (XI¹ A 141), 5035 (XI² A 203), 5181 (I C 85), 6076 (VIII¹ A 415), 6087 (455), 6171 (IX A 81), 6172 (83), 6241 (236), 6356 (X¹ A 138), 6443 (X¹ A 538), 6466 (617), 6653 (X³ A 249), 6793 (X⁴ A 474), 6860 (XI¹ A 69), 6863 (76), 6911 (551), 6912 (559), 6921 (XI² A 36), 6950 (374).

—Christianity and Judaism. 2208 (I A 49), 2217 (IX A 424), 2218 (X³ A 139), 2219 (157), 2220 (230), 2221 (293), 2222 (X⁴ A 572), 2224 (XI¹ A 139), 2225 (151), 2227 (184), 2511 (X² A 364), 2517 (X³ A 138), 2519 (170), 2601 (IX A 245), 2858 (II A 379), 2910 (XI¹ A 392), 3043 (585), 3098 (299), 3277 (II A 379), 4649 (X³ A 81), 6276 (IX A 416).

—Christianity and speculation. 1309 (II A 237), 1465 (656), 1568 (II A 48), 1570 (52), 1609 (VI B 54:30), 1610 (98:45), 1615 (X² A 431), 1617 (X⁴ A 385), 1618 (429), 1619 (XI¹ A 14), 1624 (II A 729),

1668 (VI B 53:13), 2250 (II C 44), 2251
(46), 2303 (XI² A 191), 2823 (X⁵ A 73),
3049 (VIII¹ A 331), 3072 (III A 108), 3073
(IV C 29), 3082 (V B 11:4), 3083 (IV B
35:36), 3084 (43), 3087 (VII² B 235),
3118 (X³ A 641), 3245 (I A 94), 3246 (98),
3247 (99), 3253 (II A 77), 3261 (55),
3269 (790), 3274 (434), 3276 (517),
3307 (VI B 54:33), 3329 (X² A 609), 3564
(X¹ A 561), 3576 (X⁶ B 17), 3585 (XI¹ A
202), 3592 (XI² A 216), 3595 (270), 3602
(XI¹ A 364), 3609 (X² A 430), 3612 (461),
3704 (IX A 248), 3712 (X² A 640), 3715
(X⁴ A 525), 3716 (528), 3860 (X³ A 702),
3864 (X⁵ A 134), 3865 (XI¹ A 461), 3867
(557), 4299 (XI¹ A 371).
—Dialectic of Christianity. 758 (VI A 60),
760 (VIII¹ A 492), 871 (II A 450), 1637
(V B 64), 1690 (II A 102), 1699 (136),
1822 (XI² A 267), 2448 (XI¹ A 414), 2514
(XI² A 559), 2750 (VIII¹ A 403), 2873 (X³ A
165), 4922 (XI¹ A 296), 5008 (XI² A 193).
—Existential communication (see also
COMMUNICATION). 64 (VIII¹ A 454), 106
(X³ A 96), 168 (X¹ A 346), 187 (X² A 119),
601 (X⁴ A 594), 659 (IX A 127), 663 (240),
667 (X¹ A 136), 672 (480), 674 (X² A 12),
676 (146), 761 (IX A 114), 797 (II A 791),
810 (IV A 35), 817 (X¹ A 502), 818 (523),
824 (X⁴ A 633), 1060 (X² A 606), 1061
(X³ A 150), 1957 (IX A 221), 2556 (XI² A
266), 2727 (X³ A 676), 2728 (X⁴ A 103),
2959 (X³ A 657), 3040 (XI² A 16), 3223
(XI¹ A 393), 3335 (X³ A 580), 3535 (XI¹ A
477), 4018 (X¹ A 133), 4054 (X⁴ A 397),
4056 (XI² A 106), 4566 (X⁴ A 407), 5987
(VIII¹ A 42), 6205 (IX A 171), 6212 (179),
6221 (190), 6229 (213), 6255 (IX B 63:7),
6275 (IX A 413), 6411 (X¹ A 381), 6469
(644), 6521 (X² A 157), 6523 (163), 6525
(174), 6571 (345), 6590 (525), 6592
(544), 6654 (X³ A 258), 6655 (261), 6662
(367), 6783 (X⁴ A 395).
—(S.K.). 5181 (I C 85), 5313 (II A 730),
5329 (232), 5425 (574), 6102 (VIII¹ A
507), 6167 (IX A 71), 6237 (226), 6252
(283), 6261 (310), 6262 (312), 6308 (X¹
A 39), 6401 (342), 6444 (541), 6496 (X² A
44), 6503 (75), 6586 (459), 6588 (476),
6603 (619), 6611 (X³ A 13), 6616 (77),
6618 (86), 6632 (152), 6650 (210), 6683

(483), 6684 (487), 6753 (X⁴ A 204), 6780
(383), 6798 (539), 6843 (X⁵ A 146), 6881
(XI¹ A 209), 6882 (210), 6922 (XI² A 40),
6924 (45), 6958 (399).
Christianity does not exist. 385 (X² A
16), 1148 (X⁴ A 635), 1765 (X² A 32),
2054 (XI¹ A 168), 2058 (260), 2101 (X⁴ A
392), 2902 (XI¹ A 73), 2915 (XI² A 181),
2958 (X³ A 656), 3170 (X⁵ A 10), 4816
(XI² A 382), 4978 (282), 5007 (198),
5021 (X³ A 273), 6732 (X⁴ A 55), 6734
(57), 6784 (404), 6809 (586), 6842 (X⁶ B
232, pp. 371-378), 6875 (XI³ B 49), 6878
(XI¹ A 171), 6892 (300), 6908 (505),
6918 (XI² A 21), 6934 (244).
CHRISTMAS. 543 (X⁵ A 144), 544 (145),
1893 (X³ A 776), 4331 (379), 4760 (229).
Chrysippus. 1242 (IV C 55), 2361 (IV A 12),
5593 (IV C 34), 5636 (IV A 246).
CHRYSOSTOM, Johannes. 1891 (X³ A 750),
2757 (X³ A 752), 2758 (X⁴ A 4), 3161
(X³ A 751), 4466 (745), 4665 (774), 6716
(780).
CHURCH.
—Doctrine (see also Christian doctrine;
Doctrine). 494 (IX A 461), 1226 (X⁴ A
73), 1415 (X³ A 658), 2729 (X⁵ A 102),
2772 (XI² A 22), 4566 (X⁴ A 407), 5049
(XI² A 50), 5088 (I A 59), 5089 (60), 5154
(202), 5308 (II A 714), 5788 (VI B 14),
5813 (VI A 55), 6443 (X¹ A 538), 6477
(660), 6733 (X⁴ A 56), 6753 (204).
—The established and the individual. 77
(X³ A 186), 273 (I A 28), 293 (316), 871
(II A 450), 872 (465), 1101 (III A 216),
1622 (II A 142), 1698 (114), 1699 (136),
1906 (X⁴ A 369), 1968 (II A 53), 1970
(172), 1975 (211), 1976 (223), 2011 (IX
A 450), 2013 (IX B 63:8), 2045 (X⁵ A 97),
2057 (XI¹ A 190), 2794 (I A 168), 2952
(X² A 390), 2969 (XI¹ A 64), 3229 (XI² A
431), 3722 (II A 76), 3731 (X⁴ A 30), 4070
(I A 307), 4168 (X² A 240), 4175 (478),
4176 (479), 4341 (X⁴ A 226), 4398 (I C
126), 4549 (X² A 231), 4671 (X⁴ A 169),
4742 (312), 4861 (X¹ A 407), 5337 (II A
255), 5489 (IV C 24), 6671 (X³ A 415),
6672 (416), 6720 (800), 6727 (X⁴ A 33),
6756 (233), 6761 (296), 6774 (358).
—Polemics (S.K.). 174 (X³ A 187), 374
(VIII¹ A 624), 381 (X¹ A 7), 384 (672), 470

(VIII[1] A 365), 516 (x[2] A 460), 535 (x[4] A 516), 640 (VIII[1] A 256), 1338 (V A 65), 2510 (x[2] A 334), 3135 (IX A 201), 3476 (VIII[1] A 310), 6443 (x[1] A 538), 6943 (XI[3] B 53).

—Theater. 141 (III A 110), 1051 (IX A 154), 2949 (x[2] A 294), 4828 (IV C 112), 4970 (x[3] A 561).

Church Fathers. 583 (II A 750), 2867 (x[1] A 288), 3830 (x[4] A 119), 4093 (II A 436), 6677 (x[3] A 434).

Churchyard. 5468 (III A 73).

Church year. 3789 (x[1] A 515).

Cicero. 1597 (IV C 65), 1952 (x[4] A 440), 2328 (313), 2558 (444), 3062 (442), 4288 (467), 4303 (XI[1] A 449), 5921 (VII[1] A 44), 5933 (96), 6794 (x[4] A 488).

City. 781 (x[2] A 258), 4166 (7), 4285 (x[4] A 333).

Clara Raphael. 6709 (x[3] A 678).

Claras Skriftemaal. 5162 (I A 244).

Classical (*see also* ROMANTICISM; CLASSICISM). 765 (II A 661), 852 (I A 221), 1032 (V A 6), 1565 (I A 225), 1679 (II A 37), 2317 (722), 3804 (I A 171), 3811 (219), 3815 (294), 3816 (306), 3820 (II A 669).

Claudius, Matthias. 770 (I A 146), 810 (V A 35), 818 (x[1] A 523), 4406 (II A 279), 6424 (x[1] A 494), 6731 (x[4] A 53).

Clausen, Henrik N. 36 (II C 34), 242 (I A 38), 505 (I C 19), 1305 (I A 30), 2530 (x[3] A 533), 2713 (II C 5), 2878 (x[3] A 329), 4061 (I A 93), 4243 (II A 186), 5089 (I A 60), 5181 (328), 5419 (II C 36).

Clavigo. 5808 (VI A 44).

Clement of Alexandria. 1154 (XI[2] A 380), 1724 (III B 5), 2080 (XI[2] A 125), 2878 (x[3] A 329), 3861 (x[4] A 110).

Clemmensen. 6612 (x[3] A 30).

Clergy (*see also* PASTORS). 224 (x[1] A 483), 326 (440), 470 (VIII[1] A 365), 471 (435), 597 (x[3] A 521), 622 (V A 18), 638 (VIII[1] A 6), 639 (243), 668 (x[1] A 185), 836 (VIII[1] A 10), 1003 (XI[1] A 252), 1044 (VII[1] A 216), 1220 (x[2] A 12), 1760 (IX A 437), 2065 (XI[1] A 370), 2752 (IX A 403), 2767 (VII[1] A 77), 3230 (VIII[1] A 370), 3478 (668), 3893 (IV C 77), 5451 (III A 51), 5753 (V A 95), 6065 (VIII[1] A 383), 6254 (IX A 288), 6300 (x[1] A 11), 6860 (XI[1] A 69).

Climacus. 6462 (x[1] A 594).

Clique. 1759 (IX A 420), 2027 (x[3] A 324), 4170 (x[2] A 351), 4184 (x[3] A 26), 5959 (VII[1] A 219), 6246 (IX A 258).

Clock. 5692 (IV A 151).

Closed reserve, closedupness, encapsulation. 906 (IV A 155), 4588 (VI A 46), 4591 (VII[1] A 22), 4608 (VIII[1] A 514), 5081 (I A 18), 5721 (V B 147), 5723 (148:25), 5724 (148:29), 5801 (VI A 31), 5810 (47), 5818 (61), 6131 (VIII[1] A 640), 6133 (645), 6143 (IX A 10), 6480 (x[1] A 664).

Clothes (*see also* Trousers). 6509 (x[2] A 101).

Clouds. 5764 (VI B 226).

"Clues to Illuminate the Modern Religious Confusion." 6081 (VIII[1] A 445).

Coach horn. 5290 (II A 683), 5437 (III A 15), 5438 (16), 5441 (19), 5443 (21).

Coachman. 4232 (XI[1] A 366), 4465 (x[3] A 662), 6707 (661).

Coat. 5751 (V A 93).

Cognition (*see* KNOWLEDGE).

Coherence. 540 (x[4] A 658), 2877 (x[3] A 328), 6207 (IX A 173).

Cold, Ole J. 1546 (II A 442), 5095 (I A 64), 6247 (IX A 262).

Collateral. 3278 (II A 519), 3657 (IV C 78).

"Collected Works of Consummation." 493 (IX A 414), 6271 (390), 6312 (x[1] A 45), 6317 (56), 6367 (162), 6435 (519), 6451 (567).

Collective. 2044 (x[4] A 441), 4166 (x[2] A 7).

COLLISION (*see also* Conflict; Adversity). 81 (XI[1] A 225), 305 (VIII[1] A 145), 334 (x[1] A 279), 513 (x[2] A 284), 602 (XI[1] A 546), 656 (VIII[2] B 88), 908 (IV B 67), 1166 (VIII[1] A 499), 1859 (x[2] A 317), 1866 (x[3] A 272), 1868 (277), 1869 (283), 1882 (552), 1902 (x[4] A 349), 1925 (XI[1] A 22), 1955 (577), 2003 (VIII[1] A 462), 2048 (XI[1] A 42), 2064 (369), 2080 (XI[2] A 125), 2095 (x[3] A 766), 2119 (VIII[1] A 511), 2130 (x[4] A 26), 2221 (x[3] A 293), 2453 (XI[2] A 390), 2482 (x[1] A 172), 2562 (x[5] A 86), 2571 (XI[2] A 55), 2619 (XI[1] A 253), 2642 (IX A 165), 2687 (XI[2] A 435), 2711 (x[3] A 175), 2893 (x[4] A 607), 2907 (XI[1] A 155), 2920 (XI[2] A 395), 2956 (x[3] A 262), 2976 (XI[1] A 372), 2987 (XI[2] A 89), 3082 (V B 11:4), 3097 (x[5] A 142), 3142 (x[2] A 550), 3225 (XI[2] A 177), 3639 (x[2] A 156), 3674 (x[2] A 545),

4457 (279), 4503 (XI^2 A 373), 4701 (X^5 A 85), 4725 (XI^2 A 67), 4730 (396), 4859 (X^1 A 347), 4909 (XI^1 A 351), 4933 (X^3 A 470), 4934 (471), 4952 (XI^1 A 327), 6223 (IX A 205), 6335 (X^1 A 92), 6343 (112), 6364 (156), 6384 (258), 6385 (260), 6447 (551), 6473 (X^5 A 150), 6592 (X^2 A 544), 6660 (X^3 A 318), 6725 (X^4 A 20), 6839 (X^5 A 104), 6844 (XI^2 A 283), 6867 (XI^1 A 125), 6937 (XI^2 A 251), 6950 (374), 6957 (XI^3 B 120).

Color. 2844 (VII^1 B 209), 5218 (II A 625).

Columbus, Christopher. 322 (IX A 59), 1228 (X^4 A 81), 2906 (XI^1 A 154), 4302 (448).

Combinateur. 6562 (X^2 A 285).

Comedy (*see also* TRAGEDY). 125 (I A 198), 150 (V B 148:17), 1670 (I A 145), 2819 (VII^1 A 199), 5192 (I C 124), 5247 (132), 5546 (III C 37), 5559 (III A 198), 5617 (IV A 61).

Comic, the (*see also* HUMOR; Irony). 48 (V A 25), 150 (V B 148:17), 492 (IX A 394), 622 (V A 18), 732 (IV A 94), 770 (I A 146), 1626 (208), 1851 (X^1 A 179), 2799 (I A 300), 3894 (IV A 166), 4400 (II A 163), 4823 (I A 34), 5162 (244), 5247 (II A 132), 6507 (IV C 126), 5608 (127), 5744 (V A 109), 5820 (VI A 75), 5835 (95), 5975 (VIII^1 A 15), 6288 (IX A 471), 6293 (IX B 68).

Coming into existence (*see* CHANGE).

Commentaries. 202 (I A 54), 203 (55), 210 (X^2 A 555), 211 (556), 2890 (X^4 A 428), 3021 (403), 3026 (VIII^2 B 15), 3597 (XI^2 A 376), 4548 (X^2 A 145), 5436 (II C 10).

Commerce. 3 (IV A 6).

Commitment. 4894 (X^3 A 393).

Common man. 236 (X^1 A 135), 991 (X^3 A 714), 1016 (IX A 340), 1056 (X^1 A 650), 1453 (XI^2 A 179), 1610 (VI B 98:45), 1940 (XI^2 A 434), 2082 (149), 2907 (XI^1 A 155), 2971 (234), 3534 (172), 3582 (55), 3589 (473), 3621 (213), 4164 (X^1 A 699), 4849 (VII^1 A 32), 6045 (VIII^1 A 254), 6085 (452), 6146 (IX A 25), 6158 (55), 6259 (298), 6270 (381), 6354 (X^1 A 131), 6378 (228), 6384 (258), 6474 (653), 6498 (X^2 A 48), 6504 (88), 6510 (105), 6531 (193), 6548 (251), 6611 (X^3 A 13), 6628 (142), 6916 (XI^2 A 11), 6917 (19).

COMMUNICATION (*see also* Direct com-munication, INDIRECT COMMUNICA-TION).

—Art of communication, the (S.K.). 5826 (VI A 83), 5914 (VII^1 A 127), 6005 (VIII^1 A 121), 6006 (124), 6195 (IX A 150), 6227 (213), 6230 (217), 6235 (223), 6238 (227), 6239 (229), 6415 (X^1 A 406), 6532 (X^2 A 195), 6548 (251), 6574 (372), 6577 (375), 6593 (560), 6700 (X^3 A 628), 6701 (629), 6872 (XI^1 A 136).

—Esthetic communication. 153 (VI A 118), 165 (IX A 447), 3512 (X^3 A 479).

—Ethical communication, communica-tion of inwardness. 817 (X^1 A 502), 939 (VIII^1 A 62), 1016 (IX A 340), 1038 (VI A 140), 1085 (X^3 A 464), 2293 (VII^1 A 75), 2932 (VIII^1 A 656), 3665 (91), 3695 (X^4 A 336), 4266 (VII^1 A 74), 5646 (VI B 87), 5659 (IV B 78), 6004 (VIII^1 A 120), 6342 (X^1 A 111), 6440 (531), 6521 (X^2 A 157).

—Mass communication. 2147 (VIII^1 A 136), 2150 (146), 2152 (540), 2163 (X^2 A 17), 2170 (X^3 A 723), 4111 (VII^1 A 54), 4119 (VIII^1 A 134), 4121 (245).

—Religious (Christian) communication. 7 (X^2 A 354), 187 (119), 207 (VIII^1 A 20), 322 (IX A 59), 403 (X^5 A 110), 508 (X^1 A 558), 512 (X^2 A 187), 517 (602), 519 (X^3 A 134), 591 (X^1 A 271), 761 (IX A 114), 815 (289), 818 (X^1 A 523), 824 (X^4 A 633), 1015 (IX A 44), 1056 (X^1 A 650), 1060 (X^2 A 606), 1062 (X^3 A 725), 1063 (X^4 A 5), 1414 (X^3 A 585), 1644 (X^1 A 415), 2371 (VI B 35:7), 2976 (XI^1 A 372), 3141 (X^2 A 418), 3217 (X^1 A 628), 3467 (VI A 150), 3478 (VIII^1 A 668), 3489 (X^2 A 151), 3940 (333), 4040 (X^3 A 181), 4056 (X^2 A 106), 4326 (X^1 A 417), 4862 (410), 5987 (VIII^1 A 42), 6446 (X^1 A 548), 6528 (X^2 A 184).

Communication lectures. 5996 (VIII^1 A 82).

Communion. 450 (II A 579), 550 (XI^1 A 222), 725 (X^3 A 710), 1017 (X^2 A 348), 2702 (I A 284), 3936 (X^2 A 50).

Communism. 175 (X^4 A 150), 4111 (VII^1 A 54), 4124 (299), 4127 (VIII^1 A 531), 4131 (598), 4187 (X^3 A 575), 6257 (X^6 B 41), 6310 (X^1 A 42).

Community. 450 (II A 579), 601 (X^4 A 594), 622 (V A 18), 1349 (VII^1 A 201), 1377 (IX A 315), 1698 (II A 114), 1976

(223), 2011 (IX A 450), 2056 (xi¹ A 189), 2080 (XI² A 125), 2111 (IV A 86), 2177 (II A 580), 2952 (x² A 390), 3380 (II A 538), 3915 (III C 1), 4161 (x¹ A 369), 4175 (x² A 478), 4184 (x³ A 26).

Comparison. 32 (II A 674), 924 (VI A 137), 1350 (VIII¹ A 24), 1408 (x³ A 264), 2066 (XI¹ A 384), 2986 (XI² A 88), 2999 (167), 3895 (VI A 132), 6270 (IX A 381).

Compassion. 488 (IX A 300), 533 (x⁴ A 452), 1316 (II A 407), 2675 (IX A 149), 2768 (VIII¹ A 209), 3777 (XI¹ A 143), 4634 (x⁴ A 574), 6510 (x² A 105).

Compendium. 5232 (II A 607), 5233 (609), 5243 (120).

Complement. 6854 (XI³ B 15).

Complicity. 6581 (x² A 415).

"Compounded Feelings." 2416 (VIII¹ A 680), 6140 (679).

Comprehensive plan. 6204 (IX A 169), 6207 (173), 6231 (218), 6242 (241), 6255 (IX B 63:7), 6346 (x¹ A 116), 6360 (146), 6388 (266), 6407 (351), 6505 (x² A 89), 6511 (106), 6520 (150), 6597 (601), 6654 (x³ A 258).

Compromise. 305 (VIII¹ A 145).

Concept. 2 (II A 469), 1057 (x² A 328), 1067 (XI² A 63), 1130 (x¹ A 368), 2987 (XI² A 89), 3005 (214), 4146 (IX A 31), 4334 (x³ A 241), 6652 (239), 6921 (XI² A 36).

Concept of Anxiety, The. 52 (V B 55:4), 98 (55:10), 102 (x² A 22), 1248 (V B 55:26), 1249 (56:2), 1553 (43), 1554 (44), 2740 (55:6), 3302 (55:3), 3962 (53:27), 3963 (53:28), 3964 (53:38), 4023 (x¹ A 637), 4989 (V B 53:25), 5714 (V A 102), 5715 (103), 5716 (104), 5717 (105), 5718 (106), 5719 (107), 5720 (108), 5726 (V B 47:13), 5732 (V A 34), 5844 (VI A 128).

Concept of Irony, The (see also Dissertation). 1726 (III B 7), 2280 (IV A 198), 4238 (XI² A 108), 4243 (II A 186), 4281 (x³ A 477), 5484 (III B 2), 5504 (L., Doc. XV).

Concern (*see* Care).

Concluding Unscientific Postscript. 7 (x¹ A 354), 493 (IX A 414), 566 (VII¹ A 161), 1038 (VI A 140), 2291 (VII¹ A 31), 3085 (VI B 45), 3467 (VI A 150), 3468 (151), 3469 (152), 4037 (x² A 482), 4110 (VII¹ A 20), 4319 (VII¹ C 1), 4454 (x¹ A 134), 4537 (VI B 19:1-10), 4550 (x² A 299), 5767 (VI B 231), 5786 (VI A 146), 5787-92 (VI B 13-18), 5850 (89), 5851 (90), 5855 (VI A 141), 5863 (VII¹ B 69), 5865 (83), 5871 (VII¹ A 2), 5872 (3), 5881 (VII¹ B 211), 5884 (VII¹ A 26), 5887 (VII¹ B 98), 5915 (128), 5997 (VIII¹ A 84), 6030 (L. 152), 6242 (IX A 241), 6347 (x¹ A 118), 6356 (138), 6366 (161), 6444 (541), 6458 (584), 6475 (x⁶ B 105), 6498 (x² A 48), 6523 (163), 6566 (x⁶ B 127), 6567 (245), 6594 (x² A 586), 6596 (x⁶ B 128), 6654 (x³ A 258), 6660 (318), 6690 (555), 6795 (x⁴ A 511), 6843 (x⁵ A 146), 6854 (XI³ B 15).

Concrete, concreteness, concretion. 1041 (VII¹ A 48), 1606 (V B 41), 1997 (VIII¹ A 9), 2324 (x² A 235), 3301 (V B 14 pp. 73-76).

Conditions (*see also* UNCONDITIONED). 975 (x¹ A 430), 2974 (XI¹ A 325), 4442 (VIII¹ A 78).

Confession. 598 (x³ A 697), 685 (344), 1226 (x⁴ A 73), 3920 (VIII¹ A 266), 3955 (x³ A 711), 4056 (XI² A 106), 4307 (x³ A 425), 4930 (IX A 351), 5153 (I A 194), 5205 (II A 20).

Confidant. 6072 (VIII¹ A 394), 6287 (IX A 467), 6372 (x¹ A 183).

Confidence. 339 (x¹ A 364), 1200 (II A 326).

Confirmation. 494 (IX A 461), 589 (x¹ A 38), 3101 (XI² A 81).

Conflict (*see also* COLLISION). 444 (II A 365), 792 (VIII¹ A 155), 838 (73), 839 (74), 1129 (x¹ A 367).

Conformity. 223 (IX A 475), 1081 (x² A 180), 1541 (I A 340), 1839 (VIII¹ A 349), 1882 (x³ A 552), 2470 (IX A 145), 2939 (143), 3004 (XI² A 211), 3558 (x¹ A 666), 4703 (XI² A 297).

Confucius. 6324 (x¹ A 73).

Confusion. 471 (VIII¹ A 435), 622 (V A 18), 649 (VIII² B 81), 654 (86), 1648 (XI¹ A 72), 2333 (XI² A 37), 2467 (IX A 11), 2570 (XI² A 54), 3141 (x² A 418), 3203 (VII² B 257:12), 3337 (XI² A 347), 3486 (x² A 21), 3884 (XI² A 20), 4721 (XI¹ A 561), 6075 (VIII¹ A 414), 6081 (445), 6862 (XI¹ A 72), 6919 (XI² A 31).

Confusion of categories. 953 (VIII¹ A 398).

Congregation. 595 (x⁵ B 245), 600 (x⁴ A 246), 2011 (IX A 450), 2952 (x² A 390), 2969 (XI¹ A 64), 3408 (VII¹ A 137), 3423 (VIII² B 143), 4175 (x² A 478), 4176 (479), 4341 (x⁴ A 226), 5489 (III C 24).

Conradi, Carl. 5327 (II C 53).

CONSCIENCE. 183 (VIII¹ A 416), 503 (x¹ A 467), 534 (x⁴ A 470), 1264 (x³ A 618), 1348 (VII¹ A 143), 1382 (x¹ A 20), 1486 (x⁴ A 618), 1527 (VI A 49), 1556 (5), 1586 (II A 815), 1613 (VIII¹ A 283), 1960 (x³ A 659), 2040 (x⁴ A 370), 2130 (26), 2461 (VII¹ A 192), 2550 (XI¹ A 193), 2825 (II A 633), 3029 (IX A 244), 3214 (VII¹ A 10), 3362 (XI² A 7), 4005 (III A 226), 4018 (x¹ A 133), 4064 (I A 180), 4213 (x⁴ A 187), 4431 (VII¹ A 45), 4690 (x⁴ A 620), 4874 (x³ A 664), 4935 (x⁴ A 18), 4936 (19), 5595 (IV C 42), 6012 (VIII¹ A 158), 6488 (x² A 3), 6686 (x³ A 526), 6728 (x⁴ A 36), 6842 (x⁶ B 232 pp. 371-378).

Consciousness. 267 (IV A 60), 446 (II A 443), 781 (x² A 258), 854 (I A 254), 1672 (158), 1946 (II A 387), 2284 (IV A 49), 2830 (III A 78), 3130 (x² A 594), 3261 (II C 55), 3273 (II A 440), 3702 (VI B 54:19).

Consequences. 91 (II A 18), 1205 (VII¹ A 141), 4468 (x⁴ A 59).

Conservative, conservatism. 1000 (x⁴ A 563), 6335 (x¹ A 92), 6343 (112).

Consistency. 2520 (x³ A 211), 3045 (I A 45), 3598 (II A 763), 5893 (VII¹ A 106), 5896 (109), 6015 (VIII¹ A 170).

Consolation. 299 (III C 6), 472 (VIII¹ A 493), 541 (x⁵ A 36), 659 (IX A 127), 1421 (x³ A 790), 2885 (722), 3502 (130), 4395 (I A 321), 4578 (II A 332), 4595 (VIII¹ A 85), 4605 (463), 4606 (464), 4607 (468), 4652 (x³ A 131), 4707 (XI¹ A 208), 4756 (x³ A 185), 5494 (III A 103), 6262 (IX A 312).

Constantius, Constantin. 3794 (IV A 169), 5704 (178), 5755 (V A 110), 5804 (IV A 41), 5805 (VI B 41:10), 5823 (IV A 78), 6472 (x⁵ A 149).

Contemplation. 1634 (III B 15), 3879 (XI¹ A 178).

CONTEMPORANEITY. 343 (x¹ A 624), 761 (IX A 114), 961 (314), 973 (x¹ A 393), 1050 (VIII¹ A 320), 1051 (IX A 154), 1291 (VI A 21), 1640 (IX A 112), 1644 (x¹ A 415), 1649 (XI² A 234), 1654 (x² A 451), 1793 (x³ A 670), 1851 (x¹ A 179), 1862 (x² A 361), 1864 (x³ A 171), 1867 (276), 1888 (712), 2093 (x² A 602), 2354 (VI B 35:30), 2430 (x² A 247), 2500 (x¹ A 595), 2635 (VIII¹ A 396), 2670 (338), 2722 (x³ A 594), 3353 (IX A 133), 3473 (VII² B 235 p. 88), 3578 (x⁴ A 532), 3610 (x² A 446), 3611 (447), 4059 (XI² A 343), 4444 (VIII¹ A 160), 4507 (x⁴ A 435), 4549 (x² A 231), 4622 (IX A 336), 4881 (x⁴ A 609), 4961 (VIII¹ C 3:5), 4984 (XI¹ A 555), 4998 (x³ A 47), 6238 (IX A 227), 6275 (413), 6529 (x² A 191), 6667 (x³ A 399), 6839 (x⁴ A 104).

Contemporaries. 623 (V A 19), 1643 (IX B 45:4), 1927 (XI¹ A 41), 3353 (IX A 133), 4183 (x² A 643), 4705 (XI¹ A 9), 4901 (x⁴ A 613), 5270 (II A 189), 5423 (567), 5650 (IV A 91), 5995 (VIII¹ A 81), 6009 (139), 6263 (IX A 321), 6959 (XI² A 409).

Content. 138 (II A 425).

Contentment. 5464 (III A 67).

Contingency. 1023 (II A 612), 1036 (VI A 136), 1210 (VIII¹ A 459), 1292 (VI A 93), 1672 (I A 158), 1697 (II A 112), 5153 (I A 194), 5161 (235), 5187 (335).

Continuity (see also DISCONTINUITY). 773 (III A 4), 898 (IV A 82), 907 (213), 915 (VI A 7), 972 (x¹ A 360), 1028 (IV C 92), 1136 (x² A 371), 1444 (XI² A 53), 1633 (III B 14), 1977 (II A 207), 2358 (x¹ A 361), 3031 (IX A 322), 3073 (IV C 29), 3263 (II C 57), 3276 (II A 517), 4090 (II A 783), 4242 (XI³ B 126), 4803 (x⁵ A 65), 4991 (x¹ A 436), 5605 (IV C 123).

CONTRADICTION. 20 (x⁵ A 120), 161 (VIII¹ A 88), 1302 (I A 2), 1761 (V A 85), 1917 (x⁵ A 9), 2803 (x² A 529), 2813 (VII¹ A 191), 3073 (IV C 29), 5593 (34), 5646 (IV A 87).

Contrasts. 516 (x² A 460), 702 (IV A 5), 704 (192), 1578 (II A 454), 2930 (VIII¹ A 471), 2931 (477), 4575 (I A 85).

Conversation. 793 (x³ A 729), 1279 (II A 22), 5189 (I A 338), 5373 (II A 386), 5731 (V B 72:22), 5763 (VI B 225), 6259 (IX A 298), 6270 (381), 6605 (x² A 627), 6896 (XI¹ A 383), 6917 (XI² A 19), 6957 (XI³ B 120).

"Conversation with My Wife." 6584 (x⁵ A 165).

Conversion. 420 (I A 174), 1178 (104),

1206 (VII¹ A 167), 2080 (XI² A 125), 4621 (IX A 330), 4734 (II A 477), 4750 (X¹ A 484).

Conviction. 247 (VIII¹ A 405), 822 (X⁴ A 222), 2296 (VII¹ A 215), 3608 (X¹ A 481).

Copenhagen. 5687 (IV A 140), 5912 (VII¹ A 125), 5930 (90), 6018 (VIII¹ A 174), 6034 (224), 6168 (IX A 72), 6200 (159), 6254 (288), 6285 (458), 6288 (471), 6309 (X¹ A 41), 6382 (247), 6474 (653), 6738 (X⁴ A 87), 6819 (646).

Copernicus, Nicolaus. 1303 (I A 21), 2458 (II A 289), 5270 (189).

Cordiality. 2685 (XI² A 427).

CORRECTIVE. 1135 (X² A 207), 2046 (X⁵ A 121), 2513 (X² A 558), 2521 (X³ A 217), 2550 (XI¹ A 193), 2763 (198), 3299 (V A 46), 3567 (X¹ A 679), 3625 (XI² A 162), 5000 (XI¹ A 226), 6467 (X¹ A 640), 6531 (X² A 193), 6574 (X⁶ B 121), 6693 (X³ A 565), 6863 (XI¹ A 76).

Corrodi, Heinrich. 2100 (X⁴ A 219), 5333 (II A 241).

Corruption. 405 (XI¹ A 308), 2809 (VII¹ A 186), 3209 (XI¹ A 552), 3888 (II A 297), 6101 (VIII¹ A 504), 6911 (X¹ A 551).

Corsair, The. 1258 (X² A 159), 2048 (XI¹ A 42), 2146 (VII¹ A 122), 2941 (IX A 277), 3034 (X² A 117), 4152 (IX A 364), 4237 (XI² A 85), 5853 (VI B 192), 5854 (193), 5860 (VII¹ B 1), 5861 (5), 5862 (6), 5863 (69), 5872 (VII¹ A 3), 5884 (26), 5887 (98), 5888 (99), 5889 (101), 5890 (103), 5891 (104), 5892 (105), 5894 (107), 5896 (109), 5898 (111), 5899 (112), 5901 (114), 5914 (127), 5929 (85), 5937 (147), 5942 (156), 5943 (157), 5946 (164), 5957 (214), 5966 (229), 5998 (VIII¹ A 99), 5999 (100), 6010 (153), 6031 (218), 6039 (233), 6045 (254), 6088 (458), 6099 (655), 6105 (544), 6106 (545), 6123 (595), 6160 (IX A 64), 6177 (100), 6191 (139), 6204 (169), 6225 (209), 6258 (293), 6282 (432), 6285 (458), 6286 (463), 6313 (X¹ A 46), 6351 (123), 6356 (138), 6373 (187), 6377 (206), 6382 (247), 6385 (260), 6386 (262), 6389 (272), 6458 (584), 6474 (653), 6493 (X² A 25), 6498 (48), 6504 (88), 6548 (251), 6549 (252), 6574 (X⁶ B 121), 6580 (413), 6592 (X² A 544), 6594 (586), 6602 (605), 6611 (X³ A 13),

6619 (88), 6621 (90), 6628 (142), 6680 (450), 6727 (X⁴ A 33), 6743 (167), 6748 (X⁶ B 171), 6749 (173, pp. 274-276), 6780 (X⁴ A 383), 6795 (511), 6843 (X⁵ A 146), 6886 (XI¹ A 242), 6901 (439), 6935 (XI² A 248).

Cosmism. 2712 (X³ A 588).

Cosmopolitanism. 4063 (I A 139).

Counterfeiting analogy. 6921 (XI² A 36), 6967 (437).

Courage. 490 (IX A 350), 1200 (II A 326), 1324 (III A 101), 1372 (IX A 182), 1644 (III A 217), 2179 (213), 2180 (III C 18), 2987 (XI² A 89), 3907 (X³ A 31), 3912 (601), 4183 (X² A 643), 4381 (X⁴ A 462).

"Courtesan's Diary, The." 5675 (IV A 128), 5677 (129).

Courtesy. 2134 (XI¹ A 21).

Courtier analogy. 6930 (XI² A 121).

Cows. 5242 (II A 119), 5472 (III A 79), 5841 (VI A 104).

Crazy Peter. 5164 (I A 249).

Creation. 278 (II A 93), 296 (419), 1237 (752), 1299 (X² A 563), 1307 (II A 622), 1309 (237), 1310 (758), 1345 (VII¹ A 62), 1348 (143), 1387 (X¹ A 203), 1391 (605), 1399 (X² A 241), 1673 (I A 190), 1981 (II A 474), 2099 (XI¹ A 491), 2273 (II A 550), 2888 (X⁴ A 260), 3245 (II A 94), 3385 (III A 86), 5326 (II A 229).

Cremation. 337 (X¹ A 354).

Crime, criminal. 70 (IX A 80), 897 (IV A 73), 2564 (XI¹ A 65), 2807 (VII¹ A 182), 2945 (X¹ A 231), 3690 (X⁴ A 214), 4297 (XI¹ A 318), 4371 (IX A 334), 4565 (X⁴ A 379), 4911 (XI¹ A 516), 4953 (XI² A 86), 6967 (437), 6969 (439).

Cripples. 6469 (X¹ A 644).

Crisis. 2034 (X³ A 763), 4363 (XI² A 378), 4815 (318).

Crisis and a Crisis in the Life of an Actress, The. 6060 (VIII¹ A 339), 6209 (IX A 175), 6211 (178), 6212 (179), 6213 (180), 6215 (184), 6218 (187), 6220 (189), 6223 (205), 6229 (216), 6231 (218), 6232 (219), 6238 (227), 6242 (241), 6246 (258).

Criterion. 40 (IV C 32), 150 (V B 148:17), 528 (X⁴ A 28), 532 (212), 1138 (X³ A 298), 1176 (XI¹ A 522), 1289 (II A 278), 1375 (IX A 254), 1773 (III A 242), 1804 (XI¹ A 197), 1858 (X² A 255), 2067 (XI¹ A

415), 2467 (IX A 11), 2529 (X³ A 516), 4035 (X² A 473), 4308 (VII¹ A 235).

Criticism. 139 (II A 539), 158 (VII¹ A 159), 793 (X³ A 729), 839 (VIII¹ A 74), 1048 (234), 1177 (I A 88), 1297 (IX A 275), 2509 (X² A 263), 2666 (XI¹ A 511), 2834 (VI A 90), 4628 (IX A 425), 5157 (I A 223), 5926 (VII¹ A 55), 6093 (VIII¹ A 481).

Critics. 120 (I A 90), 122 (106), 158 (VII¹ A 159), 159 (242), 2149 (VIII¹ A 140), 2151 (399), 5698 (IV A 167).

Cromwell, Oliver. 1606 (V B 41), 3973 (VI A 67).

Cross. 423 (II A 82), 1237 (752).

Crowd (*see also* Many; Mass; NUMBERS; Public). 1617 (X⁴ A 385), 1825 (XI³ B 199), 2004 (VIII¹ A 482), 2016 (X¹ A 286), 2018 (X² A 179), 2022 (457), 2030 (X³ A 476), 2050 (XI¹ A 81), 2065 (370), 2066 (384), 2165 (X³ A 231), 2514 (X² A 559), 2566 (XI¹ A 486), 2652 (X¹ A 200), 2732 (XI¹ A 489), 3147 (X³ A 132), 3860 (702), 4118 (VIII¹ A 123), 4132 (599), 4134 (606), 4166 (X² A 7), 4173 (394), 4216 (X⁴ A 268), 4285 (333), 4295 (X⁵ A 133), 4880 (X⁴ A 391), 4885 (XI¹ A 352), 4911 (516), 4912 (517), 4941 (453), 5948 (VII¹ A 176), 5979 (VIII¹ A 23), 6225 (IX A 209), 6243 (243), 6255 (IX B 63:7), 6344 (X¹ A 113), 6389 (272), 6486 (676), 6580 (X² A 413), 6680 (X³ A 450), 6873 (XI¹ A 137).

Crows. 3705 (IX A 365).

Crucifixion. 305 (VIII¹ A 145), 337 (X¹ A 354), 358 (X⁴ A 506), 460 (VIII¹ A 102), 2415 (610), 4279 (X³ A 253), 4360 (XI² A 279), 6050 (VIII¹ A 271), 6373 (X¹ A 187).

Cruelty. 6203 (IX A 168).

Crusades. 4082 (II A 272), 4295 (X⁵ A 133).

Culture. 581 (I A 108), 616 (XI² A 341), 2437 (X⁴ A 482), 2712 (X³ A 588), 3582 (XI¹ A 55), 4471 (X⁴ A 235), 4764 (137).

Cupboard, tall. 6037 (VIII¹ A 229), 6245 (IX A 255), 6472 (X⁵ A 149), 6762 (X⁴ A 299), 6789 (X⁶ B 259).

Cups. 5052 (L. 120a).

Curiosity. 302 (VII¹ A 79), 460 (VIII¹ A 102), 1055 (X¹ A 193).

Curse. 5517 (III A 161), 5874 (VII¹ A 5).

Curtius, Michael C. 4835 (IV C 119), 5606 (124).

Custom. 938 (VII¹ A 251).

Customs Clerk. 4539 (VI A 64).

"Cycle of Ethical-Religious Essays." 6229 (IX A 216), 6238 (227), 6256 (X⁶ B 40), 6325 (X¹ A 74), 6334 (90), 6336 (94), 6337 (95), 6346 (116), 6358 (140), 6387 (263), 6527 (X⁶ B 41).

Cynicism. 6160 (IX A 64).

Cyprian, Thascius C. 543 (X⁵ A 144), 1924 (XI¹ A 4), 2663 (X⁴ A 109), 3467 (VI A 150), 3596 (XI² A 368).

Dailyness. 1374 (IX A 247).

Damnation. 5275 (II A 629), 5276 (630).

Dance, dancer. 133 (II A 180), 1079 (IX A 12), 3064 (X⁵ A 159), 6591 (X² A 534), 6731 (X⁴ A 53), 6919 (XI² A 31).

Danger. 3417 (VIII¹ A 367), 4932 (X² A 531), 6180 (IX A 122), 6372 (X¹ A 183), 6386 (262).

Danish Pantheon. 5767 (VI B 231).

Danzel, Wilhelm. 5768 (VI A 4).

Darwin, Erasmus. 5578 (IV C 6).

Daub, Karl. 62 (VIII¹ A 244), 279 (II A 97), 616 (624), 899 (IV A 92), 1233 (II A 74), 1683 (79), 2229 (IX A 470), 3605 (II A 96), 4030 (X² A 436), 4555 (401), 5514 (III C 26).

David, Christian G. Nathan. 1831 (X⁴ A 533), 5749 (V A 91).

Davidius, Johan. 5582 (IV A 15).

Dead, the. 1273 (X⁵ A 13), 1665 (III A 129), 2855 (I A 298), 3605 (II A 96), 4432 (VII¹ A 57), 4796 (X² A 261), 4806 (XI¹ A 329).

DEATH. 245 (I A 138), 246 (VIII¹ A 168), 253 (IV A 187), 275 (210), 416 (I A 95), 429 (II A 234), 496 (X¹ A 190), 534 (X⁴ A 470), 568 (VIII¹ A 470), 805 (III A 96), 816 (X¹ A 248), 841 (VIII¹ A 543), 1005 (XI¹ A 528), 1095 (I A 44), 1270 (X⁴ A 245), 1472 (X² A 198), 1474 (223), 1523 (II A 716), 1525 (555), 1655 (X² A 452), 1723 (III B 4), 1949 (IX A 391), 2134 (XI¹ A 21), 2246 (I A 112), 2405 (VIII¹ A 51), 2407 (89), 2850 (474), 2908 (XI¹ A 157), 3904 (II A 153), 3908 (X³ A 35), 3915 (III C 1), 3951 (X³ A 706), 3994 (II A 63), 4039 (X³ A 180), 4042 (341), 4046 (X⁴ A 133), 4354 (XI¹ A 558), 4419 (IV A 18), 4458 (II A 313), 4484 (XI¹ A 478), 4513 (X³ A 14), 4639 (X² A 53), 4798 (X³ A 47), 4885 (XI¹

A 352), 5126 (I C 79), 5185 (I A 332), 5256 (II A 647), 5292 (685), 5298 (696), 5451 (III A 51), 5470 (75), 5800 (VI A 29), 5878 (VII¹ A 11), 5900 (113), 5948 (176), 5995 (VIII¹ A 81), 6026 (207), 6369 (X¹ A 166), 6612 (X³ A 30), 6741 (X⁴ A 154).

—Death (S. K.). 5335 (II A 243), 5490 (III A 90), 5665 (L. 82), 5999 (VIII¹ A 100), 6001 (116), 6006 (124), 6009 (139), 6051 (276), 6104 (533), 6106 (545), 6108 (549), 6152 (IX A 42), 6193 (144), 6194 (492), 6200 (159), 6211 (178), 6220 (189), 6221 (190), 6222 (203), 6227 (213), 6229 (216), 6232 (219), 6238 (227), 6242 (241), 6250 (276), 6259 (298), 6319 (X¹ A 61), 6327 (78), 6359 (143), 6380 (239), 6382 (247), 6383 (250), 6388 (266), 6391 (281), 6415 (406), 6418 (424), 6540 (X² A 212), 6541 (213), 6555 (277), 6574 (X⁶ B 121), 6583 (X² A 427), 6607 (X³ A 3), 6609 (8), 6663 (X⁶ B 93), 6664 (X³ A 381), 6842 (X⁶ B 232), 6898 (XI¹ A 423).

Death struggle. 731 (XI² A 422), 3173 (XI¹ A 86), 4725 (XI² A 67).

Deceiver. 2536 (X⁴ A 237), 4260 (IV A 124), 4315 (X⁵ A 35), 4882 (X⁴ A 653), 5517 (III A 161), 5521 (166), 5528 (172), 5538 (180), 5569 (207), 5653 (IV A 97), 5689 (142).

Deception. 624 (V A 47), 649 (VIII² B 81:22), 653 (85:22-24), 1031 (III A 188), 1482 (X³ A 784), 2977 (XI¹ A 373), 4812 (554), 4840 (V A 80), 4890 (X⁴ A 297), 5569 (III A 207), 6374 (X¹ A 192), 6389 (272), 6408 (366), 6533 (X² A 196).

Decision. 390 (X² A 453), 469 (VIII¹ A 359), 539 (X⁴ A 648), 668 (X¹ A 185), 912 (V A 72), 934 (VII¹ A 138), 946 (VIII¹ A 223), 962 (IX A 346), 1046 (VIII¹ A 127), 1103 (III A 128), 1147 (X⁴ A 634), 1174 (X³ A 506), 1269 (X⁴ A 197), 2292 (VII¹ A 34), 3093 (X² A 501), 3360 (X⁴ A 416), 3608 (X¹ A 481), 3658 (IV C 89), 4428 (V A 12), 4438 (VII² B 266:26), 4441 (VIII¹ A 67), 4491 (XI² A 73), 4537 (VI B 19:1-10), 4816 (XI² A 382), 5792 (VI B 18), 6021 (VIII¹ A 185), 6041 (246), 6112 (560), 6212 (IX A 179), 6326 (X¹ A 77).

Decline (see Fall).

Dedication. 5948 (VII¹ A 176), 6068 (VIII¹

B 116), 6112 (VIII¹ A 560), 6583 (X² A 427), 6637 (X⁶ B 162), 6638 (163), 6639 (164), 6641 (169), 6675 (X⁵ B 263).

Deep. 838 (VIII¹ A 73).

Defense. 1131 (X¹ A 395).

Defense against Christianity. 3680 (X³ A 232).

Defiance. 744 (IV A 165), 1974 (II A 652).

Definition. 2261 (II A 348), 5600 (IV C 83).

Degree. 1405 (X² A 644).

Democracy. 3219 (XI¹ A 51), 4113 (VII¹ A 163).

DEMONIC. 133 (II A 180), 292 (767), 663 (IX A 240), 1637 (V B 64), 1721 (III A 46), 1730 (III B 16), 3690 (X⁴ A 214), 4093 (II A 436), 4178 (X² A 490), 4643 (236), 5705 (IV A 181), 6257 (X⁶ B 41), 6432 (X¹ A 513), 6433 (517), 6842 (X⁶ B 232).

Demoralization. 1487 (X⁴ A 619), 1500 (XI² A 100), 1761 (X¹ A 198), 1956 (XI² A 237), 3963 (X⁴ A 517), 4149 (IX A 303), 4202 (X⁴ A 63), 6018 (VIII¹ A 174), 6191 (IX A 139), 6845 (XI² A 288).

Demosthenes. 2328 (X⁴ A 313).

Dencker, Elise. 5544 (L. 56), 6472 (X⁵ A 149:26).

Denmark. 405 (XI¹ A 308), 2763 (198), 3620 (199), 4127 (VIII¹ A 531), 4149 (IX A 303), 4180 (X² A 498), 4242 (XI³ B 126), 5904 (VII¹ A 117), 5906 (119), 5909 (124), 6077 (VIII¹ A 417), 6171 (IX A 81), 6188 (134), 6199 (156), 6204 (169), 6208 (174), 6223 (205), 6259 (298), 6282 (432), 6290 (484), 6299 (X¹ A 9), 6454 (584), 6609 (X³ A 8), 6738 (X⁴ A 87), 6912 (XI¹ A 559), 6958 (XI² A 399).

Den Stundesløse. 4823 (I A 34).

De occultis non judicat ecclesia. 3639 (X² A 156), 5813 (VI A 55), 5814 (56), 5815 (57), 5816 (58), 5817 (59), 5818 (61), 5875 (VII¹ A 6), 5882 (21), 6037 (VIII¹ A 229).

De omnibus dubitandum est (see Johannes Climacus).

Dependence. 1252 (VII¹ A 210), 1254 (VIII¹ A 522).

Depersonalization (see also Egoity, I). 673 (X¹ A 566), 3215 (2), 4356 (XI² A 62).

Depression (see also MELANCHOLY). 3645 X² A 296), 4404 (II A 721).

DESCARTES, René. 657 (VIII² B 89), 774 (IV

A 72), 1033 (V A 30), 1846 (IX A 49), 2292 (VII¹ A 34), 2338 (IV C 11), 3270 (II A 353), 4321 (VII¹ C 3), 5181 (I A 328), 5573 (IV A 1), 5574 (2), 5588 (IV C 10).

Desire. 115 (X⁵ A 31), 2114 (V B 227:5), 3374 (II A 334), 6648 (X³ A 194).

Desk, high. 6787 (X⁶ B 253).

DESPAIR. 9 (X⁶ B 78), 68 (VIII² B 168:5), 205 (II A 479), 226 (X³ A 463), 503 (X¹ A 467), 806 (III B 45:1), 903 (IV A 131), 907 (213), 924 (VI A 137), 1003 (XI¹ A 252), 1179 (I C 58), 1180 (I A 227), 1182 (II A 29), 1183 (50), 1315 (402), 1406 (507), 1757 (IX A 399), 1761 (X¹ A 148), 1923 (X⁵ A 139), 2388 (III A 89), 2551 (XI¹ A 297), 3127 (V A 44), 3247 (I A 99), 3628 (VII¹ A 130), 3915 (III C 1), 3994 (II A 63), 3999 (584), 4010 (VIII¹ A 64), 4013 (497), 4016 (IX A 341), 4025 (X² A 74), 4028 (404), 4151 (IX A 354), 4368 (331), 4375 (X¹ A 478), 4448 (IX A 37), 4594 (VIII¹ A 32), 4657 (X³ A 305), 5257 (II A 648), 5400 (509), 5431 (806), 5454 (III A 54), 6137 (VIII¹ A 652), 6138 (653), 6227 (IX A 213), 6277 (421), 6278 (498), 6279 (499).

Detective story. 6833 (X⁶ B 226).

Determinism (see Fatalism; Fate; Necessity).

Devil (see also Satan). 292 (II A 767), 416 (I A 95), 486 (IX A 292), 856 (II A 34), 1339 (V A 89), 1433 (X⁵ A 39), 1447 (XI² A 130), 1449 (133), 2253 (II A 698), 3188 (XI³ B 197), 3247 (I A 99), 3648 (XI¹ A 2), 3989 (I A 3), 4005 (III A 226), 5229 (II A 601), 5640 (IV A 76).

DIALECTIC, DIALECTICAL.

—Dialectic of Christianity. 9 (X⁶ B 78), 73 (X² A 406), 164 (IX A 110), 185 (X¹ A 5), 255 (IX A 32), 301 (IV A 33), 348 (X² A 136), 373 (VIII¹ A 547), 434 (II A 252), 483 (IX A 147), 486 (292), 520 (X³ A 172), 641 (VIII¹ A 293), 1139 (X³ A 332), 1140 (333), 1261 (X² A 428), 1337 (V A 50), 1373 (IX A 242), 1472 (X² A 198), 1485 (X⁴ A 419), 1786 (X³ A 312), 1790 (524), 1822 (XI² A 267), 1852 (X¹ A 246), 1862 (X² A 361), 1884 (X³ A 615), 1902 (X⁴ A 349), 1905 (366), 2095 (X³ A 766), 2116 (VI B 98:77), 2225 (XI¹ A 151), 2419 (IX A 306), 2474 (433), 2484 (X¹ A 213), 2502

(651), 2512 (X² A 448), 2518 (X³ A 153), 2532 (X⁴ A 7), 2556 (XI² A 266), 2873 (X³ A 165), 2906 (XI¹ A 154), 3026 (VIII² B 15), 3037 (X³ A 622), 3078 (IV A 116), 3123 (X⁵ A 75), 3218 (X² A 312), 3881 (XI¹ A 181), 4027 (X² A 405), 4110 (VII¹ A 20), 4373 (X¹ A 452), 4421 (IV C 94), 4551 (X² A 301), 4586 (V A 49), 4589 (VI A 48), 4610 (VIII¹ A 579), 5611 (580), 4779 (480), 4782 (X² A 549), 4855 (IX A 304), 5007 (XI² A 192), 5008 (193), 6002 (VIII¹ A 119), 6061 (347), 6167 (IX A 71).

—Dialectic of communication. 649 (VIII² B 81), 650 (82), 651 (83), 652 (84), 653 (85), 655 (87), 664 (IX A 257), 2371 (VI B 35:7), 3665 (VIII¹ A 91), 5914 (VII¹ A 127), 5972 (VIII¹ A 4), 5975 (15), 5979 (23), 5996 (82), 5997 (84).

—Dialectic of existence. 46 (V A 16), 710 (X⁵ A 106), 768 (V A 70), 771 (VIII¹ A 59), 808 (IV C 105), 905 (IV A 149), 931 (VII¹ A 35), 936 (172), 1091 (XI¹ A 409), 1123 (VIII¹ A 649), 1152 (XI² A 115), 1247 (V A 90), 1526 (121), 1676 (I A 239), 2345 (V C 1), 2353 (VI A 33), 3306 (145), 4109 (VII¹ A 17), 4245 (III B 27), 4430 (V A 123), 4888 (XI² A 508), 5118 (I A 120), 5272 (II C 39), 6006 (VIII¹ A 124).

—Dialectic of reflection. 38 (III A 25), 641 (VIII¹ A 293), 2296 (VII¹ A 215), 2813 (191).

—Dialectic (S.K.). 2950 (X² A 369), 6136 (VIII¹ A 651), 6137 (652), 6227 (IX A 213), 6228 (214), 6236 (225), 6242 (241), 6350 (X¹ A 211), 6506 (X² A 90), 6523 (163), 6566 (X⁶ B 127), 6595 (X² A 596), 6681 (X³ A 453), 6878 (XI¹ A 171), 6924 (XI² A 45).

—Hegelian dialectic. 1565 (I A 225), 1566 (229), 1567 (317), 3265 (II A 706), 3278 (519), 3306 (VI A 145), 4070 (I A 307), 5092 (72), 5181 (328).

"Dialectical Result of a Literary Police-operation, The." 6282 (IX A 432).

Dialectician. 9 (X⁶ B 78), 373 (VIII¹ A 547), 761 (IX A 114), 2467 (11), 6577 (X² A 375).

Dialectician, criminal. 1963 (XI¹ A 335).

Dialogue. 673 (X¹ A 566).

"Diapsalmata." 5629 (IV A 216).

"Diary of a Street Inspector." 5564 (III A 245).

Diavolo, Fra. 5061 (I A 11).
Die Lucinde. 3846 (I C 69).
Diez, Friedrich. 5137 (I C 89).
"Difference between a Genius and an Apostle, The." 6220 (IX A 189).
Differences. 22 (I A 74), 46 (V A 16), 69 (IX A 76), 106 (x³ A 96), 107 (97), 108 (x⁴ A 387), 389 (x² A 139), 528 (x⁴ A 28), 975 (x¹ A 430), 989 (x³ A 104), 991 (714), 1008 (VII¹ A 245), 1012 (VIII² B 31:20), 1013 (31:22), 1016 (IX A 340), 1018 (XI² A 122), 1073 (V A 213:2), 1340 (V B 5:8), 1383 (x¹ A 59), 1436 (XI¹ A 5), 1609 (VI B 54:30), 1993 (VII¹ B 199), 2076 (XI¹ A 576), 2372 (VI B 136), 2679 (XI² A 91), 2793 (x² A 341), 2988 (XI² A 90), 3081 (V B 5:10), 4483 (XI¹ A 475), 4502 (XI² A 112).
Dignity. 394 (x³ A 137).
Dio Cassius. 4105 (IV A 13).
Diodorus, Cronus. 5593 (IV C 34).
Diogenes. 1703 (II A 141), 6022 (VIII¹ A 197), 6063 (L. 150), 6160 (IX A 64).
Diogenes Laertius. 1482 (x³ A 784), 2558 (x⁴ A 444), 2592 (IV A 237), 4246 (III B 30), 4249 (IV A 202).
Dion. 4418 (IV A 10).
Dionysius. 5352 (II A 275).
Direct communication. (*see also* COMMUNICATION, INDIRECT COMMUNICATION). 677 (x² A 367), 2015 (x¹ A 218), 2528 (x² A 510), 5826 (VI A 83), 6230 (IX A 217), 6234 (222), 6235 (223), 6239 (229), 6248 (265), 6345 (x¹ A 115), 6352 (126), 6361 (147), 6366 (161), 6372 (183), 6383 (250), 6388 (266), 6393 (300), 6415 (406), 6532 (x² A 195), 6577 (375), 6701 (x³ A 629), 6769 (x⁴ A 323), 6770 (x⁶ B 4:3), 6786 (145, pp. 202-203), 6842 (232).
Disappointment. 6883 (XI¹ A 214).
Disciples. 338 (x¹ A 355), 343 (624), 350 (x² A 311), 400 (x⁴ A 200), 461 (VIII¹ A 129), 462 (130), 658 (IX A 79), 690 (V B 18), 695 (x³ A 653), 2194 (VIII¹ A 300), 2728 (x⁴ A 103), 2868 (x¹ A 482), 2907 (XI¹ A 155), 2975 (346), 3772 (x⁵ A 58), 3776 (XI¹ A 116), 5790 (VI B 16), 6837 (x⁵ A 72).
Discipleship (*see also* IMITATION). 695 (x³ A 653), 1867 (276), 1874 (338), 1884 (615), 1885 (666), 1887 (668), 1891 (750), 1892 (767), 1904 (x⁴ A 354), 2092 (x² A 578), 3018 (x³ A 496).
Discipline. 188 (x² A 396), 1893 (x³ A 776), 2542 (x⁴ A 451), 3406 (VII¹ A 133), 4106 (V A 77), 4465 (x³ A 662), 4526 (XI¹ A 167), 5424 (II A 572).
DISCONTINUITY (*see also* Continuity; CONTRADICTION; Contrast; LEAP). 401 (x⁵ A 42), 542 (98), 554 (XI¹ A 324), 560 (XI² A 49), 611 (IX A 56), 773 (III A 4), 838 (VIII¹ A 73), 839 (74), 1005 (XI¹ A 528), 1152 (XI² A 115), 1247 (V A 90), 1444 (XI² A 53), 1702 (II A 140), 1925 (XI¹ A 22), 1955 (577), 2217 (IX A 424), 2345 (V C 1), 2707 (II A 468), 2850 (VIII¹ A 474), 2908 (XI¹ A 157), 3031 (IX A 322), 3073 (IV C 29), 3100 (XI² A 52), 3263 (II C 57), 3276 (II A 517), 3339 (XI¹ A 347), 3650 (495), 4242 (XI³ B 126), 4489 (XI² A 29), 4696 (x⁵ A 11), 4806 (XI¹ A 329), 4949 (x⁴ A 487), 5161 (I A 235).
Discourse. 638 (VIII¹ A 6), 641 (293), 643 (362), 5686 (IV B 159:6), 5729 (V A 27), 5735 (39), 5741 (62).
"Discourses at the Communion on Fridays." 6111 (VIII¹ A 559), 6407 (x¹ A 351), 6487 (678), 6494 (x² A 39), 6495 (40), 6515 (126), 6519 (148), 6545 (217), 6676 (x⁵ B 264), 6772 (x⁴ A 351), 6777 (373), 6779 (380).
Discovery. 960 (IX A 111).
Discretion. 4913 (XI¹ A 526).
Discrimination. 1993 (VII¹ B 199).
Disgust. 6932 (XI² A 206).
Dishonesty. 654 (VIII² B 86), 845 (XI¹ A 326).
Disintegration. 6255 (IX B 63:7), 6581 (x² A 415).
Disinterestedness. 6077 (VIII¹ A 417).
Disquiet (*see also* Unrest). 3824 (x³ A 6).
Dissertation (S.K.) (see also *Concept of Irony, The*). 4238 (XI² A 108), 4281 (x³ A 477), 4289 (x⁴ A 490), 5262 (II A 166), 5322 (749), 5393 (482), 5504 (L., Doc. XV), 5626 (IV A 70).
Dissipation (*see also* Distraction; Diversion). 2991 (XI² A 109).
Dissonance. 5161 (I A 235).
Distance.
—Christianity at a distance. 305 (VIII¹ A

145), 1913 (x^4 A 521), 1929 (xi^1 A 158), 1932 (391), 2131 (x^4 A 151), 2132 (x^5 A 51), 2435 (x^3 A 741), 2515 (58), 2671 (57), 2897 (x^5 A 78), 2993 (xi^2 A 127), 3430 (ix A 417), 3500 (x^3 A 102), 3512 (479), 3866 (xi^1 A 465), 4572 (xi^2 A 196), 6850 (321).

—Distance from God. 272 (x^2 A 320), 692 (ix A 153), 761 (114), 1167 (viii^1 A 537), 1330 (iv A 106), 1348 (vii^1 A 143), 1385 (x^1 A 64), 1393 (x^2 A 72), 1441 (xi^1 A 464), 1453 (xi^2 A 179), 1454 (180), 1900 (x^4 A 321), 2093 (x^2 A 602), 2096 (xi^1 A 268), 2561 (x^5 A 47), 2853 (x^4 A 483), 3099 (xi^2 A 51), 4477 (x^5 A 24), 4571 (xi^2 A 97), 4903 (x^5 A 17), 4904 (40), 6167 (ix A 71), 6665 (x^3 A 389).

—Distance from the ideal. 987 (x^2 A 546), 1049 (viii^1 A 292), 1873 (x^3 A 331).

—Esthetic (poetic) distance (see also Poet-existence). 816 (x^1 A 248), 817 (502), 819 (x^2 A 137), 826 (xi^1 A 394), 827 (570), 828 (xi^2 A 48), 830 (331), 1043 (vii^1 A 140), 1051 (ix A 154), 1063 (x^4 A 5), 1458 (v A 57), 1828 (x^3 A 616), 1830 (479), 2107 (xi^1 A 160), 2237 (x^2 A 517), 3579 (x^4 A 614), 4360 (xi^2 A 279), 4470 (x^4 A 160), 4881 (609), 5206 (ii A 21), 5287 (207), 6150 (ix A 39), 6727 (x^4 A 33), 6839 (x^5 A 104), 6844 (xi^2 A 283), 6957 (xi^3 B 120).

Distinctions. 693 (x^1 A 132), 1016 (ix A 340), 1017 (x^2 A 348), 1018 (xi^2 A 122), 2051 (xi^1 A 82), 2817 (vii^1 A 197), 3645 (x^2 A 296), 4914 (xi^1 A 568).

Distraction (see also Dissipation; Diversion). 356 (x^3 A 655), 6042 (viii^1 A 249), 6043 (250).

Ditlevsen, Niels C. 3858 (ii A 796).

Diversion (see also Dissipation; Distraction). 806 (iii B 45:1), 2991 (xi^2 A 109), 4177 (x^2 A 486), 4373 (x^1 A 452), 5761-5765 (vi B 222-27), 6234 (ix A 222), 6497 (x^2 A 45).

Diversity. 2688 (viii^1 A 239).

Divine. 327 (x^1 A 49), 360 (x^4 A 514), 833 (ii A 351), 1677 (i A 256), 1734 (iii B 23).

Divorce. 2610 (x^3 A 113).

Dizziness. 749 (viii^2 B 168:6).

Doctrine. (see also Christian Doctrine; CHURCH: Doctrine). 178 (x^5 A99), 383 (x^1 A 460), 482 (ix A 105), 600 (x^4 A

246), 1132 (x^1 A 554), 2334 (xi^2 A 128), 2335 (129), 2626 (172), 3018 (x^3 A 496), 3279 (ii A 529), 3539 (xi^2 A 249), 3870 (117), 4544 (viii^1 A 535), 4548 (x^2 A 145), 4550 (299), 4558 (x^3 A 593), 5049 xi^2 A 50), 6702 (x^3 A 635), 6703 (636), 6727 (x^4 A 33), 6753 (204), 6780 (383), 6808 (584), 6917 (xi^2 A 19).

Dog. 920 (vi A 72), 6622 (x^3 A 94).

Dogma. 3273 (ii A 440), 3279 (529).

Dogmatics. 273 (i A 28), 412 (27), 627 (vi A 17), 693 (x^1 A 132), 795 (i A 150), 972 (x^1 A 360), 1303 (i A 21), 1304 (29), 3253 (ii A 77), 3273 (440), 3279 (529), 3850 (199), 3851 (242), 4398 (i c 126), 4774 (ii A 110), 5277 (ii c 12-24), 5299 (26-28), 5514 (iii c 26), 6475 (x^6 B 105).

DON JUAN. 1670 (i A 145), 3856 (ii A 123), 5084 (i c 52), 5148 (i A 184), 5170 (i c 109), 5290 (ii A 683), 5314 (732), 5315 (733), 5426 (575), 6727 (x^4 A 33).

—As a character. 803 (iii A 94), 4355 (xi^2 A 41), 4387 (i A 122), 5174 (i A 266), 5823 (vi A 78), 6727 (x^4 A 33).

—As a life-tendency. 795 (i A 150), 907 (iv A 213), 1179 (i c 58), 1180 (i A 227), 1181 (292), 1183 (i c 50), 2206 (66), 5110 (61), 5705 (iv A 181).

—The opera. 133 (ii A 180), 803 (iii A 94), 2785 (i A 240), 2786 (270), 2787 (278), 2788 (291), 2789 (ii A 491), 4397 (i c 125), 4416 (iii A 189), 5144 (i A 169), 5226 (ii A 598), 5699 (iv A 170).

DON QUIXOTE. 175 (x^4 A 150), 317 (viii^1 A 519), 416 (i A 95), 536 (x^4 A 581), 1562 (xi^1 A 501), 1670 (i A 145), 1762 (x^2 A 32), 1781 (x^1 A 646), 3047 (v B 1:6), 3568 (x^2 A 633), 4387 (i A 122), 5319 (ii A 740).

Donatists. 1198 (x^4 A 171), 4299 (xi^1 A 371).

Döring, Heinrich. 5122 (i c 75), 5124 (77).

Dorner, Isaak A. 1531 (x^2 A 500).

Dot analogy. 6907 (xi^1 A 497).

Double (see also Double-thinker). 5390 (ii A 444).

Double-danger. 493 (xi^1 A 414), 653 (viii^2 B 85:18), 1897 (x^4 A 274), 3760 (316), 4216 (268), 6270 (ix A 381), 6548 (x^2 A 251).

Double-movement. 5507 (iii A 147).

Double-reflection. 632 (VI B 38), 649 (VIII² B 81:18), 653 (85:21), 5865 (VII¹ B 83), 5887 (VII¹ A 98), 6171 (IX A 81).

Double-thinker. 5239 (II A 115).

DOUBT. 254 (VI A 9), 638 (VIII¹ A 6), 734 (IV B 2:16), 758 (VI A 60), 891 (IV B 13:18-19), 1044 (VII¹ A 216), 1100 (III A 39), 1178 (I A 104), 1244 (IV C 60), 1544 (II A 214), 1587 (III A 1), 1637 (V B 64), 1902 (X⁴ A 349), 1998 (VIII¹ A 331), 2004 (482), 2292 (VII¹ A 34), 2489 (X¹ A 324), 3049 (VIII¹ A 331), 3107 (X³ A 544), 3284 (III A 107), 3558 (X¹ A 666), 4457 (X² A 279), 5065 (I C 25:26), 5092 (I A 72), 5484 (III A 103), 5620 (IV B 10a), 5635 (IV A 236), 6075 (VIII¹ A 414).

Dove analogy. 5238 (II A 617), 5336 (760).

Drama. 129 (II A 15), 1221 (X² A 516), 1761 (X¹ A 148), 2715 (VIII¹ A 26), 4834 (IV C 118), 4838 (122).

DREAMS. 332 (X¹ A 243), 804 (III A 95), 1019 (II A 125), 2092 (X² A 578), 2243 (I A 91), 3798 (132), 4739 (116), 5325 (II A 757), 5381 (415), 5743 (V A 71).

"Du." 673 (X¹ A 566), 4924 (IV A 80), 5980 (VIII¹ A 27).

Dualism. 704 (IV A 192).

Duality. 77 (X³ A 186), 1917 (X⁵ A 9), 2698 (I A 213), 2699 (226), 4417 (IV A 4).

Dullness. 6891 (XI¹ A 294).

Dumas, Alexander. 152 (VI A 117).

Duty. 565 (XI² A 375), 863 (II A 671), 908 (IV B 67), 943 (VIII² B 30:4), 951 (VIII¹ A 319), 1004 (XI¹ A 451), 1807 (402), 2918 (XI² A 386), 3024 (XI¹ A 523), 4491 (XI² A 73), 6158 (IX A 55), 6950 (XI² A 374).

Dwarf. 848 (I A 84).

Dying to. 538 (X⁴ A 624), 559 (XI² A 47), 565 (375), 1006 (113), 1661 (X⁴ A 588), 1864 (X³ A 171), 1872 (314), 2454 (XI² A 421), 3749 (X³ A 166), 3752 (351), 3753 (352), 3754 (361), 3758 (X⁴ A 261), 3759 (266), 3768 (X⁵ A 19), 3769 (25), 3828 (X⁴ A 224), 4354 (XI¹ A 558), 4363 (XI² A 279), 4518 (X⁵ A 63), 4690 (X⁴ A 620), 6616 (X³ A 77), 6682 (472).

Earnestness. 235 (IX A 387), 379 (308), 496 (X¹ A 190), 547 (XI¹ A 91), 649 (VIII² B 81:23), 653 (85:23), 664 (IX A 257), 1743 (VI A 3), 1788 (X³ A 395), 1853 (X¹ A 455), 2108 (XI¹ A 322), 2109 (323), 2112 (V B 65), 2944 (IX A 490), 3123 (X⁵ A 75), 3140 (X² A 357), 3166 (X⁴ A 502), 3170 (X⁵ A 10), 3193 (VIII¹ A 206), 3211 (XI² A 187), 3212 (325), 3795 (V B 69), 4019 (X¹ A 195), 4482 (XI¹ A 472), 4924 (IV A 80), 5974 (VIII¹ A 13), 6574 (X⁶ B 121), 6669 (X³ A 403), 6948 (XI² A 370).

Earthly, the. 833 (II A 351).

Earthquake. 5430 (II A 805), 5612 (IV A 37).

Easter. 3957 (X⁴ A 523).

Eating. 1164 (VIII¹ A 41).

Echo. 1521 (II A 134), 2838 (VII¹ A 46), 2843 (VII¹ B 208), 3801 (I A 140), 5186 (333), 5438 (III A 16).

Ecstasy. 1579 (II A 487), 3280 (814), 6553 (X² A 273), 6560 (L. 240), 6857 (XI¹ A 47).

Edifying, the (see UPBUILDING).

Editor. 6578 (X² A 393).

EDUCATION (see also Upbringing). 93 (II A 489), 272 (X² A 320), 650 (VIII² B 82), 779 (X² A 386), 940 (VIII¹ A 143), 1171 (X¹ A 468), 1173 (X² A 454), 1174 (X³ A 506), 1401 (X² A 493), 1648 (XI¹ A 446), 1779 (X¹ A 434), 2303 (XI² A 191), 2428 (X² B 63), 2712 (X³ A 588), 2917 (XI² A 364), 3225 (177), 3693 (X⁴ A 289), 4068 (I A 289), 4111 (VII¹ A 54), 4266 (74), 4456 (X² A 80), 5648 (IV A 89), 6240 (IX A 230), 6251 (281), 6262 (312), 6431 (X¹ A 510), 6530 (X² A 192), 6533 (196), 6561 (281), 6577 (375), 6660 (X³ A 318), 6737 (X⁴ A 85), 6820 (647).

—Religious upbringing. 265 (II A 12), 398 (X³ A 505), 401 (X⁵ A 42), 519 (X³ A 134), 1163 (VIII¹ A 25), 1169 (616), 1215 (663), 1418 (X³ A 747), 2090 (VIII¹ A 43), 2187 (90), 3028 (585), 3098 (XI¹ A 299), 3373 (II A 327), 4202 (X⁴ A 63), 4577 (II A 761), 4654 (X³ A 182), 4659 (426), 5689 (IV A 142), 6371 (X¹ A 169), 6389 (272), 6390 (273), 6500 (X² A 61), 6521 (157), 6798 (X⁴ A 539).

Effort (see Striving).

Egmont (See GOETHE: Egmont).

Egoity (see also I). 532 (X⁴ A 212), 2053 (XI¹ A 148), 2906 (154), 3779 (376), 3899 (X¹ A 65), 4343 (X⁴ A 508).

Egotism. 532 (X⁴ A 212), 1004 (XI¹ A 451), 1318 (II A 410), 1408 (X³ A 264), 1614 (X² A 426), 1661 (X⁴ A 588), 1712 (II A 626), 1799 (X⁴ A 344), 1841 (VIII¹ A 432), 2037

(x⁴ A 89), 2053 (xɪ¹ A 148), 2075 (533), 2080 (xɪ² A 125), 2412 (vɪɪɪ¹ A 393), 2416 (680), 2441 (x⁵ A 34), 2452 (xɪ² A 105), 2624 (154), 2627 (176), 3545 (ɪ A 22), 3779 (xɪ¹ A 376), 3899 (x¹ A 65), 4206 (x⁴ A 83), 4238 (xɪ² A 108), 4343 (508), 4453 (x¹ A 50), 4501 (xɪ² A 111), 5000 (xɪ¹ A 226), 6006 (vɪɪɪ¹ A 124), 6319 (x¹ A 61).

Ehrenberg, Christian G. 3797 (ɪ A 131).

Eichendorff, Joseph F. v. 5480 (ʟ. 21).

Eight Paths, Nook of. 5096 (ɪ A 65), 5643 (ɪv A 81), 5699 (170).

1848, year. 1962 (x⁴ A 553), 2021 (x⁵ B 244), 2033 (117), 3360 (x⁴ A 416), 3530 (x⁵ A 62), 3716 (x⁴ A 416), 4116 (vɪɪɪ¹ A 108), 4156 (x¹ A 96), 4167 (x² A 52), 4179 (497), 4180 (498), 4185 (x³ A 346), 4193 (746), 4242 (xɪ³ B 126), 6125 (vɪɪɪ¹ A 602), 6126 (603), 6127 (666), 6128 (669), 6255 (ɪx B 63:7), 6256 (x⁶ B 40), 6370 (x¹ A 167), 6376 (202), 6444 (541), 6501 (x² A 66), 6623 (x³ A 98), 6722 (x⁴ A 8), 6801 (545), 6843 (x⁵ A 146), 6854 (xɪ³ B 15).

1842, year. 3822 (ɪɪɪ A 197).

1813, year. 5725 (v A 3).

Eiríksson, Magnus. 6596 (x⁶ B 128), 6597 (x² A 601), 6598 (x⁶ B 68), 6599 (69), 6600 (77), 6601 (82), 6709 (x³ A 678).

Eisengrün, Christian. 5205 (ɪɪ A 20).

Either/Or. 907 (ɪv A 213), 2463 (vɪɪɪ¹ A 465), 3608 (x¹ A 481), 3638 (x² A 115), 3823 (ɪv B 50:4), 4847 (ɪv A 42), 4928 (ɪɪ A 451), 4999 (xɪ¹ A 164), 5144 (ɪ A 169), 5186 (333), 5209 (ɪɪ A 36), 5237 (616), 5251 (637), 5365 (340), 5366 (341), 5371 (373), 5380 (414), 5381 (415), 5384 (421), 5388 (435), 5407 (540), 5426 (575), 5433 (824), 5447 (ɪɪɪ A 40), 5486 (ɪɪɪ c 5), 5496 (ɪɪɪ A 114), 5497 (115), 5498 (116), 5525 (170), 5531 (175), 5532 (176), 5539 (183), 5540 (187), 5541 (190), 5542 (Letter 54), 5546 (ɪɪɪ c 37), 5548 (Letter 62), 5549 (ɪɪɪ B 130), 5550 (132), 5551 (Letter 68), 5552 (ʟ. 69), 5553 (ɪɪɪ B 168), 5554 (ɪɪɪ A 220), 5555 (221), 5556 (223), 5557 (224), 5558 (225), 5561 (227), 5563 (229), 5565 (246), 5566 (ɪɪɪ B 172), 5567 (173), 5568 (189), 5569 (ɪɪɪ A

207), 5613 (ɪv A 43), 5614 (45), 5616 (56), 5626 (70), 5627 (214), 5628 (215), 5629 (216), 5630 (217), 5631 (221), 5632 (223), 5633 (231), 5634 (234), 5635 (235), 5636 (246), 5643 (81), 5669 (114), 5676 (128), 5677 (129), 5692 (151), 5697 (162), 5705 (181), 5710 (ɪv B 59), 5730 (v B 53:26), 5804 (vɪ A 41), 5805 (vɪ B 41:10), 5824 (vɪ A 79), 5830 (87), 5844 (128), 5849 (135), 5853 (vɪ B 192), 5865 (vɪɪ¹ B 83), 5866 (84), 5905 (vɪɪ¹ A 118), 5931 (92), 5997 (vɪɪɪ¹ A 84), 6046 (Letter 154), 6047 (ʟ. 156), 6048 (ʟ. 157), 6107 (vɪɪɪ¹ A 548), 6201 (ɪx A 166), 6206 (172), 6209 (175), 6227 (213), 6229 (216), 6238 (227), 6239 (229), 6242 (241), 6255 (ɪx B 63:7), 6300 (x¹ A 11), 6310 (42), 6323 (72), 6325 (74), 6330 (88), 6332 (x⁵ A 153), 6346 (x¹ A 116), 6356 (138), 6357 (139), 6361 (147), 6363 (152), 6374 (192), 6388 (266), 6394 (309), 6404 (x⁶ B 84), 6407 (x¹ A 351), 6410 (377), 6413 (402), 6444 (541), 6500 (x² A 61), 6593 (560), 6770 (x⁶ B 4:3), 6823 (x⁴ A 663), 6843 (x⁵ A 146), 6882 (xɪ¹ A 210), 6918 (xɪ² A 21), 6945 (xɪ³ B 55).

Either/Or (name). 6947 (xɪ³ B 57).

Either/Or. 449 (ɪɪ A 577), 756 (ɪɪɪ B 179: 27), 801 (ɪɪɪ A 218), 805 (96), 1812 (xɪ¹ A 476), 1925 (22), 2649 (ɪx B 63:13), 3943 (x³ A 107), 4202 (x⁴ A 63), 4494 (xɪ³ B 148), 4508 (x⁴ A 436), 6705 (x³ A 647), 6823 (x⁴ A 663), 6841 (x⁵ A 119), 6944 (xɪ³ B 54), 6946 (56), 6947 (57).

Eleatics. 193 (ɪɪ c 37), 3290 (ɪv A 20).

Eloquence. 598 (x³ A 697), 681 (648), 822 (x⁴ A 222), 824 (633), 828 (xɪ² A 48), 1062 (x³ A 725), 1063 (x⁴ A 5), 4972 (x³ A 677).

Elves. 31 (ɪɪ A 646), 860 (173), 2785 (ɪ A 240), 3996 (ɪɪ A 65), 4401 (169), 5270 (189).

Elvira (*see also* DAN JUAN). 2624 (xɪ² A 154), 2785 (ɪ A 240), 2789 (ɪɪ A 491), 5541 (ɪɪɪ A 190).

Empedocles. 702 (ɪv A 5), 3896 (vɪɪ¹ A 47), 4510 (ɪɪ A 331).

Emperor. 4103 (ɪv A 7).

Empirical, the. 1189 (ɪ A 302).

Empiricism. 252 (ɪ A 316), 1075 (x⁵ A 76),

2250 (II C 44), 2254 (II A 247), 2275 (III A 9).

Empiricus, Sextus. 2280 (IV A 198).

Encouragement. 6214 (IX A 183).

Endurance. 915 (VI A 7).

Enemies. 295 (II A 388), 874 (502), 1207 (VIII¹ A 114), 1211 (475), 2419 (IX A 306), 3337 (XI¹ A 161), 3338 (162), 3429 (IX A 328), 4506 (X⁴ A 434), 4507 (435), 4622 (IX A 336), 4648 (X² A 513).

Energy. 6023 (VIII¹ A 200).

Engagement (S.K.). 5515 (III A 159), 5517 (161), 5519 (164), 5521 (166), 5529 (173), 5532 (176), 5534 (178), 5542 (L. 54), 5548 (L. 62), 5551 (L. 68), 5628 (IV A 215), 5642 (79), 5664 (107), 5689 (142), 5693 (152), 5748 (V A 88), 5769 (VI A 8), 6135 (VIII¹ A 650), 6247 (IX A 262), 6250 (276), 6343 (X¹ A 112), 6389 (272), 6426 (494), 6429 (497), 6432 (513), 6453 (569), 6472 (X⁵ A 149), 6473 (150), 6479 (X¹ A 663), 6482 (677), 6485 (671), 6537 (L. 239), 6541 (X² A 213), 6583 (427), 6666 (X³ A 391), 6826 (X⁵ A 21).

Engagements. 6954 (XI³ B 93).

Engel, Johann J. 5822 (VI A 77).

Engelbrecht, Wolf F. 5089 (I A 60).

English. 3362 (XI² A 7).

Enjoyment. 1005 (XI¹ A 528).

ENTHUSIASM. 1749 (VIII¹ A 169), 2998 (XI² A 159), 3053 (X² A 133), 3360 (X⁴ A 416), 3835 (XI¹ A 440), 4302 (448).

ENVY. 970 (X¹ A 321), 1224 (XI² A 3), 2166 (X³ A 275), 2599 (VIII¹ A 369), 2664 (XI¹ A 114), 2973 (287), 2986 (XI² A 88), 4149 (IX A 303), 4227 (XI¹ A 93), 4596 (VIII¹ A 96), 4663 (X³ A 931), 5906 (VII¹ A 119), 5912 (125), 5930 (90), 5940 (154), 5959 (219), 5995 (VIII¹ A 81), 5998 (99), 6031 (218), 6263 (IX A 321), 6609 (X³ A 8), 6706 (650), 6856 (XI¹ A 6), 6886 (242).

Epic poetry. 1565 (I A 225), 5604 (IV C 107), 5605 (123).

Epictetus. 3040 (XI² A 16), 3863 (X⁴ A 409), 4514 (X³ A 643), 4516 (X⁴ A 576).

Epicureanism. 372 (VIII¹ A 392), 602 (XI¹ A 546), 1619 (14), 3530 (X⁵ A 62), 3771 (53), 3878 (XI¹ A 165), 4728 (XI² A 136), 4803 (X⁵ A 65), 6876 (XI¹ A 149), 6891 (294).

Epicurus. 726 (X⁴ A 60), 1000 (563), 3378 (II A 423), 3906 (X³ A 29), 3908 (35), 4362 (XI² A 353), 5593 (IV C 34), 6793 (X⁴ A 474), 6863 (XI¹ A 76).

Epigram. 402 (X⁵ A 107), 403 (110), 602 (XI¹ A 546), 1267 (X⁴ A 99), 1276 (XI² A 119), 1619 (XI¹ A 14), 2763 (198), 3207 (X⁵ A 111), 3209 (XI¹ A 552), 3317 (X⁵ A 113), 3617 (XI² A 305), 3878 (XI¹ A 165), 4306 (VIII¹ A 40), 4725 (XI² A 67), 4728 (136), 5037 (223), 5614 (IV A 45), 5893 (VII¹ A 106), 5958 (218), 6108 (VIII¹ A 549), 6273 (IX A 408), 6255 (IX B 63:7), 6876 (XI¹ A 15), 6891 (294).

Epitaph. 5916 (VII¹ A 40).

Epitaph (S.K.). 2004 (VIII¹ A 482), 6009 (139).

EQUALITY. 63 (VIII¹ A 268), 457 (VII¹ A 144), 492 (IX A 394), 989 (X³ A 104), 999 (X⁴ A 549), 1207 (VIII¹ A 114), 1993 (VII¹ B 199), 2033 (X⁵ B 117), 2450 (XI² A 8), 2679 (91), 2769 (X¹ A 55), 2817 (VII¹ A 197), 3066 (XI¹ A 196), 3528 (X⁴ A 671), 3561 (XI² A 46), 4131 (VIII¹ A 598), 4158 (X¹ A 269), 4198 (X⁴ A 41), 4206 (83), 4447 (VIII¹ B 76:6,7,9,10,12), 5975 (VIII¹ A 15), 6167 (IX A 71), 6299 (X¹ A 9), 6340 (107), 6384 (258), 6499 (X² A 56).

Erasmus, Desiderius. 153 (VI A 118), 3163 (X⁴ A 332), 3761 (326), 4781 (X² A 548).

Erasmus Montanus. 1105 (IV A 24), 4823 (I A 34), 5186 (333), 5263 (II A 167).

Erdmann, Johann E. 772 (II C 47), 1972 (41), 2250 (44), 2251 (46), 2361 (IV A 12), 2362 (26), 3998 (II A 90), 5271 (II C 38), 5272 (39), 5273 (40), 5274 (II A 193), 5278 (II C 42-49), 5283 (49), 5579 (IV C 8), 5597 (44).

Eremita, Victor (*see* Victor Eremita).

Erigena, Johannes Scotus. 3959 (II A 797).

Error. 924 (VI A 137).

Erslew, Thomas H. 5773 (VI B 8:1-2).

Esaias Strandsand. 6066 (VIII¹ A 384).

Esau. 418 (I A 97), 1315 (II A 402), 2743 (IX A 35).

Escape. 4546 (X¹ A 30).

Eschatology. 5421 (II A 561).

Eschenmayer, Karl A. v. 1191 (II A 592).

Escricht, Daniel F. 4062 (I A 133).

Esrom. 163 (VIII¹ A 621), 5096 (I A 65), 5746 (V A 84).

Essence. 1057 (x² A 328), 1825 (XI³ B 199), 3548 (II A 399).

Essentialism. 977 (x¹ A 580), 6423 (476).

Essentials. 1015 (IX A 44), 3570 (x³ A 121), 3571 (122).

Established, the (see also Established order). 507 (x¹ A 547), 593 (552), 3220 (XI¹ A 97), 4861 (x¹ A 407), 4878 (x⁴ A 337), 6184 (IX A 129), 6467 (x¹ A 640), 6618 (x³ A 86), 6753 (x⁴ A 204), 6754 (228), 6774 (358), 6778 (377), 6787 (x⁶ B 253).

Established order. 1415 (x³ A 658), 1788 (395), 2528 (510), 4225 (XI¹ A 30), 4237 (XI² A 85), 6325 (x¹ A 74), 6343 (112), 6344 (113), 6531 (x² A 193), 6577 (375), 6699 (x³ A 599), 6705 (647), 6943 (XI³ B 53).

ESTHETIC, THE; ESTHETICISM. 69 (IX A 76), 108 (x⁴ A 387), 124 (I A 175), 141 (III A 110), 152 (VI A 117), 226 (x³ A 463), 228 (II A 581), 403 (x⁵ A 110), 492 (IX A 394), 508 (x¹ A 558), 539 (x⁴ A 648), 546 (XI¹ A 70), 621 (II A 463), 634 (VI B 60:2), 635 (129), 663 (IX A 240), 675 (x² A 19), 681 (x³ A 648), 721 (IX B 233), 853 (I A 222), 885 (III A 135), 899 (IV A 92), 942 (VIII¹ A 189), 949 (312), 953 (398), 961 (IX A 314), 963 (372), 973 (x¹ A 393), 975 (430), 1016 (IX A 340), 1031 (IV A 188), 1041 (VII¹ A 48), 1051 (IX A 154), 1062 (x³ A 725), 1063 (x⁴ A 5), 1087 (518), 1414 (x³ A 585), 1462 (x⁴ A 582), 1736 (III A 98), 1758 (IX A 400), 1893 (x³ A 776), 1901 (x⁴ A 340), 1932 (XI¹ A 391), 2105 (x⁵ A 162), 2107 (XI¹ A 160), 2263 (II A 404), 2294 (VII¹ A 76), 2313 (II A 159), 2324 (x² A 235), 2393 (III B 106), 2394 (114), 2423 (x¹ A 489), 2437 (x⁴ A 482), 2586 (III A 117), 2853 (x⁴ A 483), 2895 (x⁵ A 48), 2907 (XI¹ A 155), 3037 (x³ A 622), 3059 (II A 789), 3305 (VI A 133), 3488 (x² A 149), 3506 (x³ A 246), 3538 (XI² A 71), 3570 (x³ A 121), 4430 (VI A 123), 4437 (VII² B 256:19), 4454 (x¹ A 134), 4467 (x³ A 791), 4562 (x⁴ A 283), 4668 (153), 4726 (XI² A 72), 4826 (IV C 110), 4849 (VII¹ A 32), 4881 (x⁴ A 609), 4971 (x³ A 570), 4972 (677), 5048 (XI² A

35), 5634 (IV A 234), 5804 (41), 6209 (IX A 175), 6223 (205), 6239 (229), 6249 (271), 6255 (IX B 63:7), 6363 (152), 6431 (x¹ A 510), 6461 (593), 6466 (617), 6475 (x⁶ B 105), 6592 (x² A 544).

Esthetics. 143 (IV C 104), 581 (I A 108), 1012 (VIII¹ B 31:20), 1013 (31:22), 1895 (x⁴ A 148), 2134 (XI¹ A 21), 2283 (IV C 99), 3489 (x² A 151), 3804 (I A 171), 4454 (x¹ A 134), 5608 (IV C 127), 6844 (XI² A 283).

ETERNAL, the. 28 (I A 334), 161 (VIII¹ A 88), 169 (x¹ A 432), 206 (IV A 143), 227 (I C 40), 235 (IX A 387), 311 (VIII¹ A 371), 463 (157), 496 (x¹ A 190), 539 (x⁴ A 648), 602 (XI¹ A 546), 717 (VII¹ A 145), 747 (VIII¹ B 154:3), 828 (XI² A 48), 879 (II A 578), 946 (VIII¹ A 223), 947 (236), 949 (312), 1003 (XI¹ A 252), 1018 (XI² A 122), 1473 (x² A 219), 1501 (XI¹ A 182), 1635 (IV C 35), 1933 (XI¹ A 396), 1937 (x¹ A 588), 1944 (I A 171), 1987 (V A 60), 1996 (VII¹ B 158:3), 2004 (VIII¹ A 482), 2080 (XI¹ A 125), 2112 (V B 65), 2113 (66), 2114 (227:5), 2222 (x⁴ A 572), 2599 (VIII¹ A 369), 2711 (x³ A 175), 2740 (V B 55:6), 2799 (I A 300), 2915 (XI¹ A 181), 2970 (227), 2974 (325), 2982 (514), 3093 (x² A 501), 3802 (I A 142), 3815 (294), 4159 (x¹ A 350), 4482 (XI¹ A 472), 4600 (VIII¹ A 191), 4696 (x⁵ A 11), 4712 (XI¹ A 377), 4789 (II A 437), 4799 (x³ A 286), 4800 (320), 4810 (XI¹ A 468), 4815 (318), 4816 (382), 4856 (IX A 326), 4918 (XI¹ A 205), 4923 (I A 201), 5009 (VIII¹ A 104), 5010 (105), 5276 (II A 630), 5792 (VI B 18), 6179 (IX A 108), 6269 (379).

Eternal life. 3097 (x⁵ A 142), 4703 (XI² A 297).

ETERNITY. 206 (IV A 143), 539 (x⁴ A 648), 547 (XI¹ A 91), 564 (XI² A 315), 1018 (122), 1250 (VII¹ A 71), 1853 (x¹ A 455), 1955 (XI¹ A 577), 2203 (x⁴ A 183), 2222 (572), 2565 (XI¹ A 435), 2668 (XI² A 262), 2673 (x⁴ A 520), 2856 (II A 149), 3098 (XI¹ A 299), 3868 (583), 3915 (III C 1), 3951 (x³ A 706), 3955 (711), 4234 (XI¹ A 536), 4242 (XI³ B 126), 4448 (IX A 37), 4527 (XI¹ A 212), 4589 (VI A 48), 4797 (x¹ A 581), 4801 (x³ A 390), 4803 (x⁵ A 65), 4804 (XI¹ A 3), 4808 (419), 4809

(420), 4812 (554), 4813 (XI^2 A 76), 4814
(123), 4923 (I A 201), 4940 (X^5 A 41),
5234 (II A 611), 5849 (VI A 135), 6152
(IX A 42), 6256 (X^6 B 40), 6262 (312),
6850 (XI^2 A 321), 6947 (XI^3 B 57), 6958
(XI^2 A 399), 6967 (437).

ETHICAL, THE; ETHICAL CONSCIOUSNESS,
THE. 108 (X^4 A 387), 634 (VI B 60:2), 649
(VIII^2 B 81:5), 650 (82:12,13), 653 (85),
656 (88), 774 (IV A 72), 1085 (X^3 A 464),
1090 (X^4 A 652), 1731 (III B 19), 1745
(VI A 38), 1757 (IX A 399), 1901 (X^4 A
340), 1991 (VI A 102), 2324 (X^2 A 235),
2808 (VII^1 A 183), 3130 (X^2 A 594), 3340
(IV A 35), 4433 (VII^1 A 68), 4437 (VII^2 B
256:19), 5632 (IV A 223), 5634 (234),
5804 (VI A 41), 6645 (X^3 A 189), 6719
(799).

Ethics. 53 (V B 196), 54 (198), 150 (148:
17), 151 (VI A 43), 167 (X^1 A 198), 220 (II
A 128), 221 (130), 231 (VII^1 A 165), 232
(178), 233 (VIII^1 A 368), 236 (X^1 A 135),
242 (I A 38), 249 (VIII^1 A 526), 250 (X^4 A
76), 261 (IV C 87), 604 (V A 5), 631 (VI A
149), 684 (X^1 A 51), 774 (IV A 72), 790 (I
A 197), 808 (IV C 105), 809 (106), 817 (X^1
A 502), 819 (X^2 A 137), 827 (XI^1 A 570),
838 (VIII^1 A 73), 1008 (VII^1 A 245), 1042
(80), 1048 (VIII^1 A 234), 1049 (292),
1088 (X^4 A 590), 1240 (III A 48), 1247 (V
A 90), 1249 (V B 56:2), 1262 (X^2 A 438),
1263 (518), 1269 (X^4 A 177), 1281 (II A
175), 1537 (XI^2 A 4), 1548 (III B 20), 1593
(III C 33), 1606 (V B 44), 1607 (VI B 40:3),
1676 (I A 239), 1743 (VI A 3), 1758 (IX A
400), 1761 (X^1 A 148), 1773 (III A 242),
1776 (IX A 202), 1779 (X^1 A 434), 1967 (I
A 337), 1984 (III A 136), 1993 (VII^1 B
199), 1994 (VII^1 A 149), 2286 (VI B 40:5),
2292 (VII^1 A 34), 2345 (V C 1), 2349 (7),
2352 (12), 2587 (III A 144), 2595 (VIII^1 A
52), 2675 (IX A 149), 2807 (VII^1 A 182),
2813 (191), 2823 (X^5 A 73), 2846 (VII^2 B
256:20), 2874 (X^3 A 169), 3076 (IV A 62),
3077 (103), 3214 (VII^1 A 110), 3287 (III B
183), 3309 (VII^1 A 152), 3318 (X^3 A 437),
3328 (X^2 A 608), 3329 (609), 3488 (149),
3503 (X^3 A 141), 3549 (IV C 40), 3608
(X^1 A 481), 3638 (X^2 A 115), 3639 (156),
3870 (XI^2 A 117), 3871 (362), 3875 (XI^1 A
112), 3877 (144), 3882 (182), 3890 (II A

464), 3978 (IV A 28), 4030 (X^2 A 436),
4060 (I A 42), 4196 (X^4 A 31), 4265 (VII^1
A 69), 4281 (X^3 A 477), 4300 (XI^1 A 428),
4319 (VII^1 C 1), 4327 (X^1 A 652), 4430
(VI A 123), 4433 (VII^1 A 68), 4436 (VII^1 B
192:15), 4444 (VIII^1 A 214), 4448 (IX A
37), 4454 (X^1 A 134), 4467 (X^3 A 791),
4476 (X^4 A 461), 4479 (X^5 A 95), 4480
(XI^1 A 456), 4483 (475), 4511 (IV C 54),
4790 (IV A 184), 4801 (X^3 A 390), 4831
(IV C 115), 4929 (VIII^1 A 66), 4944 (XI^1 A
521), 4946 (IV A 160), 5459 (III A 59),
5586 (IV A 25), 5637 (71), 5669 (114),
5748 (V A 88), 5941 (VII^1 A 155), 5975
(VIII^1 A 15), 6227 (IX A 213), 6253 (285),
6302 (X^1 A 15), 6425 (488), 6445 (546),
6582 (X^2 A 425), 6703 (X^3 A 636), 6793
(X^4 A 474).

—Aristotelian ethics. 113 (IV C 21), 114
(27), 115 (X^5 A 31), 116 (32), 143 (IV C
104), 4104 (IV A 9), 5591 (IV C 22).

—Christian ethics. 84 (XI^1 A 385), 85
(386), 107 (X^3 A 97), 108 (X^4 A 387), 195
(II A 367), 212 (X^3 A 60), 218 (I A 301),
228 (II A 581), 229 (III A 87), 283 (II A
594), 301 (IV A 33), 377 (IX A 199), 383
(X^1 A 460), 385 (X^2 A 16), 387 (58), 396
(X^3 A 282), 446 (II A 443), 451 (IV A 27),
457 (VII^1 A 144), 464 (VIII^1 A 214), 465
(215), 480 (IX A 28), 485 (284), 486
(292), 489 (329), 492 (394), 498 (X^1 A
301), 507 (547), 512 (X^2 A 187), 513
(284), 514 (420), 538 (X^4 A 624), 560 (XI^2
A 49), 561 (102), 612 (X^2 A 57), 639 (VIII^1
A 243), 640 (256), 778 (7), 1020 (II A
235), 1135 (X^2 A 207), 1139 (X^3 A 322),
1140 (323), 1142 (X^4 A 114), 1154 (XI^2 A
380), 1176 (XI^1 A 522), 1186 (I C 50),
1193 (X^2 A 563), 1201 (III A 215), 1207
(VIII^1 A 114), 1216 (675), 1286 (X^3 A
263), 1310 (II A 758), 1399 (X^2 A 241),
1445 (XI^1 A 98), 1462 (X^4 A 582), 1473
(X^2 A 219), 1474 (223), 1475 (239), 1480
(X^3 A 353), 1482 (X^3 A 784), 1483 (X^4 A
134), 1488 (X^5 A 7), 1490 (54), 1496
(109), 1510 (VIII^1 A 333), 1518 (XI^1 A
176), 1530 (X^2 A 481), 1654 (451), 1690
(II A 102), 1787 (X^3 A 347), 1793 (670),
1802 (XI^1 A 130), 1807 (402), 1819 (XI^2 A
264), 1822 (267), 1823 (271), 1834 (III A
132), 1839 (VIII^1 A 349), 1840 (350),

1841 (432), 1842 (449), 1851 (x¹ A 179), 1853 (455), 1855 (673), 1857 (x² A 47), 1862 (361), 1880 (x³ A 454), 1884 (615), 1886 (667), 1892 (767), 1895 (x⁴ A 148), 1901 (340), 1902 (349), 1912 (500), 1914 (656), 1918 (x⁵ A 27), 1919 (44), 1939 (xI² A 358), 1948 (vII¹ A 244), 1955 (xI¹ A 577), 2026 (x³ A 116), 2027 (324), 2034 (763), 2053 (xI¹ A 148), 2092 (x² A 578), 2130 (x⁴ A 26), 2380 (II A 24), 2403 (vII¹ A 225), 2404 (226), 2419 (IX A 306), 2423 (x¹ A 489), 2428 (x² A 63), 2432 (x³ A 19), 2434 (739), 2435 (741), 2449 (xI¹ A 459), 2461 (vII¹ A 192), 2534 (x⁴ A 25), 2541 (394), 2580 (II A 375), 2601 (IX A 245), 2604 (x¹ A 310), 2607 (485), 2617 (xI¹ A 150), 2643 (IX A 325), 2650 (x¹ A 16), 2654 (382), 2682 (xI² A 326), 2772 (22), 2793 (x² A 341), 2974 (xI¹ A 325), 2976 (372), 3014 (x¹ A 396), 3023 (xI¹ A 339), 3029 (IX A 244), 3032 (427), 3113 (x³ A 632), 3153 (267), 3668 (IX A 163), 3677 (x³ A 125), 3852 (x² A 416), 4042 (x³ A 341), 4052 (x¹ A 17), 4152 (IX A 364), 4163 (x¹ A 632), 4183 (x² A 643), 4185 (x³ A 346), 4206 (x⁴ A 83), 4226 (xI¹ A 54), 4503 (xI² A 373), 4524 (x⁴ A 639), 4544 (vIII¹ A 535), 4553 (x² A 336), 4623 (IX A 349), 4688 (x⁴ A 593), 4689 (611), 4700 (x⁵ A 81), 4859 (x¹ A 347), 4951 (x³ A 617), 5014 (401), 5015 (589), 5050 (x² A 568), 6050 (vIII¹ A 271), 6500 (x² A 61), 6503 (75), 6511 (106), 6793 (x⁴ A 474), 6946 (xI³ B 56).
—Communication of the ethical (*see also* COMMUNICATION: Ethical communication, Communication of inwardness). 632 (vI B 38), 648 (vIII² B 79), 649 (81), 650 (82), 651 (83), 652 (84), 653 (85), 654 (86), 657 (89), 668 (x¹ A 185), 673 (566), 676 (x² A 146), 815 (IX A 289), 828 (xI² A 48), 1087 (x⁴ A 518), 1830 (479), 2161 (x¹ A 341), 2298 (vIII¹ A 479).
—Religious ethics. 184 (vIII¹ A 436), 185 (x¹ A 5), 219 (II A 127), 1026 (III A 26), 1106 (IV C 82), 1109 (IV B 76), 1121 (vIII¹ A 19), 1129 (x¹ A 367), 1166 (vIII¹ A 499), 1232 (I A 205), 1348 (vII¹ A 143), 1350 (vIII¹ A 24), 1354 (77), 1356 (111), 1375 (IX A 254), 1380 (441), 1383 (x¹ A 59), 1412 (x³ A 421), 1784 (238), 2017

(x¹ A 463), 2116 (vI B 98:77), 2117 (vIII¹ A 76), 2118 (vIII² B 91:13), 2122 (x² A 46), 2179 (III A 213), 2184 (232), 2301 (x⁴ A 247), 2407 (vIII¹ A 89), 2424 (x¹ A 514), 2771 (x⁴ A 263), 2898 (x⁵ A 96), 2993 (xI² A 127), 3078 (IV A 116), 3378 (II A 423), 3394 (IV A 171), 3415 (vIII¹ A 342), 3794 (IV A 169), 4170 (x² A 351), 4202 (x⁴ A 68), 4364 (vI A 2), 4588 (46), 6075 (vIII¹ A 414).
Ethics, imperative and indicative. 1312 (II A 391), 1908 (x⁴ A 459), 2202 (x⁵ A 156).
Eudæmonism. 1510 (vIII¹ A 333), 3878 (xI¹ A 165), 3881 (181), 3882 (182), 5636 (IV A 246).
Eulenspiegel, Till. 3540 (xI² A 281), 5082 (I A 51), 5110 (I C 61), 6614 (x³ A 67).
"Eulogy of Autumn." 6060 (vIII¹ A 339).
Euthanasia. 6036 (vIII¹ A 228).
Eve. 282 (II A 197), 1659 (x³ A 787), 5730 (v B 53:26).
Evening. 56 (vI B 49).
Evil. 305 (vIII¹ A 145), 486 (IX A 292), 636 (vII¹ A 91), 874 (II A 502), 966 (IX A 419), 1185 (II A 605), 1249 (v B 56:2), 1251 (vII¹ A 181), 1262 (x² A 438), 1302 (I A 2), 1447 (xI² A 130), 1614 (x² A 426), 1653 (353), 1940 (xI² A 434), 2499 (x¹ A 545), 3041 (xI¹ A 204), 3089 (vIII¹ A 11), 4028 (x² A 404), 4401 (II A 169), 5227 (599), 5231 (603), 5586 (IV A 25), 5607 (IV C 126), 5979 (vIII¹ A 23), 6191 (IX A 139), 6224 (208), 6235 (223).
Ewald, Johannes. 4731 (IV A 48), 5134 (I C 87), 5316 (II A 736), 5480 (L. 21).
Exaggeration. 6912 (xI¹ A 559).
Examination. 73 (x² A 406), 156 (vII¹ A 51), 251 (x⁴ A 473), 481 (IX A 51), 637 (vII¹ A 123), 1052 (IX A 358), 1066 (xI¹ A 353), 1297 (IX A 275), 1422 (x⁴ A 132), 1439 (xI¹ A 359), 1650 (xI² A 235), 1654 (x² A 451), 1925 (xI¹ A 22), 1937 (588), 2449 (459), 3210 (xI² A 38), 3359 (x³ A 461), 3624 (xI¹ A 437), 4702 (x⁵ A 114), 4856 (IX A 326), 4977 (x⁵ A 18), 6150 (IX A 39), 6273 (408), 6591 (x² A 534), 6969 (xI² A 439).
Examination (S.K.). 5092 (I A 72), 5385 (II A 422), 5394 (490), 5396 (495), 5397 (497), 5406 (534), 5432 (807), 5434

(576), 5446 (III A 35), 5468 (73), 5626 (IV A 70).

Examiner. 1447 (XI² A 130), 2027 (X³ A 324).

Example (see IMITATION; Prototype).

Exception, the (see also EXTRAORDINARY, THE). 996 (X⁴ A 184), 1123 (VIII¹ A 649), 1300 (X³ A 499), 2183 (III A 194), 2607 (X¹ A 485), 2664 (XI¹ A 114), 4474 (X⁴ A 335), 4590 (VI A 80), 4599 (VIII¹ A 161), 6357 (X¹ A 139).

Excursions. 5746 (V A 84), 5912 (VII¹ A 125), 6013 (VIII¹ A 163), 6105 (544).

Excuses. 2053 (XI¹ A 148).

Exegesis (see Interpretation; Commentaries).

EXIST, EXISTENCE (see also CHANGE; Coming into existence; STAGES). 54 (V B 198), 55 (VI A 102), 106 (X³ A 96), 126 (I A 212), 148 (IV A 173), 152 (VI A 117), 176 (X⁴ A 537), 193 (II C 37), 197 (IV C 100), 226 (X³ A 463), 253 (IV A 187), 294 (II A 369), 381 (X¹ A 7), 703 (IV A 57), 705 (V A 88), 730 (XI² A 200), 759 (VIII¹ A 84), 895 (IV C 86), 898 (IV A 82), 925 (VI B 54:3), 973 (X¹ A 393), 977 (580), 1009 (VII¹ A 134), 1074 (X¹ A 238), 1123 (VIII¹ A 649), 1439 (XI¹ A 359), 1445 (XI² A 98), 1452 (175), 1544 (II A 214), 1593 (III C 33), 1606 (V B 41), 1616 (X³ A 786), 1635 (IV C 35), 1731 (III B 19), 2036 (X⁴ A 29), 2049 (XI¹ A 60), 2301 (X⁴ A 247), 2331 (XI¹ A 361), 3308 (VII¹ A 82), 3561 (XI² A 46), 3693 (X⁴ A 289), 3796 (I A 130), 3877 (XI¹ A 144), 4460 (X² A 642), 5402 (II A 512), 6015 (VIII¹ A 170), 6391 (X¹ A 281), 6423 (476), 6736 (X⁴ A 64), 6803 (557).

—Christian existence. 187 (X² A 119), 482 (IX A 105), 484 (207), 485 (284), 511 (X² A 141), 517 (603), 523 (X³ A 285), 579 (I A 57), 580 (58), 606 (VIII¹ A 128), 949 (312), 965 (IX A 418), 1142 (X⁴ A 114), 1143 (123), 1152 (XI² A 115), 1660 (X⁴ A 329), 1865 (X³ A 207), 2066 (XI¹ A 384), 2103 (500), 2359 (XI² A 103), 2724 (XI¹ A 186), 2853 (X⁴ A 483), 3018 (X³ A 496), 3084 (VI B 43), 3095 (X³ A 424), 3141 (X² A 418), 3192 (VI A 153), 3479 (X¹ A 6), 3509 (X³ A 307), 3513 (484), 3531 (X⁵ A 117), 3643 (XI¹ A 289), 3685

(X³ A 545), 3716 (X⁴ A 528), 3731 (30), 3757 (X³ A 560), 3860 (702), 3870 (XI² A 117), 4185 (X³ A 346), 4561 (X⁴ A 112), 4565 (379), 4566 (407), 4568 (X⁵ A 84), 4661 (X³ A 500), 4856 (IX A 326), 4918 (XI² A 205), 6521 (X² A 157), 6716 (X³ A 760), 6753 (X⁴ A 204).

—Communication of existence. 630 (VI A 147), 633 (VI B 40:45), 637 (VII¹ A 123), 644 (VIII¹ A 448), 646 (554), 649 (VIII² B 81), 650 (82), 653 (85), 656 (88), 663 (IX A 240), 676 (X² A 146), 678 (466), 3694 (X⁴ A 295), 5914 (VII¹ A 127).

—Dream-existence. 804 (III A 95).

—Existence of God. 254 (VI A 9), 1342 (VI A 121), 1334 (V A 7), 1347 (VII¹ A 139), 1348 (143).

—Poet-existence. 817 (X¹ A 502), 4464 (X³ A 512).

EXISTENTIAL. 180 (XI¹ A 237), 322 (IX A 59), 385 (X² A 16), 513 (284), 600 (X⁴ A 246), 674 (X² A 12), 686 (X⁴ A 24), 818 (X¹ A 523), 827 (XI¹ A 520), 934 (VII¹ A 138), 997 (X⁴ A 320), 1086 (32), 1375 (IX A 254), 1792 (X³ A 576), 1828 (616), 1895 (X⁴ A 148), 1912 (500), 1931 (XI¹ A 338), 2296 (VII¹ A 215), 2531 (X³ A 605), 2805 (XI¹ A 217), 2881 (X³ A 541), 2974 (XI¹ A 325), 3166 (X⁴ A 502), 3488 (X² A 149), 3574 (X⁴ A 236), 3673 (X²·A 541), 4058 (XI² A 319), 4312 (X⁴ A 484), 4553 (X² A 336), 4568 (X⁵ A 84), 4572 (XI² A 196), 6499 (X² A 56), 6780 (X⁴ A 383), 6792 (472), 6903 (XI¹ A 460).

Existing. 633 (VI B 40:45), 5794 (35:15), 5795 (35:19), 5796 (35:24).

Expectations. 879 (II A 578), 1031 (IV A 188), 1665 (III A 129), 1666 (130), 4691 (X⁴ A 623), 5614 (IV A 45).

EXPERIENCE. 124 (I A 175), 252 (316), 513 (X² A 284), 1097 (II A 190), 1116 (VI A 148), 1269 (X⁴ A 177), 1707 (II A 192), 1797 (X⁴ A 146), 1902 (349), 2251 (II C 46), 2275 (III A 9), 2298 (VIII¹ A 479), 2500 (X¹ A 595), 2532 (X⁴ A 7), 5100 (I A 75).

Experts. 1071 (IV A 59).

Explanation. 5900 (VII¹ A 113).

Expression. 485 (IX A 284), 949 (VIII¹ A 312), 1234 (II A 280), 1414 (X³ A 585), 1995 (VII¹ A 205).

Exstaticus. 5434 (II A 576).

Extensity, Extensiveness (see also INTEN-SITY; Intensiveness). 2056 (XI¹ A 189), 2100 (X⁴ A 219), 2101 (392), 2102 (X⁵ A 26), 2103 (XI¹ A 500), 2104 (XI² A 64), 2448 (XI¹ A 414), 2994 (XI² A 146), 3201 (X⁴ A 541), 6656 (X³ A 265), 6763 (X⁴ A 300), 6813 (604), 6907 (XI¹ A 497).

Externality. 889 (III A 202), 949 (VIII¹ A 312), 2129 (X⁴ A 21), 2131 (151).

EXTRAORDINARY, THE (see also Exception). 89 (XI² A 139), 108 (X⁴ A 387), 110 (418), 178 (X⁵ A 99), 234 (VIII² B 13:61-63), 329 (X¹ A 201), 525 (X³ A 649), 794 (XI¹ A 410), 1786 (X³ A 312), 1901 (X⁴ A 340), 1914 (556), 1939 (XI² A 358), 2020 (X⁶ B 52:1), 2046 (X⁵ A 121), 2095 (X³ A 766), 2432 (19), 2760 (X⁴ A 531), 3347 (X³ A 16), 3498 (48), 4469 (X⁴ A 125), 4550 (X² A 299), 4640 (128), 4646 (272), 4672 (X⁴ A 189), 4701 (X⁵ A 85), 4719 (XI¹ A 541), 4968 (X³ A 15), 5961 (VII¹ A 221), 6182 (IX A 125), 6335 (X¹ A 92), 6336 (94), 6343 (112), 6345 (115), 6346 (116), 6394 (309), 6418 (424), 6500 (X² A 61), 6511 (106), 6740 (X⁴ A 130), 6771 (339), 6820 (647), 6872 (XI¹ A 136), 6888 (275), 6901 (439).

Eye. 5076 (I A 17).

Eye of God. 6012 (VIII¹ A 158).

Faber, Friedrich. 5761 (VI B 222).

Fact, factuality. 2255 (II A 264).

Fairy story. 265 (II A 12), 1238 (456), 3270 (353), 5287 (207), 5843 (VI A 125), 5988 (VIII¹ A 44), 6294 (L. 195).

FAITH. 5 (IV A 108), 8 (X² A 592), 9 (X⁶ B 78), 48 (V A 25), 49 (28), 73 (X² A 406), 77 (X³ A 186), 170 (X² A 380), 180 (XI¹ A 237), 206 (IV A 143), 252 (I A 316), 254 (VI A 9), 255 (IX A 32), 321 (57), 326 (440), 507 (X¹ A 547), 576 (X³ A 765), 692 (IX A 153), 705 (V A 68), 810 (35), 869 (II A 447), 957 (VIII¹ A 509), 972 (X¹ A 360), 976 (457), 1031 (IV A 188), 1045 (VII¹ A 217), 1199 (X⁴ A 172), 1202 (III C 16), 1250 (VII¹ A 71), 1266 (X⁴ A 13), 1347 (VII¹ A 139), 1401 (X² A 493), 1411 (X³ A 374), 1452 (XI² A 175), 1530 (X² A 481), 1559 (225), 1610 (VI B 98:45), 1753 (IX A 151), 1861 (X² A 347), 1872 (X³ A 314), 1877 (409), 1880 (454), 1881 (455), 1892 (767), 1942 (VIII¹ A 643), 2118 (VIII² B 91:13), 2119 (VIII¹ A 511), 2122 (X² A 46), 2126 (X³ A 356), 2136 (XI¹ A 488), 2137 (VII¹ A 207), 2180 (III C 18), 2205 (XI² A 114), 2251 (II C 46), 2252 (48), 2283 (IV C 99), 2302 (X⁴ A 310), 2419 (IX A 306), 2422 (X¹ A 487), 2423 (489), 2467 (IX A 11), 2468 (22), 2474 (433), 2475 (X¹ A 10), 2480 (85), 2484 (213), 2495 (420), 2504 (X² A 123), 2532 (X⁴ A 7), 2543 (XI² A 301), 2715 (VIII¹ A 26), 2803 (X² A 529), 2810 (VII¹ A 188), 2820 (200), 2877 (X³ A 328), 3070 (II A 755), 3073 (IV C 29), 3103 (VII¹ A 151), 3315 (X² A 432), 3456 (X³ A 531), 3608 (X¹ A 481), 3610 (X² A 446), 3611 (447), 3628 (VII¹ A 130), 3659 (X⁵ A 14), 3710 (X² A 624), 3712 (640), 3714 (X⁴ A 357), 3840 (276), 3860 (X³ A 702), 3951 (706), 4040 (181), 4055 (XI¹ A 562), 4070 (I A 307), 4286 (X⁴ A 334), 4368 (IX A 331), 4370 (333), 4550 (X² A 301), 4610 (VIII¹ A 579), 4686 (X⁴ A 579), 4761 (X³ A 240), 4855 (IX A 304), 4876 (X⁴ A 42), 4896 (356), 4902 (636), 5049 (XI² A 50), 5056 (I C 9), 5181 (I A 328), 5521 (III A 166), 5664 (IV A 107), 5712 (V A 100), 5779 (VI C 2), 5964 (VII¹ A 224), 6091 (L. 167), 6135 (VIII¹ A 650), 6275 (IX A 413), 6574 (X⁶ B 121), 3575 (X² A 372), 6595 (596), 6597 (601), 6698 (X³ A 591).

Faithfulness, faithlessness. 5520 (III A 165), 5531 (175).

Falcon. 5846 (VI A 130).

Falk, Johannes. 5121 (I C 74), 5123 (76).

Fall, the. 510 (X² A 37), 830 (XI² A 331), 1309 (II A 237), 4349 (XI¹ A 363), 6881 (209), 6882 (210).

FAMILY. 56 (VI B 49), 91 (II A 18), 267 (IV A 60), 268 (V A 2), 269 (VI A 96), 270 (IX A 395), 271 (X² A 97), 272 (320), 316 (VIII¹ A 469), 398 (X³ A 505), 457 (VII¹ A 144), 475 (IX A 5), 519 (X³ A 134), 568 (VIII¹ A 470), 647 (564), 786 (257), 787 (258), 841 (543), 939 (62), 1215 (663), 1258 (X² A 159), 1374 (IX A 247), 1392 (X¹ A 629), 1779 (434), 1875 (X³ A 378), 2187 (VIII¹ A 90), 2425 (X¹ A 635), 2428 (X² A 63), 2607 (X¹ A 485), 2627 (XI² A 176), 2865 (X¹ A 221), 3407 (VII¹ A 136), 3446

(x^2 A 496), 3621 (xi^1 A 213), 3841 (x^4 A 277), 3939 (x^2 A 325), 3999 (II A 584), 4009 (VI A 105), 4161 (x^1 A 369), 4600 (viii^1 A 191), 5431 (II A 806), 5690 (IV A 144), 6106 (viii^1 A 545), 6612 (x^3 A 30).

Family (S.K.). 5328 (II A 231), 5430 (805), 5431 (806), 5690 (IV A 144), 6298 (x^1 A 8), 6379 (234).

Fanaticism. 1399 (x^2 A 241), 2379 (xi^2 A 39).

Fanatics. 1234 (II A 280), 6466 (x^1 A 617).

Fantasy. 2166 (x^3 A 275).

Farinelli. 5542 (L. 54).

Fashion designer. 5681 (IV A 135), 5682 (136), 5683 (137), 5684 (138), 5685 (139), 6858 (xi^1 A 49).

Fasting. 1065 (x^4 A 207), 2976 (xi^1 A 372), 4709 (340), 6116 (viii^1 A 570).

Fat of rams. 5385 (II A 422).

Fatalism. 1565 (I A 225), 2737 (II A 89), 4551 (x^2 A 301).

Fate (*see also* Necessity). 1242 (IV C 55), 1248 (V B 55:26), 1263 (x^2 A 518), 4173 (394), 4796 (x^1 A 261).

Fathers. 1155 (III C 7), 1161 (VI A 24), 1175 (x^3 A 792), 1366 (IX A 34), 1371 (116), 1374 (247), 1392 (x^1 A 629), 1396 (x^2 A 186), 1413 (x^3 A 581), 2622 (xi^2 A 150), 2851 (IX A 19), 3939 (x^2 A 325), 3949 (x^3 A 213), 5488 (III C 12), 6612 (x^3 A 30).

Father (S.K.) (*See also* Kierkegaard, Michael P.). 740 (II A 485), 1490 (x^5 A 54), 3841 (x^4 A 277), 5205 (II A 20), 5328 (231), 5335 (243), 5430 (805), 5664 (IV A 107), 5751 (V A 93), 5820 (VI A 75), 6019 (viii^1 A 177), 6035 (227), 6073 (397), 6131 (640), 6161 (IX A 65), 6164-67 (68-71), 6176 (99), 6178 (106), 6298 (x^1 A 8), 6308 (39), 6327 (78), 6355 (137), 6379 (234), 6389 (272), 6617 (x^3 A 78).

Father, step- (S.K.). 6178 (IX A 106), 6389 (x^1 A 272).

FAUST. 769 (II A 55), 795 (I A 150), 1186 (I C 50), 1671 (I A 154), 1968 (II A 53), 2206 (I C 66), 5077-80 (46-49), 5083-86 (51-54), 5092 (I A 72), 5110 (I C 61), 5111 (62), 5158 (100), 5159 (101), 5168-71 (107-10), 5173 (112), 5174 (I A 266), 5216 (II A 54).

Faust. 1457 (I A 233), 2703 (I C 113), 2922

(I A 165), 4387 (122), 4389 (183), 5139 (I C 96), 5160 (102), 5165 (104), 5167 (106), 5225 (II A 597), 5226 (598), 5412 (557).

Faustian letters. 5140 (I A 156), 5141 (161), 5181-88 (328-36), 5190 (339), 5191 (341), 5216 (II A 54), 5227 (599), 5228 (600), 5231 (603), 5232 (607), 5233 (609), 5235 (613), 5236 (614), 5237 (616), 5241 (118), 5249 (634).

Favorite Bible text (S.K.). 6673 (x^3 A 422), 6965 (xi^3 B 291:4).

Favorite hymn (S.K.). 6673 (x^3 A 422).

Fear. 483 (IX A 147), 1007 (xi^2 A 381), 1320 (II A 472), 2687 (xi^2 A 435), 2976 (xi^1 A 372), 3992 (II A 19), 4221 (x^5 A 136), 6394 (x^1 A 309), 6576 (x^2 A 374).

Fear and trembling. 2223 (x^5 A 132), 2383 (II A 370), 2544 (xi^2 A 303), 3369 (II A 313), 6473 (x^5 A 150), 6731 (x^4 A 53).

Fear and Trembling. 1109 (IV B 76), 1812 (xi^1 A 476), 2343 (V B 49:14), 3130 (x^2 A 594), 5485 (III C 4), 5587 (IV A 30), 5616 (56), 5625 (69), 5640 (76), 5659 (IV B 78), 5660 (79), 5665 (L. 82), 5668 (IV A 113), 5672 (122), 5674 (126), 5709 (193), 5844 (VI A 128), 6050 (viii^1 A 271), 6357 (x^1 A 139), 6404 (x^6 B 84), 6434 (L. 213), 6473 (x^5 A 150), 6491 (x^2 A 15), 6598 (x^6 B 68), 6791 (x^4 A 458), 6843 (x^5 A 146).

Fechner, Gustav T. 2852 (x^1 A 34).

Fecht, Johannes. 2368 (IV C 38).

Feeling. 14 (x^3 A 342), 47 (V A 20), 618 (II A 620), 1281 (175), 2246 (I A 112), 2261 (II A 348), 2532 (x^4 A 7), 2645 (IX A 435), 2807 (vii^1 A 182), 3542 (I A 10), 3852 (x^2 A 416), 3853 (417), 3894 (IV A 166), 5067 (I C 34), 5738 (V A 52), 5865 (vii^1 B 83), 6140 (viii^1 A 679), 6710 (x^3 A 716).

Felix de St. Vincent. 2510 (x^2 A 334), 6060 (viii^1 A 339).

Fell[d], Pouel P. 5466 (III A 71).

Fenelon, François. 818 (x^1 A 523), 3435 (291), 4638 (662), 4863 (448), 5736 (V A 45), 6426 (x^1 A 494), 6762 (x^4 A 299).

Fenger, Johannes F. 817 (x^1 A 502), 4121 (viii^1 A 245), 4126 (382), 6558 (x^6 B 130).

Fenger, Peter A. 6851 (xi^2 A 334).

Fenger, Rasmus Theodor. 4121 (vɪɪɪ¹ A 245).
Fenris wolf. 5209 (ɪɪ A 36).
Fernow, Carl L. 3242 (x³ A 683).
Ferry. 5451 (ɪɪɪ A 51).
Feuerbach, Ludwig A. 45 (v A 14), 3477 (vɪɪɪ¹ A 434), 5061 (ɪ A 11), 6523 (x² A 163).
FF. 6202 (ɪx A 167), 6387 (x¹ A 263), 6640 (x⁶ B 167).
Fibiger, Mathilde. 6709 (x³ A 678).
FICHTE, Immanuel H. 657 (vɪɪɪ² B 89), 1400 (x² A 443), 2346 (v c 2), 2631 (xɪ² A 372), 3276 (ɪɪ A 517), 3277 (518), 3278 (519), 3641 (x⁴ A 74), 4037 (x² A 482), 4110 (vɪɪ¹ A 20), 4206 (x⁴ A 83), 5282 (ɪɪ A 204), 5283 (ɪɪ c 49), 5286 (50), 5332 (ɪɪ A 240), 5883 (vɪɪ¹ A 23), 6460 (x¹ A 588).
FICHTE, Johann G. 1455 (ɪ c 73), 2338 (ɪv c 11), 3545 (ɪ A 22), 5099 (68), 5102 (77), 5982 (vɪɪɪ¹ A 34).
Fiddler. 5252 (ɪɪ A 640).
Fig-tree. 5050 (x¹ A 294), 5087 (ɪ c 65).
Figaro. 4387 (ɪ A 122), 4397 (ɪ c 125), 6624 (x³ A 99).
Finitude. 183 (vɪɪɪ¹ A 416), 257 (ɪɪɪ c 30), 842 (x¹ A 48), 1003 (xɪ¹ A 252), 1035 (vɪ A 101), 1253 (vɪɪɪ¹ A 178), 1783 (x² A 510), 1823 (xɪ² A 271), 2086 (361), 3836 (10), 4004 (ɪɪɪ A 118), 4199 (x⁴ A 43), 4242 (xɪ³ B 126), 4494 (148), 4527 (xɪ¹ A 212), 4531 (431), 4905 (x⁵ A 118), 5616 (ɪv A 56).
Fire. 564 (xɪ² A 315), 4355 (41).
Fire analogy. 6932 (xɪ² A 206).
"First and Last Declaration." 5864 (vɪɪ¹ B 75), 5871 (vɪɪ¹ A 2), 5872 (3), 5942 (156), 6654 (x³ A 258).
Fischart, Johann F. 5858 (vɪɪ¹ A 241).
Fischer, Gabriel. 5580 (ɪv c 9).
Fish. 2979 (xɪ¹ A 454).
Fisherman. 846 (xɪ³ B 124).
Fishing analogy. 5259 (ɪɪ A 653).
Fists. 6093 (vɪɪɪ¹ A 481).
Fjellenstrup. 5108 (ɪ A 71).
Flattery. 6251 (ɪx A 281).
Fliegendes Blatt, ein. 2668 (ɪ A 262), 5159 (ɪ c 101), 5200 (ɪɪ A 7), 5306 (222).
Flight. 505 (x¹ A 472).

Flögel, Carl F. 231 (ɪv A 204), 4255 (208), 5371 (ɪɪ A 373), 5858 (vɪɪ¹ A 241).
Flower drawing. 5527 (L. 71).
Folksongs. 2704 (ɪɪ A 631), 5127 (ɪ c 81), 5288 (ɪɪ A 679).
Follower. 461 (vɪɪɪ¹ A 129), 1854 (x¹ A 631).
For Self-Examination. 2859 (vɪ A 111), 4283 (x⁴ A 314), 4980 (xɪ¹ A 115), 5965 (vɪɪ¹ A 227), 6682 (x³ A 472).
FORCE. 1450 (xɪ² A 170), 4323 (vɪɪ¹ A 168), 4324 (vɪɪɪ¹ A 334), 4356 (xɪ² A 62), 4506 (x⁴ A 434), 4667 (135), 6256 (x⁶ B 40), 6936 (xɪ² A 250).
Forchammer, Peter W. 4246 (ɪɪɪ B 30).
Foreknowledge. 3544 (ɪ A 20), 3546 (43), 4389 (183).
Forest (*see also* Gribskov). 48 (v A 25), 2826 (ɪɪ A 475), 6013 (vɪɪɪ¹ A 163), 6105 (544).
Forgery. 5049 (xɪ² A 50).
Forgetting. 715 (v A 56), 898 (ɪv A 82), 1307 (ɪɪ A 622), 1324 (ɪɪɪ A 101), 1535 (x³ A 775), 3447 (x² A 595), 5142 (ɪ A 162), 5219 (ɪɪ A 67), 5422 (565), 5453 (ɪɪɪ A 53), 5532 (176).
FORGIVENESS (*See also* Sin: Forgiveness of sins). 67 (vɪɪɪ¹ A 673), 502 (x¹ A 443), 637 (vɪɪ¹ A 123), 1042 (vɪɪ¹ A 80), 1100 (ɪɪɪ A 39), 1123 (vɪɪɪ¹ A 649), 1206 (vɪɪ¹ A 167), 1215 (663), 1216 (675), 1341 (vɪ B 163), 2195 (vɪɪɪ¹ A 302), 2436 (x⁴ A 309), 2483 (x¹ A 197), 2907 (xɪ¹ A 155), 3084 (vɪ B 43), 3085 (45), 3628 (vɪɪ¹ A 130), 3825 (x³ A 10), 4012 (vɪɪɪ¹ A 473), 4029 (x² A 429), 4506 (x⁴ A 434), 4507 (435), 4654 (x³ A 182), 4787 (x² A 282), 5928 (vɪɪ¹ A 78), 5963 (223), 6037 (vɪɪɪ¹ A 229), 6043 (250), 6133 (645), 6160 (ɪx A 64), 6210 (176), 6229 (216).
Form. 119 (ɪ A 86), 138 (ɪɪ A 425), 1266 (x⁴ A 13), 5116 (ɪ B 2).
Formalism. 3318 (x³ A 437).
Formula of Concord. 2459 (ɪɪ A 434), 3656 (ɪ A 243).
Fragmentation. 143 (ɪv c 104), 377 (ɪx A 199).
Francis, St. 288 (ɪɪ A 276), 5492 (ɪɪɪ A 93).
Francke, August H. 3310 (vɪɪɪ¹ A 70), 3321 (x⁴ A 84), 3322 (94).

FRANKLIN, Benjamin. 1225 (x⁴ A 67), 1226 (73), 1228-29 (81-82), 4204 (68), 4819 (66).

Frater Taciturnus. 4868 (x³ A 25), 5804 (VI A 41), 5888 (VII¹ A 99), 5939 (150), 6202 (IX A 167), 6330 (x¹ A 88).

Fredensborg. 1546 (II A 442), 5094-96 (I A 63-65), 5481 (L. 23), 5499 (III A 121), 5852 (L. 120a), 6247 (IX A 262).

Frederik VI. 5756 (V A 111).

Frederik VII. 4134 (VIII¹ A 606).

Frederiksberg Gardens. 5756 (V A 111).

Frederiksborg. 5284 (II A 205), 5331 (238).

Frederiksen, Morten. 408 (XI¹ A 529), 2543 (XI² A 301), 5061 (I A 11).

FREEDOM. 52 (V B 55:4), 68 (VIII² B 168:5), 97 (V B 53:23), 112 (IV C 20), 199 (VI B 54:21), 249 (VIII¹ A 526), 262 (V B 15:1), 267 (IV A 60), 522 (x³ A 209), 749 (VIII² B 168:6), 777 (IV B 13:21), 894 (IV C 72), 905 (IV A 149), 1356 (VIII¹ A 111), 1616 (x³ A 786), 1875 (378), 1940 (XI² A 434), 2058 (XI¹ A 260), 2185 (IV A 146), 2338 (IV C 11), 2360 (IV A 11), 2366 (IV C 36), 2509 (x² A 263), 2672 (x⁴ A 454), 3281 (III A 11), 3542 (I A 10), 3544 (20), 3549 (IV C 40), 3744 (VIII¹ A 572), 3756 (x² A 457), 3769 (x⁵ A 25), 3770 (29), 3834 (XI¹ A 271), 3844 (I C 23 in supplement XI³ p. XXIV), 4004 (III A 118), 4037 (x² A 482), 4204 (x⁴ A 68), 4495 (XI¹ A 63), 4551 (x² A 301), 4586 (V A 49), 4610 (VIII¹ A 579), 4611 (580), 4769 (x⁴ A 142), 4860 (x¹ A 348), 4877 (x⁴ A 161), 4950 (x³ A 43), 5038 (XI² A 239), 5092 (I A 72), 5634 (IV A 234), 6021 (VIII¹ A 185), 6723 (x⁴ A 9), 6966 (XI² A 436), 6969 (439).

Freedom of religion. 4817 (x⁴ A 10).

Free-thinkers. 546 (XI¹ A 70), 555 (332), 556 (333), 1144 (x⁴ A 422), 1147 (634), 1276 (XI² A 119), 1822 (267), 6523 (x² A 163), 6832 (x⁵ A 43), 6912 (XI¹ A 559).

Fremtoning (see Phomomenon).

French Revolution. 4065 (I A 246), 4134 (VIII¹ A 606), 4136 (608), 4206 (x⁴ A 83), 5638 (IV A 74).

Friends. 319 (VIII¹ A 583), 387 (x² A 58), 2697 (x³ A 523), 6384 (x¹ A 258), 6619 (x³ A 88), 6812 (x⁴ A 603).

FRIENDSHIP. 1108 (IV A 117), 2428 (x² A 63), 4577 (II A 761), 5996 (VIII¹ A 82), 6281 (IX A 428).

Fries, Jacob F. 1191 (II A 592).

Frithiof Saga. 3800 (I A 136).

From the Papers of One Still Living. 5071 (I A 41), 5339 (II A 768).

Fruit analogy. 6485 (x¹ A 671).

Fulcrum. 2665 (XI¹ A 462).

Funeral. 840 (VIII¹ A 221), 849 (I A 124).

Future. 98 (V B 55:10), 1245 (IV C 62), 1327 (III A 131), 1654 (x² A 451), 1769 (XI² A 255), 3737 (346), 4794 (VIII¹ A 147), 6006 (124), 6072 (394), 6075 (414), 6078 (424), 6108 (549), 6204 (IX A 169), 6222 (203), 6263 (321), 6555 (x² A 277), 6919 (XI² A 31).

Fædrelandet. 4180 (x² A 498), 6128 (VIII¹ A 669), 6202 (IX A 167), 6209 (175), 6619 (x³ A 88), 6621 (90), 6957 (XI³ B 120).

Fædrelandet articles. 6960 (XI³ B 128), 6961 (129), 6962 (131), 6963 (132).

Gadfly. 641 (VIII¹ A 293), 4265 (VII¹ A 69), 4268 (VIII¹ A 154), 4271 (491), 6943 (XI³ B 53).

Galle, Friedrich. 3056 (x⁴ A 413).

Galley slave. 5256 (II A 647).

Garve, Christian. 4418 (IV A 10), 5590 (IV C 18).

Gaunilo. 3615 (x⁴ A 210).

Geese. 722 (x² A 434), 1280 (II A 23), 3067 (XI² A 210), 5303 (II A 210), 5998 (VIII¹ A 99).

Geese analogy. 6906 (XI¹ A 484).

Genesis. 26 (I A 149), 107 (x³ A 97), 4407 (II A 321).

Genetic fallacy. 3483 (x¹ A 182).

GENIUS. 107 (x³ A 97), 615 (XI² A 263), 827 (XI¹ A 570), 975 (x¹ A 430), 997 (580), 1021 (II A 556), 1114 (V C 13:4), 1135 (x² A 207), 1248 (V B 55:26), 1788 (x³ A 395), 1804 (XI¹ A 197), 2092 (x² A 578), 2255 (II A 264), 2467 (IX A 11), 2495 (x¹ A 420), 2636 (VIII¹ A 418), 2653 (x¹ A 333), 2907 (XI¹ A 155), 3066 (196), 3088 (VII² B 256:9-10), 3861 (x⁴ A 110), 3877 (XI¹ A 144), 4227 (93), 4265 (VII¹ A 69), 4271 (VIII¹ A 491), 4444 (160), 4467 (x³

A 791), 4741 (727), 5695 (IV A 154), 5835 (VI A 95), 6049 (VIII¹ A 264), 6220 (IX A 189), 6254 (288), 6382 (X¹ A 247), 6401 (342), 6407 (351), 6511 (X² A 106), 6680 (X³ A 450), 6780 (X⁴ A 383), 6787 (X⁶ B 253), 6856 (XI¹ A 6), 6903 (460).

Genthe, Friedrich W. 5360 (II C 65).

Gentleness. 3332 (X¹ A 205).

Geography book. 371 (II A 236).

Gerhard, Johann. 3918 (VIII¹ A 261).

Gerhardt, Paulus. 1361 (VIII¹ A 516), 1840 (350).

German language. 5655 (L. 80), 6595 (X² A 596).

Germans. 1620 (XI¹ A 180), 1621 (183).

Germany. 4127 (VIII¹ A 531), 6596 (X⁶ B 128).

Gersdorff, Carl v. 6861 (XI¹ A 71).

Gesticulation. 969 (X¹ A 208), 4965 (X² A 143).

Gesture. 6716 (X³ A 780).

Gilbjerget. 5099 (I A 68), 5107 (70).

Gilleleie. 5094 (I A 63), 5107 (70), 5413 (II A 817).

Gilleleie letter. 5100 (I A 75).

Giving. 1204 (IV A 66).

Gjeding, Jens J. 5466 (III A 71).

Gjenboerne. 6088 (VIII¹ A 458), 6089 (654).

Gjødwad [Giødwad], Jens F. 1791 (X³ A 525), 4307 (425), 5312 (II A 728), 5997 (VIII¹ A 84), 6209 (IX A 175), 6211 (178), 6619 (X³ A 88), 6620 (89), 6621 (90).

Glasses analogy. 5281 (II A 203).

Glaucon. 5892 (VII¹ A 105).

Gnosticism. 219 (II A 127), 1309 (237), 5227 (599), 5350 (II C 60).

Goblin analogy. 5301 (II A 702).

GOD. 6 (V A 78), 14 (X³ A 342), 53 (V B 196), 65 (VIII¹ A 601), 76 (X² A 491), 200 (XI¹ A 284), 220 (II A 128), 251 (X⁴ A 473), 254 (VI A 9), 298 (II A 569), 467 (VIII¹ A 267), 532 (X⁴ A 212), 533 (452), 538 (624), 543 (X⁵ A 144), 553 (XI¹ A 293), 565 (XI² A 375), 731 (422), 741 (III A 195), 979 (X² A 23), 1102 (III A 127), 1108 (IV A 117), 1117 (VII¹ A 61), 1123 (VIII¹ A 649), 1144 (X⁴ A 422), 1155 (III C 7), 1156 (17), 1163 (VIII¹ A 25), 1168 (586), 1170 (IX A 118), 1173 (X² A 454), 1175 (X³ A 792), 1230 (I A 5), 1251 (VII¹ A 181), 1492 (X⁵ A 64),

1506 (III A 140), 1507 (143), 1508 (240), 1510 (VIII¹ A 333), 1818 (XI² A 201), 1910 (X⁴ A 492), 1940 (XI² A 434), 1960 (X³ A 659), 1983 (III A 38), 1985 (236), 2001 (VIII¹ A 262), 2034 (X³ A 763), 2038 (X⁴ A 104), 2051 (X² A 454), 2074 (X³ A 792), 2091 (VIII¹ A 676), 2097 (XI¹ A 321), 2099 (491), 2184 (III A 232), 2205 (XI² A 114), 2349 (V C 7), 2390 (III A 137), 2395 (237), 2407 (VIII¹ A 89), 2424 (X¹ A 514), 2425 (635), 2436 (X⁴ A 309), 2437 (482), 2443 (XI¹ A 279), 2444 (356), 2446 (406), 2447 (411), 2449 (459), 2450 (XI² A 8), 2452 (105), 2453 (390), 2480 (X¹ A 85), 2494 (419), 2515 (X³ A 58), 2554 (XI¹ A 572), 2560 (X⁴ A 612), 2561 (X⁵ A 47), 2562 (86), 2563 (XI¹ A 37), 2570 (XI² A 54), 2573 (118), 2574 (144), 2576 (166), 2737 (II A 89), 2851 (IX A 19), 2853 (X⁴ A 483), 2882 (X³ A 549), 2992 (XI² A 116), 3077 (IV A 103), 3081 (V B 5:10), 3084 (VI B 43), 3085 (45), 3099 (XI² A 51), 3100 (52), 3110 (X³ A 626), 3212 (XI² A 325), 3263 (II C 56), 3341 (IX A 36), 3475 (VIII¹ A 98), 3548 (II A 399), 3649 (XI¹ A 67), 3737 (XI² A 346), 3746 (IX A 486), 3844 (I C 23, in supplement XI³ p. xxxiv), 3920 (VIII¹ A 266), 3949 (X³ A 213), 4006 (IV A 189), 4189 (X³ A 603), 4321 (VII¹ C 3), 4375 (X¹ A 478), 4462 (X³ A 394), 4484 (XI¹ A 478), 4489 (XI² A 29), 4503 (373), 4571 (97), 4677 (X⁴ A 343), 4690 (620), 4713 (XI¹ A 404), 4715 (422), 4730 (XI² A 396), 4876 (X⁴ A 42), 4890 (297), 4891 (305), 4892 (XI¹ A 418), 4898 (X⁴ A 480), 5038 (XI² A 239), 6032 (VIII¹ A 219), 6075 (414), 6134 (648), 6135 (650), 6161 (IX A 65), 6215 (184), 6229 (216), 6307 (X¹ A 37), 6623 (X³ A 98), 6824 (X⁴ A 673), 6902 (XI¹ A 445), 6965 (XI³ B 291:4).

God's agent. 466 (VIII¹ A 238).

God-conception. 1312 (II A 391).

God, existence of (*see* EXISTENCE: Existence of God).

God, fear of. 2976 (XI¹ A 372).

"God's judgment." 5786 (VI A 146), 5801 (31), 5802 (32), 5810 (47), 5813-17 (55-59), 5818 (61).

God, kingdom of. 477 (IX A 13), 478 (14), 3936 (X² A 50).

God, knowledge of. 1351 (vIII¹ A 30), 2212 (II A 354).

Godliness. 1408 (x³ A 264).

God-Man (*see also* CHRIST: God-Man Paradox). 284 (II A 595), 305 (vIII¹ A 145), 333 (x¹ A 245), 357 (x⁴ A 60), 421 (I A 215), 601 (x⁴ A 594), 2898 (x⁵ A 96), 3860 (x³ A 702), 4183 (643).

God-relationship (*see also* GOD). 77 (x³ A 186), 83 (xI¹ A 358), 255 (IX A 32), 264 (x² A 561), 272 (320), 323 (IX A 103), 490 (350), 603 (xI² A 229), 698 (xI¹ A 362), 728 (565), 904 (IV A 134), 1034 (VI A 65), 1050 (vIII¹ A 320), 1200 (II A 326), 1218 (IX A 482), 1273 (x⁵ A 13), 1471 (x² A 189), 1476 (x³ A 72), 1493 (x⁵ A 101), 1509 (vIII¹ A 253), 1511 (678), 1533 (x³ A 638), 1613 (vIII¹ A 283), 1661 (x⁴ A 588), 1715 (II A 660), 1769 (xI² A 255), 1849 (IX A 323), 1896 (x⁴ A 273), 1897 (274), 1898 (275), 1943 (471), 1960 (x³ A 659), 2008 (IX A 316), 2009 (318), 2026 (x³ A 116), 2066 (xI¹ A 384), 2119 (vIII¹ A 511), 2138 (x² A 76), 2186 (vIII¹ A 12), 2202 (x⁵ A 156), 2236 (vIII¹ A 358), 2410 (196), 2418 (IX A 88), 2428 (x² A 63), 2440 (x⁴ A 655), 2607 (x¹ A 485), 2654 (382), 2898 (x⁵ A 96), 3031 (IX A 322), 3179 (xI¹ A 389), 3457 (x³ A 595), 3628 (vII¹ A 130), 3667 (IX A 121), 3705 (365), 3708 (x¹ A 330), 3718 (xI² A 66), 3838 (IX A 295), 3987 (xI² A 142), 4132 (vIII¹ A 599), 4148 (IX A 117), 4384 (xI² A 132), 4431 (vII¹ A 45), 4449 (IX A 194), 4477 (x⁵ A 24), 4479 (95), 4481 (xI¹ A 457), 4524 (x⁴ A 639), 4588 (VI A 46), 4625 (IX A 380), 4682 (x⁴ A 570), 4692 (630), 4698 (x⁵ A 30), 4724 (xI² A 66), 4911 (xI¹ A 516), 4949 (x⁴ A 487), 5649 (IV A 90), 6001 (vIII¹ A 116), 6033 (220), 6145 (IX A 23), 6158 (55), 6161 (65), 6170 (74), 6178 (106), 6235 (223), 6239 (229), 6290 (484), 6298 (x¹ A 8), 6389 (272), 6473 (x⁵ A 150), 6478 (x¹ A 661), 6486 (676), 6514 (x² A 112), 6516 (134), 6815 (x⁴ A 610), 6824 (673), 6837 (x⁵ A 72).

God's word. 215 (x⁴ A 437), 2911 (xI¹ A 395).

GOETHE (*see also* FAUST). 827 (xI¹ A 570), 1027 (III A 62), 1046 (vIII¹ A 127), 1068 (II A 58), 1541 (I A 340), 1802 (xI¹ A 130), 1804 (197), 2344 (V B 150:21), 2565 (xI¹ A 435), 3501 (x³ A 129), 3813 (I A 230), 3872 (xI¹ A 75), 3895 (VI A 132), 4386 (I A 121), 4643 (x² A 236), 5011 (vIII¹ A 106), 5117 (I A 118), 5120 (I C 72), 5121-24 (74-77), 5160 (102), 5163 (103), 5195 (118), 5373 (II A 386), 5427 (II A 82), 5897 (vII¹ A 110), 6353 (x¹ A 130), 6473 (x⁵ A 150), 6667 (x³ A 399), 6903 (xI¹ A 460).

—Egmont. 118 (I A 33), 4823 (34).

—Faust. 699 (I A 324), 1568 (II A 48), 2922 (I A 165), 4387 (I A 122), 5139 (I C 96), 5160 (102), 5167 (106), 5412 (II A 557).

—Wilhelm Meister. 1455 (I C 73), 5745 (V A 82).

Going beyond. 1615 (x² A 431), 1798 (x⁴ A 282), 2287 (VI B 42), 4302 (xI¹ A 448), 6275 (IX A 413), 6531 (x² A 193), 6596 (x⁶ B 128), 6947 (xI³ B 57).

Goldschmidt, Meïr. 827 (xI¹ A 570), 2048 (42), 4149 (IX A 494), 5888 (vII¹ A 99), 5896 (109), 5898 (111), 5937 (147), 5957 (214), 6031 (vIII¹ A 218), 6044 (252), 6099 (655), 6123 (595), 6196 (IX A 493), 6282 (432), 6321 (x¹ A 67), 6348 (120), 6351 (123), 6377 (206), 6382 (247), 6474 (653), 6493 (x² A 25), 6498 (48), 6509 (101), 6546 (228), 6548 (251), 6594 (586), 6602 (605), 6619 (x³ A 88), 6621 (90), 6743 (x⁴ A 167), 6744 (168), 6745 (195), 6746 (x⁵ A 166), 6747 (167), 6748 (x⁶ B 171), 6750 (188), 6751 (194), 6753 (x⁴ A 204), 6757 (270), 6758 (271), 6759 (272), 6773 (353), 6777 (373), 6778 (377), 6795 (511), 6842 (x⁶ B 232), 6846 (xI² A 296), 6847 (311), 6853 (xI¹ A 1), 6854 (xI³ B 15), 6886 (xI¹ A 242).

Gomarists. 5583 (IV A 16).

Good. 305 (vIII¹ A 145), 894 (IV C 72), 932 (vII¹ A 73), 971 (x¹ A 327), 1002 (x⁴ A 669), 1249 (V B 56:2), 1262 (x² A 438), 1356 (vIII¹ A 111), 2641 (IX A 141), 3503 (x³ A 141), 4028 (x² A 404), 4030 (436), 4401 (II A 169), 4436 (vII¹ B 192:15), 4483 (xI¹ A 475), 4846 (IV C 95), 4944 (xI¹ A 521), 6683 (x³ A 483).

Good and evil. 966 (IX A 419), 1348 (vII¹ A 143), 4599 (vIII¹ A 161).

Good, the highest. 4680 (x⁴ A 456).

Good sense. 1001 (x⁴ A 571).

Good works. 983 (x² A 208), 1156 (III C 17), 4468 (x⁴ A 59).

Gorgias. 4309 (x⁴ A 466), 4840 (v A 80).

Görres, Joseph v. 3810 (I A 218), 5173 (I C 112), 5182 (I A 329), 5210 (II A 40), 5321 (745), 5492 (III A 93).

Göschel, Karl F. 2024 (x² A 489).

Gospel. 295 (II A 388), 435 (277), 1483 (x⁴ A 134), 1484 (230), 2189 (VIII¹ A 180), 2190-93 (181-84), 2194 (300), 2195 (302), 2196 (322), 2197 (323), 2198 (360), 2199 (361), 2527 (x³ A 336), 2529 (516), 2533 (x⁴ A 12), 2547 (XI¹ A 77), 2554 (572), 2905 (138), 5053 (I C 7).

Gospel of Suffering. 4131 (VIII¹ A 598), 5945 (VII¹ A 160), 5964 (224), 5967 (246), 5991 (VIII¹ A 49), 6054 (308), 6101 (504).

Gothic. 755 (III A 92).

Gottsched[en], Johann C. 5580 (IV C 9).

Gossip. 812 (VII¹ A 59), 1538 (XI² A 5), 2156 (IX A 357), 2945 (x¹ A 231), 6321 (67), 6968 (XI² A 438).

Governance (see also PROVIDENCE). 188 (x² A 396), 939 (VII¹ A 62), 2092 (x² A 578), 2093 (602), 4143 (VIII¹ A 600), 4144 (667), 6112 (IX A 560), 6113 (561), 6152 (IX A 42), 6157 (54), 6161 (65), 6171 (81), 6207 (173), 6211 (178), 6352 (x¹ A 126), 6385 (260), 6388 (266), 6390 (273), 6497 (x² A 45), 6511 (106), 6522 158), 6526 (177), 6630 (x³ A 146), 6664 (381), 6797 (x⁴ A 513), 6810 (587), 6820 (647), 6895 (XI¹ A 382).

Grabbe, Christian D. 5084 (I C 52), 5315 (II A 733).

GRACE. 174 (x³ A 187), 334 (x¹ A 279), 349 (x² A 170), 401 (x⁵ A 42), 538 (x⁴ A 624), 573 (439), 606 (VIII¹ A 128), 692 (IX A 153), 763 (x² A 132), 880 (III A 23), 984 (x² A 224), 988 (x³ A 66), 993 (734), 994 (737), 1143 (x⁴ A 123), 1164 (VIII¹ A 41), 1169 (499), 1383 (x¹ A 59), 1396 (x² A 186), 1431 (x⁴ A 640), 1654 (x² A 451), 1655 (452), 1821 (XI² A 344), 1862 (x² A 361), 1867 (x³ A 276), 1875 (378), 1884 (615), 1886 (667), 1888 (712), 1902 (x⁴ A 349), 1903 (352), 1909 (491), 1910 (492), 1918 (x⁵ A 27), 1934 (XI¹ A 492), 1951 (x² A 584), 2027 (x³ A 324), 2058 (XI¹ A 260), 2066 (384), 2119 (VIII¹ A 511), 2124 (x³ A 251), 2140 (672), 2218 (139), 2551 (XI¹ A 297), 2559 (x⁴ A 446), 2711 (x³ A 175), 2898 (x⁵ A 96), 2905 (XI¹ A 138), 3043 (585), 3096 (x⁴ A 641), 3114 (x³ A 633), 3490 (x² A 218), 3497 (581), 3513 (x³ A 484), 3530 (x⁵ A 62), 3531 (117), 3546 (I A 43), 3610 (x² A 446), 3681 (x³ A 278), 3754 (361), 3767 (x⁵ A 4), 3772 (58), 3829 (x³ A 654), 3887 (II A 248), 3936 (x² A 50), 4032 (456), 4046 (x⁴ A 133), 4333 (x² A 445), 4380 (x⁴ A 431), 4479 (x⁵ A 95), 4483 (XI¹ A 475), 4523 (x⁴ A 191), 4524 (639), 4551 (x² A 301), 4653 (x³ A 148), 4680 (x⁴ A 456), 4688 (593), 4700 (x⁵ A 81), 4799 (x³ A 286), 4933 (470), 4941 (XI¹ A 453), 5962 (VII¹ A 222), 6275 (IX A 413), 6521 (x² A 157), 6528 (184), 6532 (195), 6646 (x³ A 190), 6702 (635), 6778 (x⁴ A 377), 6783 (395), 6801 (545), 6832 (x⁵ A 43), 6834 (46), 6843 (146), 6947 (XI³ B 57).

Grade analogy. 5266 (II A 677).

Gradualness. 968 (IX A 464).

GRATITUDE. 695 (x³ A 653), 993 (734), 1164 (VIII¹ A 41), 1281 (II A 175), 1407 (x³ A 247), 1414 (585), 1420 (781), 1488 (x⁵ A 7), 1502 (XI² A 226), 1504 (367), 1533 (x³ A 638), 1883 (602), 1886 (667), 1892 (767), 2054 (XI¹ A 168), 2442 (x⁵ A 50), 2497 (x¹ A 474), 2897 (x⁵ A 78), 3364 (II A 201), 3384 (III C 19), 3704 (IX A 248), 4198 (x⁴ A 41), 4329 (x² A 103), 4524 (x⁴ A 639), 4588 (VI A 46), 4592 (VII¹ A 213), 4644 (x² A 246), 4688 (x⁴ A 593), 4700 (x⁵ A 81), 5117 (I A 118), 6135 (VIII¹ A 650), 6153 (IX A 43), 6159 (62), 6161 (65), 6166 (70), 6167 (71), 6220 (189), 6266 (371), 6511 (x² A 106), 6513 (110), 6579 (411), 6603 (619), 6642 (x³ A 168), 6664 (381), 6671 (415), 6718 (789), 6721 (x⁴ A 6), 6772 (351), 6824 (673).

Great man. 321 (IX A 57), 1289 (II A 278), 4060 (I A 42).

Greatness. 322 (IX A 59), 527 (x³ A 738), 958 (VIII¹ A 671), 961 (IX A 314), 974 (x¹ A 412).

Greece. 2708 (VI A 37), 5279 (II A 200).

Greek. 182 (VIII¹ A 225), 582 (II A 269), 649 (VIII² B 81), 650 (82), 1039 (VI B 54:10), 6412 (X¹ A 385), 6595 (X² A 596).
Greek fire. 4008 (VI A 30).
Greek language. 1703 (II A 141).
Greek mentality. 5889 (VII¹ A 101).
Greek-Roman. 432 (II A 250), 433 (251).
GREEKS. 18 (III A 13), 19 (XI¹ A 307), 154 (VII¹ A 12), 199 (VI B 54:21), 932 (VII¹ A 73), 1107 (IV A 109), 1263 (X² A 518), 1306 (II A 73), 1620 (XI¹ A 180), 1680 (II A 38), 1683 (79), 1690 (102), 1695 (107), 1711 (II A 68), 1944 (I A 151), 2316 (II A 665), 3294 (IV A 54), 3300 (V A 98), 4070 (I A 307), 4073 (310), 4085 (II A 710), 4107 (VI A 1), 4398 (I C 126).
Green[e], Robert. 6320 (X¹ A 63).
Gregorius, Rimini. 5581 (IV A 14).
Gregory VIII. 1134 (X² A 54), 3787 (VIII¹ A 203).
Gregory of Nyssa. 264 (X² A 561), 2667 (XI² A 68).
Gribskov. 5096 (I A 65), 5643 (IV A 81), 5746 (V A 84).
Grimm, Brothers. 133 (II A 180), 860 (173), 3596 (XI² A 368), 4089 (II A 775), 4401 (169), 4402 (170), 5166 (I C 105).
Ground of obligation. 967 (IX A 443).
Grulich, Joseph. 5317 (II A 737).
Grundtvig, Nikolai F. S. 184 (VIII¹ A 436), 418 (I A 97), 626 (VI B 11), 787 (VIII¹ A 258), 788 (X¹ A 647), 1646 (X⁴ A 505), 1860 (X² A 326), 3035 (389), 3309 (VII¹ A 152), 3496 (X² A 382), 3686 (X³ A 696), 4121 (VIII¹ A 245), 4171 (X² A 356), 4819 (X⁴ A 66), 5035 (XI² A 203), 5044 (XI¹ A 248), 5056 (I C 9), 5088 (I A 59), 5089-5091 (60-62), 5154 (202), 5156 (220), 5181 (328), 5202 (II A 27), 5268 (182), 5356 (300), 5408 (542), 5740 (V A 58), 5752 (94), 5767 (VI B 231), 5819 (VI A 73), 5832 (VI B 235), 5933 (VII¹ A 96), 6055 (VIII¹ A 309), 6097 (487), 6106 (545), 6122 (591), 6554 (X² A 275), 6565 (307), 6657 (X³ A 304), 6723 (X⁴ A 9), 6724 (14), 6733-35 (56-58), 6847 (XI² A 311), 6851 (334), 6876 (XI¹ A 149).
Grundtvigians. 6122 (VIII¹ A 591), 6176 (IX A 99), 6558 (X⁶ B 130), 6570 (X² A 338), 6876 (XI¹ A 149).
Guadalquibir. 5397 (II A 497), 6416 (X¹ A

422), 6431 (510), 6445 (546), 6461 (593).
Guarantees. 4919 (XI² A 320).
Gudrun, Queen. 5186 (I A 333), 5224 (II A 590).
Guericke, Heinrich E. F. 3321 (X⁴ A 84), 3322 (94).
Guerillas. 6387 (X¹ A 263).
GUILT. 91 (II A 18), 247 (VIII¹ A 405), 267 (IV A 60), 356 (X³ A 655), 460 (VIII¹ A 102), 1205 (VII¹ A 141), 1248 (V B 55:26), 1423 (X⁴ A 211), 1450 (V A 57), 1537 (XI² A 4), 1653 (X² A 353), 1936 (XI¹ A 573), 1971 (II A 187), 3093 (X² A 501), 3825 (X³ A 10), 3931 (IX A 269), 4297 (XI¹ A 318), 4370 (IX A 333), 4462 (X³ A 394), 4481 (XI¹ A 457), 4664 (X³ A 732), 4683 (X⁴ A 573), 4685 (578), 4793 (VIII¹ A 75), 5641 (IV A 77), 5669 (114), 5724 (V B 148:29), 5875 (VII¹ A 6), 6291 (IX A 488), 6411 (X¹ A 381), 6581 (X² A 415), 6933 (XI² A 213).
"'Guilty?' 'Not Guilty?'" 5866 (VII¹ B 84).
Guizot, François P. 4191 (X³ A 679), 6310 (X¹ A 42).
Günther, Anton. 1190 (II A 31), 3271 (356), 3993 (117), 5276 (630), 6460 (X¹ A 588).
Gurre Castle. 5095 (I A 64).
Gutzkov, Karl. 3846 (I C 69).
Gyldenstjerne, Baron von. 5089 (I A 67).
Gyllembourg, Thomasine. 4923 (I A 201), 5867 (VII¹ B 95), 5869 (135:5), 5911 (L. 136).
Gæa. 6594 (X² A 586).

Habit. 1167 (VIII¹ A 537), 1820 (XI² A 313), 3710 (X² A 624), 3921 (VIII¹ A 285).
Hackney cabman. 6392 (X¹ A 289).
Hagen, Friedrich H. v. 5118 (I A 120), 5129 (I C 83), 5173 (112).
Hagen, Johan F. 921 (VI A 92), 5944 (VII¹ A 158).
Halt (S.K.). 6450 (X¹ A 557).
HAMANN, Johann G. 96 (III A 235), 265 (II A 12), 596 (X³ A 54), 633 (VI B 40:45), 752 (II A 654), 765 (661), 1222 (X³ A 319), 1457 (I A 233), 1681 (II A 75), 1682 (78), 1690 (102), 1693 (105), 1699 (136), 1700 (138), 1701 (139), 1713

(658), 1722 (III A 49), 2489 (x¹ A 324), 5241 (II A 118), 5328 (259), 5389 (438), 5672 (IV A 122), 5673 (123), 5674 (126).

HAMLET. 1247 (V A 90), 1578 (II A 454), 2344 (V B 150:21), 3975 (VI A 124), 3999 (II A 584), 5900 (VII¹ A 113), 6732 (x⁴ A 55), 6903 (XI¹ A 460).

Hammerich, Martin. 4307 (x³ A 425), 5128 (I C 82), 6313 (x¹ A 46).

Hand organ. 3812 (I A 228).

Happiness. 1152 (XI² A 115), 1536 (x⁴ A 396), 2416 (VIII¹ A 680), 2442 (x⁵ A 50), 2446 (XI¹ A 406), 2449 (459), 3099 (XI² A 51), 6642 (x³ A 168).

Harmony. 767 (V A 41), 2877 (x³ A 328), 4576 (I A 115).

Hartley, David. 5371 (II A 373).

"Has a Man the Right To Let Himself Be Put to Death for the Truth?" 6358 (x¹ A 140).

Hate. 875 (II A 513), 888 (III A 185), 1955 (XI¹ A 577), 2396 (IV A 195).

Haufniensis, Vigilius. 102 (x² A 22), 5732 (V A 34).

Hauser, Caspar (see Caspar Hauser).

Health. 4637 (x¹ A 645), 5301 (II A 702), 6469 (x¹ A 644), 6556 (x² A 278).

Health (S.K.). 5655 (L. 80), 5665 (L. 82), 6176 (IX A 99), 6194 (492), 6234 (222), 6258 (293), 6310 (x¹ A 42).

Hedonism. 177 (x⁵ A 94), 516 (x² A 460), 534 (x⁴ A 470), 681 (x³ A 648), 728 (XI¹ A 565), 820 (x² A 392), 947 (VIII¹ A 236), 991 (x³ A 714), 1000 (x⁴ A 563), 1509 (VIII¹ A 253), 1519 (XI² A 224), 2920 (395), 3538 (71), 4362 (353), 4697 (x⁵ A 28), 4726 (XI² A 72), 4803 (x⁵ A 65).

HEGEL, Georg W. F. 36 (II C 34), 37 (III A 3), 184 (VIII¹ A 436), 224 (IX A 483), 260 (IV C 80), 421 (I A 215), 630 (VI A 147), 633 (VI B 40:45), 654 (VIII² B 86), 657 (89), 684 (x¹ A 51), 704 (IV A 192), 734 (IV B 2:16), 852 (I A 221), 925 (VI B 54:3), 1039 (54:10), 1042 (VII¹ A 80), 1096 (I A 273), 1190 (II A 31), 1232 (I A 205), 1245 (IV C 62), 1246 (IV B 118:1), 1375 (IX A 254), 1445 (XI² A 98), 1627 (I A 242), 1738 (IV C 108), 1802 (XI¹ A 130), 1941 (V A 75), 1983 (III A 38), 2020 (x⁶ B 52:1), 2115 (VI B 53:16), 2235 (54:16), 2282 (IV C 74), 2312 (II A 158), 2345 (V C 1),

2346 (2), 2347 (3), 2349 (7), 2352 (12), 2356 (VIII¹ A 681), 2565 (XI¹ A 435), 2823 (x⁵ A 73), 3071 (II A 439), 3073 (IV C 29), 3204 (IX B 5:24), 3300 (V A 98), 3303 (VI A 15), 3306 (145), 3327 (VII¹ A 70), 3653 (V B 49:1), 3702 (VI B 54:19), 3805 (I A 200), 3809 (217), 3857 (II A 188), 4099 (573), 4238 (XI² A 108), 4281 (x³ A 477), 4398 (I C 126), 4457 (x² A 279), 4555 (401), 5035 (XI² A 203), 5044 (XI¹ A 248), 5181 (I A 328), 5200 (II A 7), 5542 (Letter 54), 5543 (L. 55), 5545 (III C 34), 5603 (IV C 101), 5697 (IV A 162), 5768 (VI A 4), 6079 (VIII¹ A 440), 6310 (x¹ A 42), 6456 (576), 6596 (x⁶ B 128), 6602 (x² A 605).

Hegelians. 852 (I A 221), 1096 (273), 1574 (II A 766), 3294 (IV A 54), 5798 (VI C 1), 6596 (x⁶ B 128).

Heiberg, Johan L. 732 (IV A 94), 752 (II A 654), 1565 (I A 225), 1613 (VIII¹ A 283), 1627 (I A 242), 1823 (XI² A 271), 1904 (x⁴ A 354), 1953 (XI¹ A 463), 2241 (I A 23), 2286 (VI B 40:5), 2347 (V C 3), 2543 (XI² A 301), 2907 (XI¹ A 155), 3532 (19), 3975 (VI A 124), 4106 (V A 77), 4180 (x² A 498), 4529 (XI¹ A 397), 4881 (x⁴ A 609), 5160 (I C 102), 5170 (109), 5192 (124), 5224 (II A 590), 5342 (771), 5652 (IV A 96), 5697 (162), 5707 (IV B 125), 5713 (V A 101), 5859 (VII² B 274:1-22), 5891 (VII¹ A 104), 5909 (124), 5910 (Letter 134), 5911 (L. 136), 1941 (VII¹ A 155), 6013 (VIII¹ A 163), 6014 (164), 6039 (233), 6058 (331), 6201 (IX A 166), 6209 (175), 6213 (180), 6218 (187), 6386 (x¹ A 262), 6412 (385), 6493 (x² A 25), 6619 (x³ A 88), 6624 (99), 6636 (x⁶ B 137), 6709 (x³ A 678), 6748 (x⁶ B 171), 6850 (XI² A 321), 6954 (XI³ B 93).

Heiberg, Luise. 3519 (x⁴ A 227), 4881 (609), 6209 (IX A 175), 6213 (180), 6293 (IX B 68).

HEINE, Heinrich. 1626 (I A 208), 1730 (III B 16), 5138 (I C 95), 5157 (I A 223).

Heise, Carl J. 1633 (III B 14), 3362 (XI² A 7), 3713 (x⁴ A 255).

Helfferich, Adolf. 1653 (x² A 353), 3941 (350).

Helliggeistes church. 6249 (IX A 271).

Heliodor, Bishop. 5580 (IV C 9).

Hell. 1940 (XI² A 434), 3589 (XI¹ A 473).
Heloise. 5609 (IV A 31), 5703 (177).
Help. 343 (X¹ A 624).
Helvig. 2220 (X³ A 230), 5106 (I A 69), 5752 (V A 94).
Helvig, Queen. 5106 (I A 69).
Henry, Paul. 2538 (X⁴ A 325), 3575 (398), 3760 (316), 4742 (312).
Heraclitus. 702 (IV A 5), 2285 (58), 3290 (20), 3873 (XI¹ A 78).
Herder, Johann G. v. 4386 (I A 121), 5117 (118), 5560 (III A 203).
Heredity. 5714 (V A 102).
Heresy. 546 (XI¹ A 70), 3722 (II A 76), 5337 (255).
Hermann, Karl F. 3284 (III A 107).
Hero. 167 (X¹ A 198), 974 (412), 1812 (XI¹ A 476), 1974 (II A 652), 2637 (IX A 46), 2801 (II A 99), 4120 (VIII¹ A 222), 4213 (X⁴ A 187), 4217 (447), 4271 (VIII¹ A 491), 6391 (X¹ A 281), 6491 (X² A 15).
Herring. 2070 (XI¹ A 455).
Hertz, Henrik. 5399 (II A 508), 5927 (VII¹ A 66), 6039 (VIII¹ A 233), 6079 (440), 6413 (X¹ A 402).
Heterogeneity. 2135 (XI¹ A 255), 2470 (IX A 145), 2671 (X³ A 57), 4183 (X² A 643), 5022 (X⁴ A 524), 6577 (X² A 375), 6916 (XI² A 11), 6932 (206), 6938 (252).
H. H. 187 (X² A 119), 1921 (X⁵ A 87), 2653 (X¹ A 333), 4278 (X² A 598), 4457 (279), 6049 (VIII¹ A 264), 6387 (X¹ A 263), 6407 (351), 6420 (441), 6447 (551), 6557 (X² A 280), 6562 (285), 6704 (X³ A 637).
Hidden Inwardness. 382 (X¹ A 249), 1390 (479), 1830 (X⁴ A 479), 1904 (354), 2359 (XI² A 103), 2470 (IX A 145), 6349 (X⁶ B 48).
Hidden virtues. 3143 (X³ A 40).
Hierax. 5334 (II C 3).
High Priest. 4652 (X³ A 131).
Hilarius Bookbinder. 4742 (X⁴ A 312), 5774 (VI A 142), 5862 (VII¹ B 6).
Hint. 6211 (IX A 178), 6526 (X² A 177).
Hiorth, Ingvar M. 6566 (X⁶ B 127).
Hiorthöy, Christian J. 6065 (VIII¹ A 383).
Historical. 73 (X² A 406), 318 (VIII¹ A 565), 389 (X² A 139), 1101 (III A 216), 1587 (1), 4781 (X² A 548), 4975 (X⁴ A 381).
HISTORY. 134 (II A 664), 214 (X⁴ A 433), 262 (V B 15:1), 322 (IX A 59), 324 (249), 516

(X² A 460), 542 (X⁵ A 98), 581 (I A 108), 588 (IX A 264), 622 (V A 18), 653 (VIII² B 85), 689 (I A 50), 691 (IX A 95), 692 (153), 693 (X¹ A 132), 696 (XI¹ A 38), 758 (VI A 60), 783 (II A 5), 907 (IV A 213), 1040 (VII¹ A 33), 1041 (48), 1050 (VIII¹ A 320), 1054 (IX A 382), 1066 (XI¹ A 353), 1087 (X⁴ A 518), 1100 (III A 39), 1105 (IV A 24), 1135 (X² A 207), 1136 (371), 1181 (I A 292), 1232 (205), 1233 (II A 74), 1245 (IV C 62), 1268 (X⁴ A 175), 1269 (177), 1412 (X³ A 421), 1445 (XI² A 98), 1587 (III A 1), 1607 (VI B 40:3), 1620 (XI¹ A 180), 1925 (22), 1927 (41), 1966 (I A 248), 1970 (II A 172), 1991 (VI A 120), 2049 (XI¹ A 60), 2061 (319), 2077 (587), 2093 (X² A 602), 2185 (IV A 146), 2212 (II A 354), 2213 (355), 2250 (II C 44), 2283 (IV C 99), 2298 (VIII¹ A 479), 2329 (XI¹ A 80), 2354 (VI B 35:30), 2366 (IV C 36), 2394 (III B 114), 2500 (X¹ A 595), 2563 (XI¹ A 37), 2724 (186), 2796 (III A 70), 2834 (VI A 90), 2856 (II A 149), 2865 (X¹ A 221), 2910 (XI¹ A 392), 3014 (X¹ A 396), 3205 (X⁴ A 522), 3209 (XI¹ A 552), 3210 (XI² A 38), 3283 (III B 12), 3301 (V B 14, pp. 73-76), 3353 (IX A 133), 3479 (X¹ A 6), 3553 (II A 558), 3578 (X⁴ A 532), 3602 (XI¹ A 364), 3628 (VII¹ A 130), 3657 (IV C 78), 3815 (I A 294), 3857 (II A 188), 3866 (XI¹ A 465), 3867 (557), 3957 (X⁴ A 523), 4068 (I A 289), 4392 (313), 4415 (II A 515), 4420 (IV C 93), 4549 (X² A 231), 4566 (X⁴ A 407), 4899 (509), 5035 (XI² A 203), 5181 (I A 328), 5307 (II A 712), 5392 (480), 5794 (VI B 35:15), 5795 (35:19), 5796 (35:24), 6282 (IX A 432), 6368 (X¹ A 163), 6580 (X² A 413), 6793 (X⁴ A 474), 6956 (XI² A 407).
Hjort, Peder. 6898 (XI¹ A 423).
Hjort, Jens M. L. 4058 (XI² A 319).
Hobbes, Thomas. 894 (IV C 72).
Höedt, Frederik L. 6313 (X¹ A 46).
Hoffmann, Ernst T. A. 217 (I A 290), 1688 (II A 627), 1699 (136), 5109 (I C 60), 5117 (I A 118), 5148 (184), 5177 (280), 5223 (II A 98), 5241 (118), 5584 (IV A 17).
Högne. 5714 (V A 102).
Hohlenberg, Frederik L. 242 (I A 38), 4061 (93), 4243 (II A 186).

Holberg, Ludwig. 118 (I A 33), 153 (VI A 118), 180 (XI¹ A 237), 1105 (IV A 24), 1247 (V A 90), 1675 (I A 238), 1743 (VI A 3), 1747 (VII¹ A 19), 1763 (x² A 304), 2539 (x⁴ A 371), 3009 (XI² A 243), 3042 (XI¹ A 482), 3185 (XI² A 148), 3188 (XI³ B 197), 3213 (175), 3438 (x¹ A 390), 3471 (VI A 156), 3540 (XI² A 281), 3563 (VIII¹ A 441), 3693 (x⁴ A 289), 3780 (XI¹ A 298), 3869 (XI² A 94), 4382 (XI¹ A 30), 4400 (II A 163), 4495 (XI¹ A 63), 4822 (I A 25), 4823 (34), 4824 (209), 5007 (XI² A 192), 5035 (203), 5191 (I A 341), 5213 (II A 44), 5263 (107), 5344 (777), 5652 (IV A 96), 6099 (VIII¹ A 655), 6196 (IX A 493), 6744 (x⁴ A 168), 6779 (380), 6819 (646), 6917 (XI² A 19), 6926 (75).

Holger the Dane. 5212 (II A 43), 5214 (45).

Holmens church. 5523 (III A 168).

Holst, Hans P. 5909 (VII¹ A 124).

Holstebro. 5466 (III A 71).

Holsten. 4138 (VIII¹ A 613).

HOLY SPIRIT. 296 (II A 419), 1020 (II A 235), 1463 (I A 37), 1916 (x⁴ A 650), 1919 (x⁵ A 44), 2460 (VI A 108), 2673 (x⁴ A 520), 2854 (I A 26), 3194 (x¹ A 392), 3445 (x² A 344), 3522 (x⁴ A 330), 3992 (II A 19), 4029 (x² A 429), 4326 (x¹ A 417), 4346 (x⁵ A 37), 4405 (II A 756), 4462 (x³ A 394), 4478 (x⁵ A 82), 4688 (x⁴ A 593), 4692 (630), 4694 (660), 4939 (x⁴ A 538), 6792 (x⁴ A 472), 6832 (x⁵ A 43), 6862 (XI¹ A 72).

Home. 6169 (IX A 73).

Home (S.K., *see also* Nytorv 2). 5330 (II A 233), 5655 (Letter 80), 6376 (x¹ A 202), 6489 (x² A 10), 6629 (x³ A 144).

Homer. 117 (I A 8), 147 (IV A 222), 751 (I A 113), 1588 (III A 6), 4834 (IV C 118), 5473 (III A 80).

Homogeneity. 3647 (x⁴ A 258).

Honesty. 174 (x³ A 187), 1812 (XI¹ A 476), 2907 (155), 3876 (140), 4186 (x³ A 529), 6557 (x² A 280), 6905 (XI¹ A 474), 6922 (XI² A 40).

HOPE. 483 (IX A 147), 903 (IV A 131), 1200 (II A 326), 3915 (III C 1), 4151 (IX A 354), 4370 (333), 4398 (I C 126), 4473 (x⁴ A 291), 4685 (578), 5257 (II A 648), 5382

(II A 416), 5401 (510), 5402 (512), 5431 (806), 5491 (III A 91), 6610 (x³ A 12), 6883 (XI¹ A 214).

Horace. 3063 (x⁴ A 448), 5543 (L. 55).

Horizon analogy. 5398 (II A 503).

Hornemann, Jens W. 5092 (I A 72).

Horses. 4009 (VI A 105), 4232 (XI¹ A 366), 4337 (x³ A 596), 4465 (662), 4585 (V A 43), 4675 (x⁴ A 222), 4676 (256), 5380 (II A 414), 5800 (VI A 29), 6392 (x¹ A 289).

Hosbach, Wilhelm. 3320 (x³ A 682).

Hostrup, Jens P. 5940 (VII¹ A 154), 6088 (VIII¹ A 458), 6089 (654), 6299 (x¹ A 9).

How. 1405 (x² A 644), 3684 (x³ A 431), 4550 (x² A 299), 4558 (x³ A 593), 4868 (25), 5791 (VI B 17), 6643 (x³ A 174), 6784 (x⁴ A 404), 6893 (XI¹ A 315).

Hugo, Victor. 820 (x² A 392), 1653 (353), 3941 (350).

Human, the. 992 (x³ A 715), 2101 (x⁴ A 392), 2999 (XI² A 167), 3647 (x⁴ A 258), 4471 (235), 4687 (583), 4800 (x³ A 320).

Humanism. 2685 (XI² A 427).

Humanity. 2875 (x³ A 214).

Hume, David. 1539 (I A 100), 1540 (237).

Humility. 267 (IV A 60), 309 (VIII¹ A 345), 1204 (IV A 66), 1337 (V A 50), 1388 (x¹ A 332), 1438 (XI¹ A 188), 1440 (381), 1647 (388), 1682 (II A 78), 1803 (XI¹ A 194), 1901 (x⁴ A 340), 1923 (x⁵ A 139), 1935 (XI¹ A 550), 2075 (533), 2081 (XI² A 135), 2085 (360), 2098 (XI¹ A 400), 2118 (VIII² B 91:13), 2482 (x¹ A 172), 2502 (651), 2679 (XI² A 91), 2682 (326), 2687 (435), 2691 (x¹ A 400), 2721 (x³ A 532), 2724 (XI¹ A 186), 2725 (187), 2726 (XI² A 339), 2907 (XI¹ A 155), 2970 (227), 3744 (VIII¹ A 572), 4623 (IX A 349), 5099 (I A 68), 5653 (IV A 97), 6837 (x⁵ A 72), 6951 (XI² A 377).

HUMOR. 422 (II A 30), 739 (484), 797 (791), 1123 (VIII¹ A 649), 1456 (I A 224), 1521 (II A 134), 1548 (III B 20), 1554 (V B 44), 1565 (I A 225), 1568 (48), 1622 (142), 1623 (143), 1668 (VI B 53:13), 1851 (x¹ A 179), 1855 (673), 2111 (IV A 86), 2116 (VI B 98:77), 3567 (x¹ A 679), 3975 (VI A 124), 4243 (II A 186), 4426 (VI A 52), 4585 (V A 43), 5073 (I A 14), 5170 (I C

109), 5177 (I A 280), 5451 (II A 51), 5693 (IV A 152), 5704 (178), 5804 (VI A 41), 5811 (53), 5975 (VIII¹ A 15), 6181 (IX A 123), 6193 (144), 6446 (X¹ A 548).

Hundrup, Ferdinand E. 5465 (III A 69).

Hutten, Ulrich v. 5359 (II C 64).

Hverdags Forfatterens Historier. 5162 (I A 244).

Den Hvide Dame [The White Lady]. 6537 (Letter 239).

Hvidt, Laurits N. 4134 (VIII¹ A 606), 4135 (607).

Hymnbook. 3469 (VI A 152), 4106 (V A 77).

Hymns. 829 (XI² A 280), 1414 (X³ A 585), 2695 (X³ A 518), 2860 (VII¹ A 83), 5404 (II A 521), 6097 (VIII¹ A 487), 6315 (X¹ A 53), 6316 (54), 6714 (X³ A 770).

Hypocrisy. 80 (X⁴ A 638), 442 (II A 338), 644 (VIII¹ A 448), 829 (XI² A 280), 1500 (100), 1816 (77), 2053 (XI¹ A 148), 2563 (37), 2677 (549), 2687 (XI² A 435), 2725 (XI¹ A 187), 2726 (XI² A 339), 4972 (X⁴ A 178).

Hypothesis. 6307 (X¹ A 37).

I (*see also* Egoity). 71 (X² A 78), 72 (79), 222 (II A 131), 1144 (X⁴ A 422), 2075 (XI¹ A 533), 2077 (587), 3219 (51), 4350 (487), 4911 (516), 6440 (X¹ A 531).

Ibsen, Peter D. 5403 (II A 520), 6310 (X¹ A 42).

IDEA. 13 (I A 206), 83 (XI¹ A 358), 118 (I A 33), 245 (138), 365 (XI¹ A 280), 416 (95), 610 (IX A 21), 1177 (I A 88), 1184 (II A 56), 1557 (VI A 6), 1648 (XI¹ A 446), 1731 (III B 19), 1940 (XI² A 434), 2038 (X⁴ A 104), 2048 (XI¹ A 42), 2049 (60), 2086 (XI² A 361), 2101 (X⁴ A 392), 2261 (II A 348), 2394 (III B 114), 2506 (X² A 173), 2952 (390), 3627 (II A 681), 3799 (I A 134), 3801 (140), 3834 (XI¹ A 271), 4066 (I A 285), 4070 (307), 4184 (X³ A 26), 4234 (XI¹ A 536), 4348 (211), 4381 (X⁴ A 462), 4401 (II A 169), 4572 (XI² A 196), 4846 (IV C 95), 5062 (I A 12), 5074 (15), 5100 (75), 5101 (76), 5181 (388), 5186 (333), 5254 (II A 642), 5259 (653), 5270 (189), 5369 (361), 5402 (512), 5648 (IV A 89), 5793 (VI B 35:14), 5885 (VII¹ A

27), 5893 (106), 5896 (109), 5900 (113), 5913 (126), 5937 (147), 5942 (156), 5987 (VIII¹ A 42), 6077 (417), 6415 (X¹ A 406), 6423 (476), 6532 (X² A 195), 6589 (488), 6715 (X³ A 771), 6725 (X⁴ A 20), 6839 (X⁵ A 104), 6866 (XI¹ A 121), 6873 (137), 6968 (XI² A 438).

Ideal. 852 (I A 221), 936 (VII¹ A 172), 964 (IX A 392), 1182 (II A 29), 1680 (38), 2661 (X³ A 511), 3067 (XI² A 210), 3188 (XI³ B 197), 4279 (X³ A 253), 5061 (I A 11), 5461 (III A 64), 6446 (X¹ A 548), 6527 (X² A 183), 6528 (X² A 184), 6668 (X³ A 402).

Idealism. 1189 (I A 302), 3257 (II A 198).

IDEALITY. 144 (IV C 109), 150 (V B 148:17), 174 (X³ A 187), 236 (X¹ A 135), 334 (279), 422 (II A 30), 512 (X² A 187), 525 (X³ A 649), 560 (XI² A 49), 603 (229), 693 (X¹ A 132), 853 (I A 222), 882 (III A 63), 954 (VIII¹ A 410), 965 (IX A 418), 977 (X¹ A 580), 987 (X² A 546), 990 (X³ A 248), 991 (714), 998 (X⁴ A 302), 1054 (IX A 382), 1067 (XI² A 63), 1135 (X² A 207), 1166 (VIII¹ A 499), 1378 (IX A 347), 1396 (X² A 186), 1438 (XI¹ A 188), 1449 (XI² A 133), 1470 (X² A 188), 1493 (X⁵ A 101), 1498 (XI² A 285), 1645 (X⁴ A 208), 1654 (X² A 451), 1666 (III A 130), 1855 (X¹ A 673), 1861 (X² A 347), 1873 (X³ A 331), 1879 (447), 1901 (X⁴ A 340), 1904 (354), 1919 (X⁵ A 44), 1922 (88), 1933 (XI¹ A 396), 2010 (IX A 356), 2014 (IX B 66), 2053 (XI¹ A 148), 2637 (IX A 46), 2684 (XI² A 278), 2685 (427), 2882 (X² A 549), 2903 (XI¹ A 107), 2910 (392), 2998 (XI² A 159), 3142 (X² A 550), 3211 (XI² A 187), 3349 (X³ A 482), 3678 (X² A 220), 3680 (232), 3828 (X⁴ A 224), 3860 (X³ A 702), 4190 (X³ A 607), 4197 (X⁴ A 40), 4198 (41), 4327 (X¹ A 652), 4373 (X¹ A 452), 4529 (XI¹ A 397), 4797 (X¹ A 581), 4992 (459), 5620 (IV B 10a), 5976 (VIII¹ A 16), 6200 (IX A 159), 6300 (X¹ A 11), 6391 (281), 6433 (517), 6505 (X² A 89), 6511 (106), 6521 (157), 6531 (193), 6532 (195), 6573 (352), 6632 (X³ A 152), 6650 (210), 6654 (258), 6672 (416), 6736 (X⁴ A 64), 6753 (204), 6761 (296).

IDEALS. 3732 (X⁴ A 38), 4912 (XI¹ A 517),

5947 (VII¹ A 169), 6423 (X¹ A 476), 6727 (X⁴ A 33), 6749 (X⁶ B 173, pp. 274-276), 6778 (X⁴ A 337), 6783 (395), 6845 (XI² A 288), 6851 (334), 6945 (XI³ B 55), 6947 (57).

Identity (*see also* Egoity; *I*; Self-knowledge). 705 (V A 68), 706 (69), 1247 (90), 2341 (74), 3545 (I A 22).

Idler. 6491 (X² A 15).

Idolatry. 4103 (IV A 7).

Idols. 1346 (VII¹ A 81).

Idum. 5466 (III A 71).

Ignorance. 113 (IV C 21), 1732 (III B 21), 1734 (23), 1735 (24), 2291 (VII¹ A 31), 2300 (X¹ A 577), 4022 (627), 4286 (X⁴ A 334), 4297 (XI¹ A 318), 4298 (334).

Illness. 5292 (II A 685).

Illusion. 551 (XI¹ A 264), 1232 (I A 205), 2129 (X⁴ A 21), 2241 (I A 23), 2949 (X² A 294), 2958 (X³ A 656), 3738 (XI² A 355), 6632 (X³ A 152), 6680 (450), 6681 (453).

Image. 1400 (X² A 443).

IMAGINATION. 4 (VIII¹ A 622), 47 (V A 20), 135 (II A 715), 268 (V A 2), 347 (X² A 86), 560 (XI² A 49), 803 (III A 94), 804 (95), 939 (VIII¹ A 62), 940 (143), 953 (398), 973 (X¹ A 393), 1043 (VII¹ A 140), 1049 (VIII¹ A 292), 1054 (IX A 382), 1347 (VII¹ A 139), 1348 (143), 1462 (X⁴ A 582), 1771 (II A 148), 2853 (X⁴ A 483), 2897 (X⁵ A 78), 3067 (XI² A 210), 3346 (X² A 202), 3347 (X³ A 16), 3839 (X⁴ A 264), 4360 (XI² A 279), 4364 (VI A 2), 4444 (VIII¹ A 160), 4470 (X⁴ A 160), 4623 (IX A 349), 4881 (X⁴ A 609), 4972 (X³ A 677), 5288 (II A 679), 5309 (717), 5392 (480), 5980 (VIII¹ A 27), 6061 (347), 6135 (650), 6150 (IX A 39), 6645 (X³ A 189), 6677 (434), 6839 (X⁵ A 104), 6844 (XI² A 283), 6919 (31).

Imago Dei. 34 (II A 362), 1614 (X² A 426).

IMITATION. 83 (XI¹ A 358), 304 (VIII¹ A 83), 330 (X¹ A 204), 334 (279), 349 (X² A 170), 397 (X³ A 420), 401 (X⁵ A 42), 496 (X¹ A 190), 572 (X² A 305), 573 (X⁴ A 439), 597 (X³ A 521), 639 (VIII¹ A 243), 692 (IX A 153), 693 (X¹ A 132), 694 (X² A 253), 695 (X³ A 653), 963 (IX A 372), 1090 (X⁴ A 652), 1135 (X² A 207), 1274 (XI¹ A 23), 1275 (24), 1385 (X¹ A 64), 1432 (X⁵ A 23), 1482 (X³ A 784), 1486 (X⁴

A 618), 1487 (619), 1494 (X⁵ A 103), 1497 (XI² A 284), 1518 (X⁵ A 176), 1654 (X² A 451), 1661 (X⁴ A 588), 1802 (X⁵ A 130), 1803 (194), 1943 (X⁴ A 471), 1962 (553), 2027 (X³ A 324), 2072 (XI¹ A 490), 2056 (X⁵ A 189), 2057 (190), 2132 (51), 2438 (X⁴ A 589), 2442 (X⁵ A 50), 2462 (VII¹ A 209), 2481 (X¹ A 154), 2503 (X² A 30), 2528 (X³ A 510), 2665 (XI¹ A 462), 2804 (X⁴ A 519), 2805 (XI¹ A 217), 2872 (X³ A 34), 2974 (XI¹ A 325), 3201 (X⁴ A 541), 3455 (X³ A 317), 3513 (484), 3570 (121), 3571 (122), 3578 (X⁴ A 532), 3583 (XI¹ A 100), 3585 (202), 3593 (XI² A 218), 3620 (XI¹ A 199), 3681 (X³ A 278), 3740 (VII¹ B 181:2), 3915 (III C 1), 4185 (X³ A 346), 4313 (X⁴ A 555), 4454 (X¹ A 134), 4473 (X⁴ A 291), 4524 (639), 4553 (X² A 336), 4661 (X³ A 500), 4688 (X⁴ A 593), 4700 (X⁵ A 81), 4728 (XI² A 136), 4867 (X² A 635), 4899 (X⁴ A 509), 4953 (XI² A 86), 4979 (XI¹ A 103), 5047 (556), 6323 (X¹ A 72), 6495 (X² A 40), 6521 (157), 6665 (X³ A 389), 6677 (434), 6685 (519), 6761 (X⁴ A 296), 6794 (488), 6802 (554), 6804 (558), 6808 (584), 6914 (XI¹ A 586), 6947 (XI³ B 57).

Immanence. 183 (VIII¹ A 416), 297 (II A 473), 704 (IV A 192), 833 (II A 351), 837 (VIII¹ A 56), 1347 (VII¹ A 139), 2235 (VI B 54:16), 2291 (VII¹ A 31), 2437 (X⁴ A 482), 3088 (VII² B 256:9-10), 3202 (II C 56), 5928 (VII¹ A 78), 5975 (VIII¹ A 15).

Immanental. 1043 (VII¹ A 140).

Immaturity. 1811 (XI¹ A 447).

IMMEDIACY (first immediacy). 48 (V A 25), 49 (28), 102 (X² A 22), 188 (369), 475 (IX A 5), 630 (VI A 147), 1044 (VII¹ A 216), 1045 (217), 1348 (143), 1373 (IX A 242), 1676 (I A 239), 1689 (II A 101), 1725 (III B 6), 2454 (XI² A 421), 2474 (IX A 433), 2809 (VII¹ A 186), 3127 (V A 44), 3130 (X² A 594), 3774 (X⁵ A 79), 3792 (IV B 10:3,4,8,9), 3969 (XI¹ A 259), 4397 (I C 125), 4589 (VI A 48), 4690 (X⁴ A 620), 5008 (XI² A 193), 5181 (I A 328), 6244 (IX A 251), 6298 (X¹ A 8), 6604 (X² A 622), 6901 (XI¹ A 439).

—Christian immediacy (*see also* Spontaneity). 8 (X² A 592), 9 (X⁶ B 78), 37 (III A 3), 38 (25), 235 (IX A 387), 972 (X¹ A

360), 1100 (III A 39), 1101 (216), 1123 (VIII¹ A 649), 1215 (663), 1335 (V A 8), 1668 (VI B 53:13), 1999 (VIII¹ A 126), 2419 (IX A 306), 2998 (XI² A 159), 3718 (XI² A 273), 4426 (VI A 52), 4457 (X² A 279), 4642 (131), 6135 (VIII¹ A 650), 6265 (IX A 343), 6969 (XI² A 439).

IMMORTALITY. 53 (V B 196), 59 (VII¹ A 206), 73 (X² A 406), 115 (X⁵ A 31), 255 (IX A 32), 754 (III A 7), 1057 (X² A 328), 1170 (IX A 118), 1189 (I A 302), 1525 (II A 555), 1541 (I A 340), 1655 (III A 129), 1818 (XI² A 201), 1825 (XI³ B 199), 2077 (XI¹ A 587), 2496 (X¹ A 439), 2617 (XI¹ A 150), 3043 (585), 3606 (V B 40:11), 3955 (X³ A 711), 4280 (315), 4427 (VI A 71), 4535 (II A 433), 5045 (XI¹ A 251), 5201 (II A 17), 6108 (VIII¹ A 549), 6956 (XI² A 407).

Immutability (see also UNCHANGEABLE-NESS). 1304 (I A 29), 1328 (IV A 102), 1332 (157), 3379 (II A 537).

Impatience. 917 (VI A 34), 2643 (IX A 325), 3038 (X³ A 674), 3686 (696).

Imperative. 512 (X² A 187), 993 (X³ A 734), 994 (737).

Impersonal use of personal. 3497 (X² A 581).

Impersonality. 2134 (XI¹ A 21), 2650 (X¹ A 16), 3219 (XI¹ A 51), 3224 (XI² A 107), 3728 (X³ A 326), 4056 (XI² A 106).

Importance. 4481 (XI¹ A 457).

Impossibility. 3341 (IX A 36), 3409 (VII¹ A 142).

Improbability. 1119 (VII¹ A 203).

Incarnation. 280 (II A 133), 284 (595), 297 (473), 301 (IV A 33), 318 (VIII¹ A 565), 421 (I A 215), 533 (X⁴ A 452), 1344 (VI B 48:81), 1635 (IV C 35), 1960 (X³ A 659), 2402 (IV A 183), 3076 (62), 5181 (I A 328), 5383 (II A 420), 6680 (X³ A 450).

In character. 6390 (X¹ A 273).

Inclosing Reserve (see Closed Reserve).

Incognito. 1331 (IV A 125), 1753 (IX A 151), 2803 (X² A 529), 3900 (X¹ A 255), 4055 (XI¹ A 562), 4198 (X⁴ A 41), 4738 (86), 5258 (II A 649), 6238 (IX A 227), 6327 (X¹ A 78), 6346 (116), 6491 (X² A 15), 6740 (X⁴ A 130), 6752 (201), 6783 (395), 6937 (XI² A 251).

Income tax. 4218 (X⁶ B 257).

Incommensurability. 1384 (X¹ A 60), 2111 (IV A 86), 5272 (II C 39).

Independence. 1252 (VII¹ A 210), 1257 (X¹ A 26), 1271 (X⁴ A 257).

Indescribable joy. 5324 (II A 228).

India. 5386 (II A 431).

Indicative. 993 (X³ A 734), 994 (737).

Indifference. 383 (X¹ A 460), 599 (X⁴ A 22), 1167 (VIII¹ A 537), 2461 (VII¹ A 192), 2681 (XI² A 323), 5350 (II C 60), 6272 (IX A 393).

Indirect. 664 (IX A 257), 1060 (X² A 257).

INDIRECT COMMUNICATION (see also COM-MUNICATION). 649 (VIII¹ B 81), 651 (83), 662 (IX A 233), 666 (X¹ A 122), 677 (X² A 367), 2015 (X¹ A 218), 4326 (417), 6230 (IX A 217), 6231 (218), 6234 (222), 6248 (265), 6463 (X¹ A 598), 6532 (X² A 195), 6577 (375), 6700 (X³ A 628), 6783 (X⁴ A 395), 6786 (X⁶ B 145, pp. 202-3).

Indirect method (see also Direct communication; INDIRECT COMMUNICA-TION. 3846 (I C 69), 5646 (IV A 87), 5826 (VI A 83), 5991 (VIII¹ A 49), 6006 (124), 6574 (X⁶ B 121).

INDIVIDUAL. 24 (I A 114), 35 (II A 383), 36 (II C 34), 43 (IV C 76), 50 (V B 14:72), 51 (53:15), 52 (55:4), 70 (IX A 80), 78 (X³ A 501), 107 (97), 127 (I A 234), 162 (VIII¹ A 122), 213 (X³ A 348), 227 (I C 40), 238 (X⁴ A 11), 267 (IV A 60), 390 (X² A 453), 410 (I A 4), 419 (172), 450 (II A 579), 463 (VIII¹ A 157), 528 (X⁴ A 28), 536 (581), 570 (IX A 472), 594 (X¹ A 579), 601 (X⁴ A 594), 603 (XI² A 229), 632 (VI B 38), 655 (VIII² B 87), 658 (IX A 79), 662 (233), 673 (X¹ A 566), 678 (X² A 466), 696 (XI¹ A 38), 720 (VIII¹ A 406), 783 (II A 5), 850 (I A 141), 851 (152), 870 (II A 449), 896 (IV C 96), 982 (X² A 201), 1016 (IX A 340), 1017 (X² A 348), 1019 (II A 125), 1041 (VII¹ A 48), 1057 (X² A 328), 1067 (XI² A 63), 1073 (V B 213:2), 1085 (X³ A 464), 1088 (X⁴ A 590), 1089 (591), 1248 (V B 55:26), 1257 (X¹ A 26), 1283 (VIII¹ A 80), 1350 (24), 1362 (524), 1371 (IX A 116), 1375 (254), 1377 (315), 1385 (X¹ A 64), 1413 (X³ A 581), 1513 (X¹ A 639), 1518 (XI¹ A 176), 1531 (X² A 500), 1587 (III A 1), 1591 (186), 1613 (VIII¹ A 283), 1614 (X² A 426), 1646 (X⁴ A 505), 1647 (XI¹ A

388), 1648 (446), 1651 (II A 731), 1670 (I A 145), 1671 (154), 1676 (239), 1680 (II A 38), 1681 (75), 1734 (III B 23), 1751 (VIII^1 A 517), 1759 (IX A 420), 1781 (X^1 A 646), 1790 (X^3 A 524), 1793 (670), 1807 (XI^1 A 402), 1818 (XI^2 A 201), 1821 (344), 1822 (267), 1825 (XI^3 B 199), 1873 (X^3 A 331), 1906 (X^4 A 369), 1925 (XI^1 A 22), 1956 (XI^2 A 237), 1960 (X^3 A 659), 2090 (VIII^1 A 43), 2103 (XI^1 A 500), 2150 (VIII^1 A 146), 2152 (540), 2154 (IX A 282), 2165 (X^3 A 231), 2166 (275), 2172 (XI^1 A 22), 2245 (I A 111), 2277 (III A 211), 2319 (222), 2324 (X^2 A 235), 2360 (IV A 11), 2439 (X^4 A 642), 2544 (XI^2 A 303), 2566 (XI^1 A 486), 2567 (589), 2568 (590), 2570 (XI^2 A 54), 2580 (II A 375), 2632 (VI A 110), 2647 (IX B 63:11), 2707 (II A 468), 2732 (XI^1 A 489), 2742 (VII^1 A 170), 2750 (VIII^1 A 403), 2821 (X^2 A 362), 2861 (VIII^1 A 248), 2882 (X^3 A 549), 2904 (XI^1 A 110), 2907 (155), 2910 (392), 2933 (VIII^1 A 538), 2938 (IX A 63), 2939 (143), 2940 (146), 2941 (277), 2950 (X^2 A 369), 2952 (390), 2953 (485), 2958 (X^3 A 656), 2962 (X^4 A 105), 2964 (225), 2973 (XI^1 A 287), 2979 (454), 2986 (XI^2 A 88), 2988 (90), 2992 (116), 2993 (127), 3004 (211), 3099 (51), 3188 (XI^3 B 197), 3214 (VII^1 A 10), 3219 (XI^1 A 51), 3380 (II A 538), 3479 (X^1 A 6), 3548 (II A 399), 3558 (IX A 666), 3559 (X^3 A 52), 3560 (XI^1 A 62), 3561 (XI^2 A 46), 3582 (XI^1 A 55), 3587 (450), 3628 (VII^1 A 130), 3657 (IV C 78), 3660 (X^2 A 116), 3664 (XI^2 A 65), 3689 (X^4 A 190), 3793 (IV A 156), 3860 (X^3 A 702), 3915 (III C 1), 3986 (X^4 A 16), 3987 (XI^2 A 142), 3991 (I A 92), 4050 (XI^2 A 14), 4063 (I A 139), 4067 (288), 4068 (289), 4069 (304), 4070 (307), 4109 (VII^1 A 17), 4110 (20), 4114 (211), 4116 (VIII^1 A 108), 4128 (551), 4129 (552), 4132 (599), 4146 (IX A 31), 4153 (445), 4157 (X^1 A 171), 4159 (350), 4163 (632), 4165 (682), 4166 (X^2 A 7), 4169 (292), 4173 (394), 4175 (478), 4183 (643), 4186 (X^3 A 529), 4190 (607), 4198 (X^4 A 41), 4206 (83), 4213 (187), 4234 (XI^1 A 536), 4265 (VII^1 A 69), 4271 (VIII^1 A 491), 4295 (X^5 A 133), 4299 (XI^1 A 371), 4302 (448), 4335 (X^3 A 493), 4348 (211), 4351 (498), 4373 (X^1 A 452), 4394 (I A 319), 4536 (V A 37), 4541 (VIII^1 A 8), 4543 (313), 4549 (X^2 A 231), 4571 (XI^2 A 97), 4667 (X^4 A 135), 4864 (X^2 A 409), 4885 (XI^1 A 352), 4887 (438), 4899 (X^4 A 509), 4918 (XI^2 A 205), 4920 (X^1 A 516), 4922 (XI^1 A 296), 4941 (453), 4942 (458), 5408 (II A 542), 5644 (IV A 83), 5948 (VII^1 A 176), 5950 (VII^1 C 5), 5990 (VIII^1 A 46), 6006 (124), 6105 (544), 6253 (IX A 285), 6432 (X^1 A 513), 6463 (598), 6486 (676), 6552 (X^2 A 261), 6580 (413), 6593 (560), 6659 (X^3 A 310), 6705 (647), 6731 (X^4 A 53), 6873 (XI^1 A 137), 6917 (XI^2 A 19), 6921 (36), 6932 (206), 6955 (406).

Individual difference. 1009 (VII^1 A 134), 2076 (XI^1 A 576).

Individual, the single. 100 (VIII^1 A 363), 436 (II A 293), 1997 (VIII^1 A 9), 5644 (IV A 83), 5975 (VIII^1 A 15), 6095 (VIII^2 B 188), 6357 (X^1 A 139), 6358 (140), 6360 (146), 6388 (266), 6552 (X^2 A 261), 6659 (X^3 A 310), 6731 (X^4 A 53), 6753 (204), 6778 (377), 6780 (383).

Individual, special. 6357 (X^1 A 6358 (140).

Individualism. 1264 (X^3 A 618).

Individuality. 117 (I A 8), 1177 (88), 1190 (II A 31), 2315 (161), 2381 (25), 5100 (I A 75).

Indulgence. 1476 (X^3 A 72).

Inexperience. 1071 (IV A 59).

INFINITE. 56 (VI B 49), 842 (X^1 A 48), 2085 (XI^2 A 360), 2086 (361), 2289 (VII^1 A 234), 4290 (X^4 A 497), 6679 (X^3 A 448).

Infinite qualitative difference. 236 (X^1 A 135), 693 (132), 1383 (59), 3087 (VII^2 B 235, pp. 66-67), 3645 (X^2 A 296).

Infinitude. 55 (VI A 102), 1253 (VIII^1 A 178), 3285 (III C 32), 4527 (XI^1 A 212), 4531 (431), 4905 (X^5 A 118).

Infinity. 1019 (II A 125), 1577 (381), 1783 (X^2 A 510), 2811 (VII^1 A 189), 3857 (II A 188).

Influence. 658 (IX A 79).

Influencing men. 3726 (VIII^1 A 103).

Information. 3855 (II A 122).

Ingemann, Bernhard S. 1953 (XI^1 A 463), 3937 (X^2 A 51), 5223 (II A 98).

Inger. 5098 (I A 67).
Ingratitude. 1515 (x³ A 627), 1516 (x⁴ A 269), 4329 (x² A 103).
Inheritance. 6019 (VIII¹ A 177).
Inkstand. 1330 (IV A 106).
Inland journey. 5726 (V B 47:13).
Innocence. 1526 (IV A 121), 3962 (V B 53:27), 4401 (II A 169).
Innocent III. 4083 (II A 274).
Insanity. 1300 (x³ A 499), 1320 (II A 472), 1524 (744), 2248 (I A 191), 3791 (II A 445), 4552 (x² A 322), 4747 (VI A 116), 5088 (I A 336), 5090 (339), 5147 (182), 5249 (II A 634), 5270 (189), 5624 (IV A 68), 5691 (147), 5695 (154), 5913 (VII¹ A 126).
Insect analogy. 6906 (XI¹ A 484).
Insignia analogy. 6933 (XI² A 213).
Insignificance. 2849 (VIII¹ A 427), 4348 (XI¹ A 211).
Inspiration. 581 (I A 108), 689 (50), 2854 (26).
INSTRUMENT. 188 (x² A 396), 466 (VIII¹ A 238), 1520 (XI² A 245), 2078 (69), 2793 (x² A 341), 3087 (VII² B 235, pp. 66-67), 3579 (x⁴ A 614), 4053 (x² A 13), 4060 (I A 42), 4460 (x² A 642), 6794 (x⁴ A 488).
Instrumentalism. 2563 (XI¹ A 37), 3632 (267).
Instrumentalist religion. 3621 (XI¹ A 213).
Insubordination. 778 (VIII¹ A 7).
Insurance. 516 (x² A 460).
Integrity. 916 (VI A 27), 1794 (x³ A 689), 4801 (390), 5009 (VIII¹ A 104).
Intellectual life. 3070 (II A 755).
Intellectualization. 6859 (XI¹ A 56).
Intelligence. 3865 (XI¹ A 461).
INTENSITY, Intensiveness (see also Extensity; Extensiveness). 2056 (XI¹ A 189), 2057 (190), 2448 (414), 2640 (IX A 126), 2994 (XI² A 146), 3201 (x⁴ A 541), 4489 (XI² A 29), 4490 (42), 4813 (76), 6656 (x³ A 265), 6763 (x⁴ A 300), 6813 (604), 6907 (XI¹ A 497).
Intensive/extensive. 1807 (XI¹ A 402), 2056 (189), 2100 (x⁴ A 219).
Intention. 865 (II A 303), 2506 (x² A 173).
Interest. 543 (x⁵ A 144), 1415 (x³ A 658), 1450 (XI² A 170), 2079 (124), 2126 (x³ A 356), 2283 (IV C 99), 2527 (x³ A 336).

Interested. 4862 (x¹ A 410).
INTERESTING. 806 (III B 45:1), 827 (XI¹ A 570), 3690 (x⁴ A 214), 3794 (IV A 169), 3883 (XI¹ A 537), 6330 (x¹ A 88), 6396 (322), 6431 (510), 6511 (x² A 106).
Interjection analogy. 5372 (II A 382).
Internality. 949 (VIII¹ A 312).
Interpretation (see also Exegesis). 80 (x⁴ A 638), 348 (x² A 136), 2888 (x⁴ A 260), 2901 (XI¹ A 26), 4554 (x² A 355), 6520 (150), 6523 (163).
Interpreter. 6574 (x⁶ B 121).
Introduction. 131 (II A 46), 643 (VIII¹ A 362).
Inversion. 1808 (XI¹ A 403), 1897 (x⁴ A 274), 4682 (570), 4696 (x⁵ A 11), 5997 (VIII¹ A 84).
"In vino veritas." 5744 (V A 109).
Involvement. 379 (IX A 308), 673 (x¹ A 566), 791 (x⁴ A 550), 2279 (III A 145), 4521 (x³ A 685), 5049 (XI² A 50), 6191 (IX A 139).
INWARDNESS. 504 (x¹ A 471), 561 (XI² A 102), 594 (x¹ A 579), 614 (XI² A 80), 757 (VI A 51), 825 (x⁶ B 233), 949 (VIII¹ A 312), 1115 (VI A 107), 1138 (x³ A 298), 1395 (x² A 169), 1477 (x³ A 106), 1484 (x⁴ A 230), 1749 (VIII¹ A 169), 1867 (x³ A 276), 1897 (x⁴ A 274), 1960 (x³ A 659), 2004 (VIII¹ A 482), 2046 (x⁵ A 121), 2202 (156), 2294 (VII¹ A 76), 2463 (VIII¹ A 465), 2503 (x² A 30), 2518 (x³ A 153), 2522 (218), 2543 (XI² A 301), 2544 (303), 2640 (IX A 126), 2749 (VI B 58:8), 2751 (IX A 362), 2957 (x³ A 451), 3201 (x⁴ A 541), 3282 (III A 24), 3521 (x⁴ A 317), 3608 (x¹ A 481), 3617 (XI² A 305), 3619 (XI¹ A 106), 3850 (II A 199), 4296 (XI¹ A 15), 4331 (x² A 379), 4385 (I A 52), 4946 (IV A 160), 5329 (II A 232), 5653 (IV A 97), 5753 (V A 95), 6372 (x¹ A 183), 6548 (x² A 251), 6589 (488), 6643 (x³ A 174), 6646 (190), 6677 (434), 6833 (x⁶ B 226).
Irenaeus. 1483 (x⁴ A 134), 4046 (133).
Irish. 5556 (III A 223).
Irony (see also HUMOR; Comic). 900 (IV A 98), 1021 (II A 556), 1063 (x⁴ A 5), 1129 (x¹ A 367), 1234 (II A 280), 1456 (I A 224), 1526 (IV A 121), 1542 (II A 2), 1548

(III B 20), 1554 (V B 44), 1565 (I A 225), 2691 (X¹ A 400), 2999 (XI² A 147), 3077 (IV A 103), 4347 (XI¹ A 34), 4359 (XI² A 246), 4870 (X³ A 432), 5160 (I C 102), 5186 (I A 333), 5274 (II A 193), 5317 (737), 5665 (Letter 82), 5937 (VII¹ A 147).
—Irony of the ethical. 250 (X⁴ A 76), 5975 (VIII¹ A 15).
—Irony of indirect communication. 454 (V A 26), 645 (VIII¹ A 466), 650 (VIII² B 82), 1063 (X⁴ A 5), 2336 (XI² A 147), 3794 (IV A 169), 5827 (VI A 84), 6006 (VIII¹ A 124).
—Irony (S.K.). 786 (VIII¹ A 257), 5894 (VII¹ A 107), 5908 (121), 5942 (156), 5974 (VIII¹ A 13), 5999 (100), 6025 (205), 6549 (X² A 252), 6721 (X⁴ A 6), 6739 (101), 6907 (XI¹ A 497).
—Socratic irony. 4243 (II A 186), 4244 (III B 8), 4269 (VIII¹ A 281), 4276 (X² A 248), 4279 (X³ A 253), 4288 (X⁴ A 467), 4293 (599), 4897 (468).
Irony, slumbering. 5209 (II A 36).
Irvingites. 1443 (XI¹ A 591).
Isaac (see also Abraham and Isaac). 374 (VIII¹ A 629), 1109 (IV B 76), 2020 (X⁴ A 338), 2222 (572), 2223 (X⁵ A 132), 2743 (IX A 35), 3714 (X⁴ A 357), 4641 (X² A 129), 4777 (II A 544), 6791 (X⁴ A 458).
Isidorus. 739 (II A 484), 2234 (486).
Isolation. 114 (IV C 27), 1034 (VI A 65), 1825 (XI³ B 199), 4050 (XI² A 14).

Jack up the price. 6531 (X² A 193).
Jacob. 418 (I A 97), 3060 (II A 545), 4777 (544), 5423 (567).
Jacob von Thyboe. 4822 (I A 25), 4824 (209).
Jacobi, Friedrich H. 633 (VI B 40:45), 810 (V A 35), 1113 (V A 40), 1114 (V C 13:4), 1191 (II A 592), 1443 (XI¹ A 591), 2349 (V C 7), 2569 (XI² A 43), 3298 (V A 31), 5728 (21), 5733 (V C 13).
Janus. 5260 (II A 662).
Jean Paul pseudonym of A. Richter. 1696 (II A 108), 3607 (VI B 25), 4580 (II A 458), 4779 (VIII¹ A 480), 5135 (I C 88), 5241 (II A 118).
Jehovah. 200 (XI¹ A 284), 297 (II A 473),

440 (329), 1346 (VII¹ A 81), 2212 (II A 354), 2734 (86), 3234 (X³ A 149), 5424 (II A 572), 6324 (X¹ A 73).
Jeppe paa Bjerget. 4823 (I A 34).
JEST. 656 (VIII² B 88), 991 (X³ A 714), 1135 (X² A 207), 1469 (X¹ A 507), 1473 (X² A 219), 1743 (VI A 3), 1909 (X⁴ A 491), 3440 (X¹ A 633), 4924 (IV A 80), 6523 (X² A 163), 6574 (X⁶ B 121).
Jesuits. 525 (X³ A 649), 1769 (XI¹ A 255), 1770 (I A 196), 2746 (II A 292), 3113 (X³ A 632), 3805 (I A 200), 6186 (IX A 131).
Jews. 1 (II A 708), 324 (IX A 249), 410 (I A 4), 440 (II A 329), 737 (I A 181), 832 (II A 100), 857 (150), 1162 (VII¹ A 58), 1859 (X² A 317), 2579 (II A 374), 2985 (XI² A 26), 4788 (II A 372), 5420 (II A 560), 6033 (VIII¹ A 220), 6324 (X¹ A 73).
Job. 118 (I A 33), 1284 (X¹ A 194), 1386 (196), 1536 (X⁴ A 396), 1797 (146), 2216 (IX A 191), 4683 (X⁴ A 573).
Johannes Climacus. 569 (IX A 460), 1059 (X² A 439), 1174 (X³ A 506), 1575 (II A 335), 3093 (X² A 501), 3110 (X³ A 626), 3567 (X¹ A 679), 4030 (X² A 436), 4037 (482), 4550 (299), 5786 (VI A 146), 5827 (84), 5850 (VI B 89), 5851 (90), 5884 (VII¹ A 26), 5944 (158), 5997 (VIII¹ A 84), 6255 (IX B 63:7), 6349 (X⁶ B 48), 6350 (X¹ A 121), 6362 (151), 6404 (X⁶ B 84), 6433 (X¹ A 517), 6434 (Letter 213), 6439 (X¹ A 530), 6442 (536), 6449 (556), 6475 (X⁶ B 105), 6519 (X² A 148), 6523 (163), 6532 (195), 6558 (X⁶ B 130), 6566 (127), 6574 (121), 6596 (128), 6597 (601), 6598 (68), 6636 (137), 6690 (X³ A 555).
Johannes Climacus. 3300 (V A 98), 5620 (IV B 10a), 5621 (1).
Johannes de Silentio. 3130 (X² A 594), 5660 (IV B 79), 5709 (IV A 193), 5786 (VI A 146), 6327 (X¹ A 78), 6434 (L. 213), 6598 (X⁶ B 68), 6601 (82), 6787 (253).
John. 22 (I A 74), 204 (II A 287), 338 (X¹ A 355), 438 (II A 307), 601 (X⁴ A 594), 1690 (II A 102), 2435 (X³ A 741), 3025 (VIII¹ A 381).
John of the Cross. 6397 (X¹ A 323).
John the Baptist. 2887 (X⁴ A 157), 3038 (X³ A 674), 5311 (II A 723), 6561 (X² A 281).

Jonah. 4395 (I A 321).

Joseph. 798 (II A 553), 1256 (IX A 109), 2670 (VIII¹ A 338), 4144 (667).

Joseph of Arimathea. 359 (X⁴ A 507).

Josephus. 1777 (IX A 423).

Josty Cafe. 419 (I A 172), 5756 (V A 111).

Journal writing. 5241 (II A 118), 5242 (119), 5243 (120), 5289 (208).

JOURNALISM (*see also* Press; Newspapers). 155 (VII¹ A 13), 655 (VIII² B 87), 1162 (VII¹ A 58), 1782 (X² A 474), 2932 (VIII¹ A 656), 2933 (538), 2945 (X¹ A 231), 2950 (X² A 369), 2955 (X³ A 21), 3152 (260), 3728 (326), 3885 (XI² A 58), 4111 (VII¹ A 54), 4119 (VIII¹ A 134), 4127 (531), 4160 (X¹ A 356), 4181 (X² A 506), 4182 (571), 4188 (X³ A 587), 4192 (690), 4235 (XI² A 23), 4880 (X⁴ A 391), 5899 (VII¹ A 112), 6007 (VIII¹ A 133), 6008 (135), 6120 (589), 6128 (669), 6204 (IX A 169), 6217 (186), 6243 (243), 6313 (X¹ A 46), 6354 (131), 6384 (258), 6474 (653), 6742 (X⁴ A 166), 6886 (XI¹ A 242), 6957 (XI³ B 120).

Journalists. 2612 (X³ A 419), 2971 (XI¹ A 234), 3855 (II A 122), 4235 (XI² A 23), 4310 (X⁴ A 469), 6968 (XI² A 438).

Journals and Papers (S.K.). 2598 (VIII¹ A 231), 5645 (IV A 85), 5712 (V A 100), 6081 (VIII¹ A 445), 6380 (X¹ A 239), 6555 (X² A 277), 6762 (X⁴ A 299), 6842 (X⁶ B 232).

Journey. 5744 (V A 109).

JOY. 80 (X⁴ A 638), 331 (X¹ A 232), 444 (II A 365), 479 (IX A 20), 625 (VI B 10), 757 (VI A 51), 1168 (VIII¹ A 586), 1414 (X³ A 585), 1657 (360), 1661 (X⁴ A 588), 1716 (II A 672), 1886 (X³ A 667), 2008 (IX A 316), 2263 (II A 404), 2332 (XI¹ A 520), 2689 (VIII¹ A 341), 2716 (39), 2827 (II A 494), 3485 (X¹ A 540), 3522 (X⁴ A 330), 3915 (III C 1), 3938 (X² A 274), 3949 (X³ A 213), 4313 (X⁴ A 555), 4343 (508), 4349 (XI¹ A 363), 4729 (XI² A 208), 4799 (X³ A 286), 5305 (II A 216), 5324 (228), 5328 (231), 5945 (VII¹ A 160), 6091 (L. 167), 6145 (IX A 23), 6278 (498), 6659 (X³ A 310), 6686 (526), 6837 (X⁵ A 72).

Joyful Notes in the Strife of Suffering. 2201 (VIII¹ A 503), 6101 (504).

JUDAISM (*see also* CHRISTIANITY: Christianity and Judaism). 6 (V A 78), 204 (II A 287), 243 (265), 244 (283), 274 (I A 53), 305 (VIII¹ A 145), 324 (IX A 249), 378 (301), 387 (X² A 58), 410 (I A 4), 414 (46), 445 (II A 376), 447 (499), 498 (X¹ A 301), 832 (II A 100), 843 (X¹ A 426), 857 (II A 150), 1006 (XI² A 113), 1027 (III A 62), 1306 (II A 73), 1333 (IV A 190), 1433 (X⁵ A 39), 1475 (X² A 239), 1639 (VIII¹ A 305), 1690 (II A 102), 1899 (X⁴ A 293), 2068 (XI¹ A 421), 2072 (490), 2107 (160), 2511 (X² A 364), 2517 (X³ A 138), 2519 (170), 2525 (302), 2531 (605), 2579 (II A 374), 2601 (IX A 245), 2617 (XI¹ A 150), 2925 (VIII¹ A 199), 2992 (XI² A 116), 3028 (VIII¹ A 585), 3039 (XI¹ A 360), 3043 (585), 3098 (299), 3272 (II A 426), 3277 (518), 4456 (X² A 80), 4460 (642), 4649 (X³ A 81), 4788 (II A 372), 5047 (XI¹ A 556), 5430 (II A 805), 5495 (III A 105), 5939 (VII¹ A 150), 6033 (VIII¹ A 220), 6276 (IX A 416), 6947 (XI³ B 57).

JUDAS. 286 (II A 258), 339 (X¹ A 364), 392 (X² A 514), 3585 (XI¹ A 202), 3672 (IX A 474), 6321 (X¹ A 67).

Judge. 287 (II A 261), 1071 (IV A 59), 2642 (IX A 165).

Judge William. 5750 (V A 92), 5804 (VI A 41), 5823 (78), 6323 (X¹ A 72), 6357 (139).

Judgment. 322 (IX A 59), 854 (I A 254), 1386 (X¹ A 196), 2032 (X³ A 687), 2222 (X⁴ A 572), 2882 (X³ A 549), 4569 (XI¹ A 201), 5154 (I A 202), 5486 (III C 5), 6317 (X¹ A 56).

Judith. 3822 (III A 197).

Julius Caesar. 910 (IV A 172).

July Revolution 1830. 5116 (I B 2).

Jürgensen, Jørgen. 5143 (I A 166).

Justice. 490 (IX A 350), 532 (X⁴ A 212), 1325 (III A 102), 1326 (104), 1465 (II A 656), 1537 (XI² A 4), 2429 (X² A 107), 4154 (IX A 449), 4398 (I C 126), 5610 (IV A 34), 5770 (VI A 10), 6425 (X¹ A 488).

Justification. 283 (II A 594), 411 (I A 6), 453 (V A 23), 1652 (IX A 337).

Justin Martyr. 428 (II A 217).

Jutland pilgrimage. 5288 (II A 679), 5437-5444 (III A 15-22), 5445 (31), 5446 (35),

5447 (40), 5448 (42), 5449 (44), 5450-5460 (50-60), 5461-5464 (64-67), 5465 (69), 5466-5470 (71-75), 5471 (77), 5472-5474 (79-81), 5475 (83), 5476 (84).

Kagerup, Søren A. 5062 (I A 12).

Kalkar, Christian A. H. 2220 (x^3 A 230), 4015 (IX A 313).

Kalundborg. 5451 (III A 51).

KANT, Immanuel. 37 (III A 3), 188 (x^2 A 396), 649 (VIII^2 B 81), 650 (82), 1057 (x^2 A 328), 1190 (II A 31), 1191 (592), 1305 (I A 30), 1541 (340), 1600 (IV C 68), 2087 (II A 47), 2252 (II C 48), 2346 (V C 2), 3089 (VIII^1 A 11), 3093 (x^2 A 501), 3558 (x^1 A 666), 3654 (VI B 54:13,14,16), 3875 (XI^1 A 112), 4830 (IV C 114), 5181 (I A 328), 5283 (II C 49), 5702 (IV A 176), 6456 (x^1 A 576).

Kayak. 5403 (II A 520), 5542 (L. 54).

Kean. 6537 (L. 239).

Kempis, Thomas a (*see* THOMAS À KEMPIS).

Kerner, Justus. 1826 (II A 612), 3993 (117), 5205 (20), 5239 (115), 5240 (116).

Key. 6345 (x^1 A 115).

Kierkegaard, Else P. 5473 (III A 80).

Kierkegaard, Hans Peter. 5757 (L. 113), 6295 (L. 196).

Kierkegaard, Henriette. 5679 (L. 83), 6057 (L. 161), 6063 (L. 150), 6091 (L. 167), 6581 (x^2 A 415).

Kierkegaard, Michael P. 663 (IX A 240), 740 (II A 485), 1490 (x^5 A 54), 3362 (XI^2 A 7), 3841 (x^4 A 277), 5205 (II A 20), 5328 (231), 5335 (243), 5430 (805), 5466 (III A 71), 5468 (73), 5474 (81), 5664 (IV A 107), 5690 (144), 5769 (VI A 8), 5820 (75), 5874 (VII^1 A 5), 5913 (126), 5915 (128), 5961 (221), 6003 (L. 149), 6019 (VIII^1 A 177), 6035 (227), 6062 (352), 6073 (397), 6076 (414), 6131 (640), 6135 (650), 6161 (IX A 65), 6164 (68), 6165 (69), 6166 (70), 6167 (71), 6173 (85), 6176 (99), 6178 (106), 6220 (189), 6222 (203), 6274 (411), 6289 (473), 6298 (x^1 A 8), 6308 (39), 6310 (42), 6327 (78), 6355 (137), 6379 (234), 6389 (272), 6409 (374), 6453 (569), 6472

(x^5 A 149), 6477 (x^1 A 660), 6482 (667), 6488 (x^2 A 3), 6617 (x^3 A 78), 6627 (128), 6638 (x^6 B 163), 6641 (169), 6666 (x^3 A 391), 6712 (742), 6748 (x^6 A 171), 6749 (173, pp. 274-6), 6757 (x^4 A 270), 6768 (322), 6777 (373), 6842 (x^6 B 232, pp. 371-8), 6853 (XI^1 A 1), 6854 (XI^3 B 15), 6855 (28), 6860 (XI^1 A 69), 6906 (484), 6958 (XI^2 A 399), 6967 (437).

Kierkegaard, Nicoline. 6617 (x^3 A 78).

Kierkegaard, Niels Andreas. 5184 (I A 331).

Kierkegaard, Peter Christian. 77 (x^3 A 186), 224 (IX A 483), 2601 (245), 4177 (x^2 A 486), 5051 (L. 2), 5513 (L. 49), 5551 (L. 68), 5679 (L. 83), 5769 (VI A 8), 6003 (L. 149), 6059 (L. 161), 6090 (L. 166), 6091 (L. 167), 6106 (VIII^1 A 545), 6176 (IX A 99), 6274 (411), 6319 (x^1 A 61), 6472 (x^5 A 149), 6516 (x^2 A 134), 6550 (256), 6553 (273), 6554 (275), 6557 (280), 6558 (x^6 B 130), 6559 (131), 6560 (L. 240), 6562 (x^2 A 285), 6570 (338), 6581 (415), 6625 (x^3 A 112), 6695 (569), 6704 (637), 6706 (650), 6857 (XI^1 A 47).

Kierkegaard, Søren Michael. 5184 (I A 331).

King (ruler). 683 (VIII^1 A 60), 1342 (VI A 121), 2402 (IV A 183), 3477 (VIII^1 A 434), 4097 (II A 531), 4143 (VIII^1 A 636), 5756 (V A 111), 6042 (VIII^1 A 249).

King analogy. 6931 (XI^2 A 134).

King, William. 2368 (IV C 38), 5586 (IV A 25), 5594 (IV C 41), 5607 (126).

King Christian VIII (*see* Christian VIII).

Kingdom. 3004 (XI^2 A 211).

Kingo, Thomas Hansen. 877 (II A 530), 2860 (VII^1 A 83), 4386 (I A 121), 5487 (III C 8), 6097 (VIII^1 A 487).

Kirketidende. 4058 (XI^2 A 319), 6322 (x^1 A 71), 6560 (L. 240).

Kissing. 307 (VIII^1 A 343), 2393 (III B 106), 2394 (114).

Kjøbenhavn Aftenpost. 5206 (II A 21).

Kjøbenhavns Flyvepost. 5206 (II A 21), 6202 (IX A 167), 6458 (x^1 A 584), 6779 (x^4 A 380), 6785 (408).

Kjøbenhavnsposten. 5344 (II A 777), 5346 (779), 6202 (IX A 167), 6964 (XI^2 A 411).

Kjøbmagergade. 2570 (XI^2 A 54).

Klim, Niels. 5344 (II A 777).

Klinger, Friedrich M. v. 5077 (I C 46), 5160 (102).

Knippelsbro. 5444 (III A 22), 5478 (L. 17), 5481 (L. 23).

Knock. 1145 (x⁴ A 455).

Knot. 6760 (x⁴ A 285).

KNOWLEDGE. 13 (I A 206), 143 (IV C 104), 425 (II A 606), 852 (I A 221), 866 (II A 306), 1055 (x¹ A 193), 1074 (238), 1094 (I A 36), 1098 (II A 194), 1099 (III A 36), 1100 (39), 1101 (216), 1125 (VIII¹ A 672), 1148 (x⁴ A 635), 1154 (XI² A 380), 1180 (I A 227), 1182 (II A 29), 1430 (x⁴ A 567), 1682 (II A 78), 1827 (V A 24), 1902 (x⁴ A 349), 2202 (x⁵ A 156), 2856 (II A 149), 2870 (x³ A 32), 3012 (VIII¹ A 69), 3099 (XI¹ A 51), 3108 (x³ A 546), 3109 (609), 3110 (626), 3118 (641), 3471 (VI A 156), 3705 (IX A 365), 4095 (II A 467), 4460 (x² A 642), 4589 (VI A 48), 4850 (VIII¹ A 141), 4953 (XI² A 86), 4975 (x⁴ A 381), 5018 (x² A 24), 5065 (I C 25:26), 5091 (I A 62), 5101 (76), 5794 (VI B 35:15).

—Communication of knowledge (see also COMMUNICATION). 648 (VIII² B 79), 649 (81), 650 (82), 2324 (x² A 235), 2341 (V A 74), 2498 (x¹ A 526), 4766 (x⁴ A 139), 5779 (VI C 2).

—Ethical, ethical-religious knowledge. 895 (IV C 86), 4785 (x² A 93).

—Knowledge and "modern philosophy." 22 (I A 74), 23 (102), 37 (III A 3), 927 (VII¹ A 15), 1040 (33), 1072 (IV C 75), 1452 (XI² A 175), 1453 (179), 1544 (II A 214), 1579 (487), 1580 (488), 1588 (III A 6), 1601 (IV C 73), 1607 (VI B 40:3), 1628 (I A 247), 1638 (VI B 35:25), 1881 (x³ A 455), 1950 (x¹ A 372), 2235 (VI B 54:16), 2807 (VII¹ A 182), 2810-2813 (188-191), 2814-2820 (194-200), 3070 (II A 755), 3089 (VIII¹ A 11), 3099 (XI² A 51), 3245 (I A 94), 3247 (99), 3283 (III B 12), 3368 (II A 309), 3576 (x⁶ B 17), 3860 (x² A 702), 4099 (II A 573), 4267 (VII¹ A 193), 4555 (x² A 401), 5101 (I A 76).

—Self-knowledge (see Self-knowledge).

—S.K. 117 (I A 8), 1040 (VII¹ A 33), 1046 (VIII¹ A 127), 1340 (V B 5:8), 1399 (x² A 241), 2844 (VII¹ B 209), 5449 (III A 44).

Koberstein, August. 2703 (I C 113).

Kofoed-Hansen, Hans P. 4029 (x² A 429), 6673 (x³ A 422).

Kold, Christian. 5052 (L. 120a), 6247 (IX A 262).

Kolderup-Rosenvinge, Janus L. A. 6197 (L. 180).

Kolthoff, Ernst. 4858 (x¹ A 159), 6454 (570), 6853 (XI¹ A 1).

Koran. 6353 (x¹ A 130).

Krag, Johan. 4258 (IV A 211).

Kruse, Laurids. 4355 (XI² A 41).

Lady Macbeth. 3972 (IV A 50), 3973 (VI A 67), 6635 (x³ A 164).

Laity. 1924 (XI¹ A 4), 2621 (313), 2622 (XI² A 150), 2793 (x³ A 341).

Lamb. 330 (x¹ A 204).

Langeland. 5473 (III A 80).

LANGUAGE. 89 (XI² A 139), 90 (140), 98 (V B 55:10), 136 (II A 352), 538 (x⁴ A 624), 623 (V A 19), 655 (VIII² B 87), 1261 (x² A 428), 1277 (XI² A 261), 1319 (II A 418), 1590 (III A 37), 1632 (II A 650), 1935 (XI¹ A 550), 1982 (II A 516), 2339 (IV C 12), 2955 (x³ A 21), 3248 (I A 127), 3281 (III A 11), 3295 (IV A 55), 3467 (VI A 150), 3494 (x² A 310), 3532 (XI¹ A 19), 3867 (557), 4056 (XI² A 106), 4058 (319), 4059 (343), 4121 (VIII¹ A 245), 4332 (x² A 424), 4732 (XI¹ A 269), 4863 (x¹ A 448), 5100 (I A 75), 5181 (328), 5186 (333), 5203 (II A 582), 5268 (182), 5364 (328), 5378 (406), 5512 (III A 155), 5612 (IV A 37), 5692 (151), 6259 (IX A 298), 6398 (x¹ A 325), 6576 (x² A 374), 6921 (XI² A 36), 6952 (XI² A 379).

Language analogy. 5267 (II A 171), 5407 (540).

Laplander. 5522 (III A 167).

Latin. 2308 (II A 111), 5069 (I C 36), 5070 (37), 5574 (IV A 2).

Laughter. 492 (IX A 394), 1706 (I A 179), 1757 (IX A 399), 1758 (400), 1759 (420), 1761 (x¹ A 148), 1855 (673), 2046 (x⁵ A 121), 2176 (II A 506), 2645 (IX A 435), 2655 (x¹ A 623), 2941 (IX A 277), 4400 (II A 163), 4582 (III A 99), 4823 (I A 34), 5176 (272), 5258 (II A 649), 5371 (373), 5953 (VII¹ B 213), 6160 (IX A 64), 6348

(x^1 A 120), 6373 (187), 6386 (262), 6943 (xi^3 B 53), 6945 (55).

Lavater, Johann C. 4993 (x^2 A 321).

Law. 242 (I A 38), 265 (II A 12), 273 (I A 28), 295 (II A 388), 297 (473), 349 (x^2 A 170), 435 (II A 277), 538 (x^4 A 624), 647 (VIII[1] A 564), 851 (I A 152), 967 (IX A 443), 1072 (IV C 75), 1216 (VIII[1] A 675), 1238 (II A 456), 1239 (457), 1264 (x^3 A 618), 1380 (IX A 441), 1464 (I A 82), 1475 (x^2 A 239), 1481 (x^3 A 410), 1482 (784), 1483 (x^4 A 134), 1484 (230), 1488 (x^5 A 7), 1490 (54), 1504 (xi^2 A 367), 1540 (I A 237), 1654 (x^2 A 451), 1773 (III A 242), 1857 (x^2 A 47), 1878 (x^3 A 411), 1884 (615), 1905 (x^4 A 366), 2066 (xi^1 A 384), 2208 (I A 49), 2209 (287), 2403 (VII[1] A 225), 2424 (x^1 A 514), 2527 (x^3 A 336), 2533 (x^4 A 12), 2554 (xi^1 A 572), 2894 (x^5 A 15), 2905 (xi^1 A 138), 3490 (x^2 A 218), 3530 (x^5 A 62), 3612 (x^2 A 461), 3772 (x^5 A 58), 4072 (I A 309), 5100 (75), 5161 (235).

Lazarus. 879 (II A 578), 987 (x^2 A 546), 1466 (II A 507), 2713 (II C 5), 2866 (x^1 A 287), 4002 (II A 311), 6270 (IX A 381).

Leaders. 597 (x^3 A 521).

Leadership. 2935 (VIII[1] A 571).

Leander. 5191 (I A 341).

LEAP. 261 (IV C 87), 385 (x^2 A 16), 653 (VIII[2] B 85), 808 (IV C 105), 972 (x^1 A 360), 1248 (V B 55:26), 1603 (IV C 81), 1607 (VI B 40:3), 2704 (II A 631), 2807 (VII[1] A 182), 3247 (I A 99), 3598 (II A 763), 4421 (IV C 94), 4806 (xi^1 A 329), 5116 (I B 2), 5787 (VI B 13), 6019 (VIII[1] A 177), 6405 (x^6 B 85).

Lear, King. 1165 (VIII[1] A 58).

Learning. 959 (IX A 104), 1013 (VIII[2] B 31:22).

Lectures. 5601 (IV C 97), 5602 (98), 5608 (127), 6004 (VIII[1] A 120), 6005 (121), 6094 (VIII[2] B 186).

Left hand. 5639 (IV A 75), 5648 (89), 6407 (x^1 A 351).

Legends. 4402 (II A 170), 5128 (I C 82), 5129 (83), 5130 (84), 5131 (85), 5209 (II A 36), 5212 (43), 5213 (44), 5214 (45), 5223 (98), 5224 (590), 5287 (207), 5426 (575), 5811 (VI A 53), 5843 (125).

Legs. 5922 (VII[1] A 50), 6285 (IX A 458),

6509 (x^2 A 101), 6609 (x^3 A 8).

LEIBNIZ, Gottfried. 40 (IV C 32), 41 (33), 43 (76), 1057 (x^2 A 328), 1241 (IV C 39), 1245 (62), 1601 (73), 1635 (35), 2339 (12), 3073 (29), 3549 (40), 3652 (71), 4027 (x^2 A 403), 4419 (IV A 18), 5579 (IV C 8), 5580 (9), 5581 (IV A 14), 5583 (16), 5584 (17), 5585 (22), 5586 (25), 5593 (IV C 34), 5594 (41), 5597 (44), 5607 (126), 5609 (IV A 31).

Leisetritt, Emanuel. 6838 (x^5 A 93).

Lemming, Carl Frederik. 617 (I A 327), 5113 (103).

Le Moine. 525 (x^3 A 649).

Lenau, Nicolaus. 133 (II A 180), 1183 (50), 5166 (I C 105), 5225 (II A 597), 5226 (598).

Leniency. 1500 (xi^2 A 100), 4693 (x^4 A 643), 6710 (x^3 A 716).

Lenore. 2306 (I A 261), 4822 (25), 4824 (209).

Lepers. 4859 (x^1 A 347), 5056 (I C 9), 5667 (IV A 111).

LESSING, Gotthold. 73 (x^2 A 406), 974 (x^1 A 412), 1637 (V B 64), 2342 (1:3), 2345 (V C 1), 2349 (7), 2354 (VI B 35:30), 2355 (98:26), 2666 (xi^1 A 511), 2720 (x^1 A 373), 3042 (xi^1 A 482), 3195 (x^1 A 401), 4302 (xi^1 A 448), 4326 (x^1 A 417), 4364 (VI A 2), 4375 (x^1 A 478), 4474 (x^4 A 335), 4826 (IV C 110), 4828 (112), 4837 (121), 5085 (I C 53), 5158 (100), 5160 (102), 5789 (VI B 15), 5790 (16), 5793 (35:14), 5794 (35:15), 5795 (35:19), 5796 (35:24).

"Let Not the Heart in Sorrow Sin." 6277 (IX A 421), 6278 (498), 6280 (500).

Letters. 131 (II A 46), 1572 (697), 5100 (I A 75), 5504 (L. Document xv), 5509 (III A 149), 5517 (161), 5526 (171), 5530 (174), 6303 (x^1 A 23).

Letters (S.K.) (*see below,* Composite Collation).

Leucippus. 5617 (IV A 61).

Levelling. 1992 (VII[1] B 121:6), 2061 (xi^1 A 319), 4230 (118), 6340 (x^1 A 107), 6706 (x^3 A 650), 6852 (xi^2 A 335).

Levin, Israel. 6625 (x^3 A 112).

Liberals. 581 (I A 108), 4088 (II A 774), 4094 (460), 4115 (VIII[1] A 79), 5181 (I A 328).

Library. 5655 (L. 80), 5665 (L. 82).

Lice. 4235 (XI^2 A 23).

Lichtenberg, George C. 3855 (II A 122), 5241 (118), 5245 (124), 6079 (VIII^1 A 440).

Lies. 495 (X^1 A 178), 1611 (VII^1 A 153), 2572 (XI^2 A 56), 3736 (XI^1 A 525), 4228 (98), 4812 (554), 6911 (551).

Life. 25 (I A 126), 265 (II A 12), 266 (41), 729 (XI^2 A 199), 859 (II A 165), 1019 (125), 1025 (725), 1152 (XI^2 A 115), 1472 (X^2 A 198), 1565 (I A 225), 3245 (94), 3772 (X^5 A 58), 4392 (I A 313), 4398 (I C 126), 5092 (I A 72), 5100 (75), 5143 (166), 5267 (II A 171), 5364 (328), 5372 (382), 5390 (444).

"Life of Christ." 6397 (X^1 A 323).

Life's meaning. 4712 (XI^1 A 377).

Life-outlook. 22 (I A 74), 154 (VII^1 A 12), 219 (II A 127), 265 (12), 841 (VIII^1 A 543), 1005 (XI^1 A 528), 1521 (II A 134), 1682 (78), 1690 (102), 1976 (223), 2579 (374), 3547 (I A 295), 5181 (329).

"Life Put to the Test." 5575 (IV A 197).

Life-weariness. 6969 (XI^2 A 439).

Liguori, Alfons M. d. 336 (X^1 A 352), 6297 (X^6 C 2), 6355 (X^1 A 137), 6362 (151).

"Lily of the Field and the Bird of the Air, The." 6633 (X^3 A 161).

Limitation. 1654 (X^2 A 451).

Limp. 1405 (X^2 A 644).

Lind, Peter. 3609 (X^2 A 430), 5152 (I A 189), 5990 (VIII^1 A 46).

Lindberg, Jacob C. 5053 (I C 2), 5089 (I A 60).

Lindner, Benjamin. 2522 (X^3 A 218).

Listening. 3478 (VIII^1 A 668), 6424 (X^1 A 483).

Literalism. 1947 (II A 424).

"Literary Quicksilver." 5688 (IV A 141).

"Literary Review." 6334 (X^1 A 90).

Literature. 120 (I A 90), 145 (IV A 130), 5293 (II A 686), 5614 (IV A 45), 6836 (X^5 A 67).

Little things. 2570 (XI^2 A 54).

Liturgy. 584 (II A 792), 5404 (521).

Living word. 5090 (I A 61), 5091 (62).

Livius. 3358 (X^3 A 460).

Loafing. 6023 (VIII^1 A 200), 6042 (249).

Lock analogy. 6802 (X^4 A 554), 6953 (XI^2 A 383).

Locomotive. 1933 (XI^1 A 396).

Lodging. 4697 (X^5 A 28).

Logic. 196 (IV C 88), 199 (VI B 54:21), 259 (IV C 48), 759 (VII^1 A 84), 1567 (I A 317), 1602 (IV C 79), 1605 (V A 73), 2341 (74), 3658 (IV C 89), 5599 (46).

"Logical Problems." 5786 (VI A 146), 5787 (VI B 13), 5850 (89).

Longing. 4409 (II A 343), 5456 (III A 56).

Longinus, Cassius. 147 (IV A 222).

Longus. 5587 (IV A 30).

Lord's Prayer. 5265 (II A 673).

Lord's Supper. 1924 (XI^1 A 4), 5332 (II A 240).

Lost penny. 3949 (X^3 A 213).

Lost sheep. 2873 (X^3 A 165), 3949 (213).

Louis Philippe. 6681 (X^3 A 453).

LOVE. 619 (II A 624), 641 (VIII^1 A 293), 1204 (IV A 66), 1978 (II A 385), 2690 (IX A 366), 3254 (II A 586).

—Christian Love. 489 (IX A 329), 612 (X^2 A 57), 835 (III A 124), 874 (II A 502), 942 (VIII^1 A 189), 943 (VIII^2 B 30:4), 944 (34:7), 945 (58:14), 991 (X^3 A 714), 1886 (667), 2033 (X^5 B 117), 2643 (IX A 325), 3031 (322), 3677 (X^3 A 125), 4206 (X^4 A 83), 4376 (X^2 A 182), 4447 (VIII^2 B 71:6,7,9,10,12), 4603 (VIII^1 A 269), 6237 (IX A 226).

—Divine Love. 307 (VIII^1 A 343), 316 (469), 514 (X^2 A 420), 532 (X^4 A 212), 538 (624), 731 (XI^2 A 422), 875 (II A 513), 900 (IV A 98), 1123 (VIII^1 A 649), 1163 (25), 1173 (X^2 A 454), 1304 (I A 29), 1312 (II A 391), 1318 (410), 1319 (418), 1328 (IV A 102), 1329 (104), 1358 (VIII^1 A 327), 1361 (516), 1368 (IX A 77), 1379 (374), 1409 (X^3 A 359), 1410 (373), 1411 (374), 1412 (421), 1426 (X^4 A 254), 1445 (XI^2 A 98), 1446 (99), 1447 (130), 1464 (I A 82), 1520 (XI^2 A 245), 2184 (III A 232), 2205 (XI^2 A 114), 2300 (X^1 A 577), 2494 (419), 3098 (XI^1 A 299), 3391 (IV B 149), 3450 (X^3 A 49), 3453 (223), 3766 (X^4 A 649), 3915 (III C 1), 4375 (X^1 A 478), 4690 (X^4 A 620), 4692 (630), 4715 (XI^1 A 422), 4730 (XI^2 A 398), 4892 (418), 5488 (III C 12), 6032 (VIII^1 A 219), 6134 (648), 6135 (650), 6215 (IX A 184), 6229 (216), 6254 (288), 6489 (X^2 A 10), 6516

(134), 6615 (x³ A 68), 6623 (98), 6771 (x⁴ A 339), 6824 (673), 6895 (xɪ¹ A 382), 6913 (560).

—Erotic, earthly love. 1370 (ɪx A 113), 2003 (vɪɪɪ¹ A 462), 2120 (ɪx A 402), 2362 (ɪv A 26), 2595 (vɪɪɪ¹ A 52), 2596 (190), 3031 (ɪx A 322), 3237 (ɪv A 95), 3388 (ɪɪɪ A 162), 3971 (ɪv A 194), 3979 (v A 51), 4021 (x¹ A 433), 4110 (vɪɪ¹ A 20), 4447 (vɪɪɪ² B 71:6,7,9,10,12), 4838 (ɪv c 122), 5587 (ɪv A 30), 5632 (233), 5694 (153), 5996 (vɪɪɪ¹ A 82).

—Familial love. 1157 (ɪɪɪ B 41:20), 1165 (vɪɪɪ¹ A 58), 4204 (x⁴ A 83).

—Love of God. 14 (x³ A 342), 220 (ɪɪ A 128), 301 (ɪv A 33), 372 (vɪɪɪ¹ A 392), 742 (ɪɪɪ A 238), 979 (x² A 182), 1155 (ɪɪɪ c 7), 1216 (vɪɪɪ¹ A 675), 1353 (63), 1367 (ɪx A 75), 1370 (113), 1409 (x³ A 359), 1410 (373), 1411 (374), 1791 (525), 1844 (vɪɪɪ¹ A 587), 1870 (x³ A 294), 2098 (xɪ¹ A 400), 2101 (x⁴ A 392), 2299 (ɪx A 438), 2480 (x¹ A 85), 2525 (x³ A 302), 2554 (xɪ¹ A 572), 3109 (x³ A 609), 3388 (ɪɪɪ A 162), 4021 (x¹ A 433), 4690 (x⁴ A 620), 4692 (630), 4700 (x⁵ A 81), 4730 (xɪ² A 398), 6229 (ɪx A 216), 6516 (x² A 134), 6902 (xɪ¹ A 445).

—Self-love. 2086 (xɪ² A 361), 2098 (xɪ¹ A 400), 2596 (vɪɪɪ¹ A 190), 4690 (x⁴ A 620), 4692 (630), 6091 (Letter 169), 6824 (x⁴ A 673).

—(S.K.). 5368 (ɪɪ A 347), 5451 (ɪɪɪ A 51), 5461 (64), 5490 (90), 5507 (147), 5515 (159), 5526 (171), 6824 (x⁴ A 673), 6899 (xɪ¹ A 424).

Lover. 167 (x¹ A 198), 5642 (ɪv A 79).

Lucian, Marcus. 1549 (ɪv A 39), 5295 (ɪɪ A 690), 5296 (691).

Lucretius, Titus. 4728 (xɪ² A 136).

Lund, A. 5164 (ɪ A 249).

Lund, Christian. 6379 (x¹ A 234), 6581 (x² A 415).

Lund, Henrich [Henrik]. 5543 (ʟ. 55), 5544 (ʟ. 56), 6369 (ʟ. 262), 6799 (ʟ. 276).

Lund, Henriette. 5527 (ʟ. 71), 5544 (ʟ. 56).

Lund, Michael. 5544 (ʟ. 56).

Lund, Peter Wilhelm. 5092 (ɪ A 72), 5150 (187), 5248 (ɪɪ A 154), (6652 (x³ A 239).

Lund, Troels. 5448 (ɪɪɪ A 42), 5466 (71).

Luno, Bianco. 5806 (ʟ. 119), 6030 (ʟ. 152), 6452 (x¹ A 568), 6594 (x² A 586), 6656 (x³ A 265).

ʟᴜᴛʜᴇʀ, Martin. 170 (x² A 380), 209 (ɪx A 442), 229 (ɪɪɪ A 87), 337 (x¹ A 354), 338 (355), 389 (x² A 139), 463 (vɪɪɪ¹ A 157), 486 (ɪx A 292), 530 (x⁴ A 115), 599 (22), 626 (vɪ B 11), 667 (x¹ A 136), 691 (ɪx A 95), 693 (x¹ A 132), 711 (xɪ¹ A 28), 816 (x¹ A 248), 825 (x⁶ B 233), 843 (x¹ A 426), 983 (x² A 208),1124 (vɪɪɪ¹ A 661), 1135 (x² A 207), 1139 (322), 1140 (323), 1143 (x⁴ A 123), 1218 (ɪx A 482), 1264 (x³ A 618), 1380 (ɪx A 441), 1397 (x² A 226), 1406 (x³ A 25), 1433 (x⁵ A 39), 1447 (xɪ² A 130), 1448 (131), 1462 (x⁴ A 582), 1473 (x² A 219), 1482 (x³ A 784), 1484 (x⁴ A 230), 1485 (419), 1486 (616), 1630 (ɪɪ A 14), 1777 (ɪx A 423), 1792 (x³ A 576), 1845 (ɪx A 7), 1852 (x¹ A 246), 1857 (x² A 47), 1862 (361), 1877 (x³ A 409), 1901 (x⁴ A 340), 1902 (349), 1903 (352), 1904 (354), 1908 (459), 1913 (521), 1922 (x⁵ A 88), 1923 (139), 2042 (x⁴ A 415), 2046 (x⁵ A 121), 2091 (vɪɪɪ¹ A 676), 2140 (x³ A 672), 2334 (xɪ² A 128), 2358 (x¹ A 361), 2422 (487), 2423 (489), 2432 (x³ A 19), 2599 (vɪɪɪ¹ A 369), 2603 (ɪx A 434), 2605 (x¹ A 440), 2616 (xɪ¹ A 129), 2629 (xɪ² A 238), 2682 (326), 2750 (vɪɪɪ¹ A 403), 2762 (xɪ¹ A 134), 2763 (198), 2799 (ɪ A 300), 2823 (x⁵ A 73), 2890 (x⁴ A 428), 2898 (x⁵ A 96), 2901 (xɪ¹ A 26), 3009 (xɪ² A 243), 3032 (ɪx A 427), 3034 (x² A 117), 3044 (xɪ² A 163), 3063 (x⁴ A 448), 3145 (x³ A 93), 3153 (267), 3158 (606), 3213 (xɪ³ B 175), 3218 (x² A 312), 3492 (230), 3496 (382), 3515 (x³ A 534), 3617 (xɪ² A 305), 3645 (x² A 296), 3677 (x³ A 125), 3686 (696), 3737 (xɪ² A 346), 3757 (x³ A 560), 3984 (x¹ A 394), 3995 (ɪɪ A 64), 4057 (xɪ² A 161), 4061 (ɪ A 93), 4220 (x⁵ A 115), 4336 (x³ A 579), 4372 (x¹ A 22), 4379 (x⁴ A 411), 4463 (x³ A 396), 4549 (x² A 231), 4566 (x⁴ A 407), 4695 (670), 4699 (x⁵ A 38), 4856 (ɪx A 326), 4890 (x⁴ A 297), 4903 (x⁵ A 17), 4949 (x⁴ A 487), 4950 (x³ A 43), 4976 (x⁴ A 406), 5000 (xɪ¹ A 226), 5156 (ɪ A 220), 5181 (328), 5332

(II A 240), 5855 (VI A 141), 6150 (IX A 39), 6243 (243), 6328 (x¹ A 80), 6503 (x² A 75), 6651 (x³ A 219), 6653 (249), 6666 (391), 6677 (434), 6686 (526), 6720 (800), 6727 (x⁴ A 33), 6794 (488), 6842 (x⁶ B 232, pp. 371-378), 6943 (XI³ B 53), 6947 (57), 6957 (120).

Lutheranism. 1397 (x² A 226), 1913 (x⁴ A 521), 2682 (XI² A 326).

Lying. 948 (VIII¹ A 291).

Lyngby. 5483 (L. 29).

Lyngbye, Hans. 5098 (I A 67), 5106 (69).

Lyric poetry. 35 (II A 383), 1565 (I A 225), 1690 (II A 102), 2005 (VIII¹ A 568), 5604 (IV C 107), 5605 (123).

Maanedsskrift. 5200 (II A 7), 5201 (17).

Macbeth. 2112 (V B 65).

Mad Maier [Meyer]. 6382 (x¹ A 247), 6498 (x² A 48), 6897 (XI¹ A 412), 6954 (XI² A 93).

Mademoiselle de Scudéry. 5584 (IV A 17).

Madness. 905 (IV A 149), 1029 (148), 1107 (109), 3896 (VII¹ A 47).

Madonna. 164 (IX A 110).

Madvig, Johan N. 2321 (V B 53:12), 3459 (x⁴ A 229), 4111 (VII¹ A 54), 5926 (55), 6429 (x¹ A 497), 6517 (x² A 147), 6526 (177), 6778 (x⁴ A 377).

Magic flute. 4397 (I C 125).

Magnanimity. 1221 (x² A 516), 1994 (VII¹ A 149).

Mahogany chest. 6518 (x⁵ B 206), 6629 (x³ A 144).

Maieutic. 649 (VIII² B 81), 650 (82), 1957 (IX A 221), 1962 (x⁴ A 553), 5893 (VII¹ A 106), 5972 (VIII¹ A 4), 5987 (42), 6234 (IX A 222), 6363 (x¹ A 152), 6374 (192), 6408 (366), 6463 (598), 6804 (x⁴ A 558).

MAJESTY. 1436 (XI¹ A 5), 1438 (188), 1447 (XI² A 130), 1449 (133), 1450 (170), 1471 (x² A 189), 2008 (IX A 316), 2079 (XI² A 124), 2447 (XI¹ A 411), 2853 (x⁴ A 483), 2906 (XI¹ A 154), 2992 (XI² A 116), 3099 (51), 4680 (x⁴ A 456), 4812 (XI¹ A 554), 4917 (XI² A 204), 6615 (x³ A 68), 6930 (XI² A 121), 6931 (134).

Majority. 166 (x¹ A 3), 938 (VII¹ A 251), 1748 (64), 2944 (IX A 490), 2963 (x⁴ A 107), 4144 (VIII¹ A 667), 4334 (x³ A 241), 4852 (IX A 4), 4873 (x³ A 652), 4962 (IX A

124), 6307 (x¹ A 37).

Malice. 4580 (II A 458).

Man. 1415 (x³ A 658), 1518 (XI¹ A 176), 3211 (XI² A 187), 3558 (x¹ A 666), 3962 (V B 53:27).

Manhood. 2067 (XI¹ A 415).

Manichaeism. 1302 (I A 2).

Mankind. 1989 (VI A 20), 2898 (x⁵ A 96), 3361 (XI¹ A 367).

Many, the (*see also* Crowd; Mass; NUMBERS; Public). 57 (VII¹ A 86), 302 (79), 303 (72), 499 (x¹ A 399), 552 (XI¹ A 265), 1748 (VII¹ A 64), 1759 (IX A 420), 1996 (VII¹ B 158:3), 2038 (x⁴ A 104), 2050 (XI¹ A 81), 2051 (82), 2103 (500), 2154 (IX A 282), 2158 (468), 2165 (x³ A 231), 2566 (XI¹ A 486), 2652 (x¹ A 220), 3915 (III C 1), 4114 (VII¹ A 212), 4221 (x⁵ A 136), 4482 (XI¹ A 472), 4851 (VIII¹ A 605), 4885 (XI¹ A 352), 6344 (x¹ A 113), 6385 (260), 6389 (272), 6580 (413).

Map analogy. 6283 (IX A 448).

Marbach, Gotthard O. 3793 (IV A 156).

Marcellinus, Ammianus. 4429 (VI A 114).

Marcus Aurelius. 429 (II A 234), 3898 (IX A 373), 4254 (IV A 207), 4516 (x⁴ A 576).

Marheineke, Philipp. 3285 (III C 32), 5052 (I C 1), 5513 (L. 49), 5514 (III C 26), 5543 (L. 55).

Market town. 6200 (IX A 159), 6309 (x¹ A 41), 6856 (XI¹ A 6).

Märklin. 3320 (x³ A 682).

MARRIAGE. 57 (VII¹ A 86), 256 (XI² A 330), 351 (x² A 319), 1172 (14), 1257 (x¹ A 26), 1374 (IX A 247), 1482 (x³ A 784), 1556 (VI A 5), 1558 (VIII¹ A 251), 1649 (XI² A 234), 1822 (267), 1823 (271), 1824 (272), 2221 (x³ A 293), 2225 (XI¹ A 151), 2393 (III B 106), 2405 (VIII¹ A 51), 2412 (393), 2417 (IX A 30), 2428 (x² A 63), 2443 (XI¹ A 279), 2503 (x² A 30), 2522 (x³ A 218), 2534 (x⁴ A 25), 2537 (324), 2599 (VIII¹ A 369), 2691 (x¹ A 400), 2697 (x³ A 523), 2908 (XI¹ A 157), 2976 (372), 2995 (XI² A 151), 3009 (243), 3041 (XI¹ A 204), 3156 (x³ A 502), 3247 (I A 99), 3621 (XI¹ A 213), 3761 (x⁴ A 326), 3969 (XI¹ A 259), 4373 (x¹ A 452), 4396 (I A 322), 4559 (x³ A 720), 4998 (XI¹ A 141), 4999 (164), 5000 (226), 5007 (XI² A 192), 5334 (II C 3),

5575 (IV A 197), 5634 (234), 5664 (107), 5680 (133), 5693 (152), 5729 (V A 27), 5947 (VII[1] A 169), 6038 (VIII[1] A 232), 6243 (IX A 243), 6306 (x[5] A 158), 6343 (x[1] A 112), 6426 (494), 6500 (x[2] A 61), 6503 (75), 6584 (x[5] A 165), 6590 (x[2] A 525), 6837 (x[5] A 72), 6876 (XI[1] A 149), 6882 (210), 6954 (XI[3] B 93).

Martensen, Hans L. 355 (x[3] A 427), 508 (x[1] A 558), 673 (566), 707 (658), 808 (IV C 105), 921 (VI A 92), 1183 (II A 50), 1570 (52), 1738 (IV C 108), 2329 (XI[1] A 80), 3107 (x[3] A 544), 3217 (x[1] A 628), 3515 (x[3] A 534), 4212 (x[4] A 186), 5061 (I A 11), 5181 (328), 5200 (II A 7), 5225 (597), 5226 (598), 5277 (II C 12-24), 5299 (26-28), 5353 (25), 5679 (Letter 83), 5712 (V A 100), 5941 (VII[1] A 155), 6039 (VIII[1] A 233), 6052 (277), 6239 (IX A 229), 6448 (x[1] A 553), 6449 (556), 6456 (576), 6460 (588), 6465 (616), 6475 (x[6] B 105), 6493 (x[2] A 25), 6547 (242), 6550 (256), 6552 (261), 6553 (273), 6554 (275), 6557 (280), 6560 (Letter 240), 6563 (x[2] A 298), 6595 (596), 6596 (x[6] B 137), 6637 (162), 6655 (x[3] A 261), 6678 (435), 6691 (565), 6709 (678), 6748 (x[6] B 171), 6787 (253), 6813 (x[4] A 604), 6857 (XI[1] A 47), 6862 (72), 6874 (142), 6875 (XI[3] B 49), 6901 (XI[1] A 439), 6938 (XI[2] A 252), 6941 (256), 6942 (257), 6947 (XI[3] B 57), 6961 (129).

Martha. 1686 (II A 84), 5015 (x[3] A 589), 5039 (x[2] A 373).

MARTYR. 124 (I A 174), 250 (x[4] A 76), 254 (I A 138), 387 (x[2] A 58), 399 (x[4] A 147), 429 (II A 234), 481 (IX A 51), 488 (300), 504 (x[1] A 471), 516 (x[2] A 460), 1052 (IX A 358), 1221 (x[2] A 516), 1266 (x[4] A 13), 1928 (XI[1] A 104), 1930 (306), 2051 (82), 2148 (VIII[1] A 137), 2421 (x[1] A 444), 2546 (XI[1] A 61), 2550 (193), 2932 (VIII[1] A 656), 2933 (538), 2993 (XI[2] A 127), 3005 (214), 3121 (x[5] A 75), 3481 (x[1] A 125), 3575 (x[4] A 398), 3579 (614), 3669 (IX A 344), 3898 (373), 3903 (XI[1] A 285), 3940 (x[2] A 333), 4057 (XI[2] A 161), 4457 (x[2] A 279), 4671 (x[4] A 169), 4817 (10), 4856 (IX A 326), 4979 (XI[1] A 103), 4980 (115), 6050 (VIII[1] A 271), 6236 (IX A 225), 6244 (251), 6253 (285), 6288 (471), 6348 (x[1]

A 120), 6371 (169), 6395 (320), 6407 (351), 6418 (424), 6521 (x[2] A 157), 6562 (285), 6742 (x[4] A 166), 6794 (488), 6906 (XI[1] A 484), 6929 (XI[2] A 101).

Martyrdom. 382 (x[1] A 249), 497 (217), 2046 (x[5] A 121), 3836 (XI[2] A 10), 3898 (IX A 373), 4166 (x[2] A 7), 4277 (449), 6371 (x[1] A 169), 6493 (x[2] A 25).

MARY. 346 (x[2] A 85), 364 (XI[1] A 45), 1079 (IX A 12), 1087 (x[3] A 518), 1190 (II A 31), 1356 (VIII[1] A 111), 1913 (x[4] A 521), 2222 (x[3] A 572), 2515 (58), 3122 (646), 3495 (x[2] A 363), 4752 (x[1] A 490), 4993 (x[2] A 321), 5015 (x[3] A 589), 5039 (x[2] A 373), 6644 (x[3] A 183).

Mass, the (see also Crowd; Many; Mass; NUMBERS; Public). 562 (XI[2] A 110), 820 (x[2] A 392), 1531 (500), 1617 (x[4] A 385), 1647 (XI[1] A 388), 1953 (463), 1956 (XI[2] A 237), 1991 (VI A 120), 2022 (x[2] A 457), 2025 (629), 2030 (x[3] A 476), 2050 (XI[1] A 81), 2055 (175), 2081 (XI[2] A 135), 2667 (68), 4118 (VIII[1] A 123), 4182 (x[2] A 571), 4197 (x[4] A 40), 4198 (41), 4849 (VII[1] A 32), 4880 (x[4] A 391), 4912 (XI[1] A 517), 5186 (I A 333).

Master. 2975 (XI[1] A 346).

Master-thief. 1953 (XI[1] A 463), 5061 (I A 11), 5062 (12), 5072 (13), 5073 (14), 5074 (15), 5075 (16), 5081 (18), 5205 (II A 20).

Matchless. 5052 (L. 120a), 6356 (II A 300).

Mathematics. 197 (IV C 100), 653 (VIII[2] B 85), 2296 (VII[1] A 215), 3295 (IV A 55).

Mathiesen, Lars. 5752 (V A 94).

Mathæus Parisiensis. 5701 (IV A 175).

Maturity. 906 (IV A 155), 911 (179), 1668 (VI B 53:13), 1811 (XI[1] A 447), 6969 (439).

May. 3822 (III A 197).

Meaning. 811 (VI A 25), 1003 (XI A 252), 1365 (VIII[1] A 670), 1544 (II A 214), 2317 (722), 2329 (XI[1] A 80), 2993 (XI[2] A 127), 2999 (167), 4712 (XI[1] A 377), 6921 (XI[2] A 36).

Means. 931 (VII[1] A 35), 4931 (x[2] A 144), 6582 (425).

Means/ends. 1787 (x[3] A 347), 2782 (503).

Mediacy. 1101 (III A 216).

Mediation. 1242 (IV C 55), 1578 (II A 454), 1603 (IV C 81), 1617 (x[4] A 385), 1633

(III B 14), 2277 (III A 211), 2437 (IX A 482), 2749 (VI B 58:8), 3072 (III A 108), 3073 (IV C 29), 3074 (84), 3294 (IV A 54), 3307 (VI B 54:33), 4857 (IX A 487), 5549 (III B 130), 5651 (IV A 93), 5944 (VII¹ A 158).

Mediator. 1424 (X⁴ A 252), 1425 (253).

MEDIOCRITY. 166 (X¹ A 3), 225 (X² A 358), 305 (VIII¹ A 145), 525 (X³ A 649), 815 (IX A 289), 850 (I A 141), 1792 (X³ A 576), 1800 (XI² A 294), 1807 (XI¹ A 402), 1812 (476), 2053 (148), 2058 (260), 2546 (61), 2575 (XI² A 152), 2599 (VIII¹ A 369), 3663 (XI¹ A 33), 4494 (XI³ B 148), 4911 (XI¹ A 516), 4918 (XI² A 205), 6077 (VIII¹ A 417), 6224 (IX A 208), 6263 (321), 6406 (X⁶ B 86), 6553 (X² A 273), 6583 (427), 6890 (XI¹ A 277), 6902 (445).

Meditation. 3685 (X³ A 545), 3864 (X⁵ A 134).

Medium. 1579 (II A 487), 1932 (XI¹ A 391), 2359 (XI² A 103), 4857 (IX A 487).

Meekness. 1193 (X² A 564), 4628 (IX A 425).

Megaphone analogy. 6008 (VIII¹ A 135).

Meier, Edvard. 4785 (XI² A 93), 6897 (XI¹ A 412).

Meiners, Christoph. 4287 (X⁴ A 463), 4309 (466), 4310 (469), 4515 (464).

Meister Floh. 5109 (I C 60).

MELANCHOLY. 739 (II A 484), 745 (V A 33), 907 (IV A 213), 992 (X³ A 715), 1535 (775), 4577 (II A 761), 5081 (I A 18), 5148 (184), 5496 (III A 114), 5512 (155), 5517 (161), 5663 (IV A 97), 5664 (107), 5724 (V B 148:29), 5737 (V A 48), 5761 (VI B 222), 5913 (VII¹ A 126), 5980 (VIII¹ A 27), 6019 (177), 6043 (250), 6132 (641), 6135 (650), 6163 (IX A 67), 6166 (70), 6227 (213), 6250 (276), 6274 (411), 6291 (488), 6326 (X¹ A 77), 6379 (234), 6420 (441), 6431 (510), 6435 (519), 6579 (X² A 411), 6603 (619), 6659 (X³ A 310), 6837 (X⁵ A 72).

Melanchthon. 3056 (X⁴ A 413).

Mellemhverandre. 5659 (IV B 78).

Members. 820 (X² A 392).

Memory. 854 (I A 254), 898 (IV A 82), 1031 (188), 1324 (III A 101), 1667 (V A 55), 2834 (VI A 90), 4429 (114), 5184 (I A 331), 5304 (II A 212), 5534 (III A 178),

5731 (V B 72:22), 6381 (L. 243).

Men. 1814 (XI¹ A 539), 3961 (II A 478), 4988 (III A 206), 4991 (X¹ A 436), 4993 (X² A 321), 4995 (X³ A 562), 5001 (XI¹ A 231), 5002 (233), 5005 (426), 5006 (XI² A 70), 5007 (192), 5008 (193).

Mensa. 3869 (XI² A 94).

Mental weakness. 4586 (V A 49).

Mephistopheles. 732 (IV A 94), 5170 (I C 109), 5171 (110), 5172 (111).

Mercifulness. 4124 (VIII¹ A 299).

Mercy. 1325 (III A 102), 2194 (VIII¹ A 300), 2523 (X³ A 221), 2768 (VIII¹ A 209), 2862 (311), 2864 (IX A 384), 3480 (X¹ A 19).

Merlin. 5714 (V A 102).

Meritoriousness. 14 (X³ A 342), 178 (X⁵ A 99), 988 (X³ A 66), 1485 (X⁴ A 419), 1533 (X³ A 638), 1914 (X⁴ A 556), 1917 (X⁵ A 9), 2094 (X³ A 764), 2477 (X¹ A 25), 4426 (VI A 52), 4459 (X² A 318).

Metaphysics. 38 (III A 25), 927 (VII¹ A 15), 1587 (III A 1), 2021 (X⁵ B 244), 2277 (III A 211), 3249 (I A 153), 4834 (IV C 118), 4837 (121).

Method. 1998 (VIII¹ A 125), 3212 (XI² A 325), 4862 (X¹ A 410), 5827 (VI A 84), 5883 (VII¹ A 23), 6662 (X³ A 367), 6719 (799).

METHODISTS.

Microscope. 1308 (II A 657), 1817 (XI² A 195), 5281 (II A 203).

Middle age. 4703 (XI² A 297).

MIDDLE AGES. 35 (II A 383), 164 (IX A 110), 380 (405), 584 (II A 792), 693 (X¹ A 132), 762 (219), 832 (II A 100), 995 (X⁴ A 176), 1090 (652), 1135 (X² A 207), 1258 (159), 1669 (I A 125), 1670 (145), 1698 (II A 114), 1839 (VIII¹ A 349), 1840 (350), 1847 (IX A 82), 1857 (X² A 47), 1893 (X³ A 776), 1914 (X⁴ A 556), 1917 (X⁵ A 9), 2005 (VIII¹ A 568), 2060 (XI¹ A 310), 2123 (X³ A 156), 2253 (II A 698), 2260 (748), 2317 (722), 2481 (X¹ A 154), 2484 (213), 2602 (IX A 246), 2605 (X¹ A 440), 2607 (485), 2608 (X² A 181), 3153 (X³ A 267), 3201 (X⁴ A 541), 3761 (326), 3801 (I A 140), 3808 (216), 3814 (262), 4402 (II A 170), 4704 (XI¹ A 8), 4710 (350), 4730 (XI² A 396), 4906 (XI¹ A 7), 5126 (I C 79), 5251 (II A 637), 6355 (X¹ A 137), 6966 (XI² A 436).

Middle axioms. 2882 (x^3 A 549).
Middle instance. 1913 (x^4 A 521).
Mikkelsen, Peer. 5061 (I A 11), 5073 (14).
Mildness. 1500 (xi^2 A 100), 3234 (x^3 A 149), 4336 (579), 6710 (716).
Mind. 1240 (III A 48).
Mini, Jacob. 5656 (IV A 105), 6332 (x^5 A 153).
Ministry. 3158 (x^3 A 606).
"Minor Works." 5954 (VII[1] B 214), 5955 (217), 5956 (218), 6217 (IX A 186).
Minority. 2963 (x^4 A 107), 4850 (VIII[1] A 141), 4852 (IX A 4), 4873 (x^3 A 652), 6260 (IX A 307), 6412 (x^1 A 385).
MIRACLES. 6 (V A 78), 499 (x^1 A 399), 1125 (VIII[1] A 672), 1213 (646), 1682 (II A 78), 1872 (x^3 A 314), 3049 (VIII[1] A 331), 3086 (VI B 98:82), 3110 (x^3 A 626), 3248 (I A 27), 3471 (VI A 156), 3485 (x^1 A 540), 3605 (II A 96), 4319 (VII[1] C 1), 4744 (x^4 A 182), 4863 (x^1 A 448).
Misanthropy. 6902 (xi^1 A 445).
Misfortune. 501 (x^1 A 438), 634 (VI B 60:2), 4575 (I A 85), 4576 (115), 5447 (III A 40), 5808 (VI A 44).
Mistletoe. 4078 (II A 703).
MISSION. 4963 (IX A 138), 6122 (VIII[1] A 591), 6356 (x^1 A 138).
Missionaries. 468 (VIII[1] A 325), 473 (528), 6851 (xi^2 A 334).
Mistreatment. 1007 (xi^2 A 381).
Misunderstanding. 26 (I A 149), 118 (33), 1671 (154), 5074 (15), 5119 (123).
M. M. 6838 (x^5 A 93).
"Models." 5754 (V A 99).
Moden Zeitung. 5104 (I A 79).
Moderation. 2121 (x^1 A 564), 5420 (II A 560).
Modern. 754 (III A 7).
Modern literature. 6836 (x^5 A 67).
Modesty. 106 (x^3 A 96), 107 (97), 108 (x^4 A 387), 989 (x^3 A 104), 1901 (x^4 A 340), 2085 (xi^2 A 360), 6333 (x^1 A 89), 6513 (x^2 A 110).
Mohammed. 124 (I A 175), 412 (27), 413 (40), 1709 (II A 591), 5212 (43), 5410 (548), 6353 (x^1 A 130).
MOHAMMEDANISM. 447 (II A 499), 2207 (I A 48), 5071 (41).
Möhler, Johann A. 1463 (I A 37), 2175 (II A 304), 5357 (II C 29-31).

Molbech, Christian K. Г. 123 (I A 129), 5134 (I C 87), 5135 (88), 5897 (VII[1] A 110), 5981 (VIII[1] A 33), 5997 (84).
Molière. 5170 (I C 109).
MOMENT (see also MOMENTARY). 579 (I A 57), 1794 (x^3 A 689), 2415 (VIII[1] A 610), 4149 (IX A 303), 4327 (x^1 A 652), 4748 (x^2 A 161), 4931 (144), 4965 (143), 5434 (II A 576), 6369 (x^1 A 166).
The Moment. 6787 (x^6 B 253).
MOMENTARY (see also MOMENT). 4594 (VIII[1] A 32), 6006 (124).
Monarchy. 4077 (II A 680), 4116 (VIII[1] A 108), 4143 (636).
Monastery. 1138 (x^3 A 298), 2111 (IV A 86), 4306 (VIII[1] A 40), 6001 (116), 6306 (x^5 A 158), 6590 (x^2 A 525).
MONASTICISM. 172 (VI A 39), 1135 (x^2 A 207), 1138 (x^3 A 298), 1385 (x^1 A 64), 1860 (x^2 A 326), 1866 (x^3 A 272), 1893 (776), 1897 (x^4 A 274), 1914 (556), 1999 (VIII[1] A 126), 2456 (I A 283), 2511 (x^2 A 364), 2521 (x^3 A 217), 2541 (x^4 A 394), 2545 (xi^2 A 304), 2603 (IX A 434), 2608 (x^2 A 181), 2711 (x^3 A 175), 2968 (xi^1 A 16), 3617 (xi^2 A 305), 3711 (x^2 A 636), 3805 (I A 200), 5014 (x^3 A 401), 6521 (x^2 A 157), 6677 (x^3 A 434), 6709 (678).
MONEY. 3 (IV A 6), 224 (IX A 483), 235 (387), 465 (VIII[1] A 216), 857 (II A 150), 897 (IV A 73), 980 (x^2 A 142), 1266 (x^4 A 13), 1271 (257), 1787 (x^3 A 347), 2144 (VII[1] A 25), 2570 (xi^2 A 54), 2954 (x^3 A 20), 3309 (VII[1] A 152), 3472 (VII[1] B 177:4), 3760 (x^4 A 316), 4086 (II A 735), 4179 (x^2 A 497), 4313 (x^4 A 555), 4359 (xi^2 A 246), 4497 (xi^1 A 102), 5151 (I A 188), 5524 (III A 169), 5548 (Letter 62), 5551 (L. 68), 5552 (L. 69), 5725 (V A 3), 5738 (5), 5868 (VII[1] B 132), 5879 (VII[1] A 18), 5881 (VII[1] B 211), 5893 (VII[1] A 106), 5966 (229), 5976 (VIII[1] A 16), 6015 (170), 6046 (L. 154), 6047 (L. 156), 6048 (L. 157), 6089 (VIII[1] A 654), 6090 (L. 166), 6131 (VIII[1] A 640), 6132 (641), 6133 (645), 6153 (IX A 43), 6176 (99), 6177 (100), 6204 (169), 6226 (211), 6268 (375), 6325 (x^1 A 74), 6336 (94), 6355 (137), 6376 (202), 6390 (273), 6401 (342), 6414 (404), 6418 (424), 6427 (495), 6474 (653), 6489 (x^2 A 10),

6493 (25), 6501 (66), 6521 (157), 6582 (425), 6585 (440), 6592 (544), 6603, (619), 6623 (x³ A 98), 6624 (99), 6762 (x⁴ A 299), 6771 (339), 6795 (511), 6801 (545), 6803 (557), 6805 (559), 6812 (603), 6820 (647), 6825 (674), 6840 (x⁵ A 105), 6843 (146), 6906 (XI¹ A 484).

Monologue. 6670 (x³ A 404).

Monotheism. 2211 (II A 71), 2734 (86), 3276 (517).

Monrad, Ditlev G. 4140 (VIII¹ A 615), 5151 (I A 188).

MONTAIGNE. 948 (VIII¹ A 291), 2848 (411), 3634 (278).

Montanism. 3548 (II A 399).

Mood. 14 (x³ A 342), 205 (II A 479), 765 (661), 766 (709), 802 (III A 219), 1238 (II A 456), 5240 (116), 5241 (118), 5336 (760).

Moore, Thomas. 4803 (x⁵ A 65).

Morality. 166 (x¹ A 3), 219 (II A 127), 242 (I A 38), 273 (28), 416 (95), 795 (150), 889 (III A 202), 2161 (x¹ A 341), 2617 (XI¹ A 150), 5067 (I C 34), 5779 (VI C 2).

Mormons. 1443 (XI¹ A 591).

Morten, Jesper. 5749 (V A 91).

Moses. 297 (II A 473), 413 (I A 40), 833 (II A 351), 859 (165), 951 (VIII¹ A 319), 1122 (619), 1540 (I A 237), 2533 (x⁴ A 12), 2734 (II A 86), 2855 (I A 298), 3234 (x³ A 149), 3377 (II A 377), 3984 (x¹ A 394), 4053 (x² A 13), 4182 (x² A 571), 4460 (642), 5013 (IX A 430), 6141 (8), 6897 (XI¹ A 412).

Moses-Joshua analogy. 859 (II A 165).

Mother. 265 (II A 12), 1158 (V A 4), 1159 (66), 1160 (83), 1835 (V B 237), 2425 (x¹ A 635), 5149 (I A 186), 5640 (IV A 76).

Motion (see also CHANGE). 161 (VIII¹ A 88), 198 (IV A 38), 258 (IV C 47), 259 (49), 263 (x² A 324), 1594 (IV C 59), 1790 (x³ A 524), 2089 (x³ A 430), 4319 (VII¹ C 1), 5601 (IV C 97), 5977 (VIII² C 1).

Motive. 2053 (XI¹ A 148).

Motte, Houdart de la. 2374 (x¹ A 371), 5223 (II A 98).

Motte-Fouqué, F. de la. 5223 (II A 98).

Motto. 6154 (IX A 48), 6184 (129).

Movement of infinity. 3608 (x¹ A 481), 4588 (VI A 46).

MOZART. 3565 (x¹ A 573), 3835 (XI¹ A 440), 4355 (XI² A 41), 4397 (I C 125), 5095 (I A 64), 5212 (II A 43), 5403 (520), 5632 (IV A 223).

Müller, Adolf. 3163 (x⁴ A 332), 3761 (326).

Müller, Julius. 76 (x² A 491), 1262 (438), 1263 (518), 1531 (500), 1614 (426), 2023 (480), 2024 (489), 3093 (501), 4028 (404), 4030 (436), 4034 (472), 4555 (401), 4556 (402).

Multiplicity. 1595 (IV C 63), 1633 (III A 14), 3301 (V B 14, pp. 73-76), 3801 (I A 140), 3802 (142), 3803 (155), 3819 (II A 638), 4063 (I A 139), 5066 (I C 26), 5694 (IV A 153).

Münch, Ernst. 5359 (II C 64).

Munchausen, Baron. 2355 (VI B 98:26).

Mundus vult decipi. 5937 (VII¹ A 147), 5938 (148), 6680 (x³ A 450).

Munscher, Wilhelm. 5333 (II A 241).

Music. 133 (II A 180), 147 (IV A 222), 784 (II A 6), 1179 (I C 58), 1627 (I A 242), 2313 (II A 159), 2316 (665), 2394 (III B 114), 2788 (I A 291), 3812 (228), 3996 (II A 65), 4416 (III A 189), 5113 (I A 103), 5136 (147), 5144 (169), 5161 (235), 5180 (297), 5226 (II A 598), 5766 (VI B 229), 5799 (VI A 28).

Mutiny. 2566 (XI¹ A 486), 3005 (XI² A 214), 3006 (215).

Mygind, Niels. 3858 (II A 796).

Mynster, Bishop Jakob P. 77 (x³ A 186), 172 (VI A 39), 265 (II A 12), 355 (x³ A 427), 376 (IX A 60), 516 (x² A 460), 663 (IX A 240), 829 (XI² A 280), 965 (IX A 418), 996 (x⁴ A 184), 1086 (32), 1087 (518), 1256 (IX A 109), 1285 (x³ A 200), 1798 (x⁴ A 282), 1804 (XI¹ A 197), 1842 (VIII¹ A 449), 1860 (x² A 326), 1922 (x⁵ A 88), 1929 (XI¹ A 158), 2125 (x³ A 334), 2488 (x¹ A 314), 2530 (x³ A 533), 2565 (XI¹ A 435), 2712 (x³ A 588), 2754 (56), 2763 (XI¹ A 198), 2772 (XI² A 22), 2910 (XI¹ A 392), 3069 (XI¹ B 109), 3119 (x³ A 642), 3348 (290), 3488 (x² A 149), 3499 (x³ A 59), 3529 (x⁵ A 57), 3530 (62), 3737 (XI² A 346), 3772 (x⁵ A 58), 4012 (VIII¹ A 473), 4056 (XI² A 106), 4058 (319), 4140 (VIII¹ A 615), 4156 (x¹ A 96), 4183 (x² A 643), 4209 (x⁴ A 126), 4226

(XI¹ A 54), 4273 (X¹ A 591), 4294 (X⁵ A 69), 4448 (IX ᵃA 37), 4483 (XI¹ A 475), 4524 (X⁴ A 639), 4549 (X² A 231), 4643 (236), 4707 (XI¹ A 208), 4878 (X⁴ A 337), 4914 (XI¹ A 568), 4963 (IX A 138), 4986 (XI² A 57), 5013 (IX A 430), 5014 (X³ A 401), 5021 (273), 5408 (II A 452), 5637 (IV A 71), 5653 (97), 5689 (142), 5832 (VI B 235), 5837 (VII¹ A 98), 5880 (VII¹ B 131), 5884 (VII¹ A 26), 5891 (104), 5928 (78), 5947 (169), 5961 (221), 6039 (VIII¹ A 233), 6053 (298), 6058 (332), 6064 (366), 6068 (VIII² B 116), 6069 (118), 6070 (VIII¹ A 388), 6071 (390), 6073 (397), 6075 (414), 6076 (415), 6087 (455), 6100 (502), 6103 (508), 6112 (560), 6126 (603), 6150 (IX A 39), 6151 (41), 6171 (81), 6172 (83), 6173 (85), 6176 (99), 6201 (166), 6219 (188), 6224 (208), 6241 (236), 6245 (255), 6281 (428), 6305 (X¹ A 33), 6318 (58), 6335 (92), 6355 (137), 6370 (167), 6378 (228), 6381 (Letter 243), 6395 (X¹ A 320), 6412 (385), 6429 (497), 6441 (535), 6444 (541), 6449 (556), 6472 (X⁵ A 149), 6477 (X¹ A 660), 6503 (X² A 75), 6517 (147), 6521 (157), 6526 (177), 6619 (X³ A 88), 6627 (128), 6637 (X⁶ B 162), 6638 (163), 6639 (164), 6641 (169), 6651 (X³ A 219), 6653 (249), 6661 (321), 6668 (402), 6678 (435), 6679 (448), 6680 (450), 6681 (453), 6682 (472), 6691 (563), 6692 (564), 6693 (565), 6697 (578), 6712 (742), 6716 (780), 6717 (782), 6719 (799), 6723 (X⁴ A 9), 6728 (36), 6731 (53), 6732 (55), 6744 (168), 6745 (195), 6746 (X⁵ A 166), 6747 (167), 6748 (X⁶ B 171), 6749 (173, pp. 274-276), 6750 (188), 6751 (194), 6753 (X⁴ A 204), 6754 (228), 6757 (270), 6758 (271), 6759 (272), 6760 (285), 6761 (296), 6762 (299), 6768 (322), 6769 (323), 6773 (353), 6774 (358), 6775 (359), 6776 (367), 6777 (373), 6778 (377), 6793 (474), 6795 (511), 6796 (512), 6802 (554), 6806 (566), 6807 (568), 6811 (592), 6813 (604), 6814 (605), 6831 (X⁵ A 33), 6833 (X⁶ B 226), 6842 (232, pp. 371-378), 6844 (XI² A 283), 6845 (288), 6846 (296), 6847 (311), 6848 (312), 6849 (314), 6853 (XI¹ A 1), 6854 (XI³ B 15), 6855 (28), 6860 (XI¹ A 69), 6864 (90), 6865 (92), 6867 (125), 6875 (XI³ B 49), 6880 (XI¹ A 206), 6890 (277), 6914 (586), 6919 (XI² A 31), 6927 (78), 6937 (251), 6938 (252), 6939 (253), 6940 (254), 6941 (256), 6942 (257), 6943 (XI³ B 53), 6945 (55), 6947 (57), 6954 (93), 6958 (XI² A 399), 6961 (XI³ B 129), 6962 (131), 6967 (XI² A 437).

"The Mysterious Family." 5690 (IV A 144).

MYSTERY. 292 (II A 767), 1682 (78), 1721 (III A 46), 3110 (X³ A 626), 4680 (X⁴ A 456), 5422 (II A 565), 5624 (IV A 68), 5688 (141).

MYSTIC, MYSTICISM. 739 (II A 484), 1972 (II C 41), 5669 (IV A 114).

MYTH, MYTHOLOGY. 573 (X⁴ A 439), 789 (X² A 455), 1629 (I A 264), 1641 (IX A 160), 1895 (X⁴ A 148), 1904 (354), 1915 (626), 2132 (X⁵ A 51), 2439 (X⁴ A 642), 2700 (I A 269), 2895 (X⁵ A 48), 3350 (143), 3530 (62), 3815 (I A 294), 4066 (285), 4394 (319), 4398 (I C 126), 4567 (X⁴ A 667), 4806 (XI¹ A 329), 5182 (I A 329), 5350 (II C 60).

Møller, Bookbinder. 6487 (X¹ A 678).

Møller, Jens. 817 (X¹ A 502), 2604 (310), 3566 (609), 5993 (VIII¹ A 68).

Møller, Nicolai. 3817 (I A 315).

Møller, Peter Ludwig. 5713 (V A 101), 5861 (VII¹ B 5), 5863 (VII¹ B 69), 5887 (VII¹ A 98), 5891 (VII¹ A 104), 5909 (124), 5926 (55), 5937 (147), 5997 (VIII¹ A 84), 6031 (218), 6080 (444), 6382 (X¹ A 247), 6474 (653), 6493 (X² A 25), 6548 (251), 6620 (X³ A 89), 6621 (90).

Møller, Poul Martin. 804 (III A 95), 1044 (VII¹ A 216), 1690 (II A 102), 2985 (XI² A 26), 3702 (VI B 54:19), 3847 (I C 70), 5201 (II A 17), 5302 (209), 5305 (216), 5478 (Letter 17), 5479 (L. 18), 5482 (L. 27), 5543 (L. 55), 5713 (V A 101), 5798 (VI C 1), 5961 (VII¹ A 221), 6888 (XI¹ A 275), 6889 (276).

Møller, Rasmus. 1997 (VIII¹ A 9), 5993 (68).

Naive, the. 123 (I A 129).

Naiveté. 654 (VIII² B 86), 3962 (V B 53:27).

Names. 985 (X² A 270), 2330 (XI¹ A 205), 3582 (55), 6823 (X⁴ A 663).

Naming. 2271 (II A 528).

Napoleon I. 246 (VIII¹ A 168), 270 (IX A 395), 2738 (II A 262), 3732 (x⁴ A 38), 4217 (447).

Napoleon, Louis. 3537 (XI² A 27), 4217 (x⁴ A 447), 4233 (XI¹ A 507).

Narcissus. 2389 (III A 120).

Nathan. 4562 (x⁴ A 283).

National Bank. 6967 (XI² A 437).

National Religion. 2045 (x⁵ A 97).

Nationalism. 431 (II A 249), 2511 (x² A 364), 2729 (x⁵ A 102), 4121 (VIII¹ A 245), 4137 (609), 4180 (x² A 498), 6125 (VIII¹ A 602), 6127 (666), 6151 (IX A 41).

Nations. 25 (I A 126), 4129 (VIII¹ A 552).

Naturalism. 772 (II C 47), 5350 (60), 6692 (x³ A 564).

Natural man. 330 (x¹ A 204), 3031 (IX A 322), 3758 (x⁴ A 261).

NATURAL SCIENCES. 3 (IV A 6), 820 (x² A 392), 928 (VII¹ A 28), 929 (29), 2324 (x² A 235), 2563 (XI¹ A 37), 3870 (XI² A 117), 4174 (x² A 395), 4267 (VII¹ A 193), 4284 (x⁴ A 319), 4332 (x² A 424), 5092 (I A 72).

NATURE. 117 (I A 8), 134 (II A 664), 157 (VII¹ A 93), 452 (V A 10), 715 (56), 799 (III A 10), 1053 (IX A 359), 1233 (II A 74), 1235 (281), 1254 (VIII¹ A 522), 1308 (II A 657), 1335 (V A 8), 1690 (II A 102), 1695 (107), 1836 (VII¹ A 208), 2263 (II A 404), 2276 (III A 68), 2288 (VII¹ A 230), 2305 (I A 251), 2437 (x⁴ A 482), 2748 (II A 483), 2816 (VII¹ A 196), 3110 (x³ A 626), 3797 (I A 131), 4284 (x⁴ A 319), 4285 (333), 4392 (I A 313), 4393 (314), 5033 (XI¹ A 566), 5092 (I A 72), 5099 (68), 5269 (II A 185), 5761 (VI B 222).

Neander August. 264 (x² A 561), 574 (x³ A 755), 1403 (x² A 569), 1665 (x³ A 774), 2722 (594), 2557 (752), 2758 (x⁴ A 4), 2822 (232), 3109 (x³ A 609), 3158 (606), 3161 (751), 4466 (745), 5015 (589), 5059 (I C 16,18), 6703 (x³ A 636).

Nebuchadnezzar. 5325 (II A 757), 5743 (V A 71).

Necessity (see also Fatalism; Fate). 199 (VI B 54:21), 262 (V B 15:1), 1232 (I A 205), 1245 (IV A 62), 1269 (x⁴ A 177), 1270 (245), 1614 (x² A 426), 2360 (IV A 11), 2366 (IV C 36), 2819 (VII¹ A 199), 3756 (x³ A 457), 3805 (I A 200), 4037 (x² A 482).

Need. 1113 (V A 40), 1137 (x³ A 184), 1414

(585), 1497 (XI² A 284), 2028 (x³ A 339), 6824 (x⁴ A 673), 6902 (XI¹ A 445).

Needle analogy. 1817 (XI² A 195), 6910 (XI¹ A 543).

Neergaard, Johan V. 3587 (XI¹ A 450).

Negative, the. 6924 (XI² A 45).

Negativity. 2282 (IV C 74), 2341 (V A 74).

Neighbor. 221 (II A 130), 222 (131), 887 (III A 184), 942 (VIII¹ A 189), 943 (VIII² B 30:4), 1207 (VIII¹ A 114), 1380 (IX A 441), 1413 (x³ A 581), 2400 (IV B 148), 2430 (x² A 247), 2434 (x³ A 739), 2435 (741), 2525 (302), 2918 (XI² A 386), 3915 (III C 1), 4163 (x¹ A 632), 4185 (x³ A 346), 4447 (VIII² B 71:6,7,9,10,12), 4603 (VIII¹ A 269), 6628 (x³ A 142).

Nemesis. 323 (IX A 103), 1165 (VIII¹ A 58).

Nepos, Cornelius. 5380 (II A 414).

Nero. 1606 (V B 41), 4105 (IV A 13), 4355 (XI² A 41).

Neues Reportium. 5827 (VI A 84).

Neuter. 850 (I A 141).

Newmann, Francis W. 6689 (x³ A 551).

Newness. 4223 (XI¹ A 17).

Newspapers (see also JOURNALISM; Press). 5116 (I B 2), 5312 (II A 728), 5340 (769).

Newspaper articles (S.K.). 6202 (IX A 167).

NEW TESTAMENT (see also BIBLE). 182 (VIII¹ A 225), 227 (I C 40), 389 (x² A 139), 410 (I A 4), 1094 (36), 1153 (XI² A 336), 1438 (XI¹ A 188), 1464 (I A 82), 1491 (x⁵ A 56), 1637 (V B 64), 1639 (II A 101), 1807 (XI¹ A 402), 1926 (27), 2048 (42), 2054 (168), 2207 (I A 48), 2222 (x⁴ A 572), 2225 (XI¹ A 151), 2300 (x¹ A 577), 2448 (XI¹ A 414), 2455 (XI² A 426), 2529 (x³ A 516), 2550 (XI¹ A 193), 2564 (65), 2628 (XI² A 231), 2656 (x¹ A 190), 2682 (XI² A 326), 2725 (XI¹ A 187), 2730 (x⁵ A 122), 2805 (XI¹ A 217), 2948 (x² A 121), 3014 (x¹ A 396), 3038 (x³ A 674), 3098 (XI¹ A 299), 3178 (344), 3192 (VI A 153), 3204 (IX B 5:2y), 3210 (XI² A 38), 3228 (402), 3570 (x³ A 121), 3597 (XI² A 376), 3613 (x³ A 193), 3621 (XI¹ A 213), 3632 (267), 3649 (67), 3761 (x⁴ A 326), 3772 (x⁵ A 58), 3777 (XI¹ A 143), 3865 (461), 3949 (x³ A 213), 4222 (XI² A 291), 4296 (XI¹ A 15), 4483 (475), 4503 (XI² A 373), 4520 (x³ A 684), 4556 (720), 4682 (x⁴ A

570), 4685 (578), 4687 (583), 4700 (x⁵ A
81), 4861 (x¹ A 407), 4906 (xi¹ A 7), 4953
(xi² A 86), 5055 (i c 7), 5057 (11-12),
6117 (viii² c 3), 6296 (x⁶ c 1), 6677 (x³ A
434), 6792 (x⁴ A 472), 6808 (584), 6831
(x⁵ A 33), 6837 (72), 6860 (xi¹ A 69),
6863 (76), 6876 (149), 6922 (xi² A 40),
6928 (79), 6932 (206), 6943 (xi³ B 53),
6950 (xi² A 374), 6956 (407).

New Testament interpretation. 3830 (x⁴ A
119).

"New Years Gift." 5707 (iv B 125), 5708
(126).

New Zealanders. 5822 (vi A 77).

Nickname. 6509 (x² A 101).

Nicodemus. 338 (x¹ A 355), 2136 (xi¹ A
488), 4024 (x² A 29), 4848 (v A 22), 4984
(xi¹ A 555), 6126 (viii¹ A 603).

Nicolaus Notabene. 5671 (iv A 119), 5707
(iv B 125), 5708 (126), 5754 (v A 99),
5828 (vi A 85), 6636 (x⁶ B 137).

Nielsen, Anne. 6209 (ix A 175), 6293 (ix B
68).

Nielsen, Michael. 5036 (xi² A 219), 5727
(L. 107), 5778 (vii¹ A 11).

Nielsen, Peter N. 5305 (ii A 216).

Nielsen, Rasmus. 77 (x³ A 186), 707 (x¹ A
658), 3459 (x⁴ A 229), 4330 (x² A 327),
4868 (x³ A 25), 5036 (xi² A 219), 5409
(ii A 546), 5798 (vi c 1), 6233 (ix A 220),
6238 (227), 6239 (229), 6246 (258), 6247
(262), 6268 (375), 6301 (x¹ A 14), 6302
(15), 6314 (52), 6335 (92), 6341 (110),
6342 (111), 6402 (343), 6403-6 (x⁶ A 83-
86), 6415 (x¹ A 406), 6429 (497), 6434
(L. 213), 6490 (x² A 11), 6550 (256),
6554 (275), 6557 (280), 6563 (298),
6566 (x⁶ B 127), 6573 (x² A 352), 6574
(x⁶ B 121), 6593 (x² A 560), 6606 (L.
257), 6607 (x³ A 3), 6610 (12), 6614
(67), 6630 (146), 6637 (x⁶ B 162), 6663
(93), 6664 (x³ A 381), 6778 (x⁴ A 377),
6843 (x⁵ A 146), 6869 (xi³ B 13).

"Night and Day or Nicodemus and
Stephen." 6789 (x⁶ B 259).

Night watchman. 5064 (i A 39), 5323 (ii A
753), 5766 (vi B 229), 5989 (viii¹ A 45).

Nineteenth century. 1764 (x³ A 228), 3727
(viii¹ A 429).

Nocturnal conversation. 6762 (x⁴ A 299),
6765 (302), 6810 (587).

Nonconformity. 2060 (xi¹ A 310).

Nonsense. 545 (xi¹ A 39), 6398 (x¹ A 325),
6866 (xi¹ A 121).

Nonviolence. 1195 (x⁴ A 127), 4667 (135).

Nook of Eight Paths (see Eight Paths).

Nord og Syd. 6099 (viii¹ A 655).

Normative. 3617 (xi² A 305).

Norms. 934 (vii¹ A 138), 936 (172), 1901
(x⁴ A 340), 2513 (x² A 558), 2607 (x¹ A
485), 2898 (x⁵ A 96).

North America. 3309 (vii¹ A 152), 4100
(iii A 106).

North Pole. 4533 (xi³ B 146).

Notary public. 5282 (ii A 204).

"A Note." 6416 (x¹ A 422).

"Notes Concerning My Work as an
Author." 6407 (x¹ A 351).

Nothing. 102 (x² A 22), 2089 (x³ A 430),
2099 (xi¹ A 491), 2797 (x² A 340).

Novalis [Georg F. P. v. Hardenberg].
2243 (i A 91), 2798 (241), 5105 (80).

Novarinus. 5580 (iv c 9).

Novels. 801 (iii A 218), 1025 (i A 148),
1700 (ii A 138), 1974 (652), 2107 (xi¹ A
160), 2314 (ii A 160), 2798 (i A 241),
3697 (128), 5178 (286), 5249 (ii A 634),
6870 (xi¹ A 131), 6879 (177).

Novelty. 1633 (iii B 14).

NUMBERS (see also Crowd; Many; Mass;
Public). 238 (x⁴ A 11), 499 (x¹ A 399),
518 (x³ A 100), 599 (x⁴ A 22), 1513 (x¹
A 639), 1800 (xi¹ A 294), 1807 (xi¹ A
402), 1825 (xi³ B 199), 1925 (xi¹ A 22),
1940 (xi² A 434), 1981 (ii A 474), 1987
(v A 60), 2010 (ix A 356), 2016 (x¹ A
286), 2025 (x² A 629), 2032 (x³ A 687),
2038 (x⁴ A 104), 2046 (x⁵ A 121), 2047
(xi¹ A 36), 2049 (60), 2050 (81), 2051
(82), 2055 (175), 2063 (368), 2065 (370),
2069 (441), 2072 (490), 2074 (518),
2082 (xi² A 149), 2084 (275), 2165 (x³ A
231), 2330 (xi¹ A 205), 2548 (108), 2566
(486), 2567 (589), 2568 (590), 2668
(xi² A 262), 2687 (435), 3209 (xi¹ A 552),
3210 (xi² A 38), 3517 (x³ A 692), 3540
(xi² A 281), 4114 (vii¹ A 212), 4118 (viii¹
A 123), 4119 (134), 4134 (606), 4144
(667), 4160 (x¹ A 356), 4166 (x² A 7),
4178 (490), 4186 (x³ A 529), 4200 (x⁴ A
47), 4201 (51), 4202 (63), 4203 (65),
4208 (102), 4227 (xi¹ A 93), 4234 (536),

4277 (x² A 449), 4299 (xI² A 371), 4334 (x³ A 241), 4348 (xI¹ A 211), 4356 (xI² A 62), 4572 (196), 4801 (x³ A 390), 4850 (vIII¹ A 141), 4851 (605), 4852 (IX A 4), 4854 (287), 4866 (x² A 463), 4873 (x³ A 652), 4874 (664), 4875 (x⁴ A 35), 4876 (42), 4879 (342), 4911 (xI¹ A 516), 4912 (517), 4941 (453), 5020 (x² A 568), 5270 (II A 189), 6580 (x² A 413), 6728 (x⁴ A 36), 6753 (204), 6873 (xI¹ A 137), 6886 (242), 6930 (xI² A 121).

Numerical. 1810 (xI¹ A 432), 4295 (x⁵ A 133), 5044 (xI¹ A 248), 6778 (x⁴ A 377).

Nuts. 2453 (xI² A 390).

Nutzhorn Ditlev A. v. 6035 (vIII¹ A 227).

Nyerup, Rasmus. 5193 (I C 116).

Nyt theologisk Tidsskrift. 6566 (x⁶ B 127).

Nytorv 2 (*see also* Home [S.K.]). 5727 (L. 107), 6035 (vIII¹ A 227), 6041 (246), 6090 (L. 166), 6268 (IX A 375), 6376 (x¹ A 202).

Nørregade. 6622 (x³ A 94), 6629 (144), 6764 (x⁴ A 301).

Oats. 5500 (III A 122).

OBEDIENCE. 184 (vIII¹ A 436), 187 (x² A 119), 955 (vIII¹ A 413), 1151 (xI² A 84), 1255 (vIII¹ A 525), 1436 (xI¹ A 5), 1844 (vIII¹ A 587), 1931 (xI¹ A 338), 2152 (vIII¹ A 540), 2471 (IX A 274), 2865 (x¹ A 221), 2872 (x³ A 34), 3049 (vIII¹ A 331), 3103 (vII¹ A 151), 3649 (xI¹ A 67), 4140 (vIII¹ A 615), 4370 (IX A 333), 4768 (x⁴ A 141), 4893 (x¹ A 625), 4939 (x⁴ A 538), 5385 (II A 422), 5893 (vII¹ A 106), 6075 (vIII¹ A 414), 6085 (452), 6108 (549), 6167 (IX A 71), 6192 (142), 6966 (xI² A 436).

Object. 1405 (x² A 644), 2430 (247), 3483 (x¹ A 182).

Objective. 1493 (x⁵ A 101), 3496 (x² A 382), 3539 (xI² A 249), 3685 (x³ A 545).

Objectivity (*see also* SUBJECTIVITY/OBJEC-TIVITY). 35 (II A 383), 187 (x² A 119), 578 (I A 56), 650 (vIII² B 82), 657 (89), 995 (x⁴ A 176), 1100 (III A 39), 1101 (216), 1117 (vII¹ A 61), 1118 (177), 1347 (139), 1793 (x³ A 670), 1905 (x⁴ A 366), 1906 (369), 1957 (IX A 221), 2293 (vII¹ A 75), 2299 (IX A 438), 2334 (xI² A 128),

2335 (129), 2628 (231), 2692 (x¹ A 642), 3513 (x³ A 484), 3548 (II A 399), 3587 (xI¹ A 450), 3716 (x⁴ A 528), 3863 (409), 4549 (x² A 231), 4558 (x³ A 593), 4565 (x⁴ A 379), 4626 (IX A 407), 5788 (vI B 14), 5791 (17), 6617 (x³ A 78), 6634 (163), 6702 (635).

Objects. 2276 (III A 68).

Obligation. 872 (II A 465), 967 (IX A 443), 1904 (x⁴ A 354).

Obscurantism. 1129 (x¹ A 367).

Observation. 381 (x¹ A 7), 1051 (IX A 154), 1055 (x¹ A 193), 3685 (x³ A 545), 5732 (v A 34), 6687 (530), 6806 (x⁴ A 566), 6813 (604).

Occident. 288 (II A 276).

Occupation. 231 (vII¹ A 165), 233 (vIII¹ A 368), 422 (II A 30), 2541 (x⁴ A 394), 2771 (263), 3309 (vII¹ A 152), 3497 (x² A 581), 3537 (xI² A 27), 3569 (x² A 637), 5009 (vIII¹ A 104).

Oedipus. 5546 (III C 37).

Oehlenschläger, Adam. 1689 (II A 101), 1709 (591), 4301 (xI¹ A 430), 5347 (II A 780), 5509 (III A 149), 5859 (vII² B 274:1-22), 6413 (x¹ A 402).

Offenbach, Schreiber. 5079 (I C 48).

OFFENSE. 9 (x⁶ B 78), 91 (II A 18), 321 (IX A 57), 322 (59), 330 (x¹ A 204), 455 (vI A 109), 507 (x¹ A 547), 510 (x² A 37), 532 (x⁴ A 212), 691 (IX A 95), 1125 (vIII¹ A 672), 1148 (x⁴ A 635), 1318 (II A 410), 1622 (142), 1623 (143), 1710 (596), 1822 (xI² A 267), 1868 (x³ A 277), 1958 (IX A 260), 2072 (xI¹ A 490), 2225 (151), 2227 (184), 2432 (x³ A 19), 2455 (xI² A 426), 2678 (1), 2723 (x⁵ A 130), 3082 (v B 11:4), 3352 (vIII¹ A 510), 3681 (x³ A 278), 3860 (702), 4018 (x¹ A 133), 4021 (433), 4035 (x² A 473), 4055 (xI¹ A 562), 4363 (xI² A 378), 4549 (x² A 231), 4610 (vIII¹ A 579), 4680 (x⁴ A 456), 5690 (IV A 144), 6167 (IX A 71), 6210 (176), 6212 (179), 6230 (217), 6243 (243), 6261 (310), 6275 (413), 6464 (x¹ A 615), 6500 (x² A 61), 6719 (x³ A 799), 6947 (xI³ B 57).

Official, officialdom. 3220 (xI¹ A 97).

Old Testament (*see also* BIBLE). 206 (IV A 143), 436 (II A 293), 1330 (IV A 106), 1464 (I A 82), 3098 (xI¹ A 299), 4407

(II A 321), 5368 (347), 5424 (572), 5640 (IV A 76), 6745 (x⁴ A 195).

Olsen, Cornelia. 5772 (VI A 12), 6713 (x³ A 769), 6472 (x⁵ A 149).

Olsen, Regine. 1832 (XI¹ A 288), 1959 (x³ A 413), 2607 (x¹ A 485), 5007 (XI² A 192), 5219 (II A 67), 5220 (68), 5368 (347), 5461 (III A 64), 5477 (L. 15), 5478 (L. 17), 5479 (L. 18), 5480 (L. 21), 5481 (L. 23), 5482 (L. 27), 5483 (L. 29), 5490 (III A 90), 5501 (133), 5502 (134), 5505 (L. 42), 5507 (III A 147), 5509 (149), 5510 (150), 5511 (151), 5513 (L. 49), 5515 (III A 159), 5516 (160), 5517 (161), 5518 (163), 5519 (164), 5521 (166), 5523 (168), 5524 (169), 5526 (171), 5528 (172), 5529 (173), 5530 (174), 5532 (176), 5533 (177), 5534 (178), 5535 (179), 5538 (180), 5541 (190), 5548 (L. 62), 5551 (L. 68), 5628 (IV A 215), 5642 (79), 5653 (97), 5664 (107), 5680 (133), 5689 (142), 5693 (152), 5748 (V A 88), 5834 (VI A 94), 5895 (VII¹ A 108), 5913 (126), 5915 (128), 5947 (169), 5949 (184), 5961 (221), 5962 (222), 5999 (VIII¹ A 100), 6035 (227), 6082 (446), 6083 (447), 6132 (641), 6135 (650), 6144 (IX A 18), 6161 (65), 6162 (66), 6163 (67), 6179 (108), 6185 (130), 6186 (131), 6187 (132), 6203 (168), 6247 (262), 6250 (276), 6273 (408), 6284 (451), 6289 (473), 6303 (x¹ A 23), 6304 (24), 6332 (x⁵ A 153), 6385 (x¹ A 260), 6388 (266), 6389 (272), 6409 (374), 6426 (494), 6453 (569), 6454 (570), 6469 (644), 6470 (648), 6471 (x⁵ A 148), 6472 (149), 6473 (150), 6476 (x¹ A 659), 6478 (661), 6479 (663), 6480 (664), 6481 (665), 6482 (667), 6483 (668), 6485 (671), 6488 (x² A 3), 6500 (61), 6502 (68), 6510 (105), 6537 (L. 239), 6538-45 (x² A 210-217), 6583 (427), 6642 (x³ A 168), 6656 (265), 6666 (391), 6673 (422), 6675 (x⁵ B 263), 6676 (264), 6713 (x³ A 769), 6714 (770), 6715 (771), 6762 (x⁴ A 299), 6763 (300), 6765 (302), 6766 (303), 6769 (323), 6771 (339), 6800 (540), 6810 (587), 6826 (x⁵ A 21), 6835 (59), 6843 (146), 6906 (XI¹ A 484).

Olsen, Terkild. 5517 (III A 161), 6203 (IX A 168), 6247 (262), 6452 (x¹ A 568), 6453

(569), 6454 (570), 6455 (571), 6470 (648), 6472 (x⁵ A 149), 6488 (x² A 3), 6489 (10), 6502 (68), 6510 (105), 6517 (147), 6526 (177), 6536 (205), 6538 (210), 6543 (215), 6656 (x³ A 265), 6713 (769), 6762 (x⁴ A 299), 6810 (587), 6843 (x⁵ A 146).

Olson, Jonas. 888 (III A 185).

Omnipotence. 1230 (I A 5), 1251 (VII¹ A 181).

Omnipresence. 1429 (x⁴ A 485), 1443 (XI¹ A 591), 1983 (III A 38), 4741 (x³ A 727), 4951 (617), 4955 (I A 164).

"On My Work as an Author." 6673 (x³ A 422), 6674 (423), 6675 (x⁵ B 263), 6749 (x⁶ B 173, pp. 274-276), 6772 (x⁴ A 351), 6779 (380), 6780 (383), 6785 (408), 6804 (558).

One thing. 4801 (x³ A 390).

Ontological argument (see ANSELM).

Ontology. 197 (IV C 100), 199 (VI B 54:21), 536 (x⁴ A 581), 1940 (XI² A 434).

"Open Confession." 6201 (IX A 166).

Open Letter, An. 6725 (x⁴ A 20).

Openness. 4591 (VII¹ A 22), 5634 (IV A 234), 5818 (VI A 61), 6480 (x¹ A 664).

Opera. 1627 (I A 242), 5179 (296).

Opinions. 3885 (XI² A 58), 4108 (VI A 26).

Opportunism. 2742 (VII¹ A 170).

Opposites. 700 (III A 112), 702 (IV A 5).

Opposition. 604 (V A 5), 1264 (x³ A 618), 4139 (VIII¹ A 614), 4225 (XI¹ A 30), 4444 (VIII¹ A 160), 4575 (I A 85), 4576 (115), 4596 (VIII¹ A 96), 4623 (IX A 349), 4689 (x⁴ A 611).

OPTIMISM (see also Pessimism). 2224 (XI¹ A 139), 2554 (572), 3039 (360), 3245 (I A 94), 3881 (XI¹ A 181), 3883 (537), 5025 (243), 5035 (XI² A 219), 6863 (XI¹ A 76), 6919 (XI² A 31).

Orators. 6412 (x¹ A 385).

Orders at sea. 6356 (x¹ A 138), 6370 (167).

Ordination. 638 (VIII¹ A 6), 3146 (x³ A 120), 3154 (325), 3477 (VIII¹ A 434), 4568 (x⁵ A 84), 6670 (x³ A 404).

Organ. 3493 (x² A 288).

Organ grinder. 5522 (III A 167).

Organic. 1983 (III A 38), 2583 (II A 470).

Organismic, the. 4160 (x¹ A 356), 4166 (x² A 7).

Orient. 288 (II A 276), 431 (249), 1019 (125), 1632 (650), 4398 (I C 126).

Oriental. 3821 (III A 113).

Origen. 1894 (x⁴ A 131), 3162 (121), 3546 (I A 43), 3851 (II A 242).

Originality. 138 (II A 425), 1150 (xI² A 18), 5114 (I A 109), 6915 (xI¹ A 593).

Original sin. 52 (v B 55:4), 94 (III A 233), 443 (II A 360), 515 (x² A 421), 1530 (481), 2024 (489), 3093 (501), 3643 (xI¹ A 289), 3989 (I A 3), 3992 (II A 119), 3994 (584), 4003 (446), 5184 (I A 331), 5275 (II A 629), 6139 (vIII² B 166).

Origins. 2284 (IV A 49).

ORTHODOX. 4820 (x⁴ A 70), 5156 (I A 220), 6728 (x⁴ A 36), 6729 (37).

ORTHODOXY. 318 (vIII¹ A 565), 428 (II A 217), 580 (I A 58), 659 (IX A 127), 660 (198), 852 (I A 221), 1642 (IX A 196), 1949 (391), 2207 (I A 48), 2903 (xI¹ A 107), 2910 (392), 2960 (x⁴ A 93), 3046 (I A 195), 3049 (vIII¹ A 331), 3133 (xI¹ A 126), 3320 (x³ A 682), 3477 (vIII¹ A 434), 3850 (II A 199), 4064 (I A 180), 4096 (II A 481), 4103 (IV A 7), 4549 (xI² A 231), 4779 (vIII¹ A 480), 4818 (x⁴ A 48), 5092 (I A 72), 5156 (220), 6107 (vIII¹ A 548), 6176 (IX A 99), 6223 (205), 6252 (283), 6643 (x³ A 174), 6880 (xI¹ A 206).

Ossian. 117 (I A 8).

Ostermann, Johannes A. 5116 (I B 2).

Others. 1020 (II A 235), 1382 (x¹ A 20), 2134 (xI¹ A 21), 2978 (387), 3179 (389), 4707 (208), 4730 (xI² A 396), 4808 (xI¹ A 419), 4942 (458).

Ought. 975 (x¹ A 430), 3503 (x³ A 141).

PAGANISM. 48 (v A 25), 141 (III A 110), 413 (I A 40), 417 (96), 428 (II A 217), 429 (234), 430 (245), 452 (v A 10), 534 (x⁴ A 470), 584 (II A 792), 714 (v A 36), 883 (III A 214), 1006 (xI² A 113), 1148 (x⁴ A 635), 1325 (III A 102), 1351 (vIII¹ A 30), 1433 (x⁵ A 39), 1512 (x¹ A 504), 1527 (vI A 49), 1539 (I A 100), 1639 (vIII¹ A 305), 1926 (xI¹ A 27), 2041 (x⁴ A 401), 2068 (xI¹ A 421), 2207 (I A 48), 2276 (II A 68), 2570 (xI² A 54), 2578 (II A 244), 2829 (76), 2830 (78), 2908 (xI¹ A 157), 2992 (xI² A 116), 3277 (II A 518), 3636 (x¹ A 461), 4006 (IV A 189), 4032 (x² A 456), 4794 (vIII¹ A 147), 5420 (II A 560), 5556 (III A 223), 6150 (IX A 39).

Pagans. 2523 (x³ A 221).

Pages. 4917 (xI² A 204).

"Pages from the Notebook of a Street Commissioner." 5678 (IV A 132).

Pain. 1653 (x² A 353), 4483 (xI¹ A 475).

Painting analogy. 6849 (xI² A 314).

Palisander cupboard. 6472 (x⁵ A 149).

Paludan-Müller, Frederik. 6748 (x⁶ B 171), 6850 (xI² A 321), 6961 (xI³ B 129).

Panorama. 5932 (vII¹ A 95).

Pantheism. 220 (II A 128), 1019 (125), 1771 (148), 1983 (III A 38), 1990 (vI A 120), 2004 (vIII¹ A 482), 2942 (IX A 294), 3849 (II A 91), 3887 (248), 3890 (464).

Paper analogy. 5379 (II A 413).

PARABLES. 1499 (xI² A 286), 1740 (IV B 96:13), 1990 (vI A 106), 2873 (x³ A 165), 2894 (x⁵ A 15), 2900 (140), 4342 (x⁴ A 486), 5777 (vI A 13).

Paradise. 92 (II A 191), 3012 (vIII¹ A 69), 3363 (II A 69).

PARADOX. 7 (x² A 354), 11 (x⁶ B 80), 183 (vIII¹ A 416), 897 (IV A 73), 900 (98), 907 (213), 1123 (vIII¹ A 649), 1144 (x⁴ A 422), 1293 (vII² B 261:8), 1340 (v B 5:8), 1447 (xI² A 130), 1501 (182), 1530 (x² A 481), 1635 (IV C 35), 1724 (III B 5), 2345 (v C 1), 2573 (xI² A 118), 3217 (x¹ A 628), 3218 (x² A 312), 3477 (vIII¹ A 434), 3565 (x¹ A 573), 3566 (609), 3793 (IV A 156), 4483 (xI¹ A 475), 4738 (x⁴ A 86), 4782 (x² A 549), 4878 (x⁴ A 337), 5664 (IV A 107), 6037 (vIII¹ A 229), 6368 (x¹ A 163), 6405 (x⁶ B 85), 6465 (x¹ A 616), 6495 (x² A 40), 6598 (x⁶ B 68), 6918 (xI² A 21), 6924 (45).

—"The Paradox." 7 (x² A 354), 11 (x⁶ B 80), 321 (IX A 57), 493 (414), 902 (IV A 112), 1123 (vIII¹ A 649), 1293 (vII² B 261:8), 1642 (IX A 196), 1668 (vI B 53: 13), 3035 (x² A 389), 3105 (x³ A 542), 3110 (626), 3473 (vII² B 235, p. 88), 4454 (x¹ A 134), 6002 (vIII¹ A 119).

Paranekroi. 5295 (II A 690).

Parentheses. 1818 (xI² A 201), 4051 (242).

Parish boundaries. 5451 (III A 51).

Parmenides. 193 (II C 37).

Parody. 1521 (II A 134), 3716 (x⁴ A 528), 4066 (I A 285), 4067 (288), 4392 (313), 4775 (II A 291), 5246 (126).

Part. 4492 (xI² A 225).

Participation. 3248 (I A 127), 4716 (xI¹ A 433).

Particular. 43 (IV C 76), 78 (x³ A 501), 977 (x¹ A 580), 2024 (x² A 489), 2059 (XI¹ A 272), 2071 (485), 2083 (XI² A 259), 2240 (I A 1).

Parties (political) (*see also* Peasant party). 4224 (XI¹ A 18).

Party. 5141 (I A 161).

PASCAL, BLAISE. 176 (x⁴ A 537), 543 (x⁵ A 144), 1930 (XI¹ A 306), 3098 (299), 4903 (x⁵ A 17), 5047 (XI¹ A 556).

Pascal, Jacqueline. 3120 (x³ A 644), 3121 (645).

Pasha. 5407 (II A 540).

PASSION (*see also* Pathos). 487 (IX A 297), 488 (300), 888 (III A 185), 896 (IV C 96), 907 (IV A 213), 1014 (VIII¹ A 665), 2096 (XI¹ A 268), 2425 (x¹ A 635), 2447 (XI¹ A 411), 2681 (XI² A 323), 2715 (VIII¹ A 26), 3127 (V A 44), 3579 (x⁴ A 614), 3608 (x¹ A 481), 3669 (IX A 344), 4149 (303), 4178 (x² A 490), 4220 (x⁵ A 115), 4405 (II A 756), 4421 (IV C 94), 4463 (x³ A 396), 4655 (245), 5791 (VI B 17), 6244 (IX A 251), 6319 (x¹ A 61), 6648 (x³ A 194).

Past. 119 (I A 86), 124 (175), 854 (254), 918 (VI A 35), 1232 (I A 205), 1245 (IV C 62), 1327 (III A 131), 2185 (IV A 146), 3247 (I A 99), 3553 (II A 558), 4788 (II A 372), 4794 (VIII¹ A 147), 5395 (II A 492).

Pastoral Seminary. 5485 (III C 4), 5486 (5), 5487 (8), 5488 (12), 5489 (24), 6370 (x¹ A 167), 6749 (x⁶ B 173, pp. 274-276), 6762 (x⁴ A 299), 6763 (300), 6777 (373), 6778 (377), 6813 (604).

Pastorate. 836 (VIII¹ A 10), 5873 (VII¹ A 4), 5947 (169), 5961 (221), 5962 (222), 5966 (229), 6016 (VIII¹ A 171), 6062 (352), 6132 (641), 6157 (IX A 54), 6227 (213), 6229 (216), 6325 (x¹ A 74), 6326 (77), 6336 (94), 6346 (116), 6356 (138), 6361 (147), 6394 (309), 6416 (422), 6426 (494), 6427 (495), 6430 (498), 6431 (510), 6474 (653), 6517 (x² A 147), 6526 (177), 6603 (619), 6646 (x³ A 190), 6656 (265), 6748 (x⁶ B 171), 6749 (173, pp. 274-276), 6762 (x⁴ A 299), 6843 (x⁵ A 146), 6935 (XI² A 248).

PASTORS (*see also* Clergy). 226 (x³ A 463), 375 (VIII² B 171:15), 381 (x¹ A 7), 384 (672), 481 (IX A 51), 386 (x² A 27), 394

(x³ A 137), 408 (XI¹ A 529), 555 (332), 556 (333), 1048 (VIII¹ A 234), 1343 (VI A 127), 1825 (XI³ B 199), 1896 (x⁴ A 273), 1924 (XI¹ A 4), 1927 (41), 1953 (463), 2065 (370), 2121 (x¹ A 564), 2127 (x³ A 357), 2128 (469), 2563 (XI¹ A 37), 2603 (IX A 434), 2613 (x³ A 468), 2621 (XI¹ A 313), 2753 (IX A 404), 2772 (XI² A 22), 2971 (XI¹ A 234), 2976 (372), 3193 (VIII¹ A 206), 3336 (XI¹ A 156), 3476 (VIII¹ A 310), 3481 (x¹ A 125), 3485 (540), 3500 (x³ A 102), 3505 (237), 3609 (x² A 430), 3747 (509), 4186 (240), 4193 (x³ A 746), 4194 (754), 4195 (773), 4240 (XI² A 352), 4275 (x² A 229), 4505 (XI² A 416), 4722 (XI¹ A 579), 4986 (XI² A 57), 4971 (x³ A 570), 5377 (II A 398), 5485 (III C 4), 5686 (IV B 159:6), 6256 (x⁶ B 40), 6257 (41), 6521 (x² A 157), 6707 (x³ A 661).

Pathos (*see also* PASSION). 653 (VIII² B 85), 808 (IV C 105), 822 (x⁴ A 222), 1769 (XI² A 255), 1878 (x³ A 411), 2339 (IV C 12), 2345 (V C 1), 2353 (VI A 33), 2645 (IX A 435), 2772 (XI² A 22), 3129 (VIII¹ A 92), 4180 (x² A 498), 4220 (x⁵ A 115), 4421 (IV C 92), 5793 (VI B 35:14), 5794 (35:15), 5795 (35:19), 5796 (35:24).

Patience. 338 (x¹ A 355), 1284 (194), 1861 (x² A 347), 3737 (XI² A 346), 4151 (IX A 354), 4370 (333), 4408 (II A 339), 4451 (IX A 342), 4633 (x¹ A 405), 5739 (V A 54), 6263 (IX A 321), 6285 (458), 6575 (x² A 372).

Patriotism. 6580 (x² A 413).

Pattern. (*see* IMITATION; Prototype).

PAUL. 438 (II A 307), 575 (x³ A 760), 601 (x⁴ A 594), 1111 (V A 1), 1877 (x³ A 409), 1911 (x⁴ A 499), 2094 (x³ A 764), 2410 (VIII¹ A 196), 2507 (x² A 244), 2600 (IX A 237), 3088 (VII² B 256:9-10), 3213 (XI³ B 175), 4455 (x¹ A 383), 5059 (I C 16, 18), 6422 (x¹ A 469), 6524 (x² A 167), 6787 (x⁶ B 253).

—Life of Paul. 505 (x¹ A 472), 663 (IX A 240), 676 (x² A 146), 1108 (IV A 117), 1318 (II A 410), 1491 (x⁵ A 56), 1623 (II A 143), 1661 (x⁴ A 588), 2093 (x² A 602), 3507 (x³ A 271), 3531 (x⁵ A 117), 3546 (I A 43), 3630 (VIII¹ A 329), 3708 (x¹ A 330), 4881 (x⁴ A 609), 4903 (x⁵ A 17), 4993 (x² A 321), 6468 (x¹ A 643).

—Writings of Paul. 214 (x⁴ A 433), 271 (x² A 97), 516 (460), 683 (vɪɪɪ¹ A 60), 797 (ɪɪ A 791), 816 (x¹ A 248), 990 (x³ A 248), 1313 (ɪɪ A 392), 1468 (x¹ A 214), 1652 (ɪx A 337), 1690 (ɪɪ A 102), 1705 (147), 1711 (608), 1768 (xɪ² A 190), 1843 (vɪɪɪ¹ A 536), 2182 (ɪɪɪ A 192), 2207 (ɪ A 48), 2300 (x¹ A 577), 2606 (445), 2635 (vɪɪɪ¹ A 396), 3807 (ɪ A 214), 3915 (ɪɪɪ c 1), 3916 (ɪv c 1), 3994 (ɪɪ A 63), 4313 (x⁴ A 555), 4352 (xɪ¹ A 524), 4521 (x³ A 685), 4644 (x² A 246), 4678 (x⁴ A 386), 4781 (x² A 548), 5945 (vɪɪ¹ A 160), 6021 (vɪɪɪ¹ A 185), 6029 (217), 6323 (x¹ A 72), 6553 (x² A 273).

Paulli, Just H. V. 1887 (x³ A 668), 3522 (x⁴ A 330), 3950 (x³ A 695), 4808 (xɪ¹ A 419), 6493 (x² A 25), 6691 (x³ A 563), 6692 (564), 6694 (568), 6800 (x⁴ A 540), 6802 (554), 6807 (568).

Peace. 611 (ɪx A 56), 2488 (x¹ A 314), 3131 (x³ A 583), 3132 (584), 3332 (x¹ A 205), 3333 (x³ A 428), 4395 (ɪ A 321), 5455 (ɪɪɪ A 55), 6169 (ɪx A 73).

Pear tree. 5050 (x¹ A 294).

Peasant party. 6735 (x⁴ A 58).

Pedersen, Christen. 5214 (ɪɪ A 45).

Peer Degn. 2539 (x⁴ A 371), 3185 (xɪ² A 148), 3438 (x¹ A 390), 3471 (vɪ A 156), 3693 (x⁴ A 289), 3869 (xɪ² A 94), 6819 (x⁴ A 646).

Pegasus. 55 (vɪ A 102).

Pelagianism. 1463 (ɪ A 37), 1565 (225).

Pelagius. 29 (ɪ A 101), 1565 (225), 4034 (x² A 472).

Penance. 3787 (vɪɪɪ¹ A 203), 6001 (116), 6157 (ɪx A 54).

Penitent. 3507 (x³ A 271), 6132 (vɪɪɪ¹ A 641), 6152 (ɪx A 42), 6177 (100), 6195 (150), 6206 (172), 6327 (x¹ A 78), 6335 (92), 6364 (156), 6389 (272), 6395 (320), 6426 (494), 6522 (x² A 158).

Penitentiary. 5025 (xɪ¹ A 243), 5037 (xɪ² A 223).

Penny. 3897 (vɪɪɪ¹ A 625).

Pentateuch. 5436 (ɪɪ c 10).

Perception. 513 (x² A 284), 2262 (ɪɪ A 390).

PERFECTIBILITY. 414 (ɪ A 46), 542 (x⁵ A 98), 1649 (xɪ² A 234), 1815 (xɪ¹ A 540), 1925 (22), 1932 (391), 2455 (xɪ² A 426), 2724 (xɪ¹ A 186), 3013 (ɪx A 273), 3099 (xɪ² A 51), 3102 (212), 3188 (xɪ³ B 197), 3223 (xɪ¹ A 393), 3594 (xɪ² A 233), 3602 (xɪ¹ A 364), 4352 (524), 4359 (xɪ² A 246), 6257 (x⁶ B 41), 6793 (x⁴ A 474), 6921 (xɪ² A 36).

Perfection. 356 (x³ A 655), 1482 (784).

Perfume. 5479 (ʟ. 18).

Periander. 5736 (v A 45).

Persecution. 305 (vɪɪɪ¹ A 145), 429 (ɪɪ A 234), 460 (vɪɪɪ¹ A 102), 616 (xɪ² A 341), 1077 (vɪɪ¹ A 174), 2633 (vɪɪ¹ A 175), 2664 (xɪ¹ A 114), 2784 (x³ A 513), 3493 (x² A 288), 4655 (x³ A 245), 4661 (500), 4671 (x⁴ A 169), 4704 (xɪ¹ A 8), 4705 (9), 4973 (x⁴ A 178), 5021 (x³ A 273), 6371 (x¹ A 169).

Perseus. 5225 (ɪɪ A 597).

PERSON. 72 (x² A 79), 180 (xɪ¹ A 237), 183 (vɪɪɪ¹ A 416), 200 (xɪ¹ A 284), 536 (x⁴ A 581), 673 (x¹ A 566), 906 (ɪv A 155), 1437 (xɪ¹ A 35), 1825 (xɪ³ B 199), 2023 (x² A 480), 2447 (xɪ¹ A 411), 2994 (xɪ² A 146), 3262 (ɪɪ c 56), 3492 (x² A 230), 3587 (xɪ¹ A 450), 3608 (x¹ A 481), 3890 (ɪɪ A 464), 4050 (xɪ² A 14), 4530 (xɪ¹ A 398), 4565 (x⁴ A 379), 4571 (xɪ² A 97), 6440 (x¹ A 531), 6780 (x⁴ A 383), 6781 (389), 6782 (390), 6803 (557), 6839 (x⁵ A 104).

Personal. 4629 (ɪx A 466), 6525 (x² A 174).

Personalism. 3497 (x² A 581), 4166 (x² A 7).

PERSONALITY. 657 (vɪɪɪ² B 89), 906 (ɪv A 155), 1452 (xɪ² A 175), 1578 (ɪɪ A 454), 1587 (ɪɪɪ A 1), 1615 (x² A 431), 1983 (ɪɪɪ A 38), 2042 (x⁴ A 415), 2152 (vɪɪɪ¹ A 540), 2163 (x² A 17), 2172 (xɪ¹ A 25), 2512 (x² A 448), 3887 (ɪɪ A 248), 3890 (464), 4056 (xɪ² A 106), 4160 (x¹ A 356), 4163 (632), 4356 (xɪ² A 62), 4548 (x² A 145), 4569 (xɪ¹ A 201), 5899 (vɪɪ¹ A 112), 6780 (x⁴ A 383), 6803 (557.

Pessimism (*see also* OPTIMISM). 1448 (xɪ² A 131), 2666 (xɪ¹ A 511), 3039 (360), 3881 (181), 4354 (558), 5025 (243), 5035 (xɪ² A 219), 6863 (xɪ¹ A 76).

PETER. 237 (x² A 194), 319 (vɪɪɪ¹ A 583), 346 (x² A 85), 462 (vɪɪɪ¹ A 130), 576 (x³ A 765), 601 (594), 959 (ɪx A 104), 1134 (x² A 54), 1864 (x³ A 171), 2094 (764), 2200

(VIII[1] A 500), 2300 (X[1] A 577), 2376 (449), 2678 (XI[2] A 1), 2685 (427), 2891 (X[3] A 526), 3507 (271), 3570 (121), 3900 (X[1] A 255), 4494 (XI[3] B 148), 4911 (XI[1] A 516), 6261 (IX A 310), 6323 (X[1] A 72), 6422 (469), 6468 (643), 6631 (X[3] A 147), 6772 (X[4] A 351), 6933 (XI[2] A 213).

Petersen, August. 2822 (X[4] A 232), 3068 (XI[3] B 43), 6755 (X[4] A 231), 6756 (233).

PETRARCH.

Phalaris. 1943 (X[4] A 471), 2872 (X[3] A 34), 6794 (X[4] A 488), 6895 (XI[1] A 382).

Pharisee. 118 (I A 33), 442 (II A 338), 855 (13), 867 (322), 1381 (IX A 476), 1542 (II A 2), 1682 (78), 1685 (81), 2209 (I A 287), 2519 (X[3] A 170), 3063 (X[4] A 448), 4165 (X[1] A 682), 4710 (XI[1] A 350).

Phenomenon. 3859 (II A 563), 6870 (XI[1] A 131).

Phidias. 2396 (IV A 195).

Philistinism. 2752 (IX A 403).

Philipsen, Philip G. 6046 (L. 154), 6047 (L. 156).

Phillip the Fair. 4081 (II A 257).

Philo. 5370 (II A 364).

Philoctetes. 5547 (III C 40).

Philosophers. 1199 (X[4] A 172), 2087 (II A 47), 2266 (523), 3243 (I A 35), 3282 (III A 24), 3309 (VII[1] A 152), 3311 (VIII[1] A 152), 3316 (X[4] A 450), 3712 (X[4] A 640), 5270 (II A 189), 6391 (X[1] A 281), 6412 (X[1] A 385).

Philosophical anthropology (*see also* ANTHROPOLOGY: Philosophy of Man). 832 (II A 100), 1463 (I A 37).

"Philosophical Deliberations." 5574 (IV A 2).

Philosophical Fragments. 2287 (VI B 42), 3085 (45), 4037 (X[2] A 482), 4262 (V B 4:3), 4263 (23:1), 5593 (IV C 34), 5675 (IV A 127), 5786 (VI A 146), 5827 (84), 5944 (VII[1] A 158), 6690 (X[3] A 555).

PHILOSOPHY. 23 (I A 102), 37 (III A 3), 199 (VI B 54:21), 263 (X[2] A 324), 581 (I A 108), 648 (VIII[2] B 79), 649 (81), 704 (IV A 192), 754 (III A 7), 755 (92), 775 (IV A 150), 896 (IV C 96), 977 (X[1] A 580), 1030 (IV A 164), 1052 (IX A 358), 1072 (III A 108), 1132 (X[1] A 554), 1232 (I A 205), 1282 (III A 119), 1304 (I A 29), 1332 (IV A 157), 1544 (II A 214), 1570 (52), 1590 (III

A 37), 1592 (III C 31), 1619 (XI[1] A 14), 1621 (183), 1692 (II A 104), 1702 (140), 1941 (V A 75), 2087 (II A 47), 2233 (I A 192), 2239 (X[2] A 539), 2277 (III A 211), 2305 (I A 251), 2313 (II A 159), 2338 (IV C 11), 2467 (IX A 11), 2957 (X[3] A 451), 3073 (IV C 29), 3074 (84), 3077 (IV A 103), 3109 (X[3] A 609), 3126 (IV C 57), 3325 (IV A 159), 3558 (X[1] A 666), 3614 (X[4] A 162), 3669 (IX A 344), 3716 (X[4] A 528), 3726 (VIII[1] A 103), 3867 (XI[1] A 557), 4131 (VIII[1] A 598), 4282 (X[4] A 250), 4398 (I C 126), 4767 (X[4] A 140), 4806 (XI[1] A 329), 5017 (VIII[1] A 409), 5102 (I A 77), 5143 (166), 5161 (235), 5181 (328), 5353 (II C 25), 5535 (III A 179), 5574 (IV A 2), 5579 (IV C 8), 5922 (VII[1] A 50), 6423 (X[1] A 476).

Philostratus. 4103 (IV A 7), 4105 (13), 4309 (X[4] A 466).

Phister, Joakim L. 6807 (X[4] A 568).

"Phister as Scipio." 6292 (IX B 67), 6293 (68), 6487 (X[1] A 678).

Phonomenon. 6748 (X[6] B 171), 6750 (188), 6751 (194).

Photographs. 4230 (XI[1] A 118).

Physicality. 6170 (IX A 74).

Physique. 6119 (VIII[1] A 577), 6484 (X[1] A 670), 6626 (X[3] A 115).

Pickpocket. 1528 (VII[1] A 87).

Piety (*see also* PIETISM). 849 (I A 124), 863 (II A 671), 3163 (X[4] A 332), 4625 (IX A 380), 6646 (X[3] A 190), 6685 (519).

Pig. 5140 (I A 156).

Pilate. 332 (X[1] A 243), 359 (X[4] A 507), 360 (514), 363 (XI[1] A 13), 1440 (XI[2] A 130), 1801 (XI[1] A 43), 3199 (X[3] A 467), 3348 (290), 4214 (X[4] A 209), 4646 (X[2] A 272), 4858 (X[1] A 159), 6156 (IX A 53), 6635 (X[3] A 164).

Pilgrim. 1093 (XI[2] A 247), 2511 (X[2] A 364).

Pin analogy. 6928 (XI[2] A 79).

Pious fraud. 6205 (IX A 171).

"Pious Phrase Book." 6065 (VIII[1] A 383), 6066 (384), 6067 (385).

Pity. 2837 (VI A 138), 4599 (VIII[1] A 161).

Plant. 923 (VI A 122), 5526 (III A 171).

PLATO. 18 (III A 13), 42 (IV C 50), 45 (V A 14), 113 (IV C 21), 180 (XI[1] A 237), 484 (IX A 207), 517 (X[2] A 603), 575 (X[3] A 760), 824 (X[4] A 633), 1059 (X[2] A 439),

1061 (x³ A 150), 1067 (xɪ² A 63), 1088 (x⁴ A 590), 1148 (635), 1154 (xɪ² A 380), 1162 (vɪɪ¹ A 58), 1635 (ɪv c 35), 2274 (ɪɪɪ A 5), 2328 (x⁴ A 313), 2339 (ɪv c 12), 2387 (ɪɪɪ A 61), 2617 (xɪ¹ A 150), 2624 (xɪ² A 154), 3088 (vɪɪ² B 256:9-10), 3362 (xɪ² A 7), 3626 (398), 3713 (x⁴ A 255), 4028 (x² A 404), 4053 (13), 4233 (xɪ¹ A 507), 4238 (xɪ² A 108), 4246 (ɪɪɪ B 30), 4253 (ɪv A 206), 4266 (vɪɪ¹ A 74), 4275 (x² A 229), 4282 (x⁴ A 250), 4285 (333), 4287 (463), 4288 (467), 4301 (xɪ¹ A 430), 4309 (x⁴ A 466), 4345 (632), 4505 (xɪ² A 416), 4827 (ɪv c 111), 5577 (ɪv A 203), 5598 (ɪv c 45), 5602 (98), 5618 (ɪv A 63), 5619 (64), 5892 (vɪɪ¹ A 105), 6300 (x¹ A 11), 6400 (338), 6412 (385), 6528 (x² A 184), 6588 (476), 6630 (x³ A 146), 6819 (x⁴ A 646), 6839 (x⁵ A 104).

Platonism. 484 (ɪx A 207), 4243 (ɪɪ A 186).

Play. 4837 (ɪv c 121), 4482 (xɪ¹ A 472).

Playing Christianity. 380 (ɪx A 405), 546 (xɪ¹ A 70), 561 (xɪ² A 102), 1932 (xɪ¹ A 391), 2853 (x⁴ A 483), 3541 (xɪ² A 289), 3624 (xɪ¹ A 437), 4056 (xɪ² A 106).

Pleasure. 803 (ɪɪɪ A 94), 947 (vɪɪɪ¹ A 236), 3323 (ɪɪɪ B 26), 4483 (xɪ¹ A 475), 5669 (ɪv A 114), 6794 (x⁴ A 488).

Plebianism. 3221 (xɪ¹ A 341).

Plessen, Colonel v. 1826 (ɪɪ A 621).

Plotinus. 1594 (ɪv c 59).

Ploug, Parmo C. 2950 (x² A 369), 6621 (x³ A 90).

Plutarch. 69 (ɪx A 76), 1369 (78), 3342 (239), 3636 (x¹ A 461), 4247 (ɪv A 199), 4248 (200), 4253 (206), 4259 (212), 4427 (vɪ A 71), 4510 (ɪɪ A 331), 4796 (x¹ A 261), 6147 (ɪx A 26), 6148 (27), 6180 (122).

Poet. 117 (ɪ A 8), 166 (x¹ A 3), 167 (198), 169 (432), 487 (ɪx A 297), 560 (xɪ² A 49), 896 (ɪv c 96), 958 (vɪɪɪ¹ A 671), 1027 (ɪɪɪ A 62), 1391 (x¹ A 605), 1445 (xɪ² A 98), 1462 (x⁴ A 582), 1645 (208), 1689 (ɪɪ A 101), 1792 (x³ A 576), 1796 (x⁴ A 80), 1800 (xɪ² A 294), 1812 (xɪ¹ A 476), 1942 (vɪɪɪ¹ A 643), 2038 (x⁴ A 104), 2215 (ɪɪɪ A 193), 2301 (x⁴ A 247), 2637 (ɪx A 46), 3328 (x² A 608), 3512 (x³ A 479), 3578 (x⁴ A 532), 3732 (38), 4197 (40), 4198 (41), 4275 (x² A 229), 4301 (xɪ¹ A

430), 4464 (x³ A 512), 4571 (xɪ² A 97), 4970 (x³ A 561), 5210 (ɪɪ A 40), 5604 (ɪv c 107), 5640 (ɪv A 76), 5722 (v B 148:5), 5732 (v A 34), 6061 (vɪɪɪ¹ A 347), 6224 (ɪx A 208), 6227 (213), 6277 (421), 6278 (498), 6279 (499), 6300 (x¹ A 11), 6317 (56), 6327 (78), 6336 (94), 6337 (95), 6338 (100), 6353 (130), 6364 (156), 6367 (162), 6368 (163), 6383 (250), 6390 (273), 6391 (281), 6394 (309), 6395 (320), 6400 (338), 6412 (385), 6422 (513), 6431 (510), 6437 (525), 6450 (557), 6472 (x⁵ A 149), 6491 (x² A 15), 6497 (45), 6500 (61), 6503 (75), 6505 (89), 6511 (106), 6521 (157), 6527 (183), 6528 (184), 6587 (475), 6632 (x³ A 152), 6647 (191), 6727 (x⁴ A 33), 6736 (64), 6749 (x⁶ B 173, pp. 274-276), 6753 (x⁴ A 204), 6801 (545), 6824 (673), 6834 (x⁵ A 46), 6840 (105), 6844 (xɪ² A 283), 6947 (xɪ³ B 57).

Poet (S.K.). 1812 (xɪ¹ A 476), 6809 (x⁴ A 586).

Poet-existence (see also Distance: Esthetic). 800 (ɪɪɪ A 12), 817 (x¹ A 502), 5630 (ɪv A 217).

Poetic. 6506 (x² A 90), 6508 (94), 6526 (177), 6528 (184), 6561 (281), 6572 (346), 6577 (375), 6578 (393), 6718 (x³ A 789).

Poetizing. 3022 (x⁵ A 12), 4881 (x⁴ A 609).

Poetry. 124 (ɪ A 175), 136 (ɪɪ A 352), 144 (ɪv c 109), 265 (ɪɪ A 12), 859 (165), 949 (vɪɪɪ¹ A 312), 1019 (ɪɪ A 125), 1027 (ɪɪɪ A 62), 1565 (ɪ A 225), 1625 (148), 1629 (264), 1690 (ɪɪ A 102), 1904 (x⁴ A 354), 1942 (vɪɪɪ¹ A 643), 2132 (x⁵ A 51), 2255 (ɪɪ A 264), 2439 (x⁴ A 642), 2699 (ɪ A 226), 2798 (241), 2895 (x⁵ A 48), 3651 (ɪɪ A 551), 3890 (464), 4301 (xɪ¹ A 430), 4567 (x⁴ A 667), 4827 (ɪv c 111), 4832 (116), 5117 (ɪ A 118), 5134 (ɪ c 87), 5135 (88), 5143 (ɪ A 166), 5178 (286), 5206 (ɪɪ A 21), 5303 (210), 5319 (740), 5519 (ɪɪɪ A 164), 5532 (176), 5592 (ɪv c 24), 5604 (107), 5605 (123), 5608 (127), 6353 (x¹ A 130), 6870 (xɪ¹ A 131).

Poetry, Indian. 3817 (ɪ A 315).

A Poet's Confessions. 151 (vɪ A 43).

Point of View for My Work as an Author, The. 6258 (ɪx A 293), 6259 (298),

6327 (x¹ A 78), 6329 (84), 6337 (97), 6346 (116), 6361 (147), 6383 (250), 6390 (273), 6407 (351), 6416 (422), 6431 (510), 6445 (546), 6511 (x² A 106), 6530 (192), 6583 (427), 6673 (x³ A 422).

Poison. 4705 (xi¹ A 9).

Polarity. 2082 (xi² A 149).

Polemic (S.K.). 3335 (x³ A 580).

POLEMICS. 499 (x¹ A 399), 557 (xi¹ A 349), 1131 (x¹ A 395), 2379 (xi² A 39), 2666 (xi¹ A 511), 2908 (157), 2943 (ix A 452), 3616 (xi² A 338), 4058 (319), 4667 (x⁴ A 135), 4911 (xi¹ A 516), 5891 (vii¹ A 104), 5929 (85), 5961 (221), 6412 (x¹ A 385), 6415 (406), 6740 (x⁴ A 130), 6888 (xi¹ A 275), 6889 (276).

Police. 1827 (v A 24), 2078 (xi² A 69), 4305 (v A 61), 4384 (xi² A 132), 4946 (iv A 160), 5076 (i A 17), 5678 (iv A 132), 5770 (vi A 10), 5771 (11), 6016 (viii¹ A 171).

Police agents. 4981 (xi¹ A 185), 5770 (vi A 10), 5771 (11).

Police analogy. 6930 (xi² A 121).

Politicians. 2571 (xi² A 55), 4085 (ii A 710), 4087 (754), 4090 (783), 4096 (481), 4172 (x² A 391), 4182 (571), 4215 (x⁴ A 249).

Politics (see also SOCIAL-POLITICAL THOUGHT). 1584 (ii A 811), 2130 (x⁴ A 26), 2131 (151), 2469 (ix A 96), 3477 (viii¹ A 434), 3670 (ix A 415), 3813 (i A 230), 4060 (42), 4066 (285), 4085 (ii A 710), 4086 (735), 4092 (378), 4093 (436), 4107 (vi A 1), 4150 (ix A 353), 5181 (i A 328), 5779 (vi c 2), 6255 (ix B 63:7).

Polycarp. 429 (ii A 234).

Polymath. 5376 (ii A 397).

Polytheism. 1734 (iii B 23).

Poor, the. 386 (x² A 27), 4685 (x⁴ A 578), 6045 (viii¹ A 254), 6085 (452), 6120 (589).

Pope. 309 (viii¹ A 345), 418 (i A 97), 1930 (xi¹ A 306), 2548 (108), 2854 (i A 26).

Popularity. 2539 (x⁴ A 371), 2939 (ix A 143), 2940 (146), 2994 (xi² A 146), 3303 (vi A 15), 6027 (viii¹ A 212).

Population. 3969 (xi¹ A 259).

Portefeuillen. 5688 (iv A 141), 6624 (x³ A 99).

Positive, the. 6924 (xi² A 45).

Positivity. 625 (vi B 10), 1601 (iv c 73), 2282 (74).

Possession. 2518 (x³ A 153).

POSSIBILITY. 46 (v A 16), 52 (v B 55:4), 83 (xi¹ A 358), 102 (x² A 22), 199 (vi B 54:21), 258 (iv c 47), 511 (x² A 141), 823 (x⁴ A 580), 903 (iv A 131), 934 (vii¹ A 138), 992 (x³ A 715), 1039 (vi B 54:10), 1059 (x² A 439), 1086 (x⁴ A 32), 1126 (ix A 311), 1136 (x² A 371), 1139 (x³ A 322), 1185 (ii A 605), 1245 (iv c 62), 1294 (viii¹ A 395), 1462 (x⁴ A 582), 1668 (vi B 53:13), 1831 (x⁴ A 533), 2676 (xi¹ A 250), 2980 (512), 3409 (vii¹ A 142), 3621 (xi¹ A 213), 3707 (x¹ A 66), 3774 (x⁵ A 79), 3850 (ii A 119), 4030 (x² A 436), 4037 (482), 4326 (x¹ A 417), 4383 (xi² A 33), 4462 (x³ A 394), 5205 (ii A 20), 5980 (viii¹ A 27), 6135 (650), 6229 (ix A 216), 6489 (x² A 10), 6514 (112), 6525 (174), 6536 (205).

Posterity. 4901 (x⁴ A 613), 4977 (x⁵ A 18), 5900 (vii¹ A 113), 5904 (117), 5995 (viii¹ A 81), 6072 (394), 6608 (x³ A 4), 6609 (8), 6619 (88), 6626 (115), 6631 (147).

"Postscript" (Anti-Climacus). 6349 (x⁶ B 48), 6350 (x¹ A 121).

Povelsen, Hans F. 5832 (vi B 235).

Poverty. 175 (x⁴ A 150), 1007 (xi² A 381), 1847 (ix A 82), 2522 (x³ A 218), 2608 (x² A 181), 2771 (x⁴ A 263), 3472 (vii¹ B 177:4), 3751 (x³ A 306), 3760 (x⁴ A 316), 3761 (326), 4559 (x³ A 720), 4738 (x⁴ A 86), 6120 (viii¹ A 589), 6153 (ix A 43).

Power. 638 (viii¹ A 6), 2175 (ii A 304), 2943 (ix A 452), 2976 (xi¹ A 372), 3077 (iv A 103), 3477 (viii¹ A 434), 4154 (ix A 449), 4155 (453), 4214 (x⁴ A 209), 4353 (xi¹ A 538), 4356 (xi² A 62), 4585 (v A 43), 4682 (x⁴ A 570), 4997 (x⁴ A 106), 5646 (iv A 87), 6577 (x² A 375).

P. P. 6387 (x¹ A 263).

Practical. 3864 (x⁵ A 134), 6786 (x⁶ B 145, pp. 202-203).

PRACTICALITY (see also Sensibleness). 561 (xi² A 102), 1182 (ii A 29), 1417 (x³ A 743), 1788 (345), 1801 (xi¹ A 43), 2079

(XI² A 124), 3503 (X³ A 141), 3891 (III A 139), 5100 (I A 75), 6041 (VIII¹ A 246).
Practical Life. 965 (IX A 418).
Practical people. 1076 (VII¹ A 173), 2637 (IX A 46), 3351 (VIII¹ A 188).
Practice. 3870 (XI² A 117), 5230 (II A 602), 6843 (X⁵ A 146).
Practice in Christianity. 1894 (X⁴ A 131), 3159 (X³ A 610), 3354 (IX A 140), 3685 (X³ A 545), 4190 (607), 4727 (XI² A 82), 6110 (VIII¹ A 558), 6114 (562), 6130 (637), 6149 (IX A 33), 6189 (135), 6210 (176), 6229 (216), 6238 (227), 6245 (255), 6249 (271), 6271 (390), 6278 (498), 6337 (X¹ A 95), 6361 (147), 6368 (163), 6371 (169), 6387 (263), 6416 (422), 6417 (423), 6419 (425), 6421 (450), 6431 (510), 6136 (520), 6437 (525), 6445 (546), 6455 (571), 6461 (593), 6464 (615), 6487 (678), 6505 (X² A 89), 6506 (90), 6526 (177), 6528 (184), 6534 (199), 6571 (345), 6572 (346), 6578 (393), 6664 (X³ A 381), 6666 (526), 6671 (415), 6674 (423), 6686 (526), 6687 (530), 6690 (555), 6691 (563), 6694 (568), 6695 (569), 6696 (577), 6699 (599), 6707 (661), 6721 (X⁴ A 6), 6723 (9), 6746 (X⁵ A 166), 6749 (X⁶ B 173, pp. 274-276), 6762 (X⁴ A 299), 6778 (377), 6795 (511), 6797 (513), 6813 (604), 6814 (605), 6842 (X⁶ B 232, pp. 371-378), 6854 (XI³ B 15).
Pragmatic criterion. 910 (IV A 172).
Pragmaticism. 951 (VIII¹ A 319), 2502 (X¹ A 651).
PRAYER, PRAYERS (S.K.). 217 (I A 290), 290 (II A 295), 336 (X¹ A 352), 419 (I A 172), 796 (II A 632), 955 (VIII¹ A 413), 1102 (III A 127), 1164 (VIII¹ A 41), 1168 (568), 1412 (X³ A 421), 1466 (II A 507), 1656 (X³ A 297), 1798 (X⁴ A 282), 1849 (IX A 323), 2175 (II A 304), 2257 (301), 2307 (62), 2479 (X¹ A 47), 2501 (630), 3782 (I A 81), 3944 (X³ A 108), 3916 (IV C 1), 4364 (VI A 2), 4770 (X⁴ A 143), 4956 (II A 455), 5097 (I A 66), 5455 (III A 55), 5491 (91), 5508 (148), 5530 (174), 5753 (V A 95), 5792 (VI B 18), 5949 (VII¹ A 184), 6165 (IX A 69), 6514 (X² A 112), 6648 (X³ A 194), 6837 (X⁵ A 72).

Preachers. 1452 (XI¹ A 175), 3466 (V A 17).
PREACHING (*see also* Proclamation). 101 (X¹ A 353), 320 (IX A 16), 322 (59), 429 (II A 234), 591 (X¹ A 271), 622 (V A 18), 630 (VI A 147), 647 (VIII¹ A 564), 658 (IX A 79), 659 (127), 660 (198), 681 (X³ A 648), 1062 (725), 1229 (X⁴ A 82), 1378 (IX A 347), 1429 (X⁴ A 485), 1487 (619), 1846 (IX A 49), 1896 (X⁴ A 273), 1915 (626), 1950 (X¹ A 372), 1978 (II A 385), 2439 (X⁴ A 642), 2464 (VIII¹ A 541), 2510 (X² A 334), 2516 (X³ A 127), 2671 (57), 2793 (X² A 341), 2880 (X³ A 537), 2976 (XI¹ A 372), 3017 (X³ A 384), 3037 (622), 3040 (XI² A 16), 3160 (X³ A 698), 3169 (X⁴ A 627), 3182 (XI¹ A 532), 3420 (VIII² B 107), 3434 (X¹ A 211), 3612 (X² A 461), 3631 (X⁴ A 602), 3651 (II A 551), 3826 (X³ A 559), 3940 (X² A 333), 4283 (X⁴ A 314), 4309 (466), 4313 (555), 4524 (639), 4566 (407), 4662 (X³ A 671), 4686 (X⁴ A 579), 4778 (VIII¹ A 433), 4970 (X³ A 561), 5463 (III A 66), 5752 (V A 94), 5753 (95), 5883 (VII¹ A 23), 5948 (176), 6101 (VIII¹ A 504), 6150 (IX A 39), 6189 (135), 6228 (214), 6241 (236), 6270 (381), 6552 (X² A 261), 6578 (393), 6631 (X³ A 147), 6667 (399), 6670 (404), 6716 (780), 6733 (X⁴ A 56), 6767 (318), 6802 (554), 6804 (558), 6807 (568), 6808 (584).
Preaching, street. 6150 (IX A 39), 6957 (XI³ B 120).
Precosia. 6914 (XI¹ A 586).
PREDESTINATION. 227 (I C 40), 1230 (I A 5), 1231 (7), 1302 (2), 3543 (19), 3544 (20), 3545 (22), 3546 (43), 3547 (295), 4408 (II A 339).
Preexistence. 22 (I A 74), 2088 (II A 448).
Prefaces. 5708 (IV B 126), 5726 (V B 47:13), 5754 (V A 99), 5857 (VII¹ A 233), 6636 (X⁶ B 137).
Preference. 4423 (IV B 57).
Preller, Eduard L. 5577 (IV A 201).
Premonition. 3551 (II A 32).
Pre-pledged. 6389 (X¹ A 272).
Presence. 973 (X¹ A 393), 1366 (IX A 34).
Present. 1076 (VII¹ A 173), 1232 (I A 205), 1245 (IV C 62), 2796 (III A 70), 3075 (IV A 47), 3077 (103), 3796 (I A 130), 5270 (II

A 189), 5395 (492), 5398 (503), 5640 (IV A 76), 6004 (VIII¹ A 120), 6220 (IX A 189), 6222 (203).

"Present Age." 5761 (VI B 222), 6151 (IX A 41).

PRESENTIMENT. 91 (II A 18), 92 (191), 219 (127), 3992 (19), 3999 (584), 4389 (I A 183), 5669 (IV A 114), 5690 (144).

Press (see also JOURNALISM; Newspapers). 2142 (VII² B 290), 2145 (VII¹ A 37), 2153 (IX A 200), 2154 (282), 2155 (320), 2157 (378), 2158 (468), 2165 (X³ A 231), 2650 (X¹ A 16), 2767 (VII¹ A 77), 4172 (X³ A 690), 6624 (99).

Presumptuousness. 1923 (X⁵ A 139), 4525 (X⁵ A 5).

Presupposition. 143 (IV C 104), 654 (VIII² B 86), 754 (III A 7), 768 (V A 70), 772 (II C 47), 777 (IV B 13:21), 1032 (V A 6), 1240 (III A 48), 1631 (II A 183), 2127 (X³ A 357), 2284 (IV A 49), 2341 (V A 74), 2384 (II A 462), 3281 (III A 11), 3299 (V A 46), 3306 (VI A 145), 4012 (VIII¹ A 473), 4895 (X⁴ A 350), 4898 (480), 4901 (613), 4983 (XI¹ A 544), 5100 (I A 75), 5929 (VII¹ A 85), 6423 (X² A 476).

Prevenience. 3415 (VIII¹ A 342).

Price. 6061 (VIII¹ A 347), 6464 (X¹ A 615).

Pride. 924 (VI A 137), 1388 (X¹ A 332), 3895 (VI A 132), 4029 (X² A 429), 4165 (X¹ A 682), 4637 (645), 4902 (X⁴ A 636), 6020 (VIII¹ A 179), 6021 (185), 6158 (IX A 55), 6170 (74), 6333 (X¹ A 89), 6340 (107), 6384 (258).

PRIMITIVITY. 84 (XI¹ A 385), 214 (X⁴ A 433), 216 (XI¹ A 347), 648 (VIII² B 79), 649 (81), 650 (82), 654 (86), 655 (87), 657 (89), 1028 (IV C 92), 1067 (XI² A 63), 1135 (X² A 207), 1646 (X⁴ A 505), 1648 (XI¹ A 446), 1769 (XI² A 255), 2035 (X³ A 778), 2077 (XI¹ A 587), 2080 (XI² A 125), 2298 (VIII¹ A 479), 2607 (X¹ A 485), 2907 (XI¹ A 155), 2917 (XI² A 364), 2978 (XI¹ A 387), 2999 (XI² A 167), 3088 (VII² B 256:9-10), 3220 (XI¹ A 97), 4183 (X² A 643), 4296 (XI¹ A 15), 5914 (VII¹ A 127), 6463 (X¹ A 598).

Principle of contradiction. 699 (I A 324), 1610 (VI B 98:45).

Printing. 5077 (I C 46), 5734 (V B 232:1).

Printzlau, F. F. 6537 (L. 239).

Prison. 4240 (XI² A 352), 4769 (X⁴ A 142), 5429 (II A 804).

Privat-Docent. 6748 (X⁶ B 171).

"Private Tutorials." 5772 (VI A 12), 5808 (44).

Probability. 628 (VI A 19), 824 (X⁴ A 633), 1540 (I A 237), 3342 (IX A 239), 4741 (X³ A 727), 4943 (XI¹ A 502).

"Problemata." 5658 (IV B 60).

Proclamation (see also PREACHING). 815 (IX A 289), 1489 (X⁵ A 8), 3009 (XI² A 243), 3182 (XI¹ A 532), 3489 (X² A 151), 4803 (X⁵ A 65), 4907 (XI¹ A 29), 6306 (X⁵ A 158), 6618 (X³ A 86), 6783 (X⁴ A 395), 6924 (XI² A 45).

Procreation. 4051 (XI² A 242).

Procul. 6292 (IX B 67), 6293 (68).

Prodigal son. 2875 (X³ A 214), 3939 (X² A 325), 3949 (X³ A 213).

PROFESSOR. 3 (IV A 6), 69 (IX A 76), 77 (X³ A 186), 106 (96), 176 (X⁴ A 537), 183 (VIII¹ A 416), 484 (IX A 207), 646 (VIII¹ A 554), 697 (XI¹ A 59), 982 (X² A 201), 1442 (XI¹ A 553), 1452 (XI² A 175), 1611 (VII¹ A 153), 1615 (X² A 431), 1825 (XI³ B 199), 1846 (IX A 49), 1927 (XI¹ A 41), 1940 (XI² A 434), 1956 (237), 2611 (X³ A 316), 3018 (496), 3140 (X² A 357), 3316 (X⁴ A 450), 3317 (X⁵ A 113), 3669 (IX A 344), 3864 (X⁵ A 134), 3865 (XI¹ A 461), 3866 (465), 3868 (583), 3870 (XI² A 117), 3874 (XI¹ A 111), 3883 (537), 4302 (448), 4303 (449), 4475 (X⁴ A 430), 4722 (XI¹ A 579), 4757 (X² A 202), 4901 (X⁴ A 613), 4977 (X⁵ B 18), 4986 (XI² A 57), 6302 (X¹ A 15), 6465 (616), 6574 (X⁶ B 121), 6585 (X² A 440), 6596 (X⁶ B 128), 6787 (253), 6817 (X⁴ A 628), 6818 (629), 6840 (X⁵ A 105), 6859 (XI¹ A 56), 6870 (131), 6872 (136), 6968 (XI² A 438).

PROGRESS. 317 (VIII¹ A 519), 536 (X⁴ A 581), 727 (XI¹ A 479), 1052 (IX A 358), 1443 (XI¹ A 591), 1818 (XI² A 201), 1900 (X⁴ A 321), 2471 (IX A 274), 2563 (XI¹ A 37), 2640 (IX A 126), 2975 (XI¹ A 346), 3013 (IX A 273), 3206 (X⁵ A 100), 3209 (XI¹ A 552), 3210 (XI² A 38), 3212 (325), 3334 (X³ A 574), 3577 (X⁴ A 503), 3870 (XI² A 117), 4148 (IX A 177), 4442 (IV A 52), 4918 (XI² A 205), 6056 (VIII¹ A 326), 6145 (IX A 23), 6516 (X² A 134).

Progress, backward. 6389 (x¹ A 272).

Prometheus. 649 (VIII² A 81), 1183 (II A 50), 1339 (V A 89), 1706 (II A 179), 3059 (789).

Promise. 1740 (IV B 96:13), 3024 (XI¹ A 523).

Prompter. 5040 (x⁴ A 90).

PROOF. 20 (x⁵ A 120), 73 (x² A 406), 191 (XI¹ A 436), 254 (VI A 9), 274 (I A 53), 322 (IX A 59), 455 (VI A 109), 474 (IX A 2), 659 (127), 1032 (V A 6), 1117 (VII¹ A 61), 1163 (VIII¹ A 25), 1170 (IX A 118), 1314 (II A 394), 1334 (V A 7), 1342 (VI A 121), 1358 (VIII¹ A 327), 1452 (XI² A 175), 1881 (x² A 455), 1950 (x¹ A 372), 2028 (x² A 339), 2296 (VII¹ A 215), 2341 (V A 74), 2877 (x² A 328), 3165 (x⁴ A 393), 3453 (x³ A 223), 3471 (VI A 156), 3842 (x⁴ A 279), 4535 (II A 433), 4876 (x⁴ A 42), 4897 (468), 4900 (569), 5026 (XI¹ A 254), 6108 (VIII¹ A 549), 6708 (x³ A 663), 6773 (x⁴ A 353), 6814 (605), 6966 (XI² A 436).

Proof-reading. 5881 (VII¹ B 211).

Propertius, Sextus. 2433 (x³ A 489).

Property. 5310 (II A 720), 5372 (382).

Prophet. 2858 (II A 379), 4388 (I A 167), 5436 (II C 10), 5419 (36).

Prosperity. 2196 (VIII¹ A 322).

Prose. 5178 (I A 286).

Prostitute. 5622 (IV A 65).

Protagoras. 4308 (VII¹ A 235).

PROTESTANTISM. 83 (XI¹ A 358), 164 (IX A 110), 223 (475), 252 (I A 310), 405 (XI¹ A 308), 581 (I A 108), 825 (x⁶ B 233), 830 (XI² A 331), 1463 (I A 37), 1496 (x⁵ A 109), 1512 (x¹ A 504), 1904 (x⁴ A 354), 1912 (500), 1913 (521), 1917 (x⁵ A 9), 1923 (139), 1924 (XI¹ A 4), 1976 (II A 223), 2527 (x³ A 336), 2616 (XI¹ A 129), 2622 (XI² A 150), 2763 (198), 3133 (XI¹ A 126), 3153 (x³ A 267), 3160 (698), 3183 (XI¹ A 548), 3878 (165), 4061 (I A 93), 4242 (XI³ B 126), 4814 (XI² A 123), 5007 (192), 5088 (I A 59), 6863 (XI¹ A 76), 6876 (149), 6892 (300), 6912 (559), 6932 (XI² A 206).

Protestants. 252 (I A 316).

Prototype (see also IMITATION; CHRIST: prototype). 304 (VIII¹ A 83), 330 (x¹ A 204), 334 (279), 349 (x² A 170), 692 (IX A 153), 693 (x¹ A 132), 694 (x² A 253), 1432 (x⁵ A 23), 1473 (x² A 219), 1494 (x⁵ A 103), 2481 (x¹ A 154), 2503 (x² A 30), 2643 (IX A 325), 2673 (x⁴ A 520), 2872 (x³ A 34), 3455 (317), 4454 (x¹ A 134), 4637 (645), 4650 (x³ A 114), 4670 (x⁴ A 158), 6052 (VIII¹ A 227), 6152 (IX A 42), 6252 (283), 6521 (x² A 157), 6658 (x³ A 409), 6685 (519), 6837 (x⁵ A 72), 6914 (XI¹ A 586).

Proud Henry. 5293 (II A 686).

Proverbs. 5971 (VIII¹ A 2).

PROVIDENCE (see also Governance). 741 (III A 195), 1010 (VII¹ A 180), 1117 (61), 1242 (IV C 55), 1308 (II A 657), 1347 (VII¹ A 139), 1450 (XI² A 170), 1587 (III A 1), 2083 (XI² A 259), 2139 (x² A 203), 3062 (x⁴ A 442), 3662 (x³ A 740), 4097 (II A 531).

Prudence. 1853 (x¹ A 455), 3351 (VIII¹ A 188), 3357 (x³ A 143), 3361 (XI¹ A 367), 3503 (x³ A 141), 3884 (XI² A 20), 4492 (XI² A 225), 4718 (XI¹ A 494), 6890 (277).

Prussia, King of. 5831 (VI B 233).

Prussians. 4146 (IX A 31).

Psalms. 2830 (III A 78), 4588 (VI A 46).

Pseudonymous works. 5639 (IV A 75), 5648 (89), 5803 (VI A 40), 5826 (83), 5828 (85), 6407 (x¹ A 351), 6567 (x⁶ B 245).

Pseudonyms (see also Anti-Climacus, Constantin Constantius, Esaias Strandsand, Felix de St. Vincent, FF, Frater Taciturnus, H. H., Hilarius Bookbinder, Johannes Climacus, Johannes de Silentio, Johannes the Seducer, Judge William, M.M., Nicolaus Notabene, "Phister as Scipio," P. P., Procul, Quidam, Rosenblad, Rosenpind, Simon Stylita, Victor Eremita, Victorin Victorius Victor, Vigilius Haufniensis, William Afham). 3846 (I C 69), 5657 (IV B 97:1), 5728 (V A 21), 5755 (110), 5803 (VI A 40), 5804 (41), 5827 (84), 5828 (85), 5862 (VII¹ B 75), 5865 (83), 5877 (VII¹ A 9), 5893 (106), 5896 (109), 5939 (150), 5942 (156), 5980 (VIII¹ A 27), 6037 (229), 6201 (IX A 166), 6255 (IX B 63:7), 6327 (x¹ A 78), 6357 (139), 6363 (152), 6366 (161), 6374 (192), 6387 (263), 6393 (300),

6416 (422), 6421 (450), 6431 (510), 6440 (531), 6441 (535), 6446 (548), 6461 (593), 6505 (x² A 89), 6506 (90), 6530 (192), 6553 (273), 6558 (x⁶ B 130), 6559 (131), 6560 (L. 240), 6566 (x⁶ B 127), 6567 (245), 6574 (121), 6577 (x² A 375), 6578 (393), 6590 (525), 6596 (x⁶ B 128), 6597 (x² A 601), 6602 (605), 6650 (x³ A 210), 6654 (258), 6701 (629), 6786 (x⁶ B 145, pp. 202-203), 6787 (253), 6838 (x⁵ A 93), 6893 (xi¹ A 315), 6901 (439).

Psyche. 3709 (x² A 614), 3978 (iv A 28), 4381 (x⁴ A 462).

Psychological experiment. 6870 (xi¹ A 131).

Psychology. 4151 (ix A 354), 4161 (x¹ A 369), 4538 (vi A 63), 6311 (x¹ A 43), 6710 (x³ A 716), 6726 (x⁴ A 23).

Public (see also Crowd; Many; Mass; NUMBERS). 156 (vii¹ A 51), 192 (xi² A 404), 499 (x¹ A 399), 594 (579), 938 (vii¹ A 251), 1088 (x⁴ A 590), 1089 (591), 1617 (385), 2004 (viii¹ A 482), 2018 (x² A 179), 2030 (x³ A 476), 2050 (xi¹ A 81), 2151 (viii¹ A 399), 2161 (x¹ A 341), 2165 (x³ A 231), 2514 (x² A 559), 2539 (x⁴ A 371), 2548 (xi¹ A 108), 2566 (486), 2652 (x¹ A 220), 2741 (vii¹ A 38), 2766 (67), 3064 (x⁵ A 159), 3229 (xi² A 431), 3347 (x³ A 16), 4112 (vii¹ A 63), 4116 (viii¹ A 108), 4131 (598), 4160 (x¹ A 356), 4163 (632), 4172 (x² A 391), 4173 (394), 4174 (395), 4235 (xi² A 23), 4541 (viii¹ A 8), 4873 (x³ A 652), 4880 (x⁴ A 391), 4968 (x³ A 15), 5881 (vii¹ B 211), 6105 (viii¹ A 544), 6440 (x¹ A 531), 6472 (x⁵ A 149), 6886 (xi¹ A 242).

"Public Confession." 6201 (ix A 166).

Publican. 867 (ii A 322), 4165 (x¹ A 682).

Publication. 6046 (L. 154), 6047 (L. 156), 6511 (x² A 106), 6595 (596), 6674 (x³ A 423).

Public relations. 2985 (xi² A 26).

Publishing. 2767 (vii¹ A 77), 5773 (vi B 8:1-2), 5881 (vii¹ B 211), 6048 (L. 157), 6489 (x² A 10), 6517 (147).

Pückler-Muskua. 5071 (i A 41).

Punctuation. 5981 (viii¹ A 33), 5983-86 (35-38), 5993 (68).

PUNISHMENT. 424 (ii A 83), 890 (iii A 230), 1183 (ii A 50), 1201 (iii A 215), 1268 (x⁴ A 175), 1345 (vii¹ A 62), 1367 (ix A 75), 1464 (i A 82), 1653 (x² A 353), 2208 (i A 49), 2499 (x¹ A 545), 2563 (xi¹ A 37), 2567 (589), 2576 (xi² A 166), 3995 (ii A 64), 4023 (x¹ A 637), 4073 (i A 310), 4636 (x¹ A 603), 5027 (xi¹ A 286), 5641 (iv A 77).

"Purity of Heart" (see also Upbuilding Discourses in Various Spirits). 5919 (vii¹ B 136), 5948 (vii¹ A 176).

Purpose. 112 (iv C 20), 115 (x⁵ A 31), 3627 (ii A 681).

Pythagoras. 124 (i A 175), 198 (iv A 38), 703 (57), 751 (i A 113), 790 (197), 1482 (x³ A 784), 1709 (ii A 591), 2324 (x² A 235), 2334 (xi² A 128), 2335 (129), 3289 (iv A 19), 3295 (55), 5100 (i A 75), 5616 (iv A 56), 6237 (ix A 226).

Quakers. 218 (i A 301), 4843 (ii A 296), 4874 (x³ A 664).

Qualitative. 1910 (x⁴ A 492), 2345 (v C 1).

QUALITATIVE DIFFERENCE. 77 (x³ A 186), 236 (x¹ A 135), 352 (x² A 422), 981 (178), 1349 (vii¹ A 201), 1377 (ix A 315), 1385 (x¹ A 64), 1386 (196), 1393 (x² A 64), 1416 (x³ A 694), 1431 (x⁴ A 640), 1432 (x⁵ A 23), 1433 (39), 1447 (xi² A 130), 1958 (ix A 260), 2074 (xi¹ A 518), 2561 (x⁵ A 47), 2974 (xi¹ A 325), 4696 (x⁵ A 11), 6075 (viii¹ A 414), 6076 (415).

Quality. 759 (vii¹ A 84), 1599 (iv C 67), 1600 (68), 1986 (v A 53), 2534 (x⁴ A 25), 2721 (x³ A 532), 2958 (656), 3102 (xi² A 212), 4197 (x⁴ A 40), 4234 (xi¹ A 536), 4335 (x³ A 493), 4493 (xi² A 232), 4806 (xi¹ A 329), 5594 (iv C 41).

Quantity. 759 (vii¹ A 84), 1599 (iv C 67), 1600 (68), 1986 (v A 53), 2010 (ix A 356), 2345 (v C 1), 2958 (x³ A 656), 4202 (x⁴ A 63), 4335 (x³ A 493), 4806 (xi¹ A 329), 4866 (x² A 463), 4874 (x³ A 664).

Quantity/quality. 2813 (vii¹ A 191), 5712 (v A 100).

Quarters. 6268 (ix A 375), 6472 (x⁵ A 149).

Quidam. 5804 (vi A 41), 5805 (vi B 41:10), 5834 (vi A 94), 5865 (vii¹ B 83), 5939 (vii¹ A 150), 6410 (x¹ A 377), 6604 (x² A 622).

Quiet. 4506 (x^4 A 434), 4965 (x^2 A 143), 5048 (xi^2 A 35).

Quiet hours. 2132 (x^5 A 51), 6667 (x^3 A 399), 6677 (434), 6679 (448).

Quietism. 1568 (II A 48), 2132 (x^5 A 51), 2751 (IX A 362).

Quintilian. 3512 (x^3 A 479).

Quotation (of pseudonymous works). 6567 (x^6 B 245).

Race. 51 (V B 53:15), 213 (x^3 A 348), 558 (xi^1 A 444), 783 (II A 5), 1818 (xi^2 A 201), 1906 (x^4 A 369), 2054 (xi^1 A 168), 2059 (272), 2071 (485), 2079 (xi^2 A 124), 2439 (x^4 A 642), 2566 (xi^1 A 486), 2622 (xi^2 A 150), 2664 (xi^1 A 114), 2821 (x^2 A 362), 2910 (xi^1 A 392), 3361 (367), 3643 (289), 3970 (xi^2 A 202), 5035 (203), 6932 (206).

Race analogy. 6945 (xi^3 B 55).

Rachel. 448 (II A 547), 1027 (III A 62), 5475 (V A 83).

Radical cure. 415 (I A 89), 496 (x^1 A 190), 2905 (xi^1 A 138), 3247 (I A 99), 3612 (x^2 A 461), 4299 (x^5 A 69), 4690 (x^4 A 620).

"Radical Cure." 6210 (IX A 176).

Rafn, Carl C. 265 (II A 12), 3999 (584), 5130 (I C 84), 5131 (85), 5209 (II A 36), 5224 (590), 5714 (V A 102).

Rahbek, Knud L. 4828 (IV C 112), 5212 (II A 43), 5213 (44).

Railroads. 4179 (x^2 A 497).

Rain-warners. 5842 (VI A 119).

Ramus, Petrus. 5728 (V A 21).

Randers. 5472 (III A 79).

Rank. 4666 (x^3 A 783).

Raphael. 164 (IX A 110).

Rask, Hans K. 5151 (I A 188).

Rat. 5565 (III A 246).

Rationalism. 418 (I A 97), 1304 (29), 1332 (IV A 57), 3246 (I A 98), 3808 (216), 5092 (72), 5156 (220).

Rationalists. 5156 (I A 220).

Raumer, Friedrich v. 2703 (I C 113), 5079 (48), 5083 (51), 5085 (53), 5086 (54), 5167 (106), 5169 (108), 5174 (I A 266).

Reading. 209 (IX A 442), 210 (x^2 A 555), 211 (556), 213 (x^3 A 348), 1288 (II A 26), 2564 (xi^1 A 65), 2865 (x^1 A 221), 2874 (x^3 A 169), 2884 (590), 2886 (x^4 A 122), 2897 (x^5 A 78), 2917 (xi^2 A 364), 3248 (I A 127), 3649 (xi^1 A 67), 3855 (II A 122), 5114 (I A 109), 5117 (118), 5297 (II A 693), 5413 (817), 5731 (V B 72:22), 5939 (VII^1 A 150), 5944 (158), 5948 (176), 5951 (202), 5952 (VII^1 B 212), 6095 (VIII^2 B 188), 6288 (IX A 471), 6355 (x^1 A 137), 6363 (152), 6749 (x^6 B 173, pp. 274-276), 6770 (4:3).

Reading aloud. 5825 (VI A 82), 5981 (VIII^1 A 33), 5982 (34), 6004 (120), 6627 (x^3 A 128), 6768 (x^4 A 322).

Realists. 782 (II A 4), 784 (6), 3353 (IX A 133).

REALITY (see also Actuality). 977 (x^1 A 580), 1444 (xi^2 A 53), 1544 (II A 214), 2271 (528), 2309 (155), 6846 (xi^2 A 296), 6858 (xi^1 A 155).

REASON (see also Understanding). 6 (V A 78), 7 (x^2 A 354), 47 (V A 20), 48 (25), 416 (I A 95), 486 (IX A 292), 536 (x^4 A 581), 791 (550), 810 (V A 35), 1110 (IV A 191), 1305 (I A 30), 1340 (V B 5:8), 1540 (I A 237), 1764 (x^3 A 228), 2361 (IV A 12), 2813 (VII^1 A 191), 3032 (IX A 427), 3049 (VIII^1 A 331), 3073 (IV C 29), 3109 (x^3 A 609), 3247 (I A 99), 3710 (x^2 A 624), 4080 (II A 219), 5092 (I A 72), 5997 (III A 115), 5638 (IV A 74).

Reasons. 1950 (x^1 A 372), 4752 (490), 4895 (x^4 A 350), 4900 (569).

Rebecca. 864 (II A 759).

Rebellion. 778 (VIII^1 A 7), 4582 (III A 99), 4599 (VIII^1 A 161), 5332 (II A 240).

Rebirth. 537 (x^4 A 616), 1882 (x^3 A 552), 3101 (xi^2 A 81), 3321 (x^4 A 84).

Receiving. 1204 (IV A 66).

Receptivity. 878 (II A 536).

Recognition. 15 (x^4 A 71).

Recognizability. 3099 (xi^2 A 51), 4766 (x^4 A 139), 6702 (x^3 A 635), 6740 (x^4 A 130).

Recollection (see also Remembering). 646 (VIII^1 A 554), 854 (I A 254), 947 (VIII^1 A 236), 1667 (V A 55), 2274 (III A 5), 2834 (VI A 90), 2840 (VII^1 B 205), 2845 (210), 2606 (V B 40), 3942 (x^2 A 597), 5331 (II A 238), 5368 (347), 5514 (III C 26), 5621 (IV B 1), 5671 (A 119), 5875 (VII^1 A 6), 5904 (117), 6381 (L. 243), 6414 (x^1 A 404), 6636 (x^6 B 137).

Reconciliation (*see also* Atonement). 532 (x⁴ A 212), 1207 (vIII¹ A 114), 1208 (115).

Redeemer. 287 (II A 261), 1920 (x⁵ A 45).

Redemption. 412 (I A 27), 837 (vIII¹ A 56), 857 (II A 150), 1690 (102), 1934 (xI¹ A 492), 1936 (573), 1984 (III A 136), 3245 (I A 94), 3368 (II A 309), 3628 (vII¹ A 130), 3706 (IX A 383), 4021 (x¹ A 433), 4118 (vIII¹ A 123), 4368 (IX A 331), 4370 (333), 5145 (I A 173), 5181 (328), 5275 (II A 629), 6435 (x¹ A 519).

REDOUBLING. 188 (x² A 396), 653 (vIII² B 85), 1425 (x⁴ A 253), 1431 (640), 1433 (x⁵ A 39), 1447 (xI² A 130), 1793 (x³ A 670), 1822 (xI² A 267), 1917 (x⁵ A 9), 2906 (xI¹ A 154), 3665 (vIII¹ A 91), 4571 (xI² A 97), 5007 (192), 6446 (x¹ A 548), 6878 (xI¹ A 171).

REDUPLICATION. 8 (x² A 592), 188 (396), 484 (IX A 207), 518 (x³ A 100), 646 (vIII¹ A 554), 660 (IX A 198), 666 (x¹ A 122), 965 (IX A 418), 982 (x² A 201), 995 (x⁴ A 176), 1042 (vII¹ A 80), 1049 (vIII¹ A 292), 1131 (x¹ A 395), 1793 (x⁴ A 176), 2119 (vIII¹ A 511), 2512 (x² A 448), 2803 (529), 2805 (xI¹ A 217), 3107 (x³ A 544), 3142 (x² A 550), 3349 (x³ A 482), 3483 (x¹ A 182), 3497 (x² A 581), 3705 (IX A 365), 3746 (486), 4052 (x¹ A 17), 4265 (vII¹ A 69), 4540 (72), 4553 (x² A 336), 4564 (x⁴A 346), 4934 (x³ A 471), 6224 (IX A 208), 6239 (229), 6491 (x² A 15), 6592 (544), 6593 (560), 6646 (x³ A 190), 6680 (450), 6917 (xI² A 19).

REFLECTION (*see also* Thought). 38 (III A 25), 48 (v A 25), 49 (28), 234 (vIII² B 13:61-63), 497 (x¹ A 217), 522 (x³ A 209), 615 (xI² A 263), 630 (vI A 147), 632 (vI B 38), 641 (vIII¹ A 293), 649 (vIII² B 81:21), 912 (v A 72), 942 (vIII¹ A 189), 1088 (x⁴ A 540), 1089 (541), 1123 (vIII¹ A 649), 1191 (II A 592), 1261 (x² A 428), 1298 (x¹ A 590), 1376 (IX A 305), 1624 (II A 729), 1634 (III B 15), 1680 (II A 38), 1781 (x¹ A 646), 1961 (x⁴ A 91), 1999 (vIII¹ A 126), 2004 (482), 2034 (x³ A 763), 2309-2314 (II A 155-160), 2338 (IV c 11), 2454 (xI² A 421), 2650 (x¹ A 16), 2659 (x³ A 303), 2689 (vIII¹ A 341), 2998 (xI² A 159), 3129 (vIII¹ A 92), 3130 (x²A

594), 3257 (II A 198), 3308 (vII¹A 82), 3309 (152), 3313 (vIII¹ A 627), 3447 (x² A 595), 3536 (xI¹ A 504), 3579 (x⁴ A 614), 3685 (x³ A 545), 3697 (I A 128), 3698 (II A 157), 3704 (IX A 248), 3705 (365), 3707 (x¹ A 66), 3708 (330), 3711 (x² A 636), 3715 (x⁴ A 525), 3718 (xI² A 273), 3745 (IX A 224), 3857 (II A 188), 3859 (563), 3865 (xI¹ A 461), 3879 (178), 4109 (vII¹ A 17), 4118 (vIII¹ A 123), 4143 (636), 4385 (I A 52), 4415 (II A 515), 4426 (vI A 52), 4438 (vII² B 266:26), 4457 (x² A 279), 4642 (x² A 131), 4798 (x³ A 47), 4903 (x⁵ A 17), 4927 (II A 428), 4956 (455), 4991 (x¹ A 436), 5116 (I B 2), 5411 (II A 549), 5783 (vI B 130), 6061 (vIII¹ A 347), 6074 (407), 6135 (650), 6207 (IX A 173), 6211 (178), 6212 (179), 6213 (180), 6216 (185), 6234 (222), 6235 (223), 6237 (226), 6244 (251), 6265 (343), 6293 (IX B 68), 6308 (x¹ A 39), 6326 (77), 6373 (187), 6414 (404), 6429 (497), 6435 (519), 6501 (x¹ A 66), 6511 (x² A 106), 6595 (596), 6642 (x³ A 168), 6649 (204), 6739 (x⁴ A 101), 6770 (x⁶ B 4:3), 6901 (xI¹ A 439), 6921 (xI² A 36), 6969 (439).

Reflection and object. 3257 (II A 198).

REFORM. 599 (x⁴ A 22), 4118 (vIII¹ A 123), 4153 (IX A 445), 4208 (x⁴ A 102), 6432 (x¹ A 513), 6463 (598), 6477 (660), 6581 (x² A 415), 6593 (560), 6721 (x⁴ A 6), 6727 (33), 6774 (358), 6871 (xI¹ A 133), 6921 (xI² A 36).

REFORMATION. 209 (IX A 442), 471 (vIII¹ A 435), 737 (I A 181), 786 (vIII¹ A 257), 1484 (x⁴ A 230), 1681 (II A 447), 1821 (xI² A 344), 1968 (II A 53), 2130 (x⁴ A 26), 2469 (IX A 96), 2481 (x¹ A 154), 2603 (IX A 434), 2628 (xI² A 231), 2751 (IX A 362), 2929 (vIII¹ A 461), 3799 (I A 134), 4116 (vIII¹ A 108), 4207 (x⁴ A 97), 4781 (x² A 548), 5979 (vIII¹ A 23), 6255 (IX B 63:7), 6256 (x⁶ B 40), 6367 (x¹ A 162), 6720 (x³ A 800).

Reformatory. 5990 (vIII¹ A 46).

REFORMERS. 1001 (x⁴ A 571), 1227 (77), 2514 (x² A 559), 2546 (xI¹ A 61), 3575 (x⁴ A 398), 4187 (x³ A 575), 5835 (vI A 95), 6061 (vIII¹ A 347), 6344 (x¹ A 113), 6719 (x³ A 799), 6720 (800).

Regine (*see* Olsen, Regine).

Regression. 992 (x³ A 715).

Regret. 5994 (viii¹ A 71).

Reitzel, Carl A. 5768 (vi A 4), 6030 (L. 152), 6035 (viii¹ A 227), 6048 (L. 157), 6416 (x¹ A 422), 6489 (x² A 10), 6526 (177), 6961 (xi³ B 129), 6962 (131).

Relativism. 492 (ix A 394), 815 (289), 1405 (x² A 644), 2675 (ix A 149).

Relativity. 414 (i A 46), 480 (ix A 28), 486 (292), 528 (x⁴ A 28), 815 (ix A 289), 1304 (ii A 29), 2010 (ix A 356), 4905 (x⁵ A 118), 6679 (x³ A 448).

Relaxation. 4688 (x⁴ A 593), 6013 (viii¹ A 163).

Religion. 54 (v B 198), 625 (vi B 10), 650 (viii² B 82), 653 (85), 742 (iii A 238), 757 (vi A 51), 795 (i A 150), 838 (viii¹ A 73), 941 (144), 1017 (x² A 348), 1096 (i A 273), 1097 (ii A 190), 1370 (ix A 113), 2092 (x² A 578), 2106 (x⁴ A 220), 2111 (iv A 86), 2345 (v c 1), 2793 (x² A 341), 3163 (x⁴ A 332), 3325 (iv A 159), 3614 (x⁴ A 162), 3621 (xi¹ A 213), 3632 (267), 3849 (ii A 91), 4107 (vi A 1), 4172 (x² A 391), 4364 (vi A 2), 4426 (52), 4442 (viii¹ A 78), 4722 (xi¹ A 579), 5067 (i c 34), 5637 (iv A 71), 5642 (79), 5668 (113), 5722 (v B 148:5), 5975 (viii¹ A 15), 6265 (ix A 343), 6580 (x² A 413), 6615 (x³ A 68), 6967 (xi² A 437).

Religious. 151 (vi A 43), 625 (vi B 10), 1330 (iv A 106), 1336 (v A 42), 1405 (x² A 644), 2418 (ix A 88), 3632 (xi¹ A 267), 3690 (x⁴ A 214), 4364 (vi A 2), 4464 (x³ A 512), 4467 (791), 5804 (vi A 41), 6209 (ix A 175), 6330 (x¹ A 88), 6719 (x³ A 799).

Religious address. 626 (vi B 11), 631 (vi A 149), 1036 (136), 5783-5 (vi B 130-32), 5786 (vi A 146), 6037 (viii¹ A 229).

Religious life. 237 (x² A 194), 1370 (ix A 113), 2671 (x³ A 57), 4450 (ix A 204), 4460 (x² A 642), 4650 (x³ A 114), 4722 (xi¹ A 579), 6612 (x³A 30).

Religious prototypes. 1838 (viii¹ A 335).

Religiousness. 46 (v A 16), 2116 (vi B 98:77), 4141 (viii¹ A 618), 4170 (x² A 351), 4459 (318).

Remembering (*see also* Recollection). 898 (iv A 82), 2845 (vii¹ B 210).

Remorse. 1527 (vi A 49).

Renewal. 562 (xi² A 110), 6043 (viii¹ A 250).

RENUNCIATION (*see also* Self-denial). 178 (x⁵ A 99), 462 (viii¹ A 130), 477 (ix A 13), 500 (x¹ A 427), 763 (x² A 132), 1123 (viii¹ A 649), 1258 (x² A 159), 1490 (x⁵ A 54), 1497 (xi² A 284), 1948 (vii¹ A 244), 1952 (x⁴ A 440), 2119 (viii¹ A 511), 2222 (x⁴ A 572), 2224 (xi¹ A 139), 2225 (151), 2709 (viii¹ A 592), 2974 (xi¹ A 325), 3061 (x¹ A 600), 3097 (x⁵ A 142), 3123 (75), 3334 (x³ A 574), 3761 (x⁴ A 326), 3828 (224), 3881 (xi¹ A 181), 4497 (102), 4518 (x⁵ A 63), 4529 (xi¹ A 397), 4704 (8), 4769 (x⁴ A 142), 4939 (538), 4964 (x¹ A 209), 5772 (vi A 12), 6206 (ix A 172), 6598 (x⁶ B 68), 6824 (x⁴ A 673), 6825 (674).

REPENTANCE. 237 (x² A 194), 299 (iii c 6), 902 (iv A 112), 1220 (x¹ A 12), 1315 (ii A 402), 1419 (x³ A 772), 1534 (719), 1991 (vi A 120), 2362 (iv A 26), 2390 (iii A 127), 3032 (ix A 427), 3078 (iv A 116), 3272 (ii A 426), 4825 (iii A 199), 4947 (vii¹ B 145), 4948 (146), 5143 (i A 166), 5383 (ii A 420), 5669 (iv A 114), 5961 (vii¹ A 221), 6001 (viii¹ A 116), 6002 (119), 6327 (x¹ A 78), 6364 (156), 6384 (272), 6395 (320), 6444 (541), 6472 (x⁵ A 149).

REPETITION. 804 (iii A 95), 982 (x² A 201), 1201 (iii A 215), 1246 (iv B 118:1), 4741 (x³ A 727), 5162 (i A 244), 5757 (L. 113), 5792 (vi B 18), 5823 (vi A 78), 5950 (vii¹ c 5), 5978 (viii¹ A 18), 6318 (x¹ A 58), 6472 (x⁵ A 149), 6519 (x² A 148).

Repetition. 3794 (iv A 169), 5654 (101), 5655 (L. 80), 5657 (iv B 97:1), 5665 (L. 82), 5694 (iv A 153), 5704 (178), 5757 (L. 113), 6063 (L. 150), 6357 (x¹ A 139), 6521 (x² A 157).

"Report." 5886 (vii¹ A 97), 5887 (98), 5888 (99), 5889 (101), 5890-5908 (103-121), 5909 (124).

Requirement. 489 (ix A 329), 1476 (x³ A 72), 1492 (x⁵ A 64), 1498 (xi² A 285), 3530 (x⁵ A 62), 3680 (x³ A 232), 4869 (85), 6275 (ix A 413), 6688 (x³ A 550), 6946 (xi³ B 56), 6947 (57).

Reserve (*see* Closed reserve).

Resignation. 538 (x⁴ A 624), 562 (xɪ² A 110), 724 (x³ A 724), 748 (vɪɪɪ² B 159:4), 906 (ɪv A 155), 1123 (vɪɪɪ¹ A 649), 1676 (ɪ A 239), 1870 (x³ A 294), 2180 (ɪɪɪ c 18), 2454 (xɪ² A 421), 2455 (426), 3130 (x² A 594), 3551 (ɪɪ A 32), 4398 (ɪ c 126), 5507 (ɪɪɪ A 147), 5517 (161), 5521 (166), 5903 (vɪɪ¹ A 116), 5913 (126), 6135 (vɪɪɪ¹ A 650).

Resistance. 1195 (x⁴ A 127).

Resolution (see Decision).

Response. 1647 (xɪ¹ A 388), 3415 (vɪɪɪ¹ A 342).

Responsibility. 68 (vɪɪɪ² B 168:5), 94 (ɪɪɪ A 233), 890 (230), 1232 (ɪ A 205), 2152 (vɪɪɪ¹ A 540), 2691 (x¹ A 400), 2882 (x³ A 549), 3949 (213), 4031 (x² A 437), 4348 (xɪ¹ A 211).

Rest. 2731 (xɪ¹ A 345), 4362 (xɪ² A 353).

Restlessness. 4361 (xɪ² A 317), 4362 (353), 4489 (29), 6717 (x³ A 782).

Results. 910 (ɪv A 72), 911 (179), 956 (vɪɪɪ¹ A 494), 2293 (vɪɪ¹ A 75), 3254 (ɪɪ A 586), 3296 (ɪv A 163), 3358 (x³ A 460), 3359 (461), 3630 (vɪɪɪ¹ A 329), 3644 (xɪ² A 96), 4977 (x⁵ A 18).

Resurrection. 273 (ɪ A 28), 337 (x¹ A 354), 1665 (ɪɪɪ A 129), 1682 (ɪɪ A 78), 2866 (x¹ A 287), 2867 (288), 5476 (ɪɪɪ A 84).

Retraction. 6374 (x¹ A 192).

Retrogression. 4918 (xɪ² A 205).

Return. 5528 (ɪɪɪ A 172), 5535 (179).

Reuchlin, Hermann. 525 (x³ A 649), 3037 (622), 3110 (626), 3111-3115 (630-634), 3116 (639), 3117 (640), 3119 (642), 3120 (644), 3122 (646), 3123 (x⁵ A 75).

Revelation. 204 (ɪɪ A 287), 1216 (vɪɪɪ¹ A 675), 1333 (ɪv A 190), 1335 (v A 8), 1372 (ɪx A 182), 1684 (ɪɪ A 80), 1960 (x³ A 659), 2092 (x² A 578), 2207 (ɪ A 48), 2266 (ɪɪ A 523), 2299 (ɪx A 438), 2461 (vɪɪ¹ A 192), 2882 (x³ A 549), 2899 (x⁵ A 135), 3110 (x³ A 626), 3262 (ɪɪ c 56), 3900 (x¹ A 255), 4006 (ɪv A 189), 6139 (vɪɪɪ² B 166).

Revenge. 1193 (x² A 564), 1325 (ɪɪɪ A 102), 1464 (ɪ A 82), 5258 (ɪɪ A 649).

Reviews. 5709 (ɪv A 193), 5877 (vɪɪ¹ A 9), 5936 (vɪɪ² B 242), 5944 (vɪɪ¹ A 158), 6550 (x² A 256), 6779 (x⁴ A 380).

Revolution. 6523 (x² A 163).

Reward. 911 (ɪv A 179), 1809 (xɪ¹ A 429).

Rheinwald Reportorium. 5202 (ɪɪ c 11).

Rhetoric. 824 (x⁴ A 633), 3535 (xɪ¹ A 477), 3715 (x⁴ A 525), 4283 (314), 5779-5783 (vɪ c 2-5).

Rhetorical, the. 5981 (vɪɪɪ¹ A 33), 6136 (651).

Riccoboni, Luigi. 4837 (ɪv c121).

Richard III. 6882 (xɪ¹ A 210).

Richter, Johann Paul F. (see also Jean Paul). 1696 (ɪɪ A 108).

Riddle. 5640 (ɪv A 76), 5837 (vɪ A 98).

Ride. 5251 (ɪɪ A 637), 5499 (ɪɪɪ A 121).

Ridicule. 4663 (x³ A 731).

Right hand. 5639 (ɪv A 75), 5648 (89), 6407 (x¹ A 351).

Righteousness. 1465 (ɪɪ A 656), 1537 (xɪ² A 4), 1538 (5).

Rights. 4131 (vɪɪɪ¹ A 598).

Rigor. 1422 (x⁴ A 132), 1500 (xɪ² A 100), 1502 (226), 1793 (x³ A 670), 2883 (582), 3770 (x⁵ A 29), 4336 (x³ A 579), 4982 (xɪ¹ A 191).

Rigorousness. 3017 (x³ A 384), 6614 (67), 6633 (161).

Riise, Johan C. 3540 (xɪ² A 281).

Riises Bibliothek for Ungdommen. 5104 (ɪ A 79).

Ring. 5509 (ɪɪɪ A 149), 5530 (174).

Ringkjøbing. 5467 (ɪɪɪ A 72).

Risk (see also VENTURE). 1438 (xɪ¹ A 188), 2751 (ɪx A 362), 3343 (352), 4537 (vɪ B 19:1-10), 4930 (ɪx A 351), 4931 (x² A 144).

Ritter, Heinrich. 938 (vɪɪ¹ A 251), 3896 (47), 4883 (xɪ¹ A 57), 5577 (ɪv A 201), 5921 (vɪɪ¹ A 44).

Roadblock. 1792 (x³ A 576), 4998 (47), 6642 (168).

Robert le diable. 3999 (ɪɪ A 584), 5714 (v A 102).

Romance. 5178 (ɪ A 286).

Romans. 5268 (ɪɪ A 182).

Romantic. 17 (ɪ A 137), 422 (ɪɪ A 30), 755 (ɪɪɪ A 92), 771 (vɪɪɪ¹ A 59), 832 (ɪɪ A 100), 1183 (50), 1521 (134), 1565 (ɪ A 225), 1669 (125), 1679 (ɪɪ A 37), 1680 (38), 1682 (78), 1688 (627), 3819 (638), 5061 (ɪ A 11).

ROMANTICISM. 16 (ɪ A 135), 17 (137), 421 (215), 699 (324), 852 (221), 1232 (205), 1563 (170), 1966 (248), 2304 (250), 3268 (ɪɪ A 788), 4063 (ɪ A 139), 4070

(307), 4072 (309), 4398 (I C 126), 5131 (85), 5137 (89).

Rooster. 5284 (II A 205).

Rosenblad, Willibald A. A. T. H. 5759 (VI B 194), 5786 (VI A 146).

Rosenborg and Tornebuskegade. 6489 (x² A 10), 6501 (66), 6629 (x³ A 144).

Rosenhoff, Caspar C. 5312 (II A 28), 5909 (VII¹ A 124).

Rosenkrantz, Karl. 2211 (II A 71), 2747 (II C 61), 3795 (V B 69), 5222 (II A 92).

Rosenpind, Willibald A. A. T. H. 5759 (VI B 194).

Rosenvinge, Janus L. A. Kolderup-. 762 (x¹ A 219), 2769 (55).

Rosenørn, Mathias H. 5473 (III A 80).

Roskilde. 6550 (x² A 256), 6553 (273), 6557 (280), 6558 (x⁶ B 130), 6559 (131), 6581 (x² A 415).

Ross, Mrs. 5292 (II A 685).

Rothe, Richard. 1531 (x² A 500), 3789 (x¹ A 515), 3826 (x³ A 559), 4341 (x⁴ A 226), 4994 (x³ A 554).

Rötscher, Heinrich T. 1088 (x⁴ A 590), 2344 (V B 150:21), 2350 (V C 8), 4246 (III B 30), 4840 (V A 80), 5748 (88).

Round men. 2078 (XI² A 69).

ROUSSEAU, Jean Jacques. 2595 (VIII¹ A 52), 4284 (x⁴ A 319), 6794 (488).

Routine. 1402 (x² A 494).

Royal court analogy. 5403 (II A 520).

Royal service. 6728 (x⁴ A 36), 6919 (XI² A 31).

Ruckert, Leopold I. 5068 (I C 35).

Rudelbach, Andreas G. 384 (x¹ A 672), 1014 (VIII¹ A 665), 1516 (x⁴ A 269), 1517 (278), 1584 (II A 811), 1845 (IX A 7), 2961 (x⁴ A 100), 3309 (VII¹ A 152), 3460 (x⁴ A 281), 3839 (264), 3840 (276), 3841 (277), 3842 (279), 3869 (XI² A 94), 4164 (x¹ A 669), 4209 (x⁴ A 126), 4212 (186), 4880 (x⁴ A 391), 6223 (IX A 205), 6477 (x¹ A 660), 6725 (x⁴ A 20), 6728 (36), 6729 (37), 6749 (x⁶ B 173, pp. 274-276), 6778 (x⁴ A 377), 6847 (XI² A 311), 6851 (334), 6854 (XI³ B 15).

Running. 5212 (II A 43).

Ruus, Peder. 626 (VI B 11).

Ruysbroek, Jan. 2759 (x⁴ A 374).

Rørdam, Bolette. 5219 (II A 67).

Rørdam, Peter. 5219 (II A 67), 5220 (68), 5238 (617), 5848 (VI A 134).

Rørdam family. 6472 (x⁵ A 149).

Røyen, Mads N. 5331 (II A 238).

Sack, Karl H. 5350 (II C 60).

Sacraments. 543 (x⁵ A 144), 586 (II A 522), 600 (x⁴ A 246), 1467 (VI A 154), 1493 (x⁵ A 101), 1494 (103), 1905 (x⁴ A 366), 1924 (XI¹ A 4), 2918 (XI² A 386), 5047 (XI¹ A 556).

SACRIFICE. 374 (VIII¹ A 629), 504 (x¹ A 471), 838 (VIII¹ A 73), 1087 (x⁴ A 518), 1404 (x² A 591), 2059 (XI¹ A 272), 2967 (x⁵ A 123), 3680 (x³ A 232), 4057 (XI² A 161), 4170 (x² A 351), 4700 (x⁵ A 81), 4899 (x⁴ A 509), 4906 (XI¹ A 7), 4953 (XI² A 86), 4975 (x⁴ A 381), 5885 (VII¹ A 27), 6182 (IX A 125), 6185 (130), 6485 (x¹ A 671), 6843 (x⁵ A 146), 6868 (XI¹ A 128), 6901 (439), 6943 (XI³ B 53).

Sagacity. 6661 (x³ A 321), 6890 (XI¹ A 277).

Sagas. 1670 (I A 145), 5209 (II A 36).

Sager, Hans C. 5778 (VII¹ A 11).

St. Martins Eve. 5481 (L. 23).

St. Victor, Hugo de. 1653 (x² A 353), 3941 (350).

St. Victor, Richard de. 5039 (x² A 373).

Sales, Franz v. 5580 (IV C 9).

Salt. 2667 (XI² A 68), 2974 (XI¹ A 325).

Salvation. 413 (I A 40), 434 (II A 252), 617 (I A 327), 700 (III A 112), 712 (II A 213), 832 (100), 851 (I A 152), 1108 (IV A 117), 1278 (XI² A 424), 1350 (VIII¹ A 24), 1940 (XI² A 434), 2074 (XI¹ A 518), 2176 (II A 506), 2208 (I A 49), 2388 (III A 89), 2452 (XI² A 105), 2729 (x⁵ A 102), 2856 (II A 149), 3247 (I A 99), 3547 (I A 295), 3628 (VII¹ A 130), 3633 (VI A 62), 3706 (IX A 383), 4016 (341), 4600 (VIII¹ A 191), 4691 (x⁴ A 623), 4909 (XI¹ A 351), 4922 (296), 5449 (III A 44), 5454 (54), 6496 (x² A 44), 6834 (x⁵ A 46), 6928 (XI² A 79).

Samaritan. 2523 (x³ A 221), 2862 (VIII¹ A 311), 2894 (x⁵ A 15), 3480 (x¹ A 19).

Sarah. 2672 (x⁴ A 454), 5394 (II A 490).

Sardanapalus. 4303 (XI¹ A 449), 6794 (x⁴ A 488).

Satan. 2685 (XI² A 427), 3238 (XI¹ A 375), 5323 (II A 753).

Satire. 140 (II A 571), 189 (x³ A 540), 1800 (XI² A 294), 5262 (II A 166), 6282 (IX A 432), 6907 (XI¹ A 497).

Satisfaction. 1423 (x⁴ A 211), 3750 (x³ A 266), 3994 (II A 63).

Savior. 1223 (x³ A 573).

SAVONAROLA. 1516 (x⁴ A 269), 1517 (278), 1898 (275), 3460 (281), 3838 (IX A 295), 4562 (x⁴ A 283).

Scalpel. 1817 (XI² A 195).

Scandal. 3034 (x² A 117), 6651 (x³ A 219).

Scandinavian. 5832 (VI B 235), 6904 (XI¹ A 469).

Scarf. 5482 (L. 27).

Scatteredness. 377 (IX A 199).

Schaller, Julius. 3262 (II C 56).

Scharling, Carl E. 739 (II A 484), 5674 (x⁶ B 121), 5709 (IV A 193), 5944 (VII¹ A 158).

Scheherezade. 1511 (VIII¹ A 678), 4990 (485), 6274 (IX A 411).

Schelling, Friedrich W. J. v. 1114 (V C 13:4), 1190 (II A 31), 1332 (IV A 157), 1589 (III A 34), 1604 (IV A 185), 1612 (VIII¹ A 14), 2495 (x¹ A 420), 4112 (VII¹ A 63), 5513 (L. 49), 5535 (III A 179), 5536 (III C 27), 5542 (L. 54), 5543 (L. 55), 5544 (L. 56), 5551 (L. 68), 5599 (IV C 46), 6310 (x¹ A 42), 6456 (576), 6574 (x⁶ B 121).

Schikaneder, Emanuel. 5212 (II A 43).

Schiller, Johan C. F. v. 123 (I A 129), 4560 (x³ A 756), 5982 (VIII¹ A 34).

Schimmelmann, Heinrich. 5095 (I A 64).

Schlegel, August W. 1564 (I A 211), 3811 (219), 3846 (I C 69), 4219 (x⁴ A 575), 5157 (I A 223), 5194 (I C 117), 5198 (121), 5205 (II A 20), 5714 (V A 102).

Schlegel, Johan Frederik. 4219 (x⁴ A 575), 5205 (II A 20), 5693 (IV A 152), 5714 (V A 102), 5834 (VI A 94), 6083 (VIII¹ A 447), 6273 (IX A 408), 6304 (x¹ A 24), 6454 (570), 6472 (x⁵ A 149), 6473 (150), 6478 (VIII¹ A 661), 6480 (664), 6488 (x² A 3), 6538 (210), 6502 (68), 6537 (L. 239), 6539 (x² A 211), 6542 (214), 6544 (216), 6713 (x³ A 769), 6714 (770), 6715 (771), 6762 (x⁴ A 299), 6763 (300), 6800 (540), 6843 (x⁵ A 146).

SCHLEIERMACHER, Friedrich D. 173 (x² A 264), 410 (I A 4), 603 (XI² A 229), 1096 (I A 273), 1190 (II A 31), 1563 (I A 170), 2822 (x⁴ A 232), 3547 (I A 295), 3809 (217), 4245 (III B 27), 4250 (IV A 203),

4260 (124), 4386 (I A 121), 5117 (118), 5892 (VII¹ A 105), 6460 (x¹ A 588).

Schmidt, F. A. 6861 (XI¹ A 71).

Scholars and ethics. 928 (VII¹ A 28), 929 (29).

SCHOLARSHIP AND SCIENCE. 181 (XI² A 328), 529 (x⁴ A 78), 789 (x² A 455), 928 (VII¹ A 28), 929 (29), 1042 (80), 1058 (x² A 414), 2281 (IV C 23), 2570 (XI² A 54), 2806 (I A 31), 2814 (VII¹ A 194), 2823 (x⁵ A 73), 2872 (x³ A 34), 2911 (XI¹ A 395), 3021 (x⁴ A 403), 3118 (x³ A 641), 3243 (I A 35), 3255 (II A 176), 3285 (III C 32), 3564 (x¹ A 561), 3581 (XI² A 295), 3870 (117), 4168 (x² A 240), 4493 (XI² A 232), 4776 (II A 543), 4843 (296), 4927 (428), 6448 (x¹ A 553), 6449 (556).

Scholastic. 755 (III A 92), 4927 (II A 428).

Scholasticism. 3808 (I A 216), 4775 (II A 291).

SCHOPENHAUER, ARTHUR. 111 (XI¹ A 173), 1620 (180), 1621 (183), 2550 (193), 3362 (XI² A 7), 3970 (202), 4917 (204), 4998 (XI¹ A 141), 6883 (214).

Schouw, Joakim F. 5092 (I A 72).

Schubarth, Karl E. 5139 (I C 96).

Schubert, Gotthilf H. 1695 (II A 107), 2307 (62), 3623 (XI¹ A 247), 3992 (II A 19).

Schul[t]z. 3863 (x⁴ A 409).

Schulze, Hedwig. 5541 (III A 190).

Schwab, Gustav. 5714 (V A 102).

Schwarz, Carl. 2379 (XI² A 39).

Science (see SCHOLARSHIP AND SCIENCE).

Scolding. 6617 (x³ A 78).

Scott, Walter. 1687 (II A 85).

Scribe, Augustin E. 92 (x² A 79), 118 (I A 33), 744 (IV A 165), 970 (x¹ A 321), 1761 (148), 2241 (I A 23), 2410 (VIII¹ A 196), 4389 (I A 183), 4588 (VI A 46), 5548 (L. 62), 6395 (x¹ A 320), 6709 (x³ A 678).

Scriver, Christian. 726 (x⁴ A 60), 2325 (197), 2327 (199), 3200 (17), 3456 (x³ A 531), 3951 (706), 4468 (x⁴ A 59), 6644 (x³ A 183).

Scruples. 1817 (XI² A 195).

Sea. 2831 (III A 151), 2832 (152), 5095 (I A 64).

Sea-sickness. 5451 (III A 51).

Seasons. 5269 (II A 185).

Second coming. 340 (x¹ A 447), 6921 (xɪ² A 36).

Second hand. 1441 (xɪ¹ A 464).

Second spontaneity (*see* Spontaneity).

Second time. 479 (ɪx A 20), 3672 (474).

Secret. 5261 (ɪɪ A 164), 5624 (ɪv A 68), 5645 (85), 6078 (vɪɪɪ¹ A 424).

Secret agent. 2125 (x³ A 334), 2646 (ɪx A 495), 2661 (x³ A 511), 4953 (xɪ² A 86), 5770 (vɪ A 10), 5771 (11), 6192 (ɪx A 142), 6198 (155), 6221 (190), 6325 (x¹ A 74), 6752 (x⁴ A 201), 6887 (xɪ¹ A 258), 6894 (378), 6922 (xɪ² A 40), 6930 (121), 6936 (250).

Secret machinery. 6562 (x² A 285).

"The Secrets of a Heart." 5808 (vɪ A 44).

Sects. 219 (ɪɪ A 127), 535 (x⁴ A 516), 1226 (73), 2687 (xɪ² A 435), 3184 (xɪ¹ A 584), 4391 (ɪ A 282), 4861 (x¹ A 407), 5227 (ɪɪ A 599).

Secular, the. 3749 (x³ A 166), 3761 (x⁴ A 326), 4937 (290).

Secularism. 317 (vɪɪɪ¹ A 519), 326 (ɪx A 440), 386 (x² A 27), 387 (58), 394 (x³ A 137), 510 (x² A 37), 599 (x⁴ A 22), 612 (x² A 57), 2217 (ɪx A 424), 2511 (x² A 364), 2513 (558), 2518 (x³ A 153), 2528 (510), 2563 (xɪ¹ A 37), 2599 (vɪɪɪ¹ A 369), 2753 (ɪx A 404), 3032 (ɪx A 427), 3061 (x¹ A 600), 3149 (x³ A 242), 6859 (xɪ¹ A 56).

Security. 77 (x³ A 186), 376 (ɪx A 60), 1402 (x² A 494), 4204 (x⁴ A 68), 4327 (x¹ A 652), 4482 (xɪ¹ A 472), 4489 (xɪ² A 29), 4659 (x³ A 426), 4941 (xɪ¹ A 453), 4942 (458), 5962 (vɪɪ¹ A 222).

Sedentary piety. 3550 (x⁴ A 180).

Seducer. 4999 (xɪ¹ A 164), 5694 (ɪv A 153), 5730 (v ʙ 53:26), 5747 (v A 87), 5755 (110), 5804 (vɪ A 41), 5865 (vɪɪ¹ ʙ 83).

"The Seducer's Diary." 806 (ɪɪɪ ʙ 45:1), 2393 (106), 5633 (ɪv A 231), 5676 (128), 5677 (129), 5865 (vɪɪ¹ ʙ 83), 6330 (x¹ A 88), 6336 (94), 6388 (266), 6472 (x⁵ A 149), 6843 (146).

"The Seducer's Diary, No. 2." 5705 (ɪv A 181).

Seduction. 3706 (ɪx A 383).

Seeing. 2302 (x⁴ A 310).

Seek first. 477 (ɪx A 13), 478 (14), 3179 (xɪ¹ A 389), 3180 (390).

Seeking. 960 (ɪx A 111).

SELF (*see also* Egoity; *I*). 71 (x² A 78), 72 (79), 180 (xɪ¹ A 237), 200 (284), 343 (x¹ A 624), 377 (ɪx A 199), 906 (ɪv A 155), 911 (179), 934 (vɪɪ¹ A 138), 1026 (ɪɪɪ A 26), 1050 (vɪɪɪ¹ A 320), 1205 (vɪɪ¹ A 141), 1372 (ɪx A 182), 1789 (x³ A 509), 1791 (525), 1793 (670), 1820 (xɪ² A 313), 2053 (xɪ¹ A 148), 2075 (533), 2627 (xɪ² A 176), 2906 (xɪ¹ A 154), 3191 (ɪɪɪ c 23), 3214 (vɪɪ¹ A 10), 3287 (ɪɪɪ ʙ 183), 3587 (xɪ¹ A 450), 3771 (x⁵ A 53), 3772 (58), 3779 (xɪ¹ A 376), 4021 (x¹ A 433), 4178 (x² A 490), 4260 (ɪv A 124), 4343 (x⁴ A 508), 4350 (xɪ¹ A 487), 4394 (ɪ A 319), 4398 (ɪ c 126), 4408 (ɪɪ A 339), 4410 (357), 4411 (358), 4427 (vɪ A 71), 4433 (vɪɪ¹ A 68), 4520 (x³ A 684), 4548 (x² A 145), 4571 (xɪ² A 97), 4826 (ɪv c 110), 4899 (x⁴ A 509), 5272 (ɪɪ c 39), 5320 (ɪɪ A 742), 5432 (807), 5493 (ɪɪɪ A 97), 5636 (ɪv A 246), 6137 (vɪɪɪ¹ A 652), 6138 (653), 6161 (ɪx A 65).

Self-concern. 1174 (x³ A 506).

Self-denial (*see also* RENUNCIATION). 463 (vɪɪɪ¹ A 157), 1490 (x⁵ A 54), 1682 (ɪɪ A 78), 4450 (ɪx A 204), 6146 (25), 6235 (223), 6645 (x³ A 189).

Self-hate. 3771 (x⁵ A 53), 3779 (xɪ¹ A 376), 6432 (x¹ A 513).

Selfishness. 3538 (xɪ² A 71), 3545 (ɪ A 22), 4384 (xɪ² A 132), 4726 (72), 6235 (ɪx A 223).

Self-knowledge. 42 (ɪv c 50), 53 (v ʙ 196), 73 (ɪ A 8), 890 (ɪɪɪ A 230), 898 (ɪv A 82), 1020 (ɪɪ A 235), 1351 (vɪɪɪ¹ A 30), 1393 (x² A 72), 1405 (644), 1488 (x⁵ A 7), 3902 (x⁴ A 412), 4472 (251), 4562 (283), 5651 (ɪv A 93).

Self-love. 2037 (x⁴ A 89), 2384 (ɪɪ A 462), 2412 (vɪɪɪ¹ A 393), 2415 (610), 3771 (x⁵ A 53).

Self-torment. 6011 (vɪɪɪ¹ A 156), 6272 (ɪx A 393).

SENECA. 2016 (x¹ A 286), 3498 (x³ A 48), 4684 (x⁴ A 574), 4868 (x³ A 25), 4939 (x⁴ A 538).

Sensibleness (*see also* PRACTICALITY). 1001 (x⁴ A 571), 4401 (ɪɪ A 169), 5669 (ɪv A 114).

Sensuality. 1051 (IX A 154), 5669 (IV A 114).

Sentimental, the. 123 (I A 129).

Sentimentality. 566 (VII¹ A 161), 1285 (X³ A 200), 2804 (X⁴ A 519), 3125 (I A 117), 6261 (IX A 310).

Seriousness (see also Earnestness). 6168 (IX A 72).

Sermon on the Mount. 297 (II A 473), 950 (VIII¹ A 316).

SERMONS. 584 (II A 792), 620 (393), 638 (VIII¹ A 6), 639 (243), 640 (256), 3478 (668), 4011 (284), 4644 (X² A 246), 5634 (IV A 234), 5637 (71).

Sermons (S.K.). 855 (II A 13), 2891 (X⁴ A 526), 2892 (527), 4802 (X³ A 699), 4890 (X⁴ A 297), 4891 (305), 5644 (IV A 83), 5653 (97), 5686 (IV B 159:6), 5689 (IV A 142), 6249 (IX A 271), 6359 (X¹ A 143), 6612 (X³ A 30), 6749 (X⁶ B 173, pp. 274-276), 6767 (X⁴ A 318), 6768 (322), 6769 (323), 6790 (X⁶ B 260), 6965 (XI³ B 291:4).

Serpent. 2472 (IX A 377).

Servant. 1389 (X¹ A 408), 2117 (VIII¹ A 76).

Servetus. 3575 (X⁴ A 398).

Serving. 3540 (XI² A 281).

Serving the truth. 3355 (IX A 409).

Seven-league boots. 848 (I A 84), 968 (IX A 464).

Seventh day. 440 (II A 329).

70,000 fathoms. 1142 (X⁴ A 114), 1402 (X² A 494), 4937 (X⁴ A 290), 5792 (VI B 18), 5961 (VII¹ A 221).

SEX. 45 (V A 14), 78 (X³ A 501), 2617 (XI¹ A 150), 2626 (XI² A 172), 3177 (XI¹ A 230), 4009 (VI A 105).

Sextus Empiricus. 42 (IV C 50), 2348 (V C 6), 4844 (IV C 52), 4845 (53), 5602 (98).

Sexuality. 2624 (XI² A 154), 2629 (238).

SHAKESPEARE. 49 (V A 28), 226 (X³ A 463), 619 (IX A 45), 910 (IV A 172), 965 (IX A 418), 1165 (VIII¹ A 58), 1247 (V A 90), 1562 (XI¹ A 501), 3088 (VII² B 256:9-10), 4599 (VIII¹ A 161), 4773 (II A 34), 4871 (X³ A 478), 5429 (II A 804), 5675 (IV A 127), 5715 (V A 103), 5892 (VII¹ A 105), 5900 (113), 6279 (IX A 499), 6339 (X¹ A 104), 6635 (X³ A 164), 6732 (X⁴ A 55), 6882 (XI¹ A 210), 6903 (460).

Sharing. 4716 (XI¹ A 433).

Sheep. 3897 (VIII¹ A 625).

Shelley, Percy Bysshe. 1339 (V A 89), 5716 (104).

Shepherd. 2891 (X⁴ A 526), 5874 (VII¹ A 5).

Ship. 4808 (XI¹ A 419), 4809 (420), 5507 (III A 147).

Ship analogy. 6008 (VIII¹ A 135), 6731 (X⁴ A 53).

Shoe analogy. 5291 (II A 684).

Shoes. 6916 (XI² A 11).

Shoot. 5140 (I A 156), 5141 (161).

Shrewdness. 1961 (X⁴ A 91), 3355 (IX A 409), 3503 (X³ A 141).

Sibbern, Frederik C. 194 (II A 305), 1279 (22), 2206 (I C 66), 3103 (VII¹ A 152), 3278 (II A 519), 5513 (L. 49), 5543 (L. 55), 5769 (VI A 8), 6196 (IX A 493), 6472 (X⁵ A 149), 6696 (X³ A 577), 6800 (X⁴ A 540), 6888 (XI¹ A 275), 6889 (276).

Sickness. 1095 (I A 44), 1653 (X² A 353), 1817 (XI² A 195), 3992 (II A 19), 4329 (X² A 103), 4389 (I A 183).

Sickness unto death. 4002 (II A 311).

Sickness unto Death, The. 68 (VIII² B 168:5), 69 (IX A 76), 102 (X² A 22), 747 (VIII² B 154:3), 748 (159:4), 749 (168:6), 3423 (143), 4020 (X¹ A 384), 4029 (X² A 429), 6110 (VIII¹ A 558), 6134 (648), 6136 (651), 6137 (652), 6138 (653), 6139 (VIII² B 166), 6229 (IX A 216), 6238 (227), 6271 (390), 6337 (X¹ A 95), 6361 (147), 6416 (422), 6431 (510), 6434 (L. 213), 6436 (X¹ A 520), 6437 (525), 6438 (529), 6439 (530), 6445 (546), 6451 (567), 6452 (568), 6457 (583), 6487 (678), 6501 (X² A 66), 6517 (147), 6526 (177), 6535 (204), 6671 (X³ A 415), 6689 (551), 6690 (555), 6762 (X⁴ A 299), 6797 (513), 6814 (605), 6820 (647), 6843 (X⁵ A 146).

Significance. 1365 (VIII¹ A 670), 3227 (XI² A 217).

SILENCE. 335 (X¹ A 285), 442 (II A 338), 897 (IV A 73), 2334 (XI¹ A 128), 2335 (129), 3404 (VII¹ A 131), 3460 (X⁴ A 281), 4119 (VIII¹ A 134), 4306 (40), 4434 (VII¹ B 192:12), 4798 (X³ A 47), 4859 (X¹ A 347), 5041 (X⁴ A 306), 5048 (XI² A 35), 5952 (VII¹ B 212), 5953 (213), 6152 (IX A 42),

6345 (x^1 A 115), 6352 (126), 6356 (138), 6590 (x^2 A 525), 6704 (x^3 A 637), 6706 (650), 6896 (xi^1 A 383).

Simon of Cyrene. 4580 (ii A 458), 5329 (232).

Simon Stylites. 1188 (i A 252), 1541 (340), 5659 (iv B 78).

Simple man. 69 (ix A 76).

Simplicity. 665 (ix A 439), 1017 (x^2 A 348), 3095 (x^3 A 424), 3661 (28), 5464 (iii A 67), 5937 (vii^1 A 147), 6396 (x^1 A 322).

sin (see also Original sin). 23 (i A 102), 33 (ii A 743), 41 (iv C 33), 46 (v A 16), 52 (v B 55:4), 174 (x^3 A 187), 219 (ii A 127), 334 (x^1 A 279), 443 (ii A 360), 495 (x^1 A 178), 554 (xi^1 A 324), 700 (iii A 112), 855 (ii A 13), 1238 (456), 1246 (iv B 118:1), 1268 (x^4 A 175), 1348 (vii^1 A 143), 1485 (x^4 A 419), 1534 (x^3 A 719), 1614 (x^2 A 426), 2008 (ix A 316), 2460 (vi A 108), 3029 (ix A 244), 3032 (427), 3081 (v B 5:10), 3194 (x^1 A 392), 3245 (i A 94), 3263 (ii C 57), 3376 (ii A 342), 3464 (xi^1 A 578), 3639 (x^2 A 156), 3751 (x^3 A 306), 3783 (iii A 85), 3787 (viii^1 A 203), 3793 (iv A 156), 3963 (v B 53:28), 3964 (53:38), 4297 (xi^1 A 318), 4298 (334), 4367 (viii^1 A 93), 4374 (x^1 A 477), 4472 (x^4 A 251), 4487 (xi^1 A 574), 4547 (x^1 A 223), 4586 (v A 49), 4621 (ix A 330), 4639 (x^2 A 53), 4643 (236), 4657 (x^3 A 305), 4708 (xi^1 A 311), 4969 (x^3 A 301), 5205 (ii A 20), 5231 (603), 6138 (viii^1 A 653), 6277 (ix A 421), 6278 (498), 6279 (499), 6280 (500), 6444 (x^1 A 541), 6468 (643), 6469 (644), 6689 (x^3 A 551).

—Forgiveness of sins (see also FOR-GIVENESS). 67 (viii^1 A 673), 411 (i A 6), 446 (ii A 443), 532 (x^4 A 212), 1100 (iii A 34), 1324 (101), 1471 (x^2 A 189), 1971 (ii A 187), 2391 (iii A 138), 2397 (iv B 144), 2483 (x^1 A 197), 3085 (vi B 45), 3628 (vii^1 A 130), 4536 (v A 37), 4595 (viii^1 A 85), 4654 (x^3 A 182), 6037 (viii^1 A 229), 6210 (ix A 176).

—Sin-consciousness. 452 (v A 10), 496 (x^1 A 190), 503 (467), 534 (x^4 A 470), 902 (iv A 112), 1032 (v A 6), 1100 (iii A 34), 1335 (v A 8), 1991 (vi A 120), 4486 (xi^1 A 564), 4903 (x^5 A 17), 5459 (iii A 59),

6101 (viii^1 A 504), 6261 (ix A 310).

—Sin (S.K.). 6229 (ix A 216), 6261 (310), 6266 (371), 6291 (488).

Single state. 2578 (ii A 244), 2626 (xi^2 A 172), 2629 (238), 2630 (241).

Sinner. 502 (x^1 A 443), 1020 (ii A 235), 1032 (v A 6), 1310 (ii A 758), 3995 (64), 3997 (66), 4044 (x^3 A 566), 6192 (ix A 142).

Sirach. 1739 (iv A 115), 4440 (viii^1 A 22), 5971 (2).

SITUATION. 178 (x^5 A 99), 513 (x^2 A 284), 653 (viii^2 B 85), 816 (x^1 A 248), 826 (xi^1 A 394), 941 (viii^1 A 144), 978 (x^1 A 610), 1142 (x^4 A 114), 1514 (x^2 A 206), 1880 (x^3 A 454), 1881 (455), 1902 (x^4 A 349), 1904 (354), 1908 (459), 2500 (x^1 A 595), 2600 (ix A 237), 2751 (362), 3045 (i A 45), 3488 (x^2 A 149), 3862 (x^4 A 280), 4039 (x^3 A 180), 4224 (xi^1 A 18), 4278 (x^2 A 598), 4309 (x^4 A 466), 4314 (608), 4326 (x^1 A 417), 4354 (xi^1 A 558), 4546 (x^1 A 30), 4623 (ix A 349), 4626 (407), 4798 (x^3 A 47), 4933 (470), 4934 (471).

"Six Discourses." 5778 (vi B 100).

Skaane. 4126 (vii^1 A 382).

Skepticism. 774 (iv A 72), 1147 (x^4 A 634), 1243 (iv C 56), 1328 (iv A 102), 2280 (198), 2348 (v C 6), 3702 (vi B 54:19).

Skeptics. 774 (iv A 72), 776 (iv B 5:13), 1147 (x^4 A 634), 1243 (iv C 56), 1244 (60), 1247 (v A 90), 3286 (iii A 244), 4844 (iv C 52).

Sleep. 3973 (vi A 67), 4624 (ix A 367), 5631 (iv A 221).

Slesvig-Holsten. 6125 (viii^1 A 602), 6127 (666).

Smith, Troels F. 354 (x^3 A 354).

Smule. 6346 (x^1 A 116).

Sneedorf-Birch, Frederik. 5288 (ii A 679).

Soap cellars. 5156 (i A 220).

Sobriety. 2034 (x^3 A 763).

Socialism. 6256 (x^6 B 40).

Sociality. 2008 (ix A 316), 2918 (xi^2 A 386), 4126 (viii^1 A 382), 4909 (xi^1 A 351), 6923 (xi^2 A 44).

Social life. 4070 (i A 307).

Social morality. 1819 (xi^2 A 264), 1902 (x^4 A 349), 1912 (500).

SOCIAL-POLITICAL THOUGHT. 25 (I A 126), 63 (VIII^1 A 268), 114 (IV C 27), 125 (I A 198), 162 (VIII^1 A 122), 175 (X^4 A 150), 185 (X^1 A 5), 236 (135), 321 (IX A 57), 377 (199), 450 (II A 579), 473 (VIII^1 A 528), 490 (IX A 350), 492 (394), 527 (X^3 A 738), 529 (X^4 A 78), 560 (XI^2 A 49), 561 (102), 581 (I A 108), 588 (IX A 264), 593 (X^1 A 552), 595 (X^5 B 245), 601 (X^4 A 594), 654 (VIII^2 B 86), 681 (X^3 A 648), 683 (VIII^1 A 60), 708 (X^4 A 15), 737 (I A 181), 787 (VIII^1 A 258), 871 (II A 450), 872 (465), 927 (VII^1 A 15), 977 (X^1 A 580), 978 (610), 991 (X^3 A 714), 1000 (X^4 A 563), 1001 (571), 1003 (XI^1 A 252), 1008 (VII^1 A 245), 1010 (180), 1011 (VIII^1 A 314), 1012 (VIII^2 B 31:20), 1013 (31:22), 1014 (VIII^1 A 665), 1053 (IX A 359), 1056 (X^1 A 650), 1193 (X^2 A 564), 1194 (565), 1195 (X^4 A 127), 1227 (77), 1264 (X^3 A 618), 1267 (X^4 A 99), 1298 (X^1 A 590), 1349 (VII^1 A 201), 1377 (IX A 315), 1453 (XI^2 A 179), 1541 (I A 340), 1614 (X^2 A 426), 1628 (I A 247), 1651 (II A 731), 1680 (38), 1698 (114), 1748 (VII^1 A 64), 1775 (VIII^1 A 54), 1819 (XI^2 A 264), 1956 (237), 1964 (I A 177), 1965 (178), 1967 (337), 1971 (II A 187), 1972 (II C 41), 1976 (II A 223), 1977 (267), 1983 (III A 38), 1991 (VI A 120), 1996 (VII^1 B 158:3), 2006 (IX A 91), 2010 (356), 2016 (X^1 A 286), 2017 (463), 2019 (X^2 A 265), 2021 (X^5 B 244), 2029 (X^3 A 349), 2037 (X^4 A 89), 2038 (104), 2046 (X^5 A 121), 2049 (XI^1 A 60), 2122 (X^2 A 46), 2147 (VIII^1 A 136), 2154 (IX A 282), 2158 (468), 2170 (X^3 A 723), 2245 (I A 111), 2319 (III A 222), 2470 (IX A 145), 2481 (X^1 A 154), 2509 (X^2 A 263), 2514 (559), 2558 (X^4 A 444), 2603 (IX A 434), 2609 (X^2 A 566), 2618 (XI^1 A 169), 2648 (IX B 63:12), 2686 (XI^3 B 177), 2707 (II A 468), 2727 (X^3 A 676), 2751 (IX A 362), 2760 (X^4 A 531), 2780 (X^3 A 459), 2782 (503), 2923 (VII^1 A 100), 2925 (VIII^1 A 199), 2929 (461), 2932 (656), 2933 (538), 2935 (571), 2936 (611), 2938 (IX A 63), 2941 (277), 2943 (452), 2945 (X^1 A 231), 2950 (X^2 A 369), 2951 (383), 2952 (390), 2956 (262), 2960 (X^4 A 93), 2964 (225), 2967 (X^5 A 123), 2968 (XI^1 A 16), 2973 (287), 2986 (88), 3001 (XI^2 A 169), 3005 (214), 3113 (X^3 A 632), 3136 (IX A 406), 3141 (X^2 A 418), 3147 (X^3 A 132), 3160 (698), 3201 (X^4 A 541), 3219 (XI^1 A 51), 3222 (354), 3498 (X^3 A 48), 3501 (129), 3530 (X^5 A 62), 3561 (XI^2 A 46), 3599 (X^2 A 505), 3632 (XI^1 A 267), 3670 (IX A 415), 3686 (X^3 A 696), 3689 (X^4 A 190), 3726 (VIII^1 A 103), 3729 (X^3 A 608), 3732 (X^4 A 38), 3775 (XI^1 A 79), 3777 (143), 3836 (XI^2 A 10), 3895 (VI A 132), 3898 (IX A 373), 3969 (XI^1 A 259), 4050 (XI^2 A 14), 4095 (II A 467), 4177 (X^2 A 486), 4276 (248), 4281 (X^3 A 477), 4302 (XI^1 A 448), 4323 (VII^1 A 168), 4394 (I A 319), 4442 (VIII^1 A 78), 4495 (XI^1 A 63), 4496 (74), 4497 (102), 4498 (105), 4501 (XI^2 A 111), 4502 (112), 4503 (373), 4528 (XI^1 A 266), 4572 (XI^2 A 196), 4573 (354), 4623 (IX A 349), 4730 (XI^2 A 396), 4850 (VIII^1 A 141), 4852 (IX A 4), 4864 (X^2 A 409), 4866 (463), 4875 (X^4 A 35), 4936 (19), 4943 (XI^1 A 502), 4976 (X^4 A 406), 5017 (VIII^1 A 409), 5023 (X^4 A 672), 5062 (I A 12), 5089 (60), 5090 (61), 5091 (62), 5116 (I B 2), 5181 (I A 328), 5300 (II A 700), 5332 (240), 5940 (VII^1 A 154), 5941 (155), 5957 (214), 6050 (VIII^1 A 271), 6070 (388), 6085 (452), 6105 (544), 6158 (IX A 55), 6196 (493), 6255 (IX B 63:7), 6256 (X^6 B 40), 6264 (IX A 338), 6335 (X^1 A 92), 6343 (112), 6344 (113), 6354 (131), 6392 (289), 6432 (513), 6443 (538), 6444 (541), 6580 (X^2 A 413), 6581 (415), 6582 (425), 6592 (544), 6593 (560), 6604 (622), 6679 (X^3 A 448), 6681 (453), 6699 (599), 6719 (799), 6721 (X^4 A 6), 6722 (8), 6730 (52), 6731 (53), 6735 (58), 6846 (XI^2 A 296), 6886 (XI^1 A 242), 6916 (XI^2 A 11), 6923 (44).

Society. 4070 (I A 307), 4175 (X^2 A 478), 4176 (479).

SOCRATES (see also IRONY: Socratic Irony). 19 (XI^1 A 308), 73 (X^2 A 406), 88 (XI^1 A 592), 109 (X^4 A 388), 113 (IV C 21), 154 (VII^1 A 12), 170 (X^2 A 380), 182 (VIII^1 A 225), 255 (IX A 32), 265 (II A 12), 318 (VIII^1 A 565), 358 (X^4 A 506), 373 (VIII^1 A 547), 388 (X^2 A 135), 390 (453), 649 (VIII^2 B 81), 754 (III A 7), 788 (X^1 A 647), 797 (II A 791), 820 (X^2 A 392), 840 (VIII^1 A

221), 895 (IV C 86), 914 (V B 207:3), 926 (VI B 98:46), 942 (VIII^1 A 189), 963 (IX A 372), 972 (X^1 A 360), 997 (X^4 A 320), 1054 (IX A 382), 1059 (X^2 A 439), 1060 (606), 1063 (X^4 A 5), 1162 (VII^1 A 58), 1251 (181), 1291 (VI A 21), 1373 (IX A 242), 1393 (X^2 A 72), 1430 (X^4 A 567), 1547 (III B 17), 1553 (V B 43), 1554 (44), 1555 (45), 1607 (VI B 40:3), 1673 (I A 190), 1680 (II A 38), 1682 (78), 1685 (81), 1690 (102), 1691 (103), 1700 (138), 1703 (141), 1713 (658), 1723 (III B 4), 1753 (IX A 151), 1756 (398), 1763 (X^2 A 304), 1767 (XI^2 A 189), 1824 (272), 1891 (X^3 A 750), 1957 (IX A 221), 1959 (X^3 A 413), 1962 (X^4 A 553), 1968 (II A 53), 2004 (VIII^1 A 482), 2030 (X^3 A 476), 2080 (XI^2 A 125), 2171 (X^5 A 138), 2260 (II A 748), 2286 (VI B 40:5), 2287 (42), 2300 (X^1 A 577), 2311 (II A 157), 2444 (XI^1 A 356), 2460 (VI A 108), 2514 (X^2 A 559), 2652 (X^1 A 220), 2797 (X^2 A 340), 2814 (VII^1 A 194), 2998 (XI^2 A 159), 3008 (230), 3095 (X^3 A 424), 3170 (X^5 A 10), 3194 (X^1 A 392), 3303 (VI A 15), 3306 (145), 3307 (VI B 54:33), 3317 (X^5 A 113), 3328 (X^2 A 608), 3329 (609), 3331 (X^6 C 6:1), 3352 (VIII^1 A 510), 3527 (X^4 A 597), 3529 (X^5 A 57), 3535 (XI^1 A 477), 3567 (X^1 A 679), 3683 (X^3 A 377), 3689 (X^4 A 190), 3713 (255), 3738 (XI^2 A 355), 3864 (X^5 A 134), 3871 (XI^2 A 362), 3952 (X^3 A 707), 3965 (X^2 A 536), 4118 (VIII^1 A 123), 4155 (IX A 453), 4224 (XI^1 A 18), 4309 (X^4 A 466), 4480 (XI^1 A 456), 4505 (XI^2 A 416), 4545 (IX A 363), 4555 (X^2 A 401), 4571 (XI^2 A 97), 4589 (VI A 48), 4648 (X^2 A 513), 4695 (X^4 A 670), 4740 (X^2 A 562), 4765 (X^4 A 138), 4897 (468), 4942 (XI^1 A 458), 4962 (IX A 124), 5460 (III A 60), 5613 (IV A 43), 5619 (64), 5796 (VI B 35:24), 5829 (VI A 86), 5892 (VII^1 A 105), 5899 (112), 5937 (147), 5953 (VII^1 B 213), 5979 (VIII^1 A 23), 6056 (326), 6144 (IX A 18), 6152 (42), 6228 (214), 6237 (226), 6300 (X^1 A 11), 6360 (146), 6388 (266), 6389 (272), 6392 (289), 6412 (385), 6532 (X^2 A 195), 6533 (196), 6574 (X^6 B 121), 6630 (X^2 A 146), 6719 (799), 6819 (X^4 A 646), 6839 (X^5 A 104), 6871 (XI^1 A 133), 6883 (214), 6901

(239), 6903 (460), 6919 (XI^2 A 31), 6920 (32), 6945 (XI^3 B 55).

Soldiers. 1194 (X^2 A 565).

Soldin. 1541 (I A 340), 5186 (333).

Solger, Karl W. F. 4796 (X^1 A 261).

Solitary. 1775 (VIII^1 A 54), 1969 (II A 168), 2000 (VIII^1 A 210), 2838 (VII^1 A 46), 4854 (IX A 287).

SOLITUDE. 100 (VIII^1 A 363), 125 (I A 198), 1371 (IX A 116), 1988 (V B 235), 2017 (X^1 A 463), 2442 (X^5 A 50), 4285 (X^4 A 333), 4769 (142), 4885 (XI^1 A 352), 5764 (VI B 226), 5953 (VII^1 B 213), 6318 (X^1 A 58).

Solomon. 3786 (VII^1 B 147), 5539 (III A 183), 5669 (IV A 114).

Solon. 18 (III A 13), 2739 (IV A 3), 2800 (II A 587), 4072 (I A 309), 4835 (IV C 119).

Sonorous figure (see Chladni figure).

SOPHISTRY. 13 (I A 206), 525 (X^3 A 649), 999 (X^4 A 549), 2102 (X^5 A 26), 3530 (62), 3883 (XI^1 A 537), 4696 (X^5 A 11), 4806 (XI^1 A 329), 5618 (IV A 63), 6792 (X^4 A 472), 6886 (XI^1 A 242).

SOPHISTS. 388 (X^2 A 135), 681 (X^3 A 648), 938 (VII^1 A 251), 1547 (III B 17), 1633 (14), 2814 (VII^1 A 194), 3329 (X^2 A 609), 3331 (X^6 C 6:1), 4294 (X^5 A 69), 4724 (XI^2 A 66), 4840 (V A 80), 5601 (III C 97), 6665 (X^3 A 389), 6719 (799).

Sophocles. 418 (I A 97).

Sorrow. 230 (III A 191), 1434 (X^5 A 55), 2178 (III A 33), 2179 (213), 2182 (192), 2388 (89), 2422 (X^1 A 487), 3466 (V A 17), 3788 (IX A 345), 4582 (III A 99), 4608 (VIII^1 A 514), 4638 (X^1 A 662), 4639 (X^2 A 53), 5384 (II A 421), 5475 (III A 83), 6278 (IX A 498), 6279 (499), 6280 (500).

Sortebro. 5099 (I A 68).

Soul (see ANTHROPOLOGY).

Soul-care. 381 (X^1 A 7).

Soup analogy. 6880 (XI^1 A 206).

Sovereignty. 1808 (XI^1 A 403), 2051 (82), 3361 (367), 4061 (I A 93).

Space. 217 (I A 290), 2240 (1).

Spandet, Niels M. 3686 (X^3 A 696), 6728 (X^4 A 36).

Spang, Peter J. 3466 (V A 17), 3488 (X^2 A 149), 5892 (VII^1 A 105).

Sparrow. 3125 (I A 117), 3443 (X^2 A 342).

Speaking. 3472 (VII¹ B 177:4), 4283 (X⁴ A 314), 6907 (XI¹ A 497).
Specialization. 143 (IV C 104).
Specification. 389 (X² A 139).
Specimen. 2048 (XI¹ A 42), 2071 (485), 2080 (XI² A 125), 4918 (205).
Specimen men. 1067 (XI² A 63), 1825 (XI³ B 199).
Spectator. 692 (IX A 153), 1051 (154), 4521 (X³ A 685), 4522 (686), 4647 (X² A 349), 5388 (II A 435), 6873 (XI¹ A 137).
Speculation. 508 (X¹ A 558), 832 (II A 100), 1042 (VII¹ A 80), 1144 (X⁴ A 422), 1707 (II A 192), 2277 (III A 211), 2461 (VII¹ A 192), 2504 (X² A 123), 3093 (501), 3094 (502), 3272 (II A 426), 3281 (III A 11), 3572 (X³ A 392), 3656 (I A 243), 4004 (III A 118), 4270 (VIII¹ A 490), 4538 (VI A 63), 5627 (IV A 214), 5788 (VI A 14), 6574 (X⁶ B 121).
Speculator. 1132 (X¹ A 554).
Speech. 25 (I A 126), 623 (V A 19), 1982 (II A 516), 3281 (III A 11), 5181 (I A 328), 5186 (333), 5493 (III A 97), 5512 (155).
Spener, Phillip J. 3320 (X³ A 682).
SPINOZA, BARUCH. 734 (IV B 2:16), 929 (VII¹ A 29), 931 (35), 1057 (X² A 328), 1261 (428), 1333 (IV A 190), 2291 (VII¹ A 31), 2292 (34), 2340 (IV C 13), 2776 (VIII¹ A 315).
SPIRIT. 67 (VIII¹ A 673), 68 (VIII² B 168:5), 69 (IX A 76), 73 (X² A 406), 78 (X³ A 501), 79 (X⁴ A 457), 81 (XI¹ A 225), 84 (385), 86 (407), 87 (408), 88 (592), 161 (VIII¹ A 88), 188 (X² A 396), 251 (X⁴ A 473), 347 (X² A 86), 475 (IX A 5), 479 (20), 565 (XI² A 375), 613 (X² A 397), 615 (XI² A 263), 913 (V B 148:38), 934 (VII¹ A 138), 971 (X¹ A 327), 972 (360), 1000 (X⁴ A 563), 1001 (571), 1119 (VII¹ A 203), 1123 (VIII¹ A 649), 1215 (663), 1409 (X³ A 359), 1414 (585), 1530 (X² A 481), 1650 (XI² A 235), 1657 (X³ A 360), 1658 (365), 1661 (X⁴ A 588), 1800 (XI² A 294), 1836 (VII¹ A 208), 1919 (X⁵ A 44), 1940 (XI² A 434), 1954 (XI¹ A 547), 1995 (VII¹ A 205), 2010 (IX A 356), 2024 (X² A 489), 2045 (X⁵ A 97), 2059 (XI¹ A 272), 2065 (370), 2074 (518), 2082 (XI² A 149), 2084 (275), 2103 (XI¹ A 500), 2124 (X³ A 251), 2222 (X⁴ A 572), 2226 (XI¹ A 152), 2274 (III A 5), 2455 (XI² A 426), 2461 (VII¹ A 192), 2502 (X¹ A 651), 2515 (X³ A 58), 2539 (X⁴ A 371), 2544 (XI² A 303), 2550 (XI¹ A 193), 2598 (VIII¹ A 231), 2622 (XI² A 150), 2666 (XI¹ A 511), 2681 (XI² A 323), 2683 (385), 2761 (XI¹ A 85), 2824 (94), 2970 (XI¹ A 227), 2980 (512), 2986 (XI² A 88), 2987 (89), 2988 (90), 3098 (XI¹ A 299), 3099 (XI² A 51), 3100 (52), 3587 (XI¹ A 450), 3754 (X³ A 361), 3757 (560), 3766 (X⁴ A 649), 3887 (II A 248), 3892 (IV C 26), 3962 (V B 53:27), 3969 (XI¹ A 259), 4006 (IV A 189), 4048 (X⁴ A 534), 4049 (XI² A 6), 4051 (242), 4108 (VI A 26), 4151 (IX A 354), 4173 (X² A 394), 4234 (XI¹ A 536), 4267 (VII¹ A 193), 4295 (X⁵ A 133), 4373 (X¹ A 452), 4379 (X⁴ A 411), 4404 (II A 721), 4409 (343), 4433 (VII¹ A 68), 4453 (X¹ A 50), 4461 (X³ A 79), 4502 (XI² A 112), 4570 (XI¹ A 380), 4624 (IX A 367), 4679 (X⁴ A 420), 4688 (593), 4690 (620), 4793 (VIII¹ A 75), 4809 (XI¹ A 420), 4812 (554), 4872 (X³ A 614), 4885 (XI¹ A 352), 4892 (418), 4897 (X⁴ A 468), 4911 (XI¹ A 516), 4942 (458), 4949 (X⁴ A 487), 5031 (XI¹ A 519), 5043 (X⁴ A 654), 5205 (II A 20), 5251 (637), 5261 (164), 5840 (VI A 103), 6127 (VIII¹ A 666), 6591 (X² A 534), 6616 (X³ A 77), 6686 (526), 6794 (X⁴ A 488), 6881 (XI¹ A 209), 6882 (210), 6969 (XI² A 439).
Spiritlessness. 2943 (IX A 452).
Spirituality. 2123 (X³ A 156), 4956 (II A 455).
SPIRITUAL TRIAL. 416 (I A 95), 610 (IX A 21), 646 (VIII¹ A 554), 884 (III A 125), 1110 (IV A 191), 1260 (X² A 243), 1421 (X³ A 790), 2008 (IX A 316), 2526 (X³ A 335), 3247 (I A 99), 4023 (X¹ A 637), 4586 (V A 49), 4662 (X³ A 671), 4899 (X⁴ A 509), 4950 (X³ A 43), 6118 (VIII¹ A 576), 6134 (648), 6230 (IX A 217), 6323 (X¹ A 72), 6385 (260), 6459 (586), 6811 (X⁴ A 592).
Sponneck, Wilhelm. 4218 (X⁶ B 257).
Spontaneity, the second (see also IMMEDIACY: Christian immediacy). 235 (IX A 387), 1101 (III A 216), 1123 (VIII¹ A 649), 1215 (663), 1942 (643), 4266 (VII¹ A 74), 4637 (X¹ A 645), 6298 (X¹ A 8).
Spruce analogy. 5238 (II A 617).

Spy (*see* Secret agent).

Staffeldt, Schack. 5670 (IV A 118).

STAGES. 67 (VIII[1] A 673), 126 (I A 212), 228 (II A 581), 446 (443), 795 (I A 150), 796 (II A 632), 798 (553), 803 (III A 94), 1123 (VIII[1] A 649), 1135 (x[2] A 207), 1142 (x[4] A 114), 1272 (656), 1348 (VII[1] A 143), 1350 (VIII[1] A 24), 1393 (x[2] A 72), 1409 (x[3] A 359), 1432 (x[5] A 23), 1537 (XI[2] A 4), 1569 (II A 49), 1668 (VI B 53:13), 1767 (XI[2] A 189), 1792 (x[3] A 572), 1793 (670), 1943 (x[4] A 471), 2034 (x[3] A 763), 2353 (VI A 33), 2693 (XI[1] A 569), 2793 (x[2] A 341), 2866 (x[1] A 287), 3039 (XI[1] A 360), 3214 (VII[1] A 10), 3225 (XI[2] A 177), 3587 (XI[1] A 450), 3598 (II A 763), 3601 (XI[1] A 113), 3660 (x[2] A 116), 3661 (x[3] A 28), 3705 (IX A 365), 3741 (VIII[1] A 211), 3788 (IX A 345), 3790 (x[2] A 360), 3895 (VI A 132), 3903 (XI[1] A 285), 3927 (VIII[1] A 635), 4067 (I A 288), 4068 (289), 4266 (VII[1] A 74), 4323 (168), 4344 (x[4] A 617), 4350 (XI[1] A 487), 4364 (VI A 2), 4590 (80), 4741 (x[3] A 727), 4807 (XI[1] A 399), 4869 (x[3] A 85), 4926 (83), 4927 (II A 428), 4933 (x[3] A 470), 4914 (XI[1] A 568), 4946 (IV A 160), 5009 (VIII[1] A 104), 5020 (x[2] A 568), 5192 (I C 124), 5634 (IV A 234), 5950 (VII[1] C 5), 5975 (VIII[1] A 15), 6969 (XI[2] A 439).

Stages On Life's Way. 4999 (XI[1] A 164), 5610 (IV A 34), 5622 (65), 5623 (67), 5624 (68), 5643 (81), 5661 (IV B 140), 5662 (141), 5663 (142), 5666 (IV A 110), 5667 (111), 5669 (114), 5671 (119), 5673 (123), 5678 (132), 5681-5685 (135-139), 5691 (147), 5699 (170), 5718 (V A 106), 5721 (V B 147), 5722 (148:5), 5723 (148:25), 5724 (148:29), 5744 (V A 109), 5745 (82), 5747 (87), 5750 (92), 5755 (110), 5804 (VI A 41), 5805 (VI B 41:10), 5823 (VI A 78), 5824 (79), 5834 (94), 5865 (VII[1] B 83), 5866 (84), 5939 (VII[1] A 150), 6330 (x[1] A 88), 6331 (x[5] A 152), 6357 (139), 6410 (377), 6472 (149), 6500 (x[2] A 61), 6521 (157), 6602 (605), 6604 (622), 6858 (XI[1] A 49), 6882 (210).

Stand, to. 4122 (VIII[1] A 279).

Standards. 987 (x[2] A 546), 4060 (I A 42), 5023 (x[4] A 672).

Star analogy. 6917 (XI[2] A 19).

Stars. 1396 (x[2] A 186), 5761 (VI B 222).

State. 593 (x[1] A 552), 1264 (x[3] A 618), 1968 (II A 53), 3155 (x[3] A 436), 3334 (574), 4070 (I A 307), 4075 (II A 668), 4076 (669), 4084 (290), 4096 (481), 4129 (VIII[1] A 552), 4174 (x[2] A 395), 4191 (x[3] A 679), 4213 (x[4] A 187), 4232 (XI[1] A 366), 4238 (XI[2] A 108), 6053 (VIII[1] A 298).

STATE CHURCH. 2904 (XI[1] A 110), 3154 (x[3] A 325), 3155 (436), 4209 (x[4] A 126), 4232 (XI[1] A 366), 4239 (XI[2] A 292), 4240 (352), 4241 (356), 4242 (XI[3] B 126), 4504 (XI[2] A 410), 6070 (VIII[1] A 388), 6322 (x[1] A 71), 6444 (541), 6570 (x[2] A 338), 6851 (XI[2] A 334).

Statistics. 238 (x[4] A 11), 927 (VII[1] A 15), 1072 (IV C 75), 2970 (XI[1] A 227).

Status. 321 (IX A 57).

Status quo (*see also* Established; Established order). 593 (x[1] A 552), 3561 (XI[2] A 46).

Steffens, Henrich. 265 (II A 12), 2236 (VIII[1] A 358), 2304 (I A 250), 2351 (V C 9), 2641 (IX A 141), 2848 (VIII[1] A 411), 3049 (331), 3551 (II A 32), 3555 (588), 4112 (VII[1] A 63), 5543 (L. 55), 5696 (IV A 158), 6059 (VIII[1] A 337).

Stenersen, Sten J. 5054 (I C 3).

STEPHEN. 170 (x[2] A 380), 300 (III C 20), 312 (VIII[1] A 374), 568 (470), 1211 (475), 1212 (476), 2510 (x[2] A 334), 3422 (VIII[1] A 546), 3630 (329), 3950 (x[3] A 695), 6865 (XI[1] A 92).

Stettin. 6035 (VIII[1] A 227).

Stiefel, Pastor Michael. 2799 (I A 300).

Stilling, Peter M. 77 (x[3] A 186), 4190 (607), 6573 (x[2] A 352), 6574 (x[6] B 121), 6590 (x[2] A 525), 6607 (x[3] A 3), 6635 (x[3] A 164), 6636 (x[6] B 137).

Stilpo. 4307 (x[3] A 425).

STOICISM. 1565 (I A 225), 3040 (XI[2] A 16), 3771 (x[5] A 53), 3848 (I A 305), 3863 (x[4] A 409), 6611 (x[3] A 13).

STOICS. 1266 (x[4] A 13), 3880 (XI[1] A 179), 3898 (IX A 373), 3903 (XI[1] A 285), 3907 (x[2] A 31), 4625 (IX A 380), 5572 (IV C 2), 6794 (x[4] A 488).

Stopping (*see also* Roadblock). 1800 (XI[2] A 294).

Storm-house. 5049 (XI[2] A 50).

Story-telling. 265 (II A 12).

Strauss, David F. 3262 (II C 56).
Streets. 5678 (IV A 132), 5763 (VI B 225), 6957 (XI³ B 120).
Strength. 966 (IX A 419), 1806 (XI¹ A 337), 4214 (X⁴ A 209).
Strenuousness. 603 (XI² A 229), 830 (331), 1376 (IX A 305), 1502 (XI² A 226), 1807 (XI¹ A 401), 3017 (X³ A 384).
Strife. 3131 (X³ A 583), 3132 (584).
STRIVING. 923 (VI A 122), 984 (X² A 224), 1139 (X³ A 322), 1140 (323), 1166 (VIII¹ A 499), 1398 (X² A 232), 1399 (241), 1462 (X⁴ A 582), 1470 (X² A 188), 1473 (219), 1474 (223), 1482 (X³ A 784), 1489 (X⁵ A 8), 1676 (I A 239), 1875 (X³ A 378), 1909 (X⁴ A 491), 1912 (500), 1914 (556), 2027 (X³ A 324), 2031 (660), 2464 (VIII¹ A 541), 2542 (X⁴ A 451), 2551 (X¹ A 297), 2711 (X³ A 175), 2724 (XI¹ A 186), 2897 (X⁵ A 78), 3096 (X⁴ A 641), 3101 (XI² A 81), 3443 (X² A 342), 3513 (X³ A 484), 3765 (X⁴ A 645), 3773 (X⁵ A 68), 3853 (X² A 417), 4032 (456), 4333 (445), 4348 (XI¹ A 211), 4473 (X⁴ A 291), 4653 (X³ A 148), 4669 (X⁴ A 156), 4899 (X⁴ A 509), 4921 (XI¹ A 261), 4982 (191), 5012 (IX A 339), 5793 (VI B 35:14), 5794 (35:15), 5796 (35:24), 6577 (X² A 375), 6595 (596), 6598 (X⁶ B 68), 6645 (X³ A 189), 6801 (X⁴ A 545), 6859 (XI¹ A 56).
Strube, Frederik C. 6267 (L. 192), 6489 (X² A 10), 6629 (X³ A 144), 6762 (X⁴ A 299), 6764 (301).
Studenstrup. 6926 (XI² A 75).
Student association. 4201 (X⁴ A 51), 5115 (I B 1), 5116 (2), 6310 (X¹ A 42), 6625 (X³ A 112).
Students. 5832 (VI B 235).
Student (S.K.). 5282 (II A 204), 5385 (422).
Style. 138 (II A 425), 5245 (124), 5939 (VII¹ A 150), 6883 (XI¹ A 214).
Subject. 1144 (X⁴ A 422), 3483 (X¹ A 182).
Subjective. 3562 (VI B 40:31), 3608 (X¹ A 481), 3685 (X³ A 545), 4475 (X⁴ A 430), 5790 (VI B 16).
Subjectivity. 35 (II A 383), 187 (X² A 119), 493 (IX A 414), 532 (X⁴ A 212), 560 (XI² A 49), 578 (I A 56), 579 (57), 580 (58), 650 (VIII² B 82), 678 (X² A 466), 960 (IX A 111), 1042 (VII¹ A 80), 1044 (216), 1100 (III A 39), 1101 (216), 1117 (VII¹ A 61), 1347 (139), 1391 (X¹ A 605), 1405 (X² A 644), 1449 (XI² A 133), 1614 (X² A 426), 1846 (IX A 49), 1858 (X² A 255), 1902 (X⁴ A 349), 1906 (369), 1992 (VII¹ B 121:6), 2043 (X⁴ A 427), 2046 (X⁵ A 121), 2048 (XI¹ A 42), 2293 (VII¹ A 75), 2299 (IX A 438), 2315 (II A 161), 2371 (VI B 35:7), 2463 (VIII¹ A 465), 2570 (XI² A 54), 2576 (166), 2628 (231), 2957 (X³ A 451), 3317 (X⁵ A 113), 3321 (X⁴ A 84), 3350 (X⁵ A 143), 3513 (X³ A 484), 3587 (XI¹ A 450), 3899 (X¹ A 65), 4037 (X² A 482), 4265 (VII¹ A 69), 4353 (XI¹ A 538), 4384 (XI² A 132), 4433 (VII¹ A 68), 4847 (IV A 42), 4859 (X¹ A 347), 4860 (348), 4861 (407), 4944 (XI¹ A 521), 5549 (III B 130), 5789 (VI B 15), 5791 (17), 5794 (35:15), 5795 (35:19), 5796 (35:24), 5883 (VII¹ A 23), 6224 (IX A 208), 6646 (X³ A 190), 6702 (635).
SUBJECTIVITY/OBJECTIVITY. 188 (X² A 396), 591 (X¹ A 271), 673 (566), 3170 (X⁵ A 10), 3492 (X² A 230), 3902 (X⁴ A 412), 4052 (X¹ A 17), 4153 (IX A 445), 4315 (X⁵ A 35), 4350 (XI¹ A 487), 4375 (X¹ A 478), 4591 (VII¹ A 22), 4886 (XI¹ A 355), 4958 (II A 452), 4959 (453), 5049 (XI² A 294), 5102 (I A 77), 5334 (II C 3), 6360 (X¹ A 146), 6614 (X³ A 67), 6687 (530).
Subjunctive. 2315 (II A 161).
Subscription publishing. 6095 (VIII² B 188).
Substitute. 4228 (XI¹ A 98).
Success. 305 (VIII¹ A 145), 608 (354), 1433 (X⁵ A 39), 1776 (IX A 202), 1794 (X³ A 689), 2217 (IX A 424), 2221 (X³ A 293), 2301 (X⁴ A 247), 2666 (XI¹ A 511), 4152 (IX A 364), 4682 (X⁴ A 570), 4743 (477), 4856 (IX A 326), 6188 (134).
Sue, Eugène. 820 (X² A 392), 995 (X⁴ A 176).
Suetonius, Paulinus. 4103 (IV A 7), 4105 (13), 4419 (18).
SUFFERING. 267 (IV A 60), 1091 (XI¹ A 411), 1345 (VII¹ A 62), 1990 (VI A 106), 1994 (VII¹ A 149), 2059 (XI¹ A 272), 2108 (322), 2109 (323), 2837 (VI A 138), 2852 (X¹ A 34), 3586 (XI¹ A 203), 3739 (VI B 59:2), 3828 (X⁴ A 224), 4475 (430), 4545

(IX A 363), 4552 (X² A 322), 4892 (XI¹ A 418), 4972 (X³ A 677), 4983 (XI¹ A 544), 5002 (233), 5016 (VIII¹ A 150), 5025 (XI¹ A 243), 5026 (254), 5027 (286), 5258 (II A 649), 5475 (III A 83), 5569 (207), 5801 (VI A 31), 5805 (VI B 41:10), 5840 (VI A 103), 6269 (IX A 379), 6425 (X¹ A 488).

—Christian suffering. 77 (X³ A 186), 86 (XI¹ A 407), 106 (X³ A 96), 107 (97), 108 (X⁴ A 387), 168 (X¹ A 346), 396 (X³ A 282), 472 (VIII¹ A 493), 479 (IX A 20), 483 (147), 486 (292), 490 (350), 496 (X¹ A 190), 501 (438), 509 (649), 534 (X⁴ A 470), 541 (X⁵ A 36), 612 (X² A 57), 615 (XI² A 263), 625 (VI B 10), 671 (X¹ A 345), 780 (X⁴ A 234), 843 (X¹ A 426), 932 (VII¹ A 73), 974 (X¹ A 412), 1045 (VII¹ A 217), 1126 (IX A 311), 1195 (X⁴ A 127), 1274 (XI¹ A 23), 1275 (XI² A 24), 1324 (III A 101), 1385 (X¹ A 64), 1447 (XI² A 130), 1449 (133), 1497 (284), 1519 (224), 1520 (245), 1532 (X³ A 284), 1653 (X² A 353), 1813 (XI¹ A 515), 1860 (X² A 326), 1865 (X³ A 207), 1866 (272), 1867 (276), 1868 (277), 1869 (283), 1898 (X⁴ A 275), 1924 (X⁵ A 87), 1940 (XI² A 434), 1943 (X⁴ A 471), 2070 (XI¹ A 455), 2097 (321), 2183 (III A 194), 2185 (IV A 146), 2203 (X⁴ A 183), 2222 (572), 2449 (XI¹ A 459), 2471 (IX A 24), 2482 (X¹ A 172), 2502 (651), 2517 (X³ A 138), 2525 (302), 2554 (XI¹ A 572), 2572 (XI² A 56), 2662 (X⁴ A 108), 2671 (X² A 57), 2689 (VIII¹ A 341), 2711 (X³ A 175), 2731 (XI¹ A 345), 2751 (IX A 362), 2885 (X³ A 722), 2907 (XI¹ A 155), 2908 (157), 3005 (XI² A 214), 3349 (X³ A 482), 3481 (X¹ A 125), 3501 (X³ A 129), 3518 (X⁴ A 124), 3528 (671), 3650 (XI¹ A 495), 3664 (XI² A 65), 3677 (X³ A 125), 3739 (VI B 59:2), 3755 (X³ A 456), 3756 (457), 3777 (XI¹ A 143), 3868 (583), 3881 (181), 3903 (285), 4042 (X³ A 341), 4043 (376), 4059 (XI² A 343), 4152 (IX A 364), 4197 (X⁴ A 40), 4343 (508), 4354 (XI¹ A 558), 4359 (XI² A 246), 4478 (X⁵ A 82), 4737 (X³ A 429), 4797 (X¹ A 581), 4803 (X⁵ A 65), 4817 (X⁴ A 10), 4855 (IX A 304), 4857 (487), 4867 (X² A 635), 4868 (X³ A 25), 4879 (X⁴ A 342), 4881 (609), 4899 (509), 4902

(636), 4950 (X³ A 43), 5021 (273), 5032 (XI¹ A 545), 6241 (IX A 236), 6252 (283), 6272 (393), 6276 (416), 6323 (X¹ A 72), 6389 (272), 6532 (X² A 195), 6793 (X⁴ A 474), 6794 (488), 6924 (XI² A 45), 6966 (436), 6968 (438).

—Christ's suffering. 299 (III C 6), 308 (VIII¹ A 344), 315 (391), 334 (279), 365 (XI¹ A 280), 368 (XI² A 25), 1661 (X⁴ A 588), 2110 (III C 25), 2753 (IX A 404), 3442 (X⁶ B 239), 3645 (X² A 296), 4214 (X⁴ A 209), 4749 (181), 4771 (144).

—Ethical suffering. 245 (I A 138), 247 (VIII¹ A 405), 248 (425), 947 (236), 964 (IX A 392), 1054 (382), 1066 (XI¹ A 353), 1166 (VIII¹ A 499), 1532 (X³ A 284), 1809 (XI¹ A 429), 2572 (XI² A 56), 2650 (X¹ A 16), 3834 (XI¹ A 271), 3872 (75), 4155 (IX A 453), 4514 (X³ A 643).

—Martyrdom (see also MARTYR). 245 (I A 138), 2650 (X¹ A 16), 2659 (X³ A 303).

—Religious suffering. 666 (X¹ A 122), 757 (VI A 51), 964 (IX A 392), 974 (X¹ A 412), 1382 (20), 1409 (X³ A 359), 1420 (781), 1433 (X⁵ A 39), 1434 (55), 1447 (XI² A 130), 1449 (133), 1532 (X³ A 284), 1536 (X⁴ A 396), 2215 (III A 193), 2222 (X⁴ A 572), 2395 (III A 237), 2560 (X⁴ A 612), 3648 (XI¹ A 2), 3705 (IX A 365), 4369 332), 4370 (333), 4375 (X¹ A 478), 4379 (X⁴ A 411), 4384 (XI² A 132), 4474 (X⁴ A 335), 4756 (X³ A 185), 4949 (X⁴ A 487), 6323 (X¹ A 72), 6837 (X⁵ A 72).

—Suffering (S.K.). 5432 (II A 807), 5562 (III A 228), 5563 (229), 6021 (VIII¹ A 185), 6045 (254), 6091 (L. 167), 6102 (VIII¹ A 507), 6214 (IX A 183), 6230 (217), 6262 (312), 6266 (371), 6284 (451), 6435 (X¹ A 519), 6444 (541), 6507 (X² A 92), 6510 (105), 6514 (112), 6579 (411), 6613 (X³ A 41), 6615 (68), 6626 (115), 6642 (168), 6718 (789), 6823 (X⁴ A 663), 6895 (XI¹ A 382), 6936 (XI² A 250).

SUICIDE. 497 (X¹ A 217), 705 (V A 68), 738 (II A 409), 992 (X³ A 715), 1183 (II A 50), 1184 (56), 1672 (I A 158), 1791 (X³ A 525), 2692 (X¹ A 642), 2725 (X³ A 216), 3880 (XI¹ A 179), 3898 (IX A 373), 4261 (V A 113), 4511 (IV C 54), 4513 (X³ A 14), 4515 (X⁴ A 464), 4581 (X⁵ A 63), 5026

(XI¹ A 254), 5183 (I A 330), 5393 (II A 482), 5515 (III A 159).

Sunlight. 712 (II A 213), 6764 (x⁴ A 301).

Sunstroke. 4479 (x⁵ A 95), 4903 (17).

Superficiality. 3604 (XI¹ A 480).

SUPERIORITY. 793 (x³ A 729), 2943 (IX A 452), 4155 (453), 4865 (x² A 435).

Superlative. 4752 (x¹ A 490).

Supernaturalism. 2252 (II C 48).

SUPERSTITION. 48 (V A 25), 1332 (IV A 157), 1764 (x³ A 228), 2743 (IX A 35), 3579 (II A 537).

Sustenance. 296 (II A 419).

Swedborg, Jesper. 1845 (IX A 7).

Swedish family. 5830 (VI A 87).

Swift, Jonathan. 701 (III A 123), 745 (V A 33), 1727 (III B 9).

Swimming. 668 (x¹ A 185), 2359 (XI² A 103), 5049 (50), 6892 (XI¹ A 300).

Symbolic books. 2870 (x³ A 32).

Symbolik des Traums. 2307 (II A 62).

Sympathy. 386 (x² A 27), 666 (x¹ A 122), 2420 (IX A 327), 2562 (x⁵ A 86), 3877 (XI¹ A 144), 3899 (x¹ A 65), 3915 (III C 1), 3929 (IX A 267), 4155 (453), 4376 (x² A 182), 4381 (x⁴ A 462), 4663 (x³ A 731), 4684 (x⁴ A 574), 4701 (x⁵ A 85), 4745 (II A 366), 4826 (IV C 110), 4909 (XI¹ A 351), 4922 (296), 6175 (IX A 87), 6241 (236), 6262 (312), 6275 (413), 6319 (x¹ A 61), 6323 (72), 6626 (x³ A 115), 6882 (XI¹ A 210), 6888 (275), 6924 (XI² A 45).

Synergism. 4004 (III A 118).

Synesius, Bishop. 5560 (III A 203).

Synthesis. 5792 (VI B 18).

System. 36 (II C 34), 972 (x¹ A 360), 1232 (I A 205), 1587 (III A 1), 1604 (IV A 185), 1616 (x³ A 786), 1702 (II A 140), 2004 (VIII¹ A 482), 2823 (x⁵ A 73), 2957 (x³ A 451), 3071 (II A 439), 3094 (x² A 502), 3221 (XI¹ A 341), 3248 (I A 127), 3250 (253), 3255 (II A 176), 3236 (177), 3268 (788), 3280 (814), 3292 (IV C 25), 3296 (IV A 163), 3304 (VI A 66), 3308 (VII¹ A 82), 3564 (x¹ A 561), 3565 (573), 3716 (x⁴ A 528), 3850 (II A 199), 3859 (563), 4099 (573), 4304 (XI¹ A 449), 4398 (I C 126), 4983 (XI¹ A 544), 5092 (I A 72), 5181 (328), 5574 (IV A 2), 6360 (x¹ A 146), 6449 (556), 6596 (x⁶ B 128), 6748 (171).

Sæding. 5437 (III A 15), 5463 (66), 5468 (73), 5470 (75), 5473 (80), 5474 (81), 5874 (VII¹ A 5).

Søborg lake. 5095 (I A 64), 5106 (69).

Sølling, Peder N. 6026 (VIII¹ A 207).

Søren. 5902 (VII¹ A 115), 6509 (x² A 101), 6551 (260), 6580 (413), 6609 (x³ A 8), 6738 (x⁴ A 87, 6879 (x¹ A 177).

Tactic. 4054 (x⁴ A 397), 6726 (23), 6739 (101).

Taifel, André. 2362 (IV A 26).

Talent. 422 (II A 30), 958 (VIII¹ A 671), 989 (x³ A 140), 990 (248), 1301 (XI¹ A 120), 1804 (197), 2907 (155), 4054 (x⁴ A 397), 4358 (XI² A 228), 5431 (II A 806), 6780 (x⁴ A 383).

Talk. 4813 (XI² A 76), 6964 (411).

Talleyrand, Charles M. de. 623 (V A 19), 2322 (V B 115:2), 3870 (XI² A 117), 4276 (x² A 248).

Tangent. 327 (x¹ A 49), 1780 (435).

Tanner. 6489 (x² A 10).

Tantalus. 5416 (II A 820).

Tarquinus Superbus. 4865 (x² A 435), 5672 (IV A 122).

Task. 3624 (XI¹ A 437), 4480 (456), 4491 (XI² A 73), 6205 (IX A 171), 6373 (x¹ A 187), 6521 (x² A 157), 6525 (174), 6533 (196), 6595 (596), 6632 (x³ A 152), 6693 (565), 6721 (x⁴ A 6), 6918 (XI² A 21).

Tauler, Johannes. 1844 (VIII¹ A 587), 4598 (117).

Tautology. 2211 (II A 71), 4898 (x⁴ A 480).

Taxes. 5300 (II A 700).

Tea. 4722 (XI¹ A 579), 4723 (580).

Teachers. 289 (II A 289), 521 (x³ A 173), 863 (II A 671), 2586 (III A 117), 2854 (I A 26), 2870 (x³ A 32), 3539 (XI² A 249), 4240 (352), 4893 (x¹ A 625), 4971 (x³ A 570), 5376 (II A 397), 5686 (IV B 159:6), 5825 (VI A 82).

Teaching. 482 (IX A 105), 581 (I A 108), 646 (VIII¹ A 554), 779 (x² A 386), 1060 (606), 2053 (XI¹ A 148), 3218 (x² A 312), 3465 (V A 12), 3772 (x⁵ A 58), 3824 (x³ A 6), 4185 (346), 4312 (x⁴ A 484), 4544 (VIII¹ A 535), 5290 (II A 683), 6360 (x¹ A 146), 6643 (x³ A 174), 6702 (635), 6748 (x⁶ B 171).

Teachings. 3539 (XI² A 249).

Tears. 448 (II A 547), 3466 (V A 17), 5475 (III A 83), 5920 (VII¹ A 43), 6806 (x⁴ A 566).

"Tears at a Grave." 5821 (VI A 76).

Teaser, teasing. 1063 (x⁴ A 5), 5187 (I A 335), 5774 (VI A 142), 5775 (143), 5776 (144).

Technicians. 1182 (II A 29).

Technology. 2819 (VII¹ A 199), 4233 (XI¹ A 507).

Tegnér, Esaias. 3800 (I A 136).

Telegraph. 6911 (XI¹ A 551).

TELEOLOGICAL SUSPENSION. 6598 (x⁶ B 68), 6718 (x³ A 789).

Teleology. 704 (IV A 192), 931 (VII¹ A 35), 2291 (31), 2295 (185), 2579 (II A 374).

Telescope. 5478 (L. 17).

Telescope drawing. 5478 (L. 17).

Temperance society. 5857 (VII¹ A 233).

Temple archive. 5483 (L. 29).

Temporal. 161 (VIII¹ A 88), 843 (x¹ A 426), 2599 (VIII¹ A 369), 4810 (XI¹ A 468), 5792 (VI B 18).

Temporality. 235 (IX A 387), 327 (x¹ A 49), 838 (VIII¹ A 73), 1501 (XI² A 182), 2004 (VIII¹ A 482), 2114 (V B 227:5), 2225 (XI¹ A 151).

Temporary, the. 4218 (x⁶ B 257).

TEMPTATION. 91 (II A 18), 102 (x² A 22), 219 (II A 127), 328 (x¹ A 127), 420 (I A 174), 429 (II A 234), 436 (293), 488 (IX A 300), 610 (21), 634 (VI B 60:2), 856 (II A 39), 3830 (x⁴ A 119), 3989 (I A 3), 4001 (II A 310), 4002 (311), 4023 (x¹ A 637), 4367 (VIII¹ A 93), 4372 (x¹ A 22), 4373 (452), 4374 (477), 4378 (x⁴ A 95), 4382 (XI² A 30), 4698 (x⁵ A 30), 5485 (III C 4).

Ten Commandments. 5265 (II A 673).

Tennemann, Wilhelm G. 42 (IV C 50), 258 (47), 1430 (x⁴ A 567), 2280 (IV A 198), 2339 (IV C 12), 2348 (V C 6), 2361 (IV A 12), 3295 (55), 4248 (200), 4511 (IV C 54), 4512 (IV A 44), 4844 (IV C 52), 4847 (IV A 42), 5572 (IV C 2), 5595 (42), 5596 (43), 5598 (45), 5600 (83), 5618 (IV A 63), 5639 (75).

Tension. 510 (x² A 37), 2500 (x¹ A 595).

TERSTEEGEN, Gerhard. 1390 (x¹ A 479), 4040 (x³ A 181), 6426 (x¹ A 494), 6762 (x⁴ A 299).

TERTULLIAN, Quintus S. F. 542 (x⁵ A 98),

559 (XI² A 47), 616 (341), 817 (x¹ A 502), 1196 (x⁴ A 145), 2379 (XI² A 39), 3790 (x³ A 298), 4095 (II A 467), 5831 (VI B 233).

Tests. 298 (II A 569), 441 (333), 1155 (III C 7), 3098 (XI¹ A 299), 3380 (II A 538), 4001 (310), 5485 (III C 4), 5575 (IV A 197), 5812 (VI A 54).

Test-trial. 4636 (x¹ A 603).

Thales. 3342 (IX A 239).

Theater. 141 (III A 110), 165 (IX A 447), 1051 (154), 1759 (420), 3698 (II A 57), 4177 (x² A 486), 4470 (x⁴ A 160), 4828 (IV C 112), 4970 (x³ A 561), 5040 (x⁴ A 90), 5049 (XI² A 294), 5182 (I A 329), 5557 (III A 224), 6150 (IX A 39), 6332 (x⁵ A 153).

Theater analogy. 6861 (XI¹ A 71).

Them. 5473 (III A 80).

Theocracy. 2225 (XI¹ A 151).

Theodorus Atheos. 5639 (IV A 75).

THEOLOGIANS. 4776 (II A 543).

Theological degree (S.K.). 5769 (VI A 8).

Theologisk Tidsskrift. 5944 (VII¹ A 158).

THEOLOGY. 305 (VIII¹ A 145), 410 (I A 4), 429 (II A 234), 1443 (XI¹ A 591), 2823 (x⁵ A 73), 3077 (IV A 103), 3118 (x³ A 641), 3195 (x¹ A 401), 3204 (IX B 5:2y), 3245 (I A 94), 3259 (II A 329), 3273 (440), 3865 (461), 3878 (XI¹ A 165), 4174 (x² A 395), 4455 (x¹ A 383), 4553 (x² A 336), 5092 (I A 72), 5418 (II C 33).

Theophilus Nicolaus. 6597 (x² A 601), 6598 (x⁶ B 68), 6599 (69), 6600 (77), 6601 (82).

Theorizing. 2043 (x⁴ A 427).

Theory. 1182 (II A 29), 2509 (x² A 263), 3716 (x⁴ A 528), 3870 (XI² A 117), 5230 (II A 602).

Theresa, St. 3435 (x¹ A 291).

Thesis. 530 (x⁴ A 115), 6842 (x⁶ B 232, p. 377), 6943 (XI³ B 53), 6947 (57).

Thief (*see also* Thieves). 285 (II A 713), 362 (x⁵ A 131), 424 (II A 83), 549 (XI¹ A 124), 4741 (x³ A 727).

Thiele, Just M. 2232 (XI¹ A 374), 2704 (II A 631), 5094 (I A 63), 5095 (64).

Thieves (*see also* Thief). 5064 (I A 39), 5076 (17).

Thinker. 3666 (VIII¹ A 201), 6400 (x¹ A 338), 6465 (616).

Thinking. 155 (VII¹ A 13), 1375 (IX A 254), 3657 (IV C 78), 3701 (IV A 51), 5951 (VII¹ A 202), 6152 (IX A 42), 6909 (XI¹ A 510).

Third. 2380 (II A 24), 2381 (25).

Third person. 71 (X² A 78), 2075 (XI¹ A 533), 2077 (587).

Thirty-fourth birthday (S.K.). 5999 (VIII¹ A 100), 6003 (L. 149).

Thisted, Jørgen O. 3510 (X³ A 364).

Tholuck, Friedrich A. G. 5435 (II C 9).

Thomas. 2302 (X⁴ A 310), 6247 (IX A 262).

THOMAS à KEMPIS. 2016 (X¹ A 286), 2691 (400), 6524 (X² A 167).

Thomsen, Grimur. 5844 (VI A 128), 5845 (129).

Thomsen, Julie. 6294 (L. 195).

Thor. 5101 (I A 76), 5128 (I C 82).

Thorn in the flesh. 2635 (VIII¹ A 396), 4368 (IX A 331), 4585 (V A 43), 4644 (X² A 246), 4654 (X³ A 182), 5913 (VII¹ A 126), 6002 (VIII¹ A 119), 6011 (156), 6021 (185), 6025 (205), 6183 (IX A 128), 6224 (208), 6396 (X¹ A 322), 6468 (643), 6492 (X² A 20), 6532 (X² A 195), 6659 (X³ A 310), 6769 (X⁴ A 323), 6837 (X⁵ A 72), 6906 (XI¹ A 484).

Thorwaldsen, Bertel. 3805 (I A 200).

Thou (see "Du").

Thought (see also REFLECTION). 195 (II A 367), 197 (IV C 100), 623 (V A 19), 633 (V B 40:45), 772 (IV A 72), 1028 (IV C 92), 1030 (IV A 164), 1033 (V A 30), 1034 (65), 1039 (V B 54:10), 1042 (VII¹ A 80), 1043 (140), 1047 (VIII¹ A 226), 1057 (X² A 328), 1129 (X¹ A 367), 1605 (V A 73), 1606 (V B 41), 2119 (VIII¹ A 511), 2235 (V B 54:16), 2261 (II A 348), 2309 (155), 2310 (156), 2311 (157), 2312 (158), 2315 (161), 2324 (X² A 235), 3049 (VIII¹ A 331), 3308 (VII¹ A 82), 3666 (VIII¹ A 201), 3855 (II A 122), 4030 (X² A 436), 4538 (VI A 63), 4539 (64), 4610 (VIII¹ A 579), 4898 (X⁴ A 480), 5188 (I A 336).

Thought, conjunctivial. 2314 (II A 160).

Thought experiment. 868 (II A 430).

Thought, indicative and conjunctivial. 2313 (II A 159).

"Thoughts That Cure Radically." 6110 (VIII¹ A 558).

"Thoughts That Wound From Behind." 6096 (VIII¹ A 486), 6107 (548), 6110 (558), 6111 (559), 6113 (561).

Thousand and One Nights. 489 (IX A 329), 3821 (III A 113), 4142 (VIII¹ A 649), 4615 (631), 4990 (485), 6109 (557).

Thread analogy. 3540 (XI² A 281), 3689 (X⁴ A 190), 6803 (557).

"Three Discourses on Imaginary Occasions." 6500 (X² A 61).

"Three Minor Ethical-Religious Essays" (see also "Two Minor Ethical-Religious Essays"). 6441 (X¹ A 535), 6640 (X⁶ B 167), 6838 (X⁵ A 93).

"Three Moral Tales." 5774 (VI A 142), 5775 (143), 5776 (144).

"Three Notes." 6325 (X¹ A 74), 6329 (84), 6346 (116), 6347 (118), 6363 (152), 6383 (250), 6407 (351), 6416 (422), 6487 (678).

Three things. 6935 (XI² A 248).

Tiberius, Claudius Nero. 4821 (X⁴ A 328).

Tidsskrift. 4243 (II A 186), 6566 (X⁶ B 127).

Tieck, Ludwig. 265 (II A 12), 1699 (136), 3806 (I A 203), 3971 (IV A 194), 4388 (I A 167), 4773 (II A 34), 5138 (I C 95), 5163 (103), 5165 (104), 6318 (X¹ A 58), 6320 (63).

TIME (see also Future; HISTORY; Past; Present). 5 (IV A 108), 206 (143), 217 (I A 290), 227 (I C 40), 229 (III A 87), 311 (VIII¹ A 371), 347 (X² A 86), 387 (58), 539 (X⁴ A 648), 547 (XI¹ A 91), 571 (X² A 283), 646 (VIII¹ A 554), 832 (II A 100), 834 (570), 842 (X¹ A 48), 843 (426), 907 (IV A 213), 911 (179), 1003 (XI¹ A 252), 1052 (IX A 358), 1108 (IV A 117), 1232 (I A 205), 1327 (III A 131), 1403 (X² A 569), 1473 (219), 1535 (X³ A 775), 1635 (IV C 35), 1638 (VI B 35:25), 1639 (VIII¹ A 305), 1937 (XI¹ A 588), 1940 (XI² A 434), 1987 (V A 60), 2061 (XI¹ A 319), 2088 (II A 448), 2394 (III B 114), 2565 (XI¹ A 435), 2739 (IV A 3), 2740 (V B 55:6), 3044 (XI² A 163), 3093 (X² A 501), 3098 (XI¹ A 299), 3430 (IX A 417), 3868 (XI¹ A 583), 3915 (III C 1), 3942 (X² A 597), 3951 (X³ A 706), 4028 (X² A 404), 4327 (X¹ A 652), 4429 (VI A 114), 4460 (X² A 642), 4511 (IV A 54), 4589 (VI A 48), 4601 (VIII¹ A 192), 4696 (X⁵ A 11), 4712 (XI¹ A 377), 4837 (IV C 121), 4922 (296), 4940 (X⁵ A 41), 5009 (VIII¹ A 104), 5010 (105), 5032

(XI¹ A 545), 5276 (II A 630), 5302 (209), 5395 (492), 5396 (495), 5849 (VI A 135), 5928 (VII¹ A 78), 6104 (VIII¹ A 533), 6369 (X¹ A 166), 6967 (XI² A 437).

Tin box. 6640 (X⁶ B 167).

Tithing. 440 (II A 329).

Tivoli. 1899 (X⁴ A 293), 6386 (X¹ A 262).

Tobit, Book of. 5419 (II C 36).

Togetherness. 4186 (X³ A 529).

Tolerance. 383 (X¹ A 460), 599 (X⁴ A 22), 3053 (X² A 133), 6122 (VIII¹ A 591).

TOLERATION.

Tongues. 2333 (XI² A 37), 2674 (XI¹ A 40), 2896 (X⁵ A 66), 4714 (XI¹ A 413).

Top. 2724 (XI¹ A 186).

Tordenskjold, Peder. 4106 (V A 77).

Tornebuskegade. 6376 (X¹ A 202), 6629 (X³ A 144).

Torture. 516 (X² A 460).

Totality. 5099 (I A 68), 6388 (X¹ A 266), 6393 (300).

Towns. 5246 (II A 126).

Toys. 268 (V A 2).

Tradition. 214 (X⁴ A 433), 654 (VIII² B 86), 977 (X¹ A 580), 2787 (I A 278), 3014 (X¹ A 396), 4188 (X³ A 587).

TRAGEDY (see also Comedy). 26 (I A 149), 118 (33), 125 (198), 150 (V B 148:17), 429 (II A 234), 1456 (I A 224), 1674 (207), 1675 (238), 2042 (X⁴ A 415), 5074 (I A 15), 5186 (333), 5247 (II A 132), 5546 (III C 37), 5576 (IV A 8), 5617 (61), 6694 (X³ A 568).

Traitor. 6523 (X² A 163).

Tramp. 5457 (III A 57), 5464 (67).

Tranquillity. 6863 (XI¹ A 76).

Transcendence. 297 (II A 473), 833 (351), 1383 (X¹ A 59), 1385 (64), 2234 (II A 486), 2437 (X⁴ A 482), 3088 (VII² B 256: 9-10), 5928 (VII¹ A 78), 6516 (X² A 134).

Transition. 554 (XI¹ A 324), 653 (VIII² B 85), 1603 (IV C 81), 2339 (12), 2353 (VI A 33), 4421 (IV C 94), 5272 (II C 39).

Translation. 2325 (X⁴ A 197), 2327 (199).

Transparence. 2119 (VIII¹ A 511), 3228 (XI² A 402).

Transparency. 1050 (VIII¹ A 320), 3105 (X³ A 542), 3224 (XI² A 107), 3228 (402), 3955 (X³ A 711), 4373 (X¹ A 452), 4384 (XI² A 132), 4434 (VII¹ A 192:12), 4564 (X⁴ A 346).

Travel. 5506 (III A 146), 5552 (L. 69), 6035

(VIII¹ A 227), 6041 (246), 6042 (249), 6043 (250), 6134 (648), 6268 (IX A 375), 6285 (458), 6325 (X¹ A 74), 6376 (202), 6383 (250), 6388 (266), 6390 (273), 6391 (281), 6416 (422), 6418 (424), 6472 (X⁵ A 149), 6489 (X² A 10), 6628 (X³ A 142), 6762 (X⁴ A 299).

Travel analogy. 5398 (II A 503).

Treason. 2571 (XI² A 55), 2575 (152).

Trekroner. 5478 (L. 17).

Trendelenburg, Friedrich A. 199 (VI B 54: 21), 263 (X² A 324), 1941 (V A 75), 2341 (74), 2352 (V C 12), 3300 (V A 98), 3306 (VI A 145), 4252 (IV A 205), 5742 (V C 11), 5977 (VIII² C 1), 5978 (VIII¹ A 18).

Trial. 610 (IX A 21), 634 (VI B 60:2), 884 (III A 125), 964 (IX A 392), 1260 (X² A 243), 1421 (X³ A 790), 2095 (766), 3579 (X⁴ A 614).

Tribulation. 4600 (VIII¹ A 191).

Trier, Seligmann M. 6267 (L. 192).

Trinity. 1615 (X² A 431).

Trolls. 5132 (I A 143), 5133 (144).

Troubadors. 5492 (III A 93).

Trousers. 5863 (VII¹ B 69), 5922 (VII¹ A 50), 5937 (147), 5998 (VIII¹ A 99), 6004 (120), 6160 (IX A 64), 6225 (209), 6379 (X¹ A 234), 6386 (262), 6458 (584), 6609 (X³ A 8), 6883 (XI¹ A 214), 6899 (424), 6916 (XI² A 11).

Trust. 1102 (III A 127), 1108 (IV A 117), 4442 (VIII¹ A 78), 6001 (116).

TRUTH. 414 (I A 46), 499 (X¹ A 399), 580 (I A 58), 591 (X¹ A 271), 641 (VIII¹ A 293), 671 (X¹ A 345), 678 (X² A 466), 753 (II A 751), 829 (XI² A 280), 930 (VII¹ A 30), 977 (X¹ A 580), 1044 (VII¹ A 216), 1049 (VIII¹ A 292), 1066 (XI¹ A 353), 1197 (X⁴ A 170), 1243 (IV C 56), 1429 (X⁴ A 485), 1445 (XI² A 98), 1542 (II A 2), 1682 (78), 1804 (XI¹ A 197), 1825 (XI³ B 199), 1957 (IX A 221), 1977 (II A 267), 1987 (V A 60), 2043 (X⁴ A 427), 2046 (X⁵ A 121), 2102 (26), 2165 (X³ A 231), 2299 (IX A 438), 2301 (X⁴ A 247), 2358 (X¹ A 361), 2463 (VIII¹ A 465), 2467 (IX A 11), 2500 (X¹ A 595), 2512 (X² A 448), 2517 (X³ A 138), 2542 (X⁴ A 451), 2650 (X¹ A 16), 2923 (VII¹ A 100), 2932 (VIII¹ A 656), 2935 (571), 2944 (IX A 490), 2963 (X⁴ A 107), 3058 (II A 676), 3070 (755), 3141 (X² A 418), 3218 (312), 3484 (X¹ A 207), 3608

(481), 3616 (XI² A 338), 3666 (VIII¹ A 201), 3668 (IX A 163), 3669 (344), 3670 (415), 3672 (474), 3694 (X⁴ A 295), 3772 (X⁵ A 58), 3852 (X² A 416), 4052 (X¹ A 17), 4112 (VII¹ A 63), 4119 (VIII¹ A 134), 4160 (X¹ A 356), 4198 (X⁴ A 41), 4228 (XI¹ A 98), 4265 (VII¹ A 69), 4267 (193), 4280 (X³ A 315), 4299 (XI¹ A 37), 4315 (X⁵ A 35), 4375 (X¹ A 478), 4433 (VII¹ A 68), 4540 (72), 4565 (X⁴ A 379), 4572 (XI¹ A 196), 4619 (IX A 270), 4649 (X³ A 81), 4653 (148), 4656 (281), 4686 (X⁴ A 579), 4728 (XI¹ A 136), 4765 (X⁴ A 138), 4944 (XI¹ A 521), 4958 (II A 452), 4962 (IX A 124), 4975 (X⁴ A 381), 4976 (406), 4986 (XI² A 57), 5020 (X² A 568), 5034 (XI¹ A 567), 5043 (X⁴ A 654), 5100 (I A 75), 5263 (II A 167), 5272 (II C 39), 5417 (II A 821), 5620 (IV B 10a), 5646 (IV A 87), 5752 (V A 92), 5788 (VI B 14), 5793 (35:14), 5794 (35:15), 5795 (35:19), 5796 (35:24), 5883 (VII¹ A 23), 5948 (176), 5964 (224), 6050 (VIII¹ A 271), 6051 (276), 6075 (414), 6224 (IX A 208), 6243 (243), 6301 (X¹ A 14), 6302 (15), 6440 (531), 6500 (X² A 61), 6646 (X³ A 190), 6680 (450), 6861 (XI¹ A 71), 6911 (551).

Tryde, Eggert C. 4565 (X⁴ A 379), 6310 (X¹ A 42), 6687 (X³ A 530).

Turtle analogy. 5063 (I A 32).

Tutti Frutti. 5071 (I A 41).

Twenty-fifth birthday (S.K.). 5429 (II A 804).

Two Ages. 4167 (X² A 52), 5867 (VII¹ B 95), 5868 (132), 5869 (135:5), 5873 (VII¹ A 4), 5877 (9), 5880 (VII¹ B 131), 5891 (VII¹ A 104), 5911 (L. 136), 6366 (X¹ A 161), 6604 (X² A 622), 6777 (X⁴ A 373), 6804 (558).

Two conditions. 698 (XI¹ A 362).

"Two Minor Ethical-Religious Essays" (*see also* "Three Minor Ethical-Religious Essays"). 3429 (X¹ A 328), 6049 (VIII¹ A 264), 6050 (271), 6079 (440), 6114 (562), 6115 (563), 6229 (IX A 216), 6264 (338), 6358 (X¹ A 140), 6399 (336), 6400 (338), 6407 (351), 6420 (441), 6429 (497), 6447 (551), 6704 (X³ A 637).

Type. 2071 (XI¹ A 485)

Typesetter. 5644 (IV A 83).

Typhon. 42 (IV C 50).

Typographical error. 6399 (X¹ A 336), 6858 (XI¹ A 49).

Tyranny. 4235 (XI² A 23).

Tyrant. 2648 (IX B 63:12), 4118 (VIII¹ A 123), 4144 (667), 4221 (X⁵ A 136), 5352 (II A 275).

Tzschirner Heinrich G. 681 (X³ A 648).

Ugly, the. 942 (VIII¹ A 189).

Ullmann, Karl. 1484 (X⁴ A 230), 2759 (374).

Ulysses. 416 (I A 95).

Umbrella. 3045 (I A 45), 5555 (III A 221), 5765 (VI B 227), 5930 (VII¹ A 90).

Uncertainty. 3765 (X⁴ A 645).

UNCHANGEABLENESS. 1304 (I A 29), 1332 (IV A 157), 1348 (VII¹ A 143), 1428 (X⁴ A 311), 4713 (XI¹ A 484), 4715 (422), 4776 (II A 543), 4777 (544), 5973 (VIII¹ A 5), 6895 (XI¹ A 382), 6965 (XI³ B 291:4).

Unconditional, the. 536 (X⁴ A 384), 975 (X¹ A 430), 2074 (XI¹ A 518), 2204 (X⁴ A 384), 3715 (525).

UNCONDITIONED, THE. 1449 (XI² A 133), 2046 (X⁵ A 121), 2555 (XI² A 194), 2571 (55), 2572 (56), 2898 (X⁵ A 96), 2998 (XI² A 159), 4528 (XI¹ A 266), 4704 (8), 4884 (146), 4918 (XI² A 205), 4933 (X³ A 470), 4939 (X⁴ A 538), 4977 (X⁵ A 18), 6773 (X⁴ A 353), 6793 (474), 6902 (XI¹ A 445), 6924 (XI² A 45), 6966 (436).

Unconscious, the. 781 (X² A 258).

Understanding (*see also* REASON). 5 (IV A 108), 77 (X³ A 186), 493 (IX A 414), 500 (X¹ A 427), 523 (X³ A 285), 645 (VIII¹ A 466), 1130 (X¹ A 368), 1132 (554), 1202 (III C 16), 1554 (V B 44), 1559 (X² A 225), 1615 (431), 1792 (X³ A 576), 1940 (XI² A 434), 2205 (114), 2290 (VII¹ A 236), 2302 (X⁴ A 310), 2461 (VII¹ A 192), 2489 (X¹ A 324), 2498 (526), 2645 (IX A 435), 2874 (X³ A 169), 3032 (XI¹ A 339), 3109 (X³ A 609), 3346 (X² A 202), 3567 (X¹ A 679), 3693 (X⁴ A 289), 3705 (IX A 365), 4476 (X⁴ A 461), 4479 (X⁵ A 95), 4491 (XI² A 73), 4765 (X⁴ A 138), 4806 (XI¹ A 329), 5915 (VII¹ A 128), 6234 (IX A 222), 6319 (X¹ A 61), 6373 (187), 6919 (XI² A 31).

Unhappiness. 877 (II A 530), 2416 (VIII¹ A 680), 2442 (X⁵ A 50), 3100 (XI² A 52), 4683 (X⁴ A 573).

Unhappy, the. 5842 (VI A 119).
Unhappy love. 2442 (x⁵ A 50), 5532 (III A 176), 5628 (IV A 215), 6473 (x⁵ A 150).
Uniformity. 2061 (XI¹ A 319).
United Brethren. 1874 (x³ A 338).
Unity. 77 (x³ A 186), 703 (IV A 57), 1247 (V A 90).
Universal, the. 4 (VIII¹ A 622), 43 (IV C 76), 69 (x¹ A 112), 107 (x³ A 97), 629 (VI A 115), 666 (x¹ A 122), 840 (VIII¹ A 221), 896 (IV C 96), 975 (x¹ A 430), 996 (x⁴ A 184), 1085 (x³ A 464), 1086 (x⁴ A 32), 1088 (590), 1089 (591), 1476 (x³ A 72), 1591 (III A 186), 1972 (II C 41), 1984 (III A 136), 2607 (x¹ A 485), 2907 (XI¹ A 155), 3559 (x³ A 52), 4198 (x⁴ A 41), 4234 (XI¹ A 536), 4271 (VIII¹ A 491), 4469 (x⁴ A 125), 4474 (335), 4599 (VIII¹ A 161), 4816 (XI² A 382), 4951 (x³ A 617), 5842 (VI A 119), 5913 (VII¹ A 126), 5961 (221), 6002 (VIII¹ A 119), 6182 (IX A 125), 6262 (312), 6343 (x¹ A 112), 6357 (139), 6358 (140), 6718 (x³ A 789).
UNIVERSALISM. 410 (I A 4), 463 (VIII¹ A 157), 1495 (x⁵ A 108), 1503 (XI² A 342), 2070 (XI¹ A 455), 3153 (x³ A 267), 3987 (XI² A 142), 4351 (XI¹ A 498), 4543 (VIII¹ A 313), 6834 (x⁵ A 46), 6917 (XI² A 19), 6934 (244), 6947 (XI³ B 57).
Universality. 419 (I A 172), 431 (II A 249), 855 (III A 135), 998 (x⁴ A 362), 1073 (V B 213:2), 1326 (III A 104), 1385 (x¹ A 64), 1413 (x³ A 581), 1607 (VI B 54:30), 1610 (98:45), 1785 (x³ A 268), 1848 (IX A 101), 1914 (x⁴ A 556), 1970 (II A 172), 1977 (267), 1978 (385), 1993 (VII¹ A 199), 2005 (VIII¹ A 568), 2007 (IX A 268), 2019 (x² A 265), 2033 (x⁵ B 117), 2048 (XI¹ A 42), 2066 (384), 2074 (518), 2080 (XI² A 125), 2183 (III A 194), 2727 (x³ A 676), 2728 (x⁴ A 103), 2817 (VII¹ A 197), 2868 (x¹ A 482), 4060 (I A 42), 5975 (VIII¹ A 15).
Universally human, the. 43 (IV C 76), 871 (II A 450), 1939 (XI² A 358), 2966 (x⁴ A 535), 4376 (x² A 182), 6227 (IX A 213), 6275 (413).
Universe. 1307 (II A 622), 1387 (x¹ A 203).
Unrest (see also Disquiet). 2920 (XI² A 395), 3806 (I A 203), 4490 (XI² A 42), 4529 (XI¹ A 397), 4530 (398), 4807 (399).

Unseen, the. 1119 (VII¹ A 203).
Unselected. 6687 (x³ A 530).
Unwashed hands. 6635 (x³ A 164).
Unworthiness. 2009 (IX A 318).
Upbringing (see also EDUCATION: Religious Upbringing). 1166 (VIII¹ A 499), 1167 (537), 1171 (x¹ A 468), 1483 (x⁴ A 134), 2187 (VIII¹ A 90), 6252 (IX A 283), 6401 (x¹ A 342).
UPBUILDING, THE. 1588 (III A 6), 4593 (VIII¹ A 31), 4847 (IV A 42), 5634 (234), 5686 (IV B 159:6), 6238 (IX A 227), 6431 (x¹ A 510), 6436 (520), 6461 (593), 6519 (x² A 148).
Upbuilding Discourses. 641 (VIII¹ A 293), 656 (VIII² B 88), 1588 (III A 6), 4261 (V A 113), 4924 (IV A 80), 5487 (III C 8), 5644 (IV A 83), 5686 (IV B 159:6), 5734 (V B 232:1), 6229 (IX A 216), 6234 (222), 6242 (241), 6388 (x¹ A 266), 6472 (x⁵ A 149), 6545 (x² A 217), 6593 (560), 6800 (x⁴ A 540).
Upbuilding Discourses in Various Spirits. 4434 (VII¹ B 192:12), 4435 (192:13), 4436 (192:15), 4947 (145), 4948 (146), 5919 (136), 5925 (150), 5934 (192:1-2), 5945 (VII¹ A 160), 5948 (176), 5956 (218), 5970 (VIII¹ A 1), 5972 (4), 5975 (15), 5976 (16), 5997 (84), 6014 (164), 6795 (x⁴ A 511).
Urania. 3975 (VI A 124), 5859 (VII² B 274: 1-22).
Urban life (see also City). 2853 (x⁴ A 483).
Ussing, Johan L. 4795 (VIII¹ A 193).
Uticensis, Cato. 2755 (x³ A 216).
Utility. 849 (I A 124).
Utopianism. 5835 (VI A 95).

Valdemar Atterdag, King. 5095 (I A 64).
Valla, Laurentius. 2864 (IX A 384).
Value, values. 249 (VIII¹ A 526), 612 (x² A 57), 999 (x⁴ A 549), 1152 (XI² A 115).
Vaudeville. 5294 (II A 688).
Vellum copies. 6472 (x⁵ A 149).
Ventriloquism. 1541 (I A 340), 3224 (XI² A 107), 4056 (106).
VENTURE (see also Risk). 185 (x¹ A 5), 321 (IX A 57), 385 (x² A 16), 536 (x⁴ A 581), 561 (XI² A 102), 606 (VIII¹ A 128), 1046 (127), 1142 (x⁴ A 114), 1145 (455), 1259 (x² A 160), 1904 (x⁴ A 354), 1916 (650), 1992 (VII¹ B 121:6), 2121 (x¹ A 564),

2279 (III A 145), 2301 (x⁴ A 247), 2359 (XI² A 103), 2509 (x² A 263), 2679 (XI² A 91), 2902 (XI¹ A 73), 3099 (XI² A 51), 3108 (x³ A 546), 3156 (502), 3343 (IX A 352), 3705 (365), 3746 (486), 3830 (x⁴ A 119), 3831 (120), 3899 (x¹ A 65), 4058 (XI² A 319), 4330 (x² A 327), 4376 (182), 4378 (x⁴ A 95), 4379 (411), 4381 (462), 4460 (x² A 642), 4479 (x⁵ A 95), 4492 (XI² A 225), 4519 (x¹ A 429), 4674 (x⁴ A 239), 4690 (620), 4692 (630), 4757 (x³ A 202), 4890 (x⁴ A 297), 4899 (509), 4919 (XI² A 320), 4977 (x⁵ A 18), 5031 (XI¹ A 519), 5044 (248), 6372 (x¹ A 183), 6385 (260), 6391 (281), 6418 (424), 6501 (x² A 66), 6522 (158), 6623 (x³ A 98), 6812 (x⁴ A 603), 6862 (XI¹ A 72).

Venus. 2626 (XI² A 172), 4381 (x⁴ A 462).

Vespasian, Titus Flavius. 1447 (XI² A 130), 3686 (x³ A 696).

Vesterport. 5932 (VII¹ A 95).

Veterinary. 1649 (XI² A 234).

Victor Eremita. 5699 (IV A 170), 5705 (181), 5755 (V A 110), 5804 (VI A 41), 5823 (78), 5853 (VI B 192), 5860 (VII¹ B 1), 6413 (x¹ A 402).

Victorin Victorius Victor. 6787 (x⁶ B 253).

Victory. 4594 (VIII¹ A 32), 4699 (x⁵ A 38), 5885 (VII¹ A 27).

Vidocq, Eugene F. 4741 (x³ A 727).

Villamedina, Count. 2362 (IV A 26).

Vindex, Gaius Julius. 4105 (IV A 13).

Vinet, Alexander. 2039 (x⁴ A 188), 3171 (XI¹ A 53), 3689 (x⁴ A 190), 3694 (295), 4211 (185), 4212 (186), 4213 (187).

Violinist. 5252 (II A 640).

Violinist analogy. 6850 (XI² A 321).

Virgil. 2305 (I A 251), 6082 (VIII¹ A 446).

Virgilius. 4399 (II A 152).

Virgin birth. 276 (I A 232).

Virtue. 895 (IV C 86), 1218 (IX A 482).

Virtuosity. 4475 (x⁴ A 430).

Visby, Carl H. 3131 (x³ A 583), 3215 (x¹ A 2), 3495 (x² A 363), 3682 (x³ A 299), 4146 (IX A 31), 4639 (x² A 53).

Vita ante acta. 6192 (IX A 142).

Vivisection. 731 (XI¹ A 422), 6966 (XI² A 436).

VOCATION (*see also* CALL, CALLING). 1367 (IX A 75), 2711 (x³ A 175), 2793 (x² A 341), 4597 (VIII¹ A 113), 5014 (x³ A

401), 5368 (II A 347), 5403 (520), 6153 (IX A 43), 6837 (x⁵ A 72).

Voight, B. F. 6861 (XI¹ A 71).

Voight, Johannes. 5358 (II C 63).

Vollmer, W. 4394 (I A 319).

Voltaire, Francois. 3647 (x⁴ A 258).

VOLUNTARY, THE. 175 (x⁴ A 150), 1258 (x² A 159), 1259 (160), 1875 (x³ A 378), 1885 (666), 1908 (x⁴ A 459), 2509 (x² A 263), 3201 (x⁴ A 541), 3755 (x³ A 456), 3756 (457), 3759 (x⁴ A 266), 3761 (326), 4354 (XI¹ A 558), 4602 (VIII¹ A 259), 4610 (579), 4627 (IX A 410), 4634 (x¹ A 416), 4676 (x⁴ A 256), 4697 (x⁵ A 28), 4839 (IV C 125).

Vor Frelsers church. 5856 (VII¹ A 231).

Vor Frue church. 6249 (IX A 271), 6836 (x⁵ A 67).

Voting. 599 (x⁴ A 22), 986 (x² A 419), 2032 (x³ A 687), 3747 (x² A 509), 4177 (486), 4199 (x⁴ A 43), 4201 (51), 4203 (65), 4208 (102), 4852 (IX A 4), 4874 (x³ A 464), 4875 (x⁴ A 35), 6561 (x² A 281), 6631 (x³ A 147), 6728 (x⁴ A 36), 6731 (53).

Vox populi. 6307 (x¹ A 37).

Vulgarity. 2945 (x¹ A 231).

Wading analogy. 5637 (IV A 71).

Wagner (*Faust*). 4387 (I A 122).

Wahlgreen. 6339 (x¹ A 104).

Walking. 1835 (V B 237), 4870 (x³ A 432), 5398 (II A 503), 5763 (VI B 225), 5892 (VII¹ A 105), 5893 (106), 5894 (107), 5931 (92), 5937 (147), 5941 (155), 5943 (157), 6013 (VIII¹ A 163), 6063 (L. 150), 6074 (VIII¹ A 407), 6086 (453), 6105 (544), 6259 (IX A 298), 6270 (381), 6332 (x⁵ A 153), 6489 (x² A 10), 6498 (48), 6499 (56), 6568 (315), 6580 (413), 6781 (x⁴ A 389), 6782 (390), 6800 (540), 6885 (XI¹ A 216), 6916 (XI² A 11).

Walsh. 2696 (x³ A 520).

Wandering Jew. 795 (I A 150), 1179 (I C 58), 1184 (II A 56), 2206 (I C 66), 2210 (I A 299), 5087 (I C 65), 5109 (60), 5110 (61), 5111 (62), 5112 (64), 5131 (85), 5193 (116), 5194 (117), 5195 (118), 5196 (119), 5197 (120), 5198 (121), 5217 (II A 61), 5367 (346), 5797 (VI B 40: 33), 6523 (x² A 163).

Want. 167 (x¹ A 198).

War. 1193 (x¹ A 564), 1194 (565), 1196 (x⁴ A 145), 4137 (VIII¹ A 609), 4141 (618), 4146 (IX A 31), 4180 (x² A 498), 4874 (x³ A 664), 6259 (IX A 298), 6386 (x¹ A 262).

Warren, Samuel. 5199 (I C 123), 6175 (IX A 87).

Wasted lives. 6969 (XI² A 439).

Watch. 1817 (XI² A 195).

Watchman. 6836 (x⁵ A 67).

Watermark analogy. 5200 (II A 7).

Way. 361 (x⁴ A 659), 2916 (XI² A 316).

Weakness. 1491 (x⁵ A 56), 1806 (XI¹ A 337), 6484 (x¹ A 670).

Wealth. 1010 (VII¹ A 180), 1312 (II A 391).

Weather analogy. 6968 (XI² A 438).

Weber, Carl Maria v. 5095 (I A 64), 5654 (IV A 101).

Wednesday. 5483 (L. 29).

Weeping. 3466 (V A 17), 4582 (III A 99), 4823 (I A 34), 5260 (II A 662).

Weigel, Valentin. 3446 (x² A 496).

Weil, Gustav. 1034 (VI A 65), 5811 (53), 5812 (54).

Weis, Carl M. 5937 (VII¹ A 147).

Weisse, Christian H. 5713 (V A 101).

Werder, Karl. 257 (III C 30), 3285 (32), 5537 (28-29), 5543 (L. 55).

Werner, Zacharias. 1134 (x² A 54), 2867 (x¹ A 288), 3934 (x² A 26), 3935 (28), 4025 (74), 4274 (67), 5050 (x¹ A 294).

Wesley, John. 2695 (x³ A 518), 2697 (523).

Wessel, Johann. 3575 (x⁴ A 398).

Wessel, Johan H. 3362 (XI² A 7), 6874 (XI¹ A 142).

Wessenberg, Ignaz H. v. 2041 (x⁴ A 401), 4772 (402).

Westphaler, Gert. 5035 (XI² A 203), 6196 (IX A 493).

Wette, Wilhelm M. L. de. 872 (II A 465), 4095 (467).

Whale. 2070 (XI¹ A 455).

What. 4550 (x² A 299), 4558 (x³ A 593), 5791 (VI B 17).

What We Learn From the Lilies of the Field and the Birds of the Air. 5953 (VII¹ B 213), 5970 (VIII¹ A 1), 5976 (16), 6388 (x¹ A 266), 6407 (351), 6422 (469), 6457 (583), 6486 (676).

Whole. 2360 (IV A 11), 4492 (XI² A 225).

Whole/half. 2683 (XI² A 385).

Wholeness. 5063 (I A 32).

Wieland, Christoph M. 1830 (x⁴ A 479), 3328 (x² A 608), 3530 (x⁵ A 62), 4278 (x² A 598), 6036 (VIII¹ A 228), 6813 (x⁴ A 604).

Wild birds. 6445 (x¹ A 546).

Wild geese. 3065 (XI¹ A 195), 3066 (196), 5303 (II A 210).

Wilhelm Meister (see GOETHE: *Wilhelm Meister).*

Will. 115 (x⁵ A 31), 513 (x² A 284), 776 (IV B 5:13), 777 (13:21), 973 (VII¹ A 393), 989 (x³ A 104), 1094 (I A 36), 1095 (44), 1241 (IV C 39), 1243 (56), 1244 (60), 1272 (x⁴ A 656), 1273 (x⁵ A 13), 3194 (x¹ A 392), 3658 (IV C 89), 4433 (VII¹ A 68), 4944 (XI¹ A 521), 5038 (XI² A 239), 5616 (IV A 56), 5634 (234), 5648 (89), 6966 (XI² A 436).

William Afham. 5823 (VI A 78).

Willingness. 2628 (XI² A 231).

Window analogy. 6684 (x³ A 487).

Wine. 439 (II A 317), 552 (XI¹ A 265), 5290 (II A 683).

Winning men. 4897 (x⁴ A 468).

Winsløv, Carl. 732 (IV A 94).

Winther, R. V. Christian. 5116 (I B 2), 5428 (II A 803), 5909 (VII¹ A 124), 6413 (x¹ A 402), 6900 (XI¹ A 425).

Wisdom. 271 (x² A 97), 4888 (XI¹ A 508).

WIT. 1706 (II A 179), 1720 (562), 1765 (XI¹ A 343), 5102 (I A 77), 5219 (II A 67), 5247 (132), 5349 (782), 5405 (533), 6399 (x¹ A 336), 6605 (x² A 627).

Without authority. 2653 (x¹ A 333), 5646 (IV A 87), 5686 (IV B 159:6), 5903 (VII¹ A 116), 6220 (IX A 189), 6256 (x⁶ B 40), 6257 (41), 6271 (IX A 390), 6317 (x¹ A 56), 6325 (74), 6338 (100), 6367 (162), 6526 (x² A 177), 6533 (196), 6577 (375), 6587 (475), 6616 (x³ A 77), 6655 (261), 6665 (389), 6753 (x⁵ A 166), 6936 (XI² A 250), 6947 (XI³ B 57).

WITNESS. 106 (x³ A 96), 168 (x¹ A 346), 382 (249), 441 (II A 333), 462 (VIII¹ A 130), 616 (XI² A 341), 670 (x¹ A 235), 1385 (64), 1520 (XI² A 245), 1657 (x³ A 360), 1897 (x⁴ A 274), 1898 (275), 1901 (340), 1905 (366), 1957 (IX A 221), 2961 (x⁴ A 100), 2966 (535), 3319 (x³ A 556), 3367 (II A 308), 3484 (x¹ A 207), 3487 (x² A 95), 3499 (x³ A 59), 3680 (232), 3940 (x² A 333), 3982 (VIII¹ A 3), 4054 (x⁴ A 397),

4152 (IX A 364), 4169 (x^2 A 292), 4239
(xi^2 A 292), 4315 (x^5 A 35), 4459 (x^2 A
318), 4597 (viii^1 A 113), 4653 (x^3 A 148),
4699 (x^5 A 38), 4820 (x^4 A 70), 4881
(609), 4904 (x^5 A 40), 4949 (x^4 A 487),
5018 (x^2 A 24), 5019 (31), 5964 (vii^1 A
224), 6256 (x^6 B 40), 6257 (41), 6305 (x^1
A 33), 6521 (x^2 A 157), 6582 (425), 6727
(x^4 A 33), 6875 (xi^1 B 49), 6938 (xi^2 A
252), 6939 (253).

Wolf, Johann W. 5876 (vii^1 A 7).

WOMAN/MAN.

Women. 95 (III A 234), 97 (V B 53:23), 387
(x^2 A 58), 1157 (III B 41:20), 1814 (xi^1 A
539), 1823 (xi^2 A 271), 1832 (xi^1 A 288),
2386 (II A 498), 3177 (xi^1 A 230), 3211
(xi^2 A 187), 3961 (II A 478), 3979 (V A
51), 4021 (x^1 A 433), 4151 (IX A 354),
5730 (V B 53:26), 5755 (V A 110), 6030
(L. 152), 6531 (x^2 A 193), 6709 (x^3 A
678), 6727 (x^4 A 33), 6904 (xi^1 A 469).

Wonder. 48 (V A 25), 1341 (VI B 163), 1522
(II A 298), 2292 (vii^1 A 34), 3284 (III A
107), 3559 (x^3 A 52), 5588 (IV C 10).

Woodcutter analogy. 6952 (xi^2 A 379).

Word, God's. 215 (x^4 A 437), 2912 (xi^1 A
452).

WORK. 236 (x^1 A 135), 683 (viii^1 A 60), 869
(II A 447), 985 (x^2 A 270), 999 (x^4 A 549),
1097 (II A 190), 1106 (IV C 82), 1156 (III
C 17), 1924 (xi^1 A 4), 2428 (x^2 A 63),
2711 (x^3 A 175), 3076 (IV A 62), 3363 (II
A 69), 3497 (x^2 A 581), 4424 (V A 76),
4524 (x^4 A 639), 5039 (x^2 A 373), 6001
(viii^1 A 116), 6023 (200), 6165 (IX A 69),
6582 (x^2 A 425).

Works. 14 (x^3 A 342), 252 (I A 316), 976
(x^1 A 457), 988 (x^3 A 66), 1106 (IV C 82),
1121 (viii^1 A 19), 1143 (x^4 A 123), 2140
(x^3 A 672), 2468 (IX A 22), 2483 (x^1 A
197), 2543 (xi^2 A 301).

"Works of Consummation." 6317 (x^1 A
56), 6517 (x^2 A 147).

Works of Love. 943 (viii^2 B 30:4), 944
(34:7), 1012 (31:20), 1013 (31:22), 2409
(viii^1 A 173), 2411 (295), 2502 (x^1 A
651), 2598 (viii^1 A 231), 3313 (627),
4122 (279), 4124 (299), 5965 (vii^1 A
227), 5972 (viii^1 A 4), 5996 (82), 6005
(121), 6032 (219), 6042 (249), 6043
(250), 6053 (298), 6055 (309), 6063 (L.

150), 6071 (viii^1 A 390), 6092 (472),
6098 (496), 6111 (559), 6112 (560),
6310 (x^1 A 42), 6366 (161), 6795 (x^4 A
511).

WORLD. 428 (II A 217), 554 (xi^1 A 324),
1048 (viii^1 A 234), 1307 (II A 622), 1327
(III A 131), 1397 (x^2 A 226), 1439 (xi^1 A
359), 1613 (viii^1 A 283), 1673 (I A 190),
1674 (207), 1677 (256), 1680 (II A 38),
1683 (78), 1700 (138), 1966 (I A 248),
2041 (x^4 A 401), 2248 (I A 191), 2388 (III
A 89), 2437 (x^4 A 482), 2825 (II A 633),
3262 (II C 56), 3264 (II A 229), 3294 (IV A
54), 3334 (x^3 A 574), 3602 (xi^1 A 364),
3876 (140), 4152 (IX A 364), 4343 (x^4 A
508), 4392 (I A 313), 4597 (viii^1 A 113),
4682 (x^4 A 570), 4709 (xi^1 A 340), 4975
(x^4 A 381), 5147 (I A 182), 5938 (vii^1 A
148), 6053 (298), 6056 (326), 6076
(415), 6224 (IX A 209), 6486 (x^1 A 676),
6582 (x^2 A 425), 6604 (622), 6661 (x^3 A
321).

World history. 637 (viii^1 A 123), 1775
(54), 4134 (606), 4917 (xi^2 A 204).

Worldliness (*see* Secularism).

World wants to be deceived, the. 4870 (x^3
A 432), 5018 (x^2 A 24), 5019 (31), 6395
(x^1 A 320), 6839 (x^5 A 104).

WORSHIP. 821 (x^3 A 151), 1159 (V A 66),
2571 (xi^2 A 55), 4524 (x^4 A 639), 4917
(xi^2 A 204), 5049 (50), 6219 (IX A 188),
6235 (223).

Writers. 121 (I A 105), 127 (234), 128
(245), 137 (II A 412), 146 (IV A 161), 156
(vii^1 A 51), 160 (viii^1 A 53), 715 (V A 56),
930 (vii^1 A 30), 2105 (x^5 A 162), 2151
(viii^1 A 399), 2237 (x^2 A 517), 2964 (x^4 A
225), 5063 (I A 32), 5241 (II A 118), 5644
(IV A 83), 6547 (x^2 A 242).

Writing (incl. S.K.'s). 637 (vii^1 A 123),
645 (viii^1 A 466), 655 (viii^2 B 87), 2410
(viii^1 A 196), 2766 (vii^1 A 67), 2767 (77),
2924 (viii^1 A 132), 3248 (I A 127), 3665
(viii^1 A 91), 4400 (II A 163), 5155 (I A
204), 5178 (286), 5188 (336), 5241 (II A
118), 5249 (634), 5266 (677), 5279
(200), 5281 (203), 5289 (208), 5290
(683), 5293 (686), 5295 (690), 5297
(693), 5298 (696), 5332 (240), 5347
(780), 5351 (270), 5361 (312), 5374
(389), 5378 (406), 5379 (413), 5387

(432), 5391 (476), 5406 (534), 5414 (818), 5415 (819), 5433 (824), 5446 (III A 35), 5457 (57), 5485 (III C 4), 5495 (III A 105), 5519 (164), 5532 (176), 5551 (L. 68), 5560 (III A 203), 5564 (245), 5565 (246), 5570 (208), 5571 (209), 5574 (IV A 2), 5576 (8), 5614 (45), 5615 (53), 5617 (61), 5638 (74), 5640 (76), 5644 (83), 5647 (88), 5665 (L. 82), 5666 (IV A 110), 5668 (113), 5669 (114), 5671 (119), 5676 (128), 5677 (129), 5678 (132), 5681 (135), 5682 (136), 5683 (137), 5684 (138), 5685 (139), 5687 (140), 5690 (144), 5693 (152), 5694 (153), 5695 (154), 5699 (170), 5703 (177), 5705 (181), 5706 (182), 5712 (V A 100), 5713 (101), 5717 (105), 5729 (27), 5735 (39), 5744 (109), 5754 (99), 5756 (111), 5762 (VI B 224), 5763 (225), 5764 (226), 5765 (227), 5770 (VI A 10), 5771 (11), 5772 (12), 5777 (13), 5778 (VI B 100), 5783 (130), 5784 (131), 5785 (132), 5786 (VI A 146), 5787 (VI B 13), 5801 (VI A 31), 5802 (32), 5803 (40), 5808 (44), 5809 (45), 5810 (47), 5813 (55), 5814 (56), 5815 (57), 5816 (58), 5817 (59), 5821 (76), 5828 (85), 5829 (86), 5830 (87), 5846 (130), 5847 (131), 5857 (VII^1 A 233), 5866 (VII^1 B 84), 5868 (132), 5873 (VII^1 A 4), 5877 (9), 5879 (18), 5881 (VII^1 B 211), 5888 (VII^1 A 99), 5891 (104), 5893 (106), 5894 (107), 5901 (114), 5904 (117), 5095 (118), 5913 (126), 5914 (127), 5915 (128), 5931 (92), 5934 (VII^1 B 192:1-2), 5939 (VII^1 A 150), 5946 (164), 5947 (169), 5951 (202), 5952 (VII^1 B 212), 5953 (213), 5962 (VII^1 A 222), 5972 (VIII^1 A 4), 5980 (27), 6001 (116), 6005 (121), 6008 (135), 6017 (172), 6037 (229), 6040 (237), 6043 (250), 6049 (264), 6060 (339), 6064 (366), 6065 (383), 6072 (394), 6078 (424), 6081 (445), 6101 (504), 6114 (562), 6128 (669), 6130 (637), 6132 (641), 6133 (645), 6136 (651), 6140 (679), 6143 (IX A 10), 6168 (72), 6174 (86), 6201 (166), 6202 (167), 6205 (171), 6209 (175), 6212 (179), 6216 (185), 6217 (186), 6220 (189), 6227 (213), 6229 (216), 6237 (226), 6238 (227), 6242 (241), 6248 (265), 6259 (298), 6268 (375), 6269 (379), 6274 (411), 6278 (498), 6280 (500), 6282 (432), 6292 (IX B 67), 6308 (X^1 A 39), 6312 (45), 6316 (54), 6317 (56), 6327 (78), 6337 (95), 6339 (104), 6356 (138), 6358 (140), 6365 (158), 6374 (192), 6375 (199), 6376 (202), 6390 (273), 6391 (281), 6394 (309), 6407 (351), 6409 (374), 6424 (483), 6428 (496), 6435 (519), 6444 (541), 6461 (593), 6505 (X^2 A 89), 6507 (92), 6512 (109), 6517 (147), 6521 (157), 6533 (196), 6543 (215), 6566 (X^6 B 127), 6571 (X^2 A 345), 6575 (372), 6584 (X^5 A 165), 6594 (X^2 A 586), 6624 (X^3 A 99), 6645 (189), 6645 (190), 6664 (381), 6732 (X^4 A 55), 6787 (X^6 B 253), 6790 (260), 6821 (X^4 A 651), 6840 (X^5 A 105), 6843 (146), 6879 (XI^1 A 177), 6883 (214), 6885 (216), 6909 (510), 6957 (XI^3 B 120).

Writing analogy. 5552 (L. 69), 6925 (XI^2 A 61).

Writing sampler. 5759 (VI B 194), 5760 (199-201), 5761 (222), 5762 (224), 5763 (225), 5764 (226), 5765 (227), 5766 (229), 5767 (231), 5786 (VI A 146), 5831 (VI B 233), 5832 (235), 5841 (VI A 104), 5859 (VII^2 B 274:1-22), 6060 (VIII^1 A 339).

"Writings of a Young Man, The." 6060 (VIII^1 A 339).

Wrong. 4628 (IX A 425).

Xanthippe. 1824 (X^2 A 272), 4249 (IV A 202).
Xenophon. 2769 (X^1 A 55), 3223 (XI^1 A 393), 3307 (VI B 54:33), 4246 (III B 30), 4288 (X^4 A 467).

You (see "Du").
Young. 623 (V A 19), 2322 (V B 115:2).
Young man. 5805 (VI B 41:10).
Youth. 693 (X^1 A 132), 804 (III A 95), 1135 (X^2 A 207), 1797 (X^4 A 146), 1811 (XI^1 A 447), 4273 (X^1 A 591), 5143 (I A 166), 5383 (II A 420), 5401 (510), 5403 (520), 5428 (803), 6170 (IX A 74), 6179 (108), 6521 (X^2 A 157), 6638 (X^6 B 163), 6811 (X^4 A 592).

ZACHAEUS. 5050 (X^1 A 294), 5228 (II A 600).

Composite Collation

This composite collation of entries in *Søren Kierkegaard's Journals and Papers,* volumes 1-6, provides a cross-reference to the *Papirer* and the *Breve*. Numbers in the left-hand columns are the standard international references to the *Papirer*. Numbers in parentheses are the serially ordered references in the present edition. References to Kierkegaard's letters appear at the end of the collation. Serial numbers are divided among the six volumes of the *Journals and Papers* as follows:

Volume 1	1-1093
Volume 2	1094-2303
Volume 3	2304-3828
Volume 4	3829-5050
Volume 5	5051-6140
Volume 6	6141-6969

Composite Collation

Volume I A	Volume I A	Volume I A	Volume I A	Volume I A
1 (2240)	45 (3045)	89 (415)	133 (4062)	179 (5146)
2 (1302)	46 (414)	90 (120)	134 (3799)	180 (4064)
3 (3989)	48 (2207)	91 (2243)	135 (16)	181 (737)
4 (410)	49 (2208)	92 (3991)	136 (3800)	182 (5147)
5 (1230)	50 (689)	93 (4061)	137 (17)	183 (4389)
6 (411)	51 (5082)	94 (3245)	138 (245)	184 (5148)
7 (1231)	52 (4385)	95 (416)	139 (4063)	186 (5149)
8 (117)	53 (274)	96 (417)	140 (3801)	187 (5150)
10 (3542)	54 (202)	97 (418)	141 (850)	188 (5151)
11 (5061)	55 (203)	98 (3246)	142 (3802)	189 (5152)
12 (5062)	56 (578)	99 (3247)	143 (5132)	190 (1673)
13 (5072)	57 (579)	100 (1539)	144 (5133)	191 (2248)
14 (5073)	58 (580)	101 (29)	145 (1670)	192 (2233)
15 (5074)	59 (5088)	102 (23)	146 (770)	194 (5153)
16 (5075)	60 (5089)	103 (5113)	147 (5136)	195 (3046)
17 (5076)	61 (5090)	104 (1178)	148 (1625)	196 (1770)
18 (5081)	62 (5091)	105 (121)	149 (26)	197 (790)
19 (3543)	63 (5094)	106 (122)	150 (795)	198 (125)
20 (3544)	64 (5095)	107 (3721)	151 (1944)	199 (27)
21 (1303)	65 (5096)	108 (581)	152 (851)	200 (3805)
22 (3545)	66 (5097)	109 (5114)	153 (3249)	201 (4923)
23 (2241)	67 (5098)	110 (2244)	154 (1671)	201 (5154)
24 (2242)	68 (5099)	111 (2245)	155 (3803)	203 (3806)
25 (4822)	69 (5106)	112 (2246)	156 (5140)	204 (5155)
26 (2854)	70 (5107)	113 (751)	158 (1672)	205 (1232)
27 (412)	71 (5108)	114 (24)	160 (2247)	206 (13)
28 (273)	72 (5092)	115 (4576)	161 (5141)	207 (1674)
29 (1304)	73 (5093)	116 (4739)	162 (5142)	208 (1624)
30 (1305)	74 (22)	117 (3125)	163 (4954)	209 (4824)
31 (2806)	75 (5100)	118 (5117)	164 (4955)	210 (275)
32 (5063)	76 (5101)	120 (5118)	165 (2922)	211 (1564)
33 (118)	77 (5102)	121 (4386)	166 (5143)	212 (126)
34 (4823)	78 (5103)	122 (4387)	167 (4388)	213 (2698)
35 (3243)	79 (5104)	123 (5119)	168 (2794)	214 (3807)
36 (1094)	80 (5105)	124 (849)	169 (5144)	215 (421)
37 (1463)	81 (3782)	125 (1669)	170 (1563)	216 (3808)
38 (242)	82 (1464)	126 (25)	171 (3804)	217 (3809)
39 (5064)	83 (1287)	127 (3248)	172 (419)	218 (3810)
40 (413)	84 (848)	128 (3697)	173 (5145)	219 (3811)
41 (5071)	85 (4575)	129 (123)	174 (420)	220 (5156)
42 (4060)	86 (119)	130 (3796)	175 (124)	221 (852)
43 (3546)	87 (3244)	131 (3797)	177 (1964)	222 (853)
44 (1095)	88 (1177)	132 (3798)	178 (1965)	223 (5157)

Volume I A	Volume I A	Volume I C	Volume I C	Volume II A
224 (1456)	290 (217)	17 (5060)	105 (5166)	43 (5212)
225 (1565)	291 (2788)	18 (5059)	106 (5167)	44 (5213)
226 (2699)	292 (1181)	19 (5058)	107 (5168)	45 (5214)
227 (1180)	294 (3815)	20 (3843)	108 (5169)	46 (131)
228 (3812)	295 (3547)	23 (3844)	109 (5170)	47 (2087)
229 (1566)	296 (5179)	25 (5065)	110 (5171)	48 (1568)
230 (3813)	297 (5180)	27-33 (5066)	111 (5172)	49 (1569)
231 (1187)	298 (2855)	31 (3990)	112 (5173)	50 (1183)
232 (276)	299 (2210)	34 (5067)	113 (2703)	51 (5215)
233 (1457)	300 (2799)	35 (5068)	116 (5193)	52 (1570)
234 (127)	301 (218)	36 (5069)	117 (5194)	53 (1968)
235 (5161)	302 (1189)	37 (5070)	118 (5195)	54 (5216)
236 (371)	304 (4069)	40 (227)	119 (5196)	55 (769)
237 (1540)	305 (3848)	46 (5077)	120 (5197)	56 (1184)
238 (1675)	306 (3816)	47 (5078)	121 (5198)	57 (3698)
239 (1676)	307 (4070)	48 (5079)	123 (5199)	58 (1068)
240 (2785)	308 (4071)	49 (5080)	124 (5192)	59 (3252)
241 (2798)	309 (4072)	50 (1186)	125 (4397)	61 (5217)
242 (1627)	310 (4073)	51 (5083)	126 (4398)	62 (2307)
243 (3656)	313 (4392)	52 (5084)	Volume II A	63 (3994)
244 (5162)	314 (4393)	53 (5085)	1 (3913)	64 (3995)
245 (128)	315 (3817)	54 (5086)	2 (1542)	65 (3996)
246 (4065)	316 (252)	56 (3845)	4 (782)	66 (3997)
247 (1628)	317 (1567)	58 (1179)	5 (783)	67 (5219)
248 (1966)	319 (4394)	60 (5109)	6 (784)	68 (5220)
249 (5164)	321 (4395)	61 (5110)	7 (5200)	69 (3363)
250 (2304)	322 (4396)	62 (5111)	11 (3251)	70 (5221)
251 (2305)	324 (699)	64 (5112)	12 (265)	71 (2211)
252 (1188)	325 (277)	65 (5087)	13 (855)	73 (1306)
253 (3250)	327 (617)	66 (2206)	14 (1630)	74 (1233)
254 (854)	328 (5181)	69 (3846)	15 (129)	75 (1681)
255 (3854)	329 (5182)	70 (3847)	17 (5201)	76 (3722)
256 (1677)	330 (5183)	72 (5120)	18 (91)	77 (3253)
261 (2306)	331 (5184)	73 (1455)	19 (992)	78 (1682)
262 (3814)	332 (5185)	74 (5121)	20 (5205)	79 (1683)
264 (1629)	333 (5186)	75 (5122)	21 (5206)	80 (1684)
265 (1678)	334 (28)	76 (5123)	22 (1279)	81 (1685)
266 (5174)	335 (5187)	77 (5124)	23 (1280)	82 (423)
267 (2745)	336 (5188)	78 (5125)	24 (2380)	83 (424)
269 (2700)	337 (1967)	79 (5126)	25 (2381)	84 (1686)
270 (2786)	338 (5189)	80 (831)	26 (1288)	85 (1687)
271 (5175)	339 (5190)	81 (5127)	27 (5207)	86 (2734)
272 (5176)	340 (1541)	82 (5128)	29 (1182)	87 (2735)
273 (1096)	341 (5191)	83 (5129)	30 (422)	88 (2736)
278 (2787) Volume I B		84 (5130)	31 (1190)	89 (2737)
279 (4390)	1 (5115)	85 (5131)	32 (3551)	90 (3998)
280 (5177)	2 (5116)	87 (5134)	33 (3552)	91 (3849)
281 (2701) Volume I C		88 (5135)	34 (4773)	92 (5222)
282 (4391)	1 (5052)	89 (5137)	35 (5208)	93 (278)
283 (2456)	2 (5053)	95 (5138)	36 (5209)	96 (3605)
284 (2702)	3 (5054)	96 (5139)	37 (1679)	97 (279)
285 (4066)	7 (5055)	100 (5158)	38 (1680)	98 (5223)
286 (5178)	9 (5056)	101 (5159)	39 (856)	99 (2801)
287 (2209)	11 (5057)	102 (5160)	40 (5210)	100 (832)
288 (4067)	12 (5057)	103 (5163)	41 (266)	101 (1689)
289 (4068)	16 (5059)	104 (5165)	42 (5211)	102 (1690)

Volume II A	Volume II A	Volume II A	Volume II A	Volume II A
103 (1691)	164 (5261)	228 (5324)	289 (2458)	347 (5368)
104 (1692)	165 (859)	229 (5326)	290 (4084)	348 (2261)
105 (1693)	166 (5262)	230 (3699)	291 (4775)	351 (833)
106 (1694)	167 (5263)	231 (5328)	292 (2746)	352 (136)
107 (1695)	168 (1969)	232 (5329)	293 (436)	353 (3270)
108 (1696)	169 (4401)	233 (5330)	294 (437)	354 (2212)
109 (3818)	170 (4402)	234 (429)	295 (290)	355 (2213)
110 (4774)	171 (5267)	235 (1020)	296 (4843)	356 (3271)
111 (2308)	172 (1970)	236 (371)	297 (3888)	357 (4410)
112 (1697)	173 (860)	237 (1309)	298 (1522)	358 (4411)
114 (1698)	174 (861)	238 (5331)	299 (3264)	359 (4412)
115 (5239)	175 (1281)	239 (3259)	300 (5356)	360 (443)
116 (5240)	176 (3255)	240 (5332)	301 (2257)	361 (5369)
117 (3993)	177 (3256)	241 (5333)	302 (2258)	362 (34)
118 (5241)	178 (4842)	242 (3851)	303 (865)	364 (5370)
119 (5242)	179 (1706)	243 (5335)	304 (2175)	365 (444)
120 (5243)	180 (133)	244 (2578)	305 (194)	366 (4745)
121 (5244)	181 (5268)	245 (430)	306 (866)	367 (195)
122 (3855)	183 (1631)	246 (4987)	307 (438)	368 (2857)
123 (3856)	184 (427)	247 (2254)	308 (3367)	369 (294)
124 (5245)	185 (5269)	248 (3887)	309 (3368)	370 (2383)
125 (1019)	186 (4243)	249 (431)	310 (4001)	371 (1576)
126 (5246)	187 (1971)	250 (432)	311 (4002)	372 (4788)
127 (219)	188 (3857)	251 (433)	312 (5361)	373 (5371)
128 (220)	189 (5270)	252 (434)	313 (3369)	374 (2579)
130 (221)	190 (1097)	255 (5337)	314 (3370)	375 (2580)
131 (222)	191 (92)	257 (4081)	315 (585)	376 (445)
132 (5247)	192 (1707)	258 (286)	316 (293)	377 (3377)
133 (280)	193 (5274)	259 (5338)	317 (439)	378 (4092)
134 (1521)	194 (1098)	260 (1573)	318 (3371)	379 (2858)
136 (1699)	195 (1708)	261 (287)	319 (5362)	380 (2706)
138 (1700)	197 (282)	262 (2738)	320 (3372)	381 (1577)
139 (1701)	198 (3257)	263 (4534)	321 (4407)	382 (5372)
140 (1702)	199 (3850)	264 (2255)	322 (867)	383 (35)
141 (1703)	200 (5279)	265 (243)	323 (4091)	385 (1978)
142 (1622)	201 (3364)	266 (3365)	324 (1833)	386 (5373)
143 (1623)	202 (5280)	267 (1977)	325 (3134)	387 (1946)
145 (2457)	203 (5281)	268 (2705)	326 (1200)	388 (295)
146 (1704)	204 (5282)	269 (582)	327 (3373)	389 (5374)
147 (1705)	205 (5284)	270 (5351)	328 (5364)	390 (2262)
148 (1771)	206 (5285)	271 (2256)	329 (440)	391 (1312)
149 (2856)	207 (5287)	272 (4082)	330 (1311)	392 (1313)
150 (857)	208 (5289)	273 (2382)	331 (4510)	393 (620)
151 (858)	209 (5302)	274 (4083)	332 (4578)	394 (1314)
152 (4399)	210 (5303)	275 (5352)	333 (441)	395 (5375)
153 (3904)	211 (1975)	276 (288)	334 (3374)	396 (3190)
154 (5248)	212 (5304)	277 (435)	335 (1575)	397 (5376)
155 (2309)	213 (712)	278 (1289)	336 (3375)	398 (5377)
156 (2310)	214 (1544)	279 (4406)	337 (3889)	399 (3548)
157 (2311)	215 (1545)	280 (1234)	338 (442)	400 (1979)
158 (2312)	216 (5305)	281 (1235)	339 (4408)	401 (1980)
159 (2313)	217 (428)	283 (244)	340 (5365)	402 (1315)
160 (2314)	218 (4403)	284 (289)	341 (5366)	404 (2263)
161 (2315)	219 (4080)	285 (3366)	342 (3376)	406 (5378)
162 (30)	222 (5306)	286 (3914)	343 (4409)	407 (1316)
163 (4400)	223 (1976)	287 (204)	346 (5367)	408 (1317)

Volume II A	Volume II A	Volume II A	Volume II A	Volume II A
409 (738)	466 (4960)	522 (586)	580 (2177)	638 (1945)
410 (1318)	467 (4095)	523 (2266)	581 (228)	639 (3819)
412 (137)	468 (2707)	524 (2267)	582 (5203)	640 (5252)
413 (5379)	469 (2582)	525 (2268)	583 (130)	641 (5253)
414 (5380)	470 (2583)	526 (2269)	584 (3999)	642 (5254)
415 (5381)	471 (2584)	527 (2270)	585 (5204)	643 (1973)
416 (5382)	472 (1320)	528 (2271)	586 (3254)	644 (5255)
417 (4579)	473 (297)	529 (3279)	587 (2800)	646 (31)
418 (1319)	474 (1981)	530 (877)	588 (3555)	647 (5256)
419 (296)	475 (2826)	531 (4097)	589 (3556)	648 (5257)
420 (5383)	476 (5391)	532 (4098)	590 (5224)	649 (5258)
421 (5384)	477 (4734)	533 (5405)	591 (1709)	650 (1632)
422 (5385)	478 (3961)	534 (5406)	592 (1191)	652 (1974)
423 (3378)	479 (205)	535 (1290)	593 (862)	653 (5259)
424 (1947)	480 (5392)	536 (878)	594 (283)	654 (752)
425 (138)	481 (4096)	537 (3379)	595 (284)	656 (1465)
426 (3272)	482 (5393)	538 (3380)	596 (1710)	657 (1308)
427 (3960)	483 (2748)	539 (139)	597 (5225)	658 (1713)
428 (4927)	484 (739)	540 (5407)	598 (5226)	659 (1714)
429 (2581)	485 (740)	541 (2272)	599 (5227)	660 (1715)
430 (868)	486 (2234)	542 (5408)	600 (5228)	661 (765)
431 (5386)	487 (1579)	543 (4776)	601 (5229)	662 (5260)
432 (5387)	488 (1580)	544 (4777)	602 (5230)	663 (2249)
433 (4535)	489 (93)	545 (3060)	603 (5231)	664 (134)
434 (2459)	490 (5394)	546 (5409)	604 (4000)	665 (2316)
435 (5388)	491 (2789)	547 (448)	605 (1185)	667 (1505)
436 (4093)	492 (5395)	548 (5410)	606 (425)	668 (4075)
437 (4789)	493 (3274)	549 (5411)	607 (5232)	669 (4076)
438 (5389)	494 (2827)	550 (2273)	608 (1711)	670 (5264)
439 (3071)	495 (5396)	551 (3651)	609 (5233)	671 (863)
440 (3273)	496 (2)	553 (798)	610 (1022)	672 (1716)
441 (2264)	497 (5397)	554 (3381)	611 (5234)	673 (5265)
442 (1546)	498 (2386)	555 (1525)	612 (1023)	674 (32)
443 (446)	499 (447)	556 (1021)	613 (5235)	675 (281)
444 (5390)	500 (4414)	557 (5412)	614 (5236)	676 (3058)
445 (3791)	501 (873)	558 (3553)	616 (5237)	677 (5266)
446 (4003)	502 (874)	559 (3554)	617 (5238)	678 (1571)
447 (869)	503 (5398)	560 (5420)	619 (4074)	679 (5288)
448 (2088)	504 (4581)	561 (5421)	620 (618)	680 (4077)
449 (870)	505 (2828)	562 (1720)	621 (1826)	681 (3627)
450 (871)	506 (2176)	563 (3859)	622 (1307)	682 (1717)
451 (4928)	507 (1466)	564 (2214)	623 (1543)	683 (5290)
452 (4958)	508 (5399)	565 (5422)	624 (619)	684 (5291)
453 (4959)	509 (5400)	566 (1663)	625 (5218)	685 (5292)
454 (1578)	510 (5401)	567 (5423)	626 (1712)	686 (5293)
455 (4956)	511 (3275)	569 (298)	627 (1688)	688 (5294)
456 (1238)	512 (5402)	570 (834)	628 (426)	689 (1718)
457 (1239)	513 (875)	571 (140)	629 (5275)	690 (5295)
458 (4580)	514 (876)	572 (5424)	630 (5376)	691 (5296)
459 (4413)	515 (4415)	573 (4099)	631 (2704)	693 (5297)
460 (4094)	516 (1982)	574 (5425)	632 (796)	694 (1719)
461 (2265)	517 (3276)	575 (5426)	633 (2825)	695 (1772)
462 (2384)	518 (3277)	576 (5434)	634 (5249)	696 (5298)
463 (621)	519 (3278)	577 (449)	635 (5250)	697 (1572)
464 (3890)	520 (5403)	578 (879)	636 (132)	698 (2253)
465 (872)	521 (5404)	579 (450)	637 (5251)	699 (3820)

Volume II A	Volume II A	Volume II C	Volume III A	Volume III A
700 (5300)	765 (291)	29 (5357)	30 (1322)	89 (2388)
701 (3258)	766 (1574)	32 (5363)	31 (5445)	90 (5490)
702 (5301)	767 (292)	33 (5418)	32 (3382)	91 (5491)
703 (4078)	768 (5339)	34 (36)	33 (2178)	92 (755)
704 (2385)	769 (5340)	36 (5419)	34 (1589)	93 (5492)
705 (4079)	770 (5341)	37 (193)	35 (5446)	94 (803)
706 (3265)	771 (5342)	38 (5271)	36 (1099)	95 (804)
708 (1)	772 (5343)	39 (5272)	37 (1590)	96 (805)
709 (766)	774 (4088)	40 (5273)	38 (1983)	97 (5493)
710 (4085)	775 (4089)	41 (1972)	39 (1100)	98 (1736)
711 (1024)	777 (5344)	42 (5278)	40 (5447)	99 (4582)
712 (5307)	778 (5345)	44 (2250)	41 (39)	100 (3977)
713 (285)	779 (5346)	46 (2251)	42 (5448)	101 (1324)
714 (5308)	780 (5347)	47 (772)	44 (5449)	102 (1325)
715 (135)	781 (5348)	48 (2252)	45 (1323)	103 (5494)
716 (1523)	782 (5349)	49 (5283)	46 (1721)	104 (1326)
717 (5309)	783 (4090)	50 (5286)	48 (1240)	105 (5495)
720 (5310)	786 (3266)	53 (5328)	49 (1722)	106 (4100)
721 (4404)	787 (3267)	54 (3260)	50 (5450)	107 (3284)
722 (2317)	788 (3268)	55 (3261)	51 (5451)	108 (3072)
723 (5311)	789 (3059)	56 (3262)	52 (5452)	109 (1203)
724 (3700)	790 (3269)	57 (3263)	53 (5453)	110 (141)
725 (1025)	791 (797)	60 (5350)	54 (5454)	111 (142)
728 (5312)	792 (584)	61 (2747)	55 (5455)	112 (700)
729 (1624)	795 (171)	62 (5355)	56 (5456)	113 (3821)
730 (5313)	796 (3858)	63 (5358)	57 (5457)	114 (5496)
731 (1651)	797 (3959)	64 (5359)	58 (5458)	115 (5497)
732 (5314)	802 (5427)	65 (5360)	59 (5459)	116 (5498)
733 (5315)	803 (5428) Volume III A		60 (5460)	117 (2586)
735 (4086)	804 (5429)	1 (1587)	61 (2387)	118 (4004)
736 (5316)	805 (5430)	2 (3723)	62 (1027)	119 (1282)
737 (5317)	806 (5431)	3 (37)	63 (882)	120 (2389)
739 (5318)	807 (5432)	4 (773)	64 (5461)	121 (5499)
740 (5319)	808 (1581)	5 (2274)	65 (5462)	122 (5500)
742 (5320)	809 (1582)	6 (1588)	66 (5463)	123 (701)
743 (33)	810 (1583)	7 (754)	67 (5464)	124 (835)
744 (1524)	811 (1584)	8 (2795)	68 (2276)	125 (884)
745 (5321)	812 (1585)	9 (2275)	69 (5465)	126 (3386)
746 (1236)	813 (1586)	10 (799)	70 (2796)	127 (1102)
747 (2259)	814 (3280)	11 (3281)	71 (5466)	128 (1103)
748 (2260)	817 (5413)	12 (800)	72 (5467)	129 (1665)
749 (5322)	818 (5414)	13 (18)	73 (5468)	130 (1666)
750 (583)	819 (5415)	15 (5437)	74 (5469)	131 (1327)
751 (753)	820 (5416)	16 (5438)	75 (5470)	132 (1834)
752 (1237)	821 (5417)	17 (5439)	76 (2829)	133 (5501)
753 (5323)	824 (5433) Volume II C	18 (5440)	77 (5470)	134 (5502)
754 (4087) Volume II C	3 (5334)	19 (5441)	78 (2830)	135 (885)
755 (3070)	5 (2713)	20 (5442)	79 (5472)	136 (1984)
756 (4405)	8 (3189)	21 (5443)	80 (5473)	137 (2390)
757 (5325)	9 (5435)	22 (5444)	81 (5474)	138 (2391)
758 (1310)	10 (5436)	23 (880)	82 (2585)	139 (3891)
759 (864)	11 (5202)	24 (3282)	83 (5475)	140 (1506)
760 (5336)	12 (5277)	25 (38)	84 (5476)	141 (2181)
761 (4577)	25 (5353)	26 (1026)	85 (3783)	142 (5503)
762 (2141)	26 (5299)	28 (881)	86 (3385)	143 (1507)
763 (3598)		29 (1321)	87 (229)	144 (2587)

Volume III A	Volume III A	Volume III B	Volume III C	Volume IV A
145 (2279)	203 (5560)	17 (1547)	34 (5545)	57 (703)
146 (5506)	204 (3389)	19 (1731)	37 (5546)	58 (2285)
147 (5507)	205 (1737)	20 (1548)	40 (5541)	59 (1071)
148 (5508)	206 (4988)	21 (1632)	Volume IV A	60 (267)
149 (5509)	207 (5569)	22 (1733)	1 (5573)	61 (5617)
150 (5510)	208 (5570)	23 (1734)	2 (5574)	62 (3076)
151 (5511)	209 (5571)	24 (1735)	3 (2739)	63 (5618)
152 (2831)	211 (2277)	26 (3323)	4 (4417)	64 (5619)
153 (2832)	212 (2278)	27 (4245)	5 (702)	65 (5622)
154 (886)	213 (2179)	30 (4246)	6 (3)	66 (1204)
155 (5512)	214 (883)	39 (2588)	7 (4103)	67 (5623)
156 (2318)	215 (1201)	41:2 (4101)	8 (5576)	68 (5624)
157 (2392)	216 (1101)	41:18 (4102)	9 (4104)	69 (5625)
158 (3387)	217 (1664)	41:20 (1157)	10 (4418)	70 (5626)
159 (5515)	218 (801)	41:25 (2589)	11 (2360)	71 (5637)
160 (5516)	219 (802)	45:1 (806)	12 (2361)	72 (774)
161 (5517)	220 (5554)	45:5 (807)	13 (4105)	73 (897)
162 (3388)	221 (5555)	106 (2393)	14 (5581)	74 (5638)
163 (5518)	222 (2319)	114 (2394)	15 (5582)	75 (5639)
164 (5519)	223 (5556)	130 (5549)	16 (5583)	76 (5640)
165 (5520)	224 (5557)	132:3 (5550)	17 (5584)	77 (5641)
166 (5521)	225 (5558)	168 (5553)	18 (4419)	78 (2591)
167 (5522)	226 (4005)	172 (5566)	19 (3289)	79 (5642)
168 (5523)	227 (5561)	173 (5567)	20 (3290)	80 (4924)
169 (5524)	228 (5562)	179:27 (756)	21 (1774)	81 (5643)
170 (5525)	229 (5563)	179:34 (2790)	22 (5585)	82 (898)
171 (5526)	230 (890)	181:9 (713)	24 (1105)	83 (5644)
172 (5528)	231 (785)	183 (3287)	25 (5586)	85 (5645)
173 (5529)	232 (2184)	189 (5568)	26 (2362)	86 (2111)
174 (5530)	233 (94)	192 (3288)	27 (451)	87 (5646)
175 (5531)	234 (95)	Volume III C	28 (3978)	88 (5647)
176 (5532)	235 (96)	1 (3915)	29 (2363)	89 (5648)
177 (5533)	236 (1985)	4 (5485)	30 (5587)	90 (5649)
178 (5534)	237 (2395)	5 (5486)	31 (5609)	91 (5650)
179 (5535)	238 (742)	6 (299)	33 (301)	92 (899)
180 (5538)	239 (4584)	7 (1155)	34 (5610)	93 (5651)
181 (4583)	240 (1508)	8 (5487)	35 (3340)	94 (732)
182 (1104)	241 (743)	9 (3383)	36 (5611)	95 (3239)
183 (5539)	242 (1773)	12 (5488)	37 (5612)	96 (5652)
184 (887)	244 (3286)	13 (1069)	38 (198)	97 (5653)
185 (888)	245 (5564)	14 (4746)	39 (1549)	98 (900)
186 (1591)	246 (5565) Volume III B	15 (587)	42 (4847)	100 (901)
187 (5540)	2 (5484)	16 (1202)	43 (5613)	101 (5654)
189 (4416)	4 (1723)	17 (1156)	44 (4512)	102 (1328)
190 (5541)	5 (1724)	18 (2180)	45 (5614)	103 (3077)
191 (230)	6 (1725)	19 (3384)	46 (1070)	104 (1329)
192 (2182)	7 (1726)	20 (300)	47 (3075)	105 (5656)
193 (2215)	8 (4244)	23 (3191)	48 (4731)	106 (1330)
194 (2183)	9 (1727)	24 (5489)	49 (2284)	107 (5664)
195 (741)	10 (1728)	25 (2110)	50 (3972)	108 (5)
196 (682)	11 (1729)	26 (5514)	51 (3701)	109 (1107)
197 (3822)	12 (3283)	28 (5537)	52 (4422)	110 (5666)
198 (5559)	14 (1633)	30 (257)	53 (5615)	111 (5667)
199 (4825)	15 (1634)	31 (1592)	54 (3294)	112 (902)
200 (2369)	16 (1730)	32 (3285)	55 (3295)	113 (5668)
202 (889)		33 (1593)	56 (5616)	114 (5669)

Volume IV A	Volume IV A	Volume IV B	Volume IV C	Volume IV C
115 (1739)	173 (148)	5:13 (776)	15 (5589)	74 (2282)
116 (3078)	174 (5700)	6 (3291)	16 (892)	75 (1072)
117 (1108)	175 (5701)	10a (5620)	17 (893)	76 (43)
118 (5670)	176 (5702)	10:3 (3792)	18 (5590)	77 (3893)
119 (5671)	177 (5703)	10:4 (3792)	19 (3784)	78 (3657)
121 (1526)	178 (5704)	10:8 (3792)	20 (112)	79 (1602)
122 (5672)	179 (911)	10:9 (3792)	21 (113)	80 (260)
123 (5673)	181 (5705)	10a (5620 in	22 (5591)	81 (1603)
124 (4260)	182 (5706)	Suppl. XI³)	23 (2281)	82 (1106)
125 (1331)	183 (2402)	13:18-19 (891)	24 (5592)	83 (5600)
126 (5674)	184 (4790)	13:23 (735)	25 (3292)	84 (3074)
127 (5675)	185 (1604)	14:6 (2320)	26 (3892)	86 (895)
128 (5676)	186 (4791)	50:4 (3823)	27 (114)	87 (261)
129 (5677)	187 (253)	57 (4423)	28 (2540)	88 (196)
130 (145)	188 (1031)	59 (5710)	29 (3073)	89 (3658)
131 (903)	189 (4006)	60 (5658)	30 (2364)	90 (240)
132 (5678)	190 (1333)	67 (908)	31 (2365)	91 (241)
133 (5680)	191 (1110)	75 (3079)	32 (40)	92 (1028)
134 (904)	192 (704)	76 (1109)	33 (41)	93 (4420)
135 (5681)	193 (5709)	78 (5659)	34 (5593)	94 (4421)
136 (5682)	194 (3971)	79 (5660)	35 (1635)	95 (4846)
137 (5683)	195 (2396)	96:1a, 1b, 1c	36 (2366)	96 (896)
138 (5684)	197 (5575)	(1550)	37 (2367)	97 (5601)
139 (5685)	198 (2280)	96:4 (1551)	38 (2368)	98 (5602)
140 (5687)	199 (4247)	96:13 (1740)	39 (1241)	99 (2283)
141 (5662)	200 (4248)	97:1 (5657)	40 (3549)	100 (197)
142 (5663)	201 (5577)	118:1 (1246)	41 (5594)	101 (5603)
143 (206)	202 (4249)	125 (5707)	42 (5595)	104 (143)
144 (5690)	203 (4250)	126 (5708)	43 (5596)	105 (808)
145 (3390)	204 (4251)	140 (5661)	44 (5597)	106 (809)
146 (2185)	205 (4252)	141 (5662)	45 (5598)	107 (5604)
147 (5691)	206 (4253)	142 (5663)	46 (5599)	108 (1738)
148 (1029)	207 (4254)	144 (2397)	47 (258)	109 (144)
149 (905)	208 (4255)	146 (2398)	48 (259)	110 (4826)
150 (2401)	209 (4256)	147 (2399)	50 (42)	111 (4827)
151 (5692)	210 (4257)	148 (2400)	52 (4844)	112 (4828)
152 (5693)	211 (4258)	149 (3391)	53 (4845)	113 (4829)
153 (5694)	212 (4259)	150 (2401)	54 (4511)	114 (4830)
154 (5695)	213 (907)	159:6 (5686)	55 (1242)	115 (4831)
155 (906)	214 (5627)	164 (3392)	56 (1243)	116 (4832)
156 (3793)	215 (5628)	165 (3393)	57 (3126)	117 (4833)
157 (1332)	216 (5629)	170 (909)	59 (1594)	118 (4834)
158 (5696)	217 (5630)	171 (3394)	60 (1244)	119 (4835)
159 (3325)	221 (5631)	173 (44)	61 (3293)	120 (4836)
160 (4946)	222 (147)	175 (3395)	62 (1245)	121 (4837)
161 (146)	223 (5632)	**Volume IV C**	63 (1595)	122 (4838)
162 (5697)	224 (2781)	1 (3916)	64 (1596)	123 (5605)
163 (3296)	230 (3326)	2 (5572)	65 (1597)	124 (5606)
164 (1030)	231 (5633)	6 (5578)	66 (1598)	125 (4839)
165 (744)	234 (5634)	8 (5579)	67 (1599)	126 (5607)
166 (3894)	236 (5635)	9 (5580)	68 (1600)	127 (5608)
167 (5698)	237 (2592)	10 (5588)	69 (4316)	**Volume V A**
169 (3794)	246 (5636)	11 (2338)	70 (3324)	1 (1111)
170 (5699)	**Volume IV B**	12 (2339)	71 (3652)	2 (268)
171 (3396)	1 (5621)	13 (2340)	72 (894)	3 (5725)
172 (910)	2:16 (734)	14 (736)	73 (1601)	4 (1158)

Volume V A	Volume V A	Volume V B	Volume V C	Volume VI A
5 (604)	64 (2593)	5:10 (3081)	3 (2347)	48 (4589)
6 (1032)	65 (1338)	11:4 (3082)	6 (2348)	49 (1527)
7 (1334)	66 (1159)	14:72-3 (50)	7 (2349)	51 (757)
8 (1335)	67 (4925)	14:73-6 (330)	8 (2350)	52 (4426)
9 (3297)	68 (705)	15:1 (262)	9 (2351)	53 (5811)
10 (452)	69 (706)	18 (690)	11 (5742)	54 (5812)
12 (3465)	70 (768)	23:1 (4263)	12 (2352)	55 (5813)
14 (45)	71 (5743)	40:11 (3606)	13 (5733)	56 (5814)
16 (46)	72 (912)	41 (1606)	13:4 (1114)	57 (5815)
17 (3466)	73 (1605)	43 (1553)	Volume VI A	58 (5816)
18 (622)	74 (2341)	44 (1554)	1 (4107)	59 (5817)
19 (623)	75 (1941)	45 (1555)	2 (4364)	60 (758)
20 (47)	76 (4424)	47:13 (5726)	3 (1743)	61 (5818)
21 (5728)	77 (4106)	49:1 (3653)	4 (5768)	62 (3633)
22 (4848)	78 (6)	49:14 (2343)	5 (1556)	63 (4538)
23 (453)	79 (3080)	53:9 (3557)	6 (1557)	64 (4539)
24 (1827)	80 (4840)	53:12 (2321)	7 (915)	65 (1034)
25 (48)	81 (4841)	53:15 (51)	8 (5769)	66 (3304)
26 (454)	82 (5745)	53:23 (97)	9 (254)	67 (3973)
27 (5729)	83 (1160)	53:25 (4989)	10 (5770)	68 (3974)
28 (49)	84 (5746)	53:26 (5730)	11 (5771)	69 (2714)
29 (1552)	85 (1741)	53:27 (3962)	12 (5772)	70 (919)
30 (1033)	86 (1742)	53:28 (3963)	13 (5777)	71 (4427)
31 (3298)	87 (5747)	53:35 (2802)	14 (105)	72 (920)
32 (1112)	88 (5748)	53:38 (3964)	15 (3303)	73 (5819)
33 (745)	89 (1339)	55:3 (3302)	16 (4587)	75 (5820)
34 (5732)	90 (1247)	55:4 (52)	17 (627)	76 (5821)
35 (810)	91 (5749)	55:6 (2740)	19 (628)	77 (5822)
36 (714)	92 (5750)	55:10 (98)	20 (1989)	78 (5823)
37 (4536)	93 (5751)	55:26 (1248)	21 (1291)	79 (5824)
38 (1636)	94 (5752)	56:2 (1249)	22 (1744)	80 (4590)
39 (5735)	95 (5753)	64 (1637)	23 (4735)	82 (5825)
40 (1113)	96 (3980)	65 (2112)	24 (1161)	83 (5826)
41 (767)	97 (149)	66 (2113)	25 (811)	84 (5827)
42 (1336)	98 (3300)	69 (3795)	26 (4108)	85 (5828)
43 (4585)	99 (5754)	115:2 (2322)	27 (916)	86 (5829)
44 (3127)	100 (5712)	116:3 (3240)	28 (5799)	87 (5830)
45 (5736)	101 (5713)	147 (5721)	29 (5800)	88 (5833)
46 (3299)	102 (5714)	148:5 (5722)	30 (4008)	89 (2833)
47 (624)	103 (5715)	148:16 (1561)	31 (5801)	90 (2834)
48 (5737)	104 (5716)	148:17 (150)	32 (5802)	91 (2835)
49 (4586)	105 (5717)	148:25 (5723)	33 (2353)	92 (921)
50 (1337)	106 (5718)	148:29 (5724)	34 (917)	93 (1292)
51 (3979)	107 (5719)	148:38 (913)	35 (918)	94 (5834)
52 (5738)	108 (5720)	150:21 (2344)	36 (2594)	95 (5835)
53 (1986)	109 (5744)	196 (53)	37 (2708)	96 (269)
54 (5739)	110 (5755)	198 (54)	38 (1745)	97 (5836)
55 (1667)	111 (5756)	207:3 (914)	39 (172)	98 (5837)
56 (715)	112 (5758)	213:2 (1073)	40 (5803)	99 (5838)
57 (1458)	113 (4261)	221 (3397)	41 (5804)	100 (5839)
58 (5740)	Volume V B	227:5 (2114)	42 (5807)	101 (1035)
59 (4007)	1:2 (2370)	232:1 (5734)	43 (151)	102 (55)
60 (1987)	1:3 (2342)	237 (1835)	44 (5808)	103 (5840)
61 (4305)	1:6 (3047)	Volume V C	45 (5809)	104 (5841)
62 (5741)	4:3 (4262)	1 (2345)	46 (4588)	105 (4009)
63 (716)	5:8 (1340)	2 (2346)	47 (5810)	106 (1990)

Volume VI A	Volume VI B	Volume VI B	Volume VII¹ A	Volume VII¹ A
107 (1115)	15 (5789)	150 (3398)	30 (930)	90 (5930)
108 (2460)	16 (5790)	154 (3399)	31 (2291)	91 (636)
109 (455)	17 (5791)	160 (3400)	32 (4849)	92 (5931)
110 (2632)	18 (5792)	161 (3401)	33 (1040)	93 (157)
111 (2859)	19:1-10 (4537)	163 (1341)	34 (2292)	95 (5932)
112 (4428)	25 (3607)	164 (3402)	35 (931)	96 (5933)
113 (922)	27:2 (456)	173 (3785)	37 (2145)	97 (5886)
114 (4429)	35:7 (2371)	175 (4425)	38 (2741)	98 (5887)
115 (620)	35:14 (5793)	192 (5853)	39 (4317)	99 (5888)
116 (4747)	35:15 (5794)	193 (5854)	40 (5916)	100 (2923)
117 (152)	35:19 (5795)	194 (5759)	41 (5917)	101 (5889)
118 (153)	35:24 (5796)	199-201 (5760)	42 (5918)	102 (3128)
119 (5842)	35:25 (1638)	222 (5761)	43 (5920)	103 (5890)
120 (1991)	35:36 (3083)	224 (5762)	44 (5921)	104 (5891)
121 (1342)	38 (632)	225 (5763)	45 (4431)	105 (5892)
122 (923)	40:3 (1607)	226 (5764)	46 (2838)	106 (5893)
123 (4430)	40:5 (2286)	227 (5765)	47 (3896)	107 (5894)
124 (3975)	40:31 (3562)	229 (5766)	48 (1041)	108 (5895)
125 (5843)	40:33 (5797)	231 (5767)	50 (5992)	109 (5896)
126 (2836)	40:45 (633)	233 (5831)	51 (156)	110 (5897)
127 (1343)	41:10 (5805)	235 (5832)	53 (5923)	111 (5898)
128 (5844)	42 (2287)	**Volume VI C**	54 (4111)	112 (5899)
129 (5845)	43 (3084)	1 (5798)	55 (5926)	113 (5900)
130 (5846)	45 (3085)	2 (5779)	56 (3403)	114 (5901)
131 (5847)	49 (56)	3 (5780)	57 (4432)	115 (5902)
132 (3895)	53:13 (1668)	4 (5781)	58 (1162)	116 (5903)
133 (3305)	53:16 (2115)	5 (5782)	59 (812)	117 (5904)
134 (5848)	54:3 (925)	**Volume VII¹ A**	61 (1117)	118 (5905)
135 (5849)	54:10 (1039)	1 (5870)	62 (1345)	119 (5906)
136 (1036)	54:12 (1608)	2 (5871)	63 (4112)	120 (5907)
137 (924)	54:16 (2235)	3 (5872)	64 (1748)	121 (5908)
138 (2837)	54:13, 14, 16 (3654)	4 (5873)	65 (4264)	122 (2146)
139 (1037)	54:19 (3702)	5 (5874)	66 (5927)	123 (637)
140 (1038)	54:21 (199)	6 (5875)	67 (2766)	124 (5909)
141 (5855)	54:30 (1609)	7 (5876)	68 (4433)	125 (5912)
142 (5774)	54:33 (3307)	8 (1459)	69 (4265)	126 (5913)
143 (5775)	58:8 (2749)	9 (5877)	70 (3327)	127 (5914)
144 (5776)	59:2 (3739)	10 (3214)	71 (1250)	128 (5915)
145 (3306)	60:2 (634)	11 (5878)	72 (4540)	129 (5924)
146 (5786)	70:13, 14, 15 (1746)	12 (154)	73 (932)	130 (3628)
147 (630)	89 (5850)	13 (155)	74 (4266)	131 (3404)
148 (1116)	90 (5851)	15 (927)	75 (2293)	132 (3405)
149 (631)	98:26 (2355)	16 (4957)	76 (2294)	133 (3406)
150 (3467)	98:45 (1610)	17 (4109)	77 (2767)	134 (1009)
151 (3468)	98:46 (926)	18 (5879)	78 (5928)	136 (3407)
152 (3469)	98:77 (2116)	19 (1747)	79 (302)	137 (3408)
153 (3192)	98:81 (1344)	20 (4110)	80 (1042)	138 (934)
154 (1467)	98:82 (3086)	21 (5882)	81 (1346)	139 (1347)
155 (3470)	100 (5778)	22 (4591)	82 (3308)	140 (1043)
156 (347)	129 (635)	23 (5883)	83 (2860)	141 (1205)
Volume VI B	130 (5783)	24 (2143)	84 (759)	142 (3409)
8:1-2 (5773)	131 (5784)	25 (2144)	85 (5929)	143 (1348)
10 (625)	132 (5785)	26 (5884)	86 (57)	144 (457)
11 (626)	136 (2372)	27 (5885)	87 (1528)	145 (717)
13 (5787)		28 (928)	88 (2839)	146 (935)
14 (5788)		29 (929)	89 (93)	147 (5937)

Volume VII¹ A	Volume VII¹ A	Volume VII¹ B	Volume VII² B	Volume VIII¹ A
148 (5938)	206 (59)	136 (5919)	270 (5969)	54 (1775)
149 (1994)	207 (2137)	145 (4947)	274:1-22 (5859)	55 (3410)
150 (5939)	208 (1836)	146 (4948)	290 (2142)	56 (837)
151 (3103)	209 (2462)	147 (3786)	Volume VIII¹ A	57 (1352)
152 (3309)	210 (1252)	150 (5925)	1 (5970)	58 (1165)
153 (1611)	211 (605)	153:5 (3629)	2 (5971)	59 (771)
154 (5940)	212 (4114)	158:3 (1996)	3 (3982)	60 (683)
155 (5941)	213 (4592)	177:4 (3472)	4 (5972)	61 (5992)
156 (5942)	214 (5957)	181:2 (3740)	5 (5973)	62 (939)
157 (5943)	215 (2296)	192:1-2 (5934)	6 (638)	63 (1353)
158 (5944)	216 (1044)	192:12 (4434)	7 (778)	64 (4010)
159 (158)	217 (1045)	192:13 (4435)	8 (4541)	65 (2717)
160 (5945)	218 (5958)	192:15 (4436)	9 (1997)	66 (4929)
161 (566)	219 (5959)	199 (1993)	10 (836)	67 (4441)
162 (567)	220 (5960)	205 (2840)	11 (3089)	68 (5993)
163 (4113)	221 (5961)	206 (2841)	12 (2186)	69 (3012)
164 (5946)	222 (5962)	207 (2842)	13 (5974)	70 (3310)
165 (231)	223 (5963)	208 (2843)	14 (1612)	71 (5994)
167 (1206)	224 (5964)	209 (2844)	15 (5975)	72 (303)
168 (4323)	225 (2403)	210 (2845)	16 (5976)	73 (838)
169 (5947)	226 (2404)	211 (5881)	17 (4439)	74 (839)
170 (2742)	227 (5965)	212 (5952)	18 (5978)	75 (4793)
171 (58)	228 (1120)	213 (5953)	19 (1121)	76 (2117)
172 (936)	229 (5966)	214 (5954)	20 (207)	77 (1354)
173 (1076)	230 (2288)	217 (5955)	22 (4440)	78 (4442)
174 (1077)	231 (5856)	218 (5956)	23 (5979)	79 (4115)
175 (2633)	232 (718)	Volume VII¹ C	24 (1350)	80 (1283)
176 (5948)	233 (5857)	1 (4319)	25 (1163)	81 (5995)
177 (1118)	234 (2289)	2 (4320)	26 (2715)	82 (5996)
178 (232)	235 (4308)	3 (4321)	27 (5980)	83 (304)
179 (937)	236 (2290)	4 (4322)	28 (746)	84 (5997)
180 (1010)	237 (4792)	5 (5950)	29 (3011)	85 (4595)
181 (1251)	238 (60)	Volume VII² B	30 (1351)	86 (2406)
182 (2807)	239 (458)	235 (5968)	31 (4593)	87 (719)
183 (2808)	241 (5858)	235 pp. 48-49 fn.	32 (4594)	88 (161)
184 (5949)	242 (159)	(3724)	33 (5981)	89 (2407)
185 (2295)	243 (459)	235 p. 63 fn.	34 (5982)	90 (2187)
186 (2809)	244 (1948)	(2669)	35 (5983)	91 (3665)
187 (1192)	245 (1008)	235 pp. 66-67	36 (5984)	92 (3129)
188 (2810)	246 (5967)	(3087)	37 (5985)	93 (4367)
189 (2811)	248 (99)	235 p. 88 (3473)	38 (5986)	94 (1355)
190 (2812)	250 (4318)	235 p. 191 (3474)	39 (2716)	95 (4443)
191 (2813)	251 (938)	235 pp. 113-14	40 (4306)	96 (4596)
192 (2461)	Volume VII¹ B	(3202)	41 (1164)	97 (2188)
193 (4267)	1 (5860)	236-70 (5935)	42 (5987)	98 (3475)
194 (2814)	5 (5861)	242 (5936)	43 (2090)	99 (5998)
195 (2815)	6 (5862)	249:4 (3725)	44 (5988)	100 (5999)
196 (2816)	69 (5863)	256:9-10 (3088)	45 (5989)	102 (460)
197 (2817)	75 (5864)	256:19 (4471)	46 (5990)	103 (3726)
198 (2818)	83 (5865)	256:20 (2846)	47 (4365)	104 (5009)
199 (2819)	84 (5866)	257:9 (3104)	48 (4366)	105 (5010)
200 (2820)	95 (5867)	257:12 (3203)	49 (5991)	106 (5011)
201 (1349)	121:6 (1992)	261:8 (1293)	50 (208)	107 (6000)
202 (5951)	131 (5880)	261:18 (3981)	51 (2405)	108 (4116)
203 (1119)	132 (5868)	261:22 (2356)	52 (2595)	109 (4117)
205 (1995)	135:5 (5869)	266:26, 28 (4438)	53 (160)	110 (2323)

Volume VIII¹ A	Volume VIII¹ A	Volume VIII¹ A	Volume VIII¹ A	Volume VIII¹ A
111 (1356)	174 (6018)	237 (6040)	299 (4124)	363 (100)
113 (4597)	177 (6019)	238 (466)	300 (2194)	364 (3416)
114 (1207)	178 (1253)	239 (2688)	302 (2195)	365 (470)
115 (1208)	179 (6020)	240 (2634)	303 (1837)	366 (6064)
116 (6001)	180 (2189)	241 (61)	304 (3414)	367 (3417)
117 (4598)	181 (2190)	243 (639)	305 (1639)	368 (233)
118 (3048)	182 (2191)	244 (62)	306 (4446)	369 (2599)
119 (6002)	183 (2192)	245 (4121)	307 (607)	370 (3230)
120 (6004)	184 (2193)	246 (6041)	308 (6054)	371 (311)
121 (6005)	185 (6021)	247 (3412)	309 (6055)	372 (3418)
122 (162)	186 (2297)	248 (2861)	310 (3476)	374 (312)
123 (4118)	188 (3351)	249 (6042)	311 (2862)	377 (313)
124 (6006)	189 (942)	250 (6043)	312 (949)	378 (314)
125 (1998)	190 (2596)	251 (1558)	313 (4543)	379 (1360)
126 (1999)	191 (4600)	252 (6044)	314 (1011)	380 (3419)
127 (1046)	192 (4601)	253 (1509)	315 (2776)	381 (3025)
128 (606)	193 (4795)	254 (6045)	316 (950)	382 (4126)
129 (461)	196 (2410)	255 (3413)	317 (179)	383 (6065)
130 (462)	197 (6022)	256 (640)	318 (2777)	384 (6066)
132 (2924)	198 (2597)	257 (786)	319 (951)	385 (6067)
133 (6007)	199 (2925)	258 (787)	320 (1050)	386 (3924)
134 (4119)	200 (6023)	259 (4602)	321 (4125)	388 (6070)
135 (6008)	201 (3666)	260 (3917)	322 (2196)	390 (6071)
136 (2147)	202 (1078)	261 (3918)	323 (2197)	391 (315)
137 (2148)	203 (3787)	262 (2001)	324 (3923)	392 (372)
139 (6009)	204 (6024)	263 (2847)	325 (468)	393 (2412)
140 (2149)	205 (6025)	264 (6049)	326 (6056)	394 (6072)
141 (4850)	206 (3193)	265 (3919)	327 (1358)	395 (1294)
143 (940)	207 (6026)	266 (3920)	329 (3630)	396 (2635)
144 (941)	208 (4445)	267 (467)	330 (306)	397 (6073)
145 (305)	209 (2768)	268 (63)	331 (3049)	398 (953)
146 (2150)	210 (2000)	269 (4603)	332 (6058)	399 (2151)
147 (4794)	211 (3741)	270 (813)	333 (1510)	403 (2750)
148 (1357)	212 (6027)	271 (6050)	335 (1838)	405 (247)
149 (2408)	214 (464)	273 (3090)	337 (6059)	406 (720)
150 (5016)	215 (465)	275 (4604)	338 (2670)	407 (6074)
152 (3311)	216 (3742)	276 (6051)	339 (6060)	409 (5017)
153 (6010)	217 (6029)	277 (6052)	340 (2718)	410 (954)
154 (4268)	218 (6031)	278 (3634)	341 (2689)	411 (2848)
155 (792)	219 (6032)	279 (4122)	342 (3415)	413 (955)
156 (6011)	220 (6033)	280 (4123)	343 (307)	414 (6075)
157 (463)	221 (840)	281 (4269)	344 (308)	415 (6076)
158 (6012)	222 (4120)	283 (1613)	345 (309)	416 (183)
159 (3411)	223 (946)	284 (4011)	346 (310)	417 (6077)
160 (4444)	224 (6034)	285 (3921)	347 (6061)	418 (2636)
161 (4599)	225 (182)	286 (2002)	349 (1839)	423 (609)
163 (6013)	226 (1047)	287 (3922)	350 (1840)	424 (6078)
164 (6014)	227 (6035)	289 (2775)	352 (6062)	425 (248)
165 (4542)	228 (6036)	291 (948)	354 (608)	427 (2849)
166 (3312)	229 (6037)	292 (1049)	356 (1359)	428 (2719)
168 (246)	230 (1209)	293 (641)	357 (469)	429 (3727)
169 (1749)	231 (2598)	294 (642)	358 (2236)	432 (1841)
170 (6015)	232 (6038)	295 (2411)	359 (952)	433 (4778)
171 (6016)	233 (6039)	296 (2926)	360 (2198)	434 (3477)
172 (6017)	234 (1048)	297 (2927)	361 (2199)	435 (471)
173 (2409)	236 (947)	298 (6053)	362 (643)	436 (184)

Volume VIII¹ A	Volume VIII¹ A	Volume VIII¹ A	Volume VIII¹ A	Volume VIII² B
437 (2413)	507 (6102)	573 (1364)	646 (1213)	107 (3420)
438 (2299)	508 (6103)	576 (6118)	647 (1214)	116 (6068)
440 (6079)	509 (957)	577 (6119)	648 (6134)	118 (6069)
441 (3563)	510 (3352)	579 (4610)	649 (1123)	133:5 (2792)
444 (6080)	511 (2119)	580 (4611)	650 (6135)	143 (3423)
445 (6081)	514 (4608)	581 (4612)	651 (6136)	154:3 (747)
446 (6082)	516 (1361)	582 (4613)	652 (6137)	159:4 (748)
447 (6083)	517 (1751)	583 (319)	653 (6138)	166 (6139)
448 (644)	518 (4609)	585 (3028)	654 (6089)	168:5 (68)
449 (1842)	519 (317)	586 (1168)	655 (6099)	168:6 (749)
450 (6084)	520 (4272)	587 (1844)	656 (2932)	168:8 (750)
452 (6085)	521 (2414)	589 (6120)	661 (1124)	171:15 (375)
453 (6086)	522 (1254)	590 (6121)	662 (4014)	186 (6094)
454 (64)	524 (1362)	591 (6122)	663 (1215)	188 (6095)
455 (6087)	525 (1255)	592 (2709)	664 (2466)	274:1-22 (5859)
456 (2928)	526 (249)	595 (6123)	665 (1014)	Volume VIII² C
458 (6088)	527 (3635)	596 (6124)	666 (6127)	1 (5977)
459 (1210)	528 (473)	597 (4614)	667 (4144)	2 (6028)
461 (2929)	529 (3050)	598 (4131)	668 (3478)	3 (6117)
462 (2003)	530 (814)	599 (4132)	669 (6128)	3:5 (4961)
463 (4605)	531 (4127)	600 (4133)	670 (1365)	Volume IX A
464 (4606)	532 (3421)	601 (65)	671 (958)	2 (474)
465 (2463)	533 (6104)	602 (6125)	672 (1125)	3 (1295)
466 (645)	535 (4544)	603 (6126)	673 (67)	4 (4852)
468 (4607)	536 (1843)	605 (4851)	675 (1216)	5 (475)
469 (316)	537 (1167)	606 (4134)	676 (2091)	6 (476)
470 (568)	538 (2933)	607 (4135)	678 (1511)	7 (1845)
471 (2930)	539 (2934)	608 (4136)	679 (6140)	8 (6141)
472 (6092)	540 (2152)	609 (4137)	680 (2416)	9 (6142)
473 (4012)	541 (2464)	610 (2415)	681 (2357)	10 (6143)
474 (2850)	543 (841)	611 (2936)	Volume VIII² B	11 (2467)
475 (1211)	544 (6105)	613 (4138)	13:61-63 (234)	12 (1079)
476 (1212)	545 (6106)	614 (4139)	15 (3026)	13 (477)
477 (2931)	546 (3422)	615 (4140)	16:8 (3703)	14 (478)
478 (1750)	547 (373)	616 (1169)	30:4 (943)	15 (3424)
479 (2298)	548 (6107)	618 (4141)	31:20 (1012)	16 (320)
480 (4779)	549 (6108)	619 (1122)	31:22 (1013)	17 (4617)
481 (6093)	551 (4128)	620 (2937)	32:22 (1113)	18 (6144)
482 (2004)	552 (4129)	621 (163)	34:7 (944)	19 (2851)
485 (4990)	554 (646)	622 (4)	36:11 (3231)	20 (479)
486 (6096)	556 (4130)	624 (4142)	40 (3027)	21 (610)
487 (6097)	557 (6109)	625 (3897)	58:14 (945)	22 (2468)
490 (4270)	558 (6110)	627 (3313)	59:20 (3743)	23 (6145)
491 (4271)	559 (6111)	629 (374)	71:6, 7, 9, 10, 12	24 (3425)
492 (760)	560 (6112)	631 (4615)	(4447)	25 (6146)
493 (472)	561 (6113)	632 (66)	79 (648)	26 (6147)
494 (956)	562 (6114)	633 (4616)	81 (649)	27 (6148)
496 (6098)	563 (6115)	634 (6129)	82 (650)	28 (480)
497 (4013)	564 (647)	635 (3927)	83 (651)	29 (4145)
498 (3925)	565 (318)	636 (4143)	84 (652)	30 (2417)
499 (1166)	566 (3051)	637 (6130)	85 (653)	31 (4146)
500 (2200)	568 (2005)	640 (6131)	86 (654)	32 (255)
502 (6100)	569 (1363)	641 (6132)	87 (655)	33 (6149)
503 (2201)	570 (6116)	642 (2465)	88 (656)	34 (1366)
504 (6101)	571 (2935)	643 (1942)	89 (657)	35 (2743)
506 (3926)	572 (3744)	645 (6133)	91:13 (2118)	36 (3341)

Volume IX A	Volume IX A	Volume IX A	Volume IX A	Volume IX A
37 (4448)	103 (323)	165 (2642)	230 (6240)	300 (488)
38 (4325)	104 (959)	166 (6201)	232 (661)	301 (378)
39 (6150)	105 (482)	167 (6202)	233 (662)	303 (4149)
40 (3976)	106 (6178)	168 (6203)	236 (6241)	304 (4855)
41 (6151)	107 (1752)	169 (6204)	237 (2600)	305 (1376)
42 (6152)	108 (6179)	171 (6205)	239 (3342)	306 (2419)
43 (6153)	109 (1256)	172 (6206)	240 (663)	307 (6260)
44 (1015)	110 (164)	173 (6207)	241 (6242)	308 (379)
46 (2637)	111 (960)	174 (6208)	242 (1373)	309 (4150)
48 (6154)	112 (1640)	175 (6209)	243 (6243)	310 (6261)
49 (1846)	113 (1370)	176 (6210)	244 (3029)	311 (1126)
50 (6155)	114 (761)	177 (1217)	245 (2601)	312 (6262)
51 (481)	115 (3426)	178 (6211)	246 (2602)	313 (4015)
53 (6156)	116 (1371)	179 (6212)	247 (1374)	314 (961)
54 (6157)	117 (4148)	180 (6213)	248 (3704)	315 (1377)
55 (6158)	118 (1170)	182 (1372)	249 (324)	316 (2008)
56 (611)	121 (3667)	183 (6214)	251 (6244)	317 (4620)
57 (321)	122 (6180)	184 (6215)	253 (3030)	318 (2009)
59 (322)	123 (6181)	185 (6216)	254 (1375)	319 (1127)
60 (376)	124 (4962)	186 (6217)	255 (6245)	320 (2155)
61 (4147)	125 (6182)	187 (6218)	257 (664)	321 (6263)
62 (6159)	126 (2640)	188 (6219)	258 (6246)	322 (3031)
63 (2938)	127 (659)	189 (6220)	260 (1958)	323 (1849)
64 (6160)	128 (6183)	190 (6221)	262 (6247)	325 (2643)
65 (6161)	129 (6184)	191 (2216)	264 (588)	326 (4856)
66 (6162)	130 (6185)	192 (3427)	265 (6248)	327 (2420)
67 (6163)	131 (6186)	193 (3428)	266 (3928)	328 (3429)
68 (6164)	132 (6187)	194 (4449)	267 (3929)	329 (489)
69 (6165)	133 (3353)	196 (1642)	268 (3930)	330 (4621)
70 (6166)	134 (6188)	198 (660)	269 (3931)	331 (4368)
71 (6167)	135 (6189)	199 (377)	270 (4619)	332 (4369)
72 (6168)	136 (3052)	200 (2153)	271 (6249)	333 (4370)
73 (6169)	137 (6190)	201 (3135)	272 (3932)	334 (4371)
74 (6170)	138 (4963)	202 (1776)	273 (3013)	336 (4622)
75 (1367)	139 (6191)	203 (6222)	274 (2471)	337 (1652)
76 (69)	140 (3354)	204 (4450)	275 (1297)	338 (6264)
77 (1368)	141 (2641)	205 (6223)	276 (6250)	339 (5012)
78 (1369)	142 (6192)	207 (484)	277 (2941)	340 (1016)
79 (658)	143 (2939)	208 (6224)	278 (4853)	341 (4016)
80 (70)	144 (6193)	209 (6225)	279 (1754)	342 (4451)
81 (6171)	145 (2470)	211 (6226)	280 (1755)	343 (6265)
82 (1847)	146 (2940)	213 (6227)	281 (6251)	344 (3669)
83 (6172)	147 (483)	214 (6228)	282 (2154)	345 (3788)
85 (6173)	148 (3314)	216 (6229)	283 (6252)	346 (962)
86 (6174)	149 (2675)	217 (6230)	284 (485)	347 (1378)
87 (6175)	150 (6195)	218 (6231)	285 (6253)	349 (4623)
88 (2418)	151 (1753)	219 (6232)	286 (2007)	350 (490)
89 (1460)	153 (692)	220 (6233)	287 (4854)	351 (4930)
91 (2006)	154 (1051)	221 (1957)	288 (6254)	352 (3343)
95 (691)	155 (6198)	222 (6234)	289 (815)	353 (4151)
96 (2469)	156 (6199)	223 (6235)	292 (486)	355 (2863)
98 (2638)	157 (1296)	224 (3745)	293 (6258)	356 (2010)
99 (6176)	159 (6200)	225 (6236)	294 (2942)	357 (2156)
100 (6177)	160 (164)	226 (6237)	295 (3838)	358 (1052)
101 (1848)	162 (4618)	227 (6238)	297 (487)	359 (1053)
102 (2639)	163 (3668)	229 (6239)	298 (6259)	360 (491)

Volume IX A	Volume IX A	Volume IX A	Volume X¹ A	Volume X¹ A
362 (2751)	426 (3431)	496 (2012)	52 (6314)	134 (4454)
363 (4545)	427 (3032)	498 (6278)	53 (6315)	135 (236)
364 (4152)	428 (6281)	499 (6279)	54 (6316)	136 (667)
365 (3705)	429 (4017)	500 (6280)	55 (2769)	137 (6355)
366 (2690)	430 (5013)	Volume IX B	56 (6317)	138 (6356)
367 (4624)	431 (2228)	5:2 y (3204)	58 (6318)	139 (6357)
368 (325)	432 (6282)	45:4 (1643)	59 (1383)	140 (6358)
371 (6266)	433 (2474)	63:7 (6255)	60 (1384)	143 (6359)
372 (963)	434 (2603)	63:8 (2013)	61 (6319)	144 (3482)
373 (3898)	435 (2645)	63:11 (2647)	62 (1128)	146 (6360)
374 (1379)	437 (1760)	63:12 (2648)	63 (6320)	147 (6361)
375 (6268)	438 (2299)	63:13 (2649)	64 (1385)	148 (1761)
377 (2472)	439 (665)	66 (2014)	65 (3899)	151 (6362)
378 (2157)	440 (326)	67 (6292)	66 (3707)	152 (6363)
379 (6269)	441 (1380)	68 (6293)	67 (6321)	154 (2481)
380 (4625)	442 (209)	Volume X¹ A	71 (6322)	156 (6364)
381 (6270)	443 (967)	2 (3215)	72 (6323)	158 (6365)
382 (1054)	445 (4153)	3 (166)	73 (6324)	159 (4858)
383 (3706)	447 (165)	5 (185)	74 (6325)	161 (6366)
384 (2864)	448 (6283)	6 (3479)	77 (6326)	162 (6367)
385 (2644)	449 (4154)	7 (381)	78 (6327)	163 (6368)
387 (235)	450 (2011)	8 (6298)	80 (6328)	164 (2230)
389 (2473)	451 (6284)	9 (6299)	84 (6329)	166 (6369)
390 (6271)	452 (2943)	10 (2475)	85 (2480)	167 (6370)
391 (1949)	453 (4155)	11 (6300)	88 (6330)	169 (6371)
392 (964)	456 (3671)	12 (1220)	89 (6333)	171 (4157)
393 (6272)	458 (6285)	14 (6301)	90 (6334)	172 (2482)
394 (492)	459 (1778)	15 (6302)	92 (6335)	173 (3232)
395 (270)	460 (569)	16 (2650)	94 (6336)	178 (495)
396 (1850)	461 (494)	17 (4052)	95 (6337)	179 (1851)
398 (1756)	462 (3432)	18 (3216)	96 (4156)	182 (3483)
399 (1757)	463 (6286)	19 (3480)	100 (6338)	183 (6372)
400 (1758)	464 (968)	20 (1382)	104 (6339)	185 (668)
402 (2120)	466 (4629)	21 (2476)	107 (6340)	187 (6373)
403 (2752)	467 (6287)	22 (4372)	108 (4630)	188 (186)
404 (2753)	468 (2158)	23 (6303)	110 (6341)	190 (496)
405 (380)	470 (2229)	24 (6304)	111 (6342)	192 (6374)
406 (3136)	471 (6288)	25 (2477)	112 (6343)	193 (1055)
407 (4626)	472 (570)	26 (1257)	113 (6344)	194 (1284)
408 (6273)	473 (6289)	30 (4546)	115 (6345)	195 (4019)
409 (3355)	474 (3672)	32 (2478)	116 (6346)	196 (1386)
410 (4627)	475 (223)	33 (6305)	118 (6347)	197 (2483)
411 (6274)	476 (1381)	34 (2852)	119 (2651)	198 (167)
412 (3344)	478 (2159)	37 (6307)	120 (6348)	199 (6375)
413 (6275)	482 (1218)	38 (589)	121 (6350)	201 (329)
414 (493)	483 (224)	39 (6308)	122 (666)	202 (6376)
415 (3670)	484 (6290)	41 (6309)	123 (6351)	203 (1387)
416 (6276)	486 (3746)	42 (6310)	124 (3983)	204 (330)
417 (3430)	487 (4857)	43 (6311)	125 (3481)	205 (3332)
418 (965)	488 (6291)	45 (6312)	126 (6352)	206 (6377)
419 (966)	490 (2944)	46 (6313)	127 (328)	207 (3484)
420 (1759)	491 (1219)	47 (2479)	128 (2160)	208 (969)
421 (6277)	492 (6194)	48 (842)	130 (6353)	209 (4964)
423 (1777)	493 (6196)	49 (327)	131 (6354)	210 (3433)
424 (2217)	494 (4452)	50 (4453)	132 (693)	211 (3434)
425 (4628)	495 (2646)	51 (684)	133 (4018)	212 (590)

Volume	X¹ A	Volume	X¹ A	Volume	X¹ A	Volume	X¹ A	Volume	X¹ A
213	(2484)	321	(970)	397	(4780)	466	(2378)	545	(2499)
214	(1468)	322	(6396)	399	(499)	467	(503)	546	(6445)
216	(669)	323	(6397)	400	(2691)	468	(1171)	547	(507)
217	(497)	324	(2489)	401	(3195)	469	(6422)	548	(6446)
218	(2015)	325	(6398)	402	(6413)	470	(3439)	550	(4783)
219	(762)	326	(2490)	403	(2493)	471	(504)	551	(6447)
220	(2652)	327	(971)	404	(6414)	472	(505)	552	(593)
221	(2865)	330	(3708)	405	(4633)	473	(506)	553	(6448)
223	(4547)	332	(1388)	406	(6415)	474	(2497)	554	(1132)
228	(6378)	333	(2653)	407	(4861)	476	(6423)	555	(1133)
231	(2945)	336	(6399)	408	(1389)	477	(4375)	556	(6449)
232	(331)	338	(6400)	409	(2162)	478	(4375)	557	(6450)
233	(721)	341	(2161)	410	(4862)	479	(1390)	558	(508)
234	(6379)	342	(6401)	412	(974)	480	(672)	561	(3564)
235	(670)	343	(6402)	415	(1644)	481	(3608)	564	(2121)
237	(3233)	345	(671)	416	(4634)	482	(2868)	565	(3033)
238	(1074)	346	(168)	417	(4326)	483	(6424)	566	(673)
239	(6380)	347	(4859)	419	(2494)	484	(4750)	567	(6451)
243	(332)	348	(4960)	420	(2495)	485	(2607)	568	(6452)
245	(333)	350	(4159)	422	(6416)	486	(4751)	569	(6453)
246	(1852)	351	(6407)	423	(6417)	487	(2422)	570	(6454)
247	(6382)	352	(336)	424	(6418)	488	(6425)	571	(6455)
248	(816)	353	(101)	425	(6419)	489	(2423)	572	(4754)
249	(382)	354	(337)	426	(843)	490	(4752)	573	(3565)
250	(6383)	355	(338)	427	(500)	492	(4753)	576	(6456)
255	(3900)	356	(4160)	428	(3933)	493	(3905)	577	(2300)
258	(6384)	360	(972)	429	(4519)	494	(6426)	579	(594)
260	(6385)	361	(2358)	430	(975)	495	(6427)	580	(977)
261	(4796)	363	(2373)	432	(169)	496	(6428)	581	(4797)
262	(6386)	364	(339)	433	(4021)	497	(6429)	583	(6457)
263	(6387)	365	(4632)	434	(1779)	498	(6430)	584	(6458)
266	(6388)	366	(6408)	435	(1780)	502	(817)	586	(6459)
268	(2946)	367	(1129)	436	(4991)	503	(341)	587	(342)
269	(4158)	368	(1130)	438	(501)	504	(1512)	588	(6460)
271	(591)	369	(4161)	439	(2496)	507	(1469)	590	(1298)
272	(6389)	370	(2491)	440	(2605)	510	(6431)	591	(4273)
273	(6390)	371	(2374)	441	(6420)	513	(6432)	593	(6461)
279	(334)	372	(1950)	443	(502)	514	(2424)	594	(6462)
281	(6391)	373	(2720)	444	(2421)	515	(3789)	595	(2500)
285	(335)	374	(6409)	445	(2606)	516	(4920)	598	(6463)
286	(2016)	376	(2492)	447	(340)	517	(6433)	600	(3061)
287	(2866)	377	(6410)	448	(4863)	519	(6435)	603	(4636)
288	(2867)	379	(2375)	449	(2376)	520	(6436)	605	(1391)
289	(6392)	381	(6411)	450	(6421)	522	(4162)	607	(4755)
291	(3435)	382	(2654)	451	(3196)	523	(818)	608	(1080)
294	(5050)	383	(4455)	452	(4373)	525	(6437)	609	(3566)
297	(2485)	384	(4020)	455	(1853)	526	(2498)	610	(978)
300	(6393)	385	(6412)	457	(976)	529	(6438)	615	(6464)
301	(498)	388	(3436)	458	(2947)	530	(6439)	616	(6465)
303	(2486)	389	(3437)	459	(4992)	531	(6440)	617	(6466)
304	(2487)	390	(3438)	460	(383)	535	(6441)	623	(2655)
309	(6394)	392	(3194)	461	(3636)	536	(6442)	624	(343)
310	(2604)	393	(973)	462	(3637)	537	(592)	625	(4893)
314	(2488)	394	(3984)	463	(2017)	538	(6443)	627	(4022)
319	(4631)	395	(1131)	464	(4635)	540	(3485)	628	(3217)
320	(6395)	396	(3014)	465	(2377)	541	(6444)	629	(1342)

Volume X¹ A	Volume X² A	Volume X² A	Volume X² A	Volume X² A
630 (2501)	19 (675)	92 (6507)	170 (349)	236 (4643)
631 (1854)	20 (6492)	93 (4785)	173 (2506)	238 (3137)
632 (4163)	21 (3486)	94 (6508)	174 (6525)	239 (1475)
633 (3440)	22 (102)	95 (3487)	177 (6526)	240 (4168)
635 (2425)	23 (979)	97 (271)	178 (981)	241 (1399)
637 (4023)	24 (5018)	101 (6509)	179 (2018)	242 (6547)
638 (2426)	25 (6493)	103 (4329)	180 (1081)	243 (1260)
639 (1513)	26 (3934)	105 (6510)	181 (2608)	244 (2507)
640 (6467)	27 (386)	106 (6511)	182 (4376)	245 (2508)
642 (2692)	28 (3935)	107 (2429)	183 (6527)	246 (4644)
643 (6468)	29 (4024)	109 (6512)	184 (6528)	247 (2430)
644 (6469)	30 (2503)	110 (6513)	186 (1396)	248 (4276)
645 (4637)	31 (5019)	112 (6514)	187 (512)	251 (6548)
646 (1781)	32 (1762)	114 (3345)	188 (1470)	252 (6549)
647 (788)	36 (1856)	115 (3638)	189 (1471)	253 (694)
648 (6470)	37 (510)	116 (3660)	190 (2656)	255 (1858)
649 (509)	38 (344)	117 (3034)	191 (6529)	256 (6550)
650 (1056)	39 (6494)	119 (187)	192 (6530)	257 (4645)
651 (2502)	40 (6495)	121 (2948)	193 (6531)	258 (781)
652 (4327)	41 (3197)	122 (4786)	194 (237)	260 (6551)
653 (6474)	42 (4784)	123 (2504)	195 (6532)	261 (6552)
655 (2869)	43 (3985)	125 (1394)	196 (6533)	262 (2431)
658 (707)	44 (6496)	126 (6515)	197 (3655)	263 (2509)
659 (6476)	45 (6497)	128 (4640)	198 (1472)	264 (173)
660 (6477)	46 (2122)	129 (4641)	199 (6534)	265 (2019)
661 (6478)	47 (1857)	131 (4642)	201 (982)	270 (985)
662 (4638)	48 (6498)	132 (763)	202 (3346)	271 (764)
663 (6479)	50 (3936)	133 (3053)	203 (2139)	272 (4646)
664 (6480)	51 (3937)	134 (6516)	204 (6535)	273 (6553)
665 (6481)	52 (4167)	135 (388)	205 (6536)	274 (3938)
666 (3558)	53 (4639)	136 (348)	206 (1514)	275 (6554)
667 (6482)	54 (1134)	137 (819)	207 (1135)	277 (6555)
668 (6483)	56 (6499)	139 (389)	208 (983)	278 (6556)
669 (4164)	57 (612)	140 (1529)	210 (6538)	279 (4457)
670 (6484)	58 (387)	141 (511)	211 (6539)	280 (6557)
671 (6485)	61 (6500)	142 (980)	212 (6540)	281 (6561)
672 (384)	63 (2428)	143 (4965)	213 (6541)	282 (4787)
673 (1855)	65 (4328)	144 (4931)	214 (6542)	283 (571)
675 (2427)	66 (6501)	145 (4548)	215 (6543)	284 (513)
676 (6486)	67 (4274)	146 (676)	216 (6544)	285 (6562)
678 (6487)	68 (6502)	147 (6517)	217 (6545)	288 (3493)
679 (3567)	72 (1393)	148 (6519)	218 (3490)	289 (2657)
680 (3091)	73 (345)	149 (3488)	219 (1473)	292 (4169)
682 (4165)	74 (4025)	150 (6520)	220 (1082)	294 (2949)
Volume X² A	75 (6503)	151 (3489)	221 (1083)	296 (3645)
3 (6488)	76 (2138)	154 (3356)	223 (1474)	298 (6563)
5 (2770)	77 (3441)	156 (3639)	224 (984)	299 (4550)
7 (4166)	78 (71)	157 (6521)	225 (1559)	301 (4551)
10 (6489)	79 (72)	158 (6522)	226 (1397)	302 (6564)
11 (6490)	80 (4456)	159 (1258)	227 (3491)	304 (1763)
12 (674)	85 (346)	160 (1259)	228 (6546)	305 (572)
13 (4053)	86 (347)	161 (4748)	229 (4275)	307 (6565)
14 (1172)	87 (3901)	162 (2505)	230 (3492)	310 (3494)
15 (6491)	88 (6504)	163 (6523)	231 (4549)	311 (350)
16 (385)	89 (6505)	167 (6524)	232 (1398)	312 (3218)
17 (2163)	90 (6506)	169 (1395)	235 (2324)	313 (4458)

Volume X^2 A	Volume X^2 A	Volume X^2 A	Volume X^2 A	Volume X^2 A
314 (2164)	389 (3035)	454 (1173)	541 (3673)	632 (3448)
315 (6568)	390 (2952)	455 (789)	544 (6592)	633 (3568)
317 (1859)	391 (4172)	456 (4032)	545 (3674)	635 (4867)
318 (4459)	392 (820)	457 (2022)	546 (987)	636 (3711)
319 (351)	393 (6578)	459 (6586)	548 (4781)	637 (3569)
320 (272)	394 (4173)	460 (516)	549 (4782)	640 (3712)
321 (4993)	395 (4174)	461 (3612)	550 (3142)	642 (4460)
322 (4552)	396 (188)	462 (391)	552 (3640)	643 (4183)
323 (2658)	397 (613)	463 (4866)	553 (3054)	644 (1405)
324 (263)	400 (4026)	464 (2710)	554 (3055)	Volume X^3 A
325 (3939)	401 (4555)	465 (1461)	555 (210)	3 (6607)
326 (1860)	402 (4556)	466 (678)	556 (211)	4 (6608)
327 (4330)	403 (4027)	467 (4033)	557 (4966)	5 (4967)
328 (1057)	404 (4028)	472 (4034)	558 (2513)	6 (3824)
333 (3940)	406 (73)	473 (4035)	559 (2514)	8 (6609)
334 (2510)	407 (74)	474 (1782)	560 (6593)	10 (3825)
336 (4553)	408 (75)	475 (6587)	561 (264)	11 (3449)
338 (6570)	409 (4864)	476 (6588)	562 (4740)	12 (6610)
340 (2797)	411 (6579)	477 (4036)	563 (1299)	13 (6611)
341 (2793)	412 (3241)	478 (4175)	564 (1193)	14 (4513)
342 (3443)	413 (6580)	479 (4176)	565 (1194)	15 (4968)
343 (3444)	414 (1058)	480 (2023)	566 (2609)	16 (3347)
344 (3445)	415 (6581)	481 (1530)	568 (5020)	19 (2432)
345 (6571)	416 (3852)	482 (4037)	569 (1403)	20 (2954)
346 (6572)	417 (3853)	483 (4038)	571 (4182)	21 (2955)
347 (1861)	418 (3141)	484 (3092)	573 (3675)	22 (4557)
348 (1017)	419 (986)	485 (2953)	578 (2092)	23 (3646)
349 (4647)	420 (514)	486 (4177)	581 (3497)	25 (4868)
350 (3941)	421 (515)	488 (6589)	582 (3015)	26 (4184)
351 (4170)	422 (352)	489 (2024)	584 (1951)	27 (1084)
352 (6573)	424 (4332)	490 (4178)	586 (6594)	28 (3661)
353 (1653)	425 (6582)	491 (76)	590 (4377)	29 (3906)
354 (7)	426 (1614)	493 (1401)	591 (1404)	30 (6612)
355 (4554)	427 (6583)	494 (1402)	592 (8)	31 (3907)
356 (4171)	428 (1261)	496 (3446)	593 (393)	32 (2870)
357 (3140)	429 (4029)	497 (4179)	594 (3130)	33 (2871)
358 (225)	430 (3609)	498 (4180)	595 (3447)	34 (2872)
360 (3790)	431 (1615)	500 (1531)	596 (6595)	35 (3908)
361 (1862)	432 (3315)	501 (3093)	597 (3942)	36 (3909)
362 (2821)	434 (722)	502 (3094)	598 (4278)	40 (3143)
363 (3495)	435 (4865)	505 (3599)	601 (6597)	41 (6613)
364 (2511)	436 (4030)	506 (4181)	602 (2093)	43 (4950)
367 (677)	437 (4031)	509 (3747)	603 (517)	47 (4798)
369 (2950)	438 (1262)	510 (1783)	604 (3748)	48 (3498)
371 (1136)	439 (1059)	513 (4648)	605 (6602)	49 (3450)
372 (6575)	440 (6585)	514 (392)	606 (1060)	51 (1560)
373 (5039)	441 (3198)	516 (1221)	608 (3328)	52 (3559)
374 (6576)	443 (1400)	517 (2237)	609 (3329)	54 (596)
375 (6577)	445 (4333)	518 (1263)	610 (3330)	56 (2754)
377 (201)	446 (3610)	519 (2238)	614 (3709)	57 (2671)
379 (4331)	447 (3611)	525 (6590)	617 (844)	58 (2515)
380 (170)	448 (2512)	529 (2803)	619 (6603)	59 (3499)
382 (3496)	449 (4277)	531 (4932)	622 (6604)	60 (212)
383 (2951)	451 (1654)	534 (6591)	624 (3710)	61 (4736)
384 (103)	452 (1655)	536 (3965)	627 (6605)	62 (3144)
386 (779)	453 (390)	539 (2239)	629 (2025)	66 (988)

Volume	X³ A	Volume	X³ A	Volume	X³ A	Volume	X³ A	Volume	X³ A
67	(6614)	148	(4653)	221	(2523)	286	(4799)	356	(2126)
68	(6615)	149	(3234)	222	(3452)	287	(4763)	357	(2127)
72	(1476)	150	(1061)	223	(3453)	288	(3508)	359	(1409)
75	(1406)	151	(821)	225	(3679)	290	(3348)	360	(1657)
77	(6616)	152	(6632)	227	(3454)	293	(2221)	361	(3754)
78	(6617)	153	(2518)	228	(1764)	294	(1870)	362	(524)
79	(4461)	154	(3504)	229	(4760)	295	(1871)	364	(3510)
81	(4649)	155	(3948)	230	(2220)	297	(1656)	365	(1658)
83	(4926)	156	(2123)	231	(2165)	298	(1138)	367	(6662)
85	(4869)	157	(2219)	232	(3680)	299	(3682)	371	(2778)
86	(6618)	161	(6633)	233	(2876)	301	(4969)	373	(1410)
88	(6619)	163	(6634)	234	(2524)	302	(2525)	374	(1411)
89	(6620)	164	(6635)	237	(3505)	303	(2659)	376	(4043)
90	(6621)	165	(2873)	238	(1784)	304	(6657)	377	(3683)
93	(3145)	166	(3749)	239	(6652)	305	(4657)	378	(1875)
94	(6622)	168	(6642)	240	(4761)	306	(3751)	381	(6664)
96	(106)	169	(2874)	241	(4334)	307	(3509)	382	(4658)
97	(107)	170	(2519)	242	(3149)	309	(6658)	383	(3016)
98	(6623)	171	(1864)	243	(3150)	310	(6659)	384	(3017)
99	(6624)	172	(520)	244	(3151)	312	(1786)	389	(6665)
100	(518)	173	(521)	245	(4655)	314	(1872)	390	(4801)
102	(3500)	174	(6643)	246	(3506)	315	(4280)	391	(6666)
104	(989)	175	(2711)	247	(1407)	316	(2611)	392	(3572)
106	(1477)	176	(3148)	248	(990)	317	(3455)	393	(4894)
107	(3943)	180	(4039)	249	(6653)	318	(6660)	394	(4462)
108	(3944)	181	(4040)	250	(723)	319	(1222)	395	(1788)
109	(3945)	182	(4654)	251	(2124)	320	(4800)	396	(4463)
110	(3946)	183	(6644)	253	(4279)	321	(6661)	398	(3573)
111	(3947)	184	(1137)	257	(353)	322	(1139)	399	(6667)
112	(6625)	185	(4756)	258	(6654)	323	(1140)	400	(1876)
113	(2610)	186	(77)	259	(4762)	324	(2027)	401	(5014)
114	(4650)	187	(174)	260	(3152)	325	(3154)	402	(6668)
115	(6626)	189	(6645)	261	(6655)	326	(3728)	403	(6669)
116	(2026)	190	(6646)	262	(2956)	328	(2877)	404	(6670)
118	(4651)	191	(6647)	263	(1286)	329	(2878)	407	(3511)
120	(3146)	192	(395)	264	(1408)	330	(2879)	409	(1877)
121	(3570)	193	(3613)	265	(6656)	331	(1873)	410	(1481)
122	(3571)	194	(6648)	266	(3750)	333	(3036)	411	(1878)
124	(3676)	199	(4041)	267	(3153)	334	(2125)	412	(2779)
125	(3677)	200	(1285)	268	(1785)	335	(2526)	413	(1959)
127	(2516)	202	(4757)	269	(1478)	336	(2527)	415	(6671)
128	(6627)	203	(4758)	270	(1479)	337	(2756)	416	(6672)
129	(3501)	204	(6649)	271	(3507)	338	(1874)	419	(2612)
130	(3502)	205	(4759)	272	(1866)	339	(2028)	420	(397)
131	(4652)	207	(1865)	273	(5021)	340	(724)	421	(1412)
132	(3147)	208	(3451)	275	(2166)	341	(4042)	422	(6673)
134	(519)	209	(522)	276	(1867)	342	(14)	423	(6674)
137	(394)	210	(6650)	277	(1868)	344	(685)	424	(3095)
138	(2517)	211	(2520)	278	(3681)	346	(4185)	425	(4307)
139	(2218)	213	(3849)	279	(2167)	347	(1787)	426	(4659)
141	(3503)	214	(2875)	280	(2168)	348	(213)	427	(355)
142	(6628)	216	(2755)	281	(4656)	349	(2029)	428	(3333)
143	(3357)	217	(2521)	282	(396)	351	(3752)	429	(4737)
144	(6629)	218	(2522)	283	(1869)	352	(3753)	430	(2089)
146	(6630)	219	(6651)	284	(1532)	353	(1480)	431	(3684)
147	(6631)	220	(3678)	285	(523)	354	(354)	432	(4870)

Volume X³ A	Volume X³ A	Volume X³ A	Volume X³ A	Volume X³ A
434 (6677)	516 (2529)	584 (3132)	652 (4873)	718 (4996)
435 (6678)	517 (2694)	585 (1414)	653 (695)	719 (1534)
436 (3155)	518 (2695)	587 (4188)	654 (3829)	720 (4559)
437 (3318)	519 (6685)	588 (2712)	655 (356)	721 (1890)
447 (1879)	520 (2696)	589 (5015)	656 (2958)	722 (2885)
448 (6679)	521 (597)	590 (2884)	657 (2959)	723 (2170)
450 (6680)	523 (2697)	591 (6698)	658 (1415)	725 (1062)
451 (2957)	524 (1790)	593 (4558)	659 (1960)	727 (4741)
452 (3910)	525 (1791)	594 (2722)	660 (2031)	729 (793)
453 (6681)	526 (6686)	595 (3457)	661 (6707)	730 (6711)
454 (1880)	529 (4186)	596 (4337)	662 (4465)	731 (4663)
455 (1881)	530 (6687)	597 (4338)	663 (6708)	732 (4664)
456 (3755)	531 (3456)	599 (6699)	664 (4874)	733 (526)
457 (3756)	532 (2721)	601 (3912)	665 (2169)	734 (993)
459 (2780)	533 (2530)	602 (1883)	666 (1885)	736 (4340)
460 (3358)	534 (3515)	603 (4189)	667 (1886)	737 (994)
461 (3359)	536 (1141)	605 (2531)	668 (1887)	738 (527)
463 (226)	537 (2880)	606 (3158)	670 (1793)	739 (2434)
464 (1085)	540 (189)	607 (4190)	671 (4662)	740 (3662)
467 (3199)	541 (2881)	608 (3729)	672 (2140)	741 (2435)
468 (2613)	542 (3105)	609 (3109)	674 (3038)	742 (6712)
469 (2128)	543 (3106)	610 (3159)	676 (2727)	743 (1417)
470 (4933)	544 (3107)	614 (4872)	677 (4972)	745 (4466)
471 (4934)	545 (3685)	615 (1884)	678 (6709)	746 (4193)
472 (6682)	546 (3108)	616 (1828)	679 (4191)	747 (1418)
476 (2030)	547 (3516)	617 (4951)	680 (6709a)	750 (1891)
477 (4281)	549 (2882)	618 (1264)	682 (3320)	751 (3161)
478 (4871)	550 (6688)	619 (1265)	683 (3242)	752 (2757)
479 (3512)	551 (6689)	622 (3037)	684 (4520)	754 (4194)
480 (2781)	552 (1882)	624 (679)	685 (4521)	755 (574)
481 (3911)	553 (2614)	625 (680)	686 (4522)	756 (4560)
482 (3349)	554 (4994)	626 (3110)	687 (2032)	760 (575)
483 (6683)	555 (6690)	627 (1515)	688 (4045)	763 (2034)
484 (3513)	556 (3319)	628 (6700)	689 (1794)	764 (2094)
487 (6684)	559 (3826)	629 (6701)	690 (4192)	765 (576)
489 (2433)	560 (3757)	630 (3111)	692 (3517)	766 (2095)
492 (4660)	561 (4970)	631 (3112)	694 (1416)	767 (1892)
493 (4335)	562 (4995)	632 (3113)	695 (3950)	769 (6713)
496 (3018)	563 (6691)	633 (3114)	696 (3686)	770 (6714)
497 (3019)	564 (6692)	634 (3115)	697 (598)	771 (6715)
498 (2660)	565 (6693)	635 (6702)	698 (3160)	772 (1419)
499 (1300)	566 (4044)	636 (6703)	699 (4802)	773 (4195)
500 (4661)	568 (6694)	637 (6704)	700 (3458)	774 (4665)
501 (78)	569 (6695)	638 (1533)	702 (3860)	775 (1535)
502 (3156)	570 (4971)	639 (3116)	705 (4339)	776 (1893)
503 (2782)	573 (1223)	640 (3117)	706 (3951)	777 (3956)
505 (398)	574 (3334)	641 (3118)	707 (3952)	778 (2035)
506 (1174)	575 (4187)	642 (3119)	708 (3953)	780 (6716)
508 (2783)	576 (1792)	643 (4514)	709 (3954)	781 (1420)
509 (1789)	577 (6696)	644 (3120)	710 (725)	782 (6717)
510 (2528)	578 (6697)	645 (3121)	711 (3955)	783 (4666)
511 (2661)	579 (4336)	646 (3122)	712 (1888)	784 (1482)
512 (4464)	580 (3335)	647 (6705)	713 (1889)	786 (1616)
513 (2784)	581 (1413)	648 (681)	714 (991)	787 (1659)
514 (3157)	582 (2883)	649 (525)	715 (992)	789 (6718)
515 (3514)	583 (3131)	650 (6706)	716 (6710)	790 (1421)

Volume X³ A	Volume X⁴ A	Volume X⁴ A	Volume X⁴ A	Volume X⁴ A
791 (4467)	58 (6735)	125 (4469)	187 (4213)	261 (3758)
792 (1175)	59 (4468)	126 (4209)	188 (2039)	263 (2771)
799 (6719)	60 (726)	127 (1195)	189 (4672)	264 (3839)
800 (6720)	62 (1064)	128 (3688)	190 (3689)	266 (3759)
Volume X⁴ A	63 (4202)	129 (3832)	191 (4523)	268 (4216)
4 (2758)	64 (6736)	130 (6740)	195 (6745)	269 (1516)
5 (1063)	65 (4203)	131 (1894)	197 (2325)	270 (6757)
6 (6721)	66 (4819)	132 (1422)	198 (2326)	271 (6758)
7 (7532)	67 (1225)	133 (4046)	199 (2327)	272 (6759)
8 (6722)	68 (4204)	134 (1483)	200 (400)	273 (1896)
9 (6723)	70 (4820)	135 (4667)	201 (6752)	274 (1897)
10 (4817)	71 (15)	137 (4764)	204 (6753)	275 (1898)
11 (238)	72 (4205)	138 (4765)	207 (1065)	276 (3840)
12 (2533)	73 (1226)	139 (4766)	208 (1645)	277 (3841)
13 (1266)	74 (3641)	140 (4767)	209 (4214)	278 (1517)
14 (6724)	75 (3687)	141 (4768)	210 (3615)	279 (3842)
15 (708)	76 (250)	142 (4769)	211 (1423)	280 (3862)
16 (3986)	77 (1227)	143 (4770)	212 (532)	281 (3460)
17 (3200)	78 (529)	144 (4771)	214 (3690)	282 (1798)
18 (4935)	80 (1796)	145 (1196)	215 (3691)	283 (4562)
19 (4936)	81 (1228)	146 (1797)	216 (3692)	284 (4563)
20 (6725)	82 (1229)	147 (399)	219 (2100)	285 (6760)
21 (2129)	83 (4206)	148 (1895)	220 (2106)	287 (3520)
22 (599)	84 (3321)	149 (531)	222 (822)	288 (104)
23 (6726)	85 (6737)	150 (175)	223 (3827)	289 (3693)
24 (686)	86 (4738)	151 (2131)	224 (3828)	290 (4937)
25 (2534)	87 (6738)	153 (4668)	225 (2964)	291 (4473)
26 (2130)	89 (2037)	154 (6741)	226 (4341)	293 (1899)
27 (3730)	90 (5040)	155 (4210)	227 (3519)	295 (3694)
28 (528)	91 (1961)	156 (4669)	228 (6754)	296 (6761)
29 (2036)	93 (2960)	157 (2887)	229 (3459)	297 (4890)
30 (3731)	94 (3322)	158 (4670)	230 (1484)	298 (3790)
31 (4196)	95 (4378)	160 (4470)	231 (6755)	299 (6762)
32 (1086)	97 (4207)	161 (4877)	232 (2822)	300 (6763)
33 (6727)	99 (1267)	162 (3614)	233 (6756)	301 (6764)
34 (687)	100 (2961)	163 (3235)	234 (780)	302 (6765)
35 (4875)	101 (6739)	166 (6742)	235 (4471)	303 (6766)
36 (6728)	102 (4208)	167 (6743)	236 (3574)	304 (1427)
37 (6729)	103 (2728)	168 (6744)	237 (2536)	305 (4891)
38 (3732)	104 (2038)	169 (4671)	238 (4673)	306 (5041)
39 (1795)	105 (2962)	170 (1197)	239 (4674)	309 (2436)
40 (4197)	106 (4997)	171 (1198)	244 (4675)	310 (2302)
41 (4198)	107 (2963)	172 (1199)	245 (1270)	311 (1428)
42 (4876)	108 (2662)	173 (4047)	246 (600)	312 (4742)
43 (4199)	109 (2663)	174 (3642)	247 (2301)	313 (2328)
47 (4200)	110 (3861)	175 (1268)	249 (4215)	314 (4283)
48 (4818)	112 (4561)	176 (995)	250 (4282)	315 (2889)
49 (577)	114 (1142)	177 (1269)	251 (4472)	316 (3760)
50 (357)	115 (530)	178 (4973)	252 (1424)	317 (3521)
51 (4201)	117 (3733)	180 (3550)	253 (1425)	318 (6767)
52 (6730)	119 (3830)	181 (4749)	254 (1426)	319 (4284)
53 (6731)	120 (3831)	182 (4744)	255 (3713)	320 (997)
54 (2535)	121 (3162)	183 (2203)	256 (4676)	321 (1900)
55 (6732)	122 (2886)	184 (996)	257 (1271)	322 (6768)
56 (6733)	123 (1143)	185 (4211)	258 (3647)	323 (6769)
57 (6734)	124 (3518)	186 (4212)	260 (2888)	324 (2537)

Volume X⁴ A	Volume X⁴ A	Volume X⁴ A	Volume X⁴ A	Volume X⁴ A
325 (2538)	393 (3165)	462 (4381)	523 (3957)	591 (1089)
326 (3761)	394 (2541)	463 (4287)	524 (5022)	592 (6811)
328 (4821)	395 (6783)	464 (4515)	525 (3715)	593 (4688)
329 (1660)	396 (1536)	466 (4309)	526 (2891)	594 (601)
330 (3522)	397 (4054)	467 (4288)	527 (2892)	596 (709)
332 (3163)	398 (3575)	468 (4897)	528 (3716)	597 (3527)
333 (4285)	401 (2041)	469 (4310)	529 (3717)	598 (4292)
334 (4286)	402 (4772)	470 (534)	530 (4291)	599 (4293)
335 (4474)	403 (3021)	471 (1943)	531 (2760)	602 (3631)
336 (3695)	404 (6784)	472 (6792)	532 (3578)	603 (6812)
337 (4878)	405 (2965)	473 (251)	533 (1831)	604 (6813)
338 (3020)	406 (4976)	474 (6793)	534 (4048)	605 (6814)
339 (6771)	407 (4566)	475 (5042)	535 (2966)	607 (2893)
340 (1901)	408 (6785)	476 (4311)	536 (3764)	608 (4314)
341 (4974)	409 (3863)	477 (4743)	537 (176)	609 (4881)
342 (4879)	410 (1907)	478 (1829)	538 (4939)	610 (6815)
343 (4677)	411 (4379)	479 (1830)	539 (6798)	611 (4689)
344 (1799)	412 (3902)	480 (4898)	540 (6800)	612 (2560)
345 (3734)	413 (3056)	481 (4681)	541 (3201)	613 (4901)
346 (4564)	414 (3600)	482 (2437)	545 (6801)	614 (3579)
349 (1902)	415 (2042)	483 (2853)	549 (999)	615 (3735)
350 (4895)	416 (3360)	484 (4312)	550 (791)	616 (537)
351 (6772)	418 (110)	485 (1429)	553 (1962)	617 (4344)
352 (1903)	419 (1485)	486 (4342)	554 (6802)	618 (1486)
353 (6773)	420 (4679)	487 (4949)	555 (4313)	619 (1487)
354 (1904)	422 (1144)	488 (6794)	556 (1914)	620 (4690)
355 (3523)	427 (2043)	489 (1146)	557 (6803)	622 (3168)
356 (4896)	428 (2890)	490 (4289)	558 (6804)	623 (4691)
357 (3714)	429 (1618)	491 (1909)	559 (6805)	624 (538)
358 (6774)	430 (4475)	492 (1910)	562 (3461)	625 (6816)
359 (6775)	431 (4380)	495 (3525)	563 (1000)	626 (1915)
360 (3524)	433 (214)	496 (3526)	565 (3462)	627 (3169)
362 (998)	434 (4506)	497 (4290)	566 (6806)	628 (6817)
366 (1905)	435 (4507)	499 (1911)	567 (1430)	629 (6818)
367 (6776)	436 (4508)	500 (1912)	568 (6807)	630 (4692)
368 (3164)	437 (215)	501 (4938)	569 (4900)	632 (4345)
369 (1906)	438 (4509)	502 (3166)	570 (4682)	633 (824)
370 (2040)	439 (573)	503 (3577)	571 (1001)	634 (1147)
371 (2539)	440 (1952)	504 (3762)	572 (2222)	635 (1148)
372 (2540)	441 (2044)	505 (1646)	573 (4683)	636 (4902)
373 (6777)	442 (3062)	506 (358)	574 (4684)	638 (80)
374 (2759)	443 (2557)	507 (359)	575 (4219)	639 (4524)
377 (6778)	444 (2558)	508 (4343)	576 (4516)	640 (1431)
379 (4565)	446 (2559)	509 (4899)	577 (4517)	641 (3096)
380 (6779)	447 (4217)	510 (3167)	578 (4685)	642 (2439)
381 (4975)	448 (3063)	511 (6795)	579 (4686)	643 (4693)
383 (6780)	450 (3316)	512 (6796)	580 (823)	644 (190)
384 (2204)	451 (2542)	513 (6797)	581 (536)	645 (3765)
385 (1617)	452 (533)	514 (360)	582 (1462)	646 (6819)
386 (4678)	454 (2672)	516 (535)	583 (4687)	647 (6820)
387 (108)	455 (1145)	517 (3763)	584 (6808)	648 (539)
388 (109)	456 (4680)	518 (1087)	586 (6809)	649 (3766)
389 (6781)	457 (79)	519 (2804)	587 (6810)	650 (1916)
390 (6782)	458 (6791)	520 (2673)	588 (1661)	651 (6821)
391 (4880)	459 (1908)	521 (1913)	589 (2438)	652 (1090)
392 (2101)	461 (4476)	522 (3205)	590 (1088)	653 (4882)

Volume X⁴ A

654	(5043)
655	(2440)
656	(1272)
658	(540)
659	(361)
660	(4694)
661	(6822)
662	(3057)
663	(6823)
667	(4567)
669	(1002)
670	(4695)
671	(3528)
672	(5023)
673	(6824)
674	(6825)

Volume X⁵ A

4	(3767)
5	(4525)
7	(1488)
8	(1489)
9	(1917)
10	(3170)
11	(4696)
12	(3022)
13	(1273)
14	(3659)
15	(2894)
17	(4903)
18	(4977)
19	(3768)
21	(6826)
22	(239)
23	(1432)
24	(4477)
25	(3769)
26	(2102)
27	(1918)
28	(4697)
29	(3770)
30	(4698)
31	(115)
32	(116)
33	(6831)
34	(2441)
35	(4315)
36	(541)
37	(4346)
38	(4699)
39	(1433)
40	(4904)
41	(4940)
42	(401)
43	(6832)
44	(1919)
45	(1920)

Volume X⁵ A

46	(6834)
47	(2561)
48	(2895)
49	(1662)
50	(2442)
51	(2132)
52	(2133)
53	(3771)
54	(1490)
55	(1434)
56	(1491)
57	(3529)
58	(3772)
59	(6835)
62	(3530)
63	(4518)
64	(1492)
65	(4803)
66	(2896)
67	(6836)
68	(3773)
69	(4294)
72	(6837)
73	(2823)
75	(3123)
76	(1075)
78	(2897)
79	(3774)
81	(4700)
82	(4478)
84	(4568)
85	(4701)
86	(2562)
87	(1921)
88	(1922)
93	(6838)
94	(177)
95	(4479)
96	(2898)
97	(2045)
98	(542)
99	(178)
100	(3206)
101	(1493)
102	(2729)
103	(1494)
104	(6839)
105	(6840)
106	(710)
107	(402)
108	(1495)
109	(1496)
110	(403)
111	(3207)
113	(3317)
114	(4702)

Volume X⁵ A

115	(4220)
116	(1435)
117	(3531)
118	(4905)
119	(6841)
120	(20)
121	(2046)
122	(2730)
123	(2967)
130	(2723)
131	(362)
132	(2223)
133	(4295)
134	(3864)
135	(2899)
136	(4221)
138	(2171)
139	(1923)
140	(2900)
142	(3097)
143	(3350)
144	(543)
145	(544)
146	(6843)
148	(6471)
149	(6472)
150	(6473)
152	(6331)
153	(6332)
156	(2202)
158	(6306)
159	(3064)
162	(2105)
163	(3138)
164	(3139)
165	(6584)
166	(6746)
167	(6747)

Volume X⁵ B

117	(2033)
206	(6518)
244	(2021)
245	(595)
263	(6675)
264	(6676)

Volume X⁶ B

4:3	(6770)
6	(6829)
7	(6830)
17	(3576)
40	(6256)
41	(6257)
48	(6349)
52:1	(2020)
68	(6598)
69	(6599)

Volume X⁶ B

77	(6600)
78	(9)
79	(10)
80	(11)
81	(12)
82	(6601)
83	(6403)
84	(6404)
85	(6405)
86	(6406)
93	(6663)
105	(6475)
121	(6574)
127	(6566)
128	(6596)
130	(6558)
131	(6559)
137	(6636)
145	(6786)
162	(6637)
163	(6638)
164	(6639)
167	(6640)
169	(6641)
171	(6748)
173	(6749)
188	(6750)
194	(6751)
226	(6833)
227	(3580)
232	(6842)
233	(825)
239	(3442)
241	(1863)
245	(6567)
253	(6787)
254	(6788)
257	(4218)
259	(6789)
260	(6790)

Volume X⁶ C

1	(6296)
2	(6297)
4	(6827)
5	(6828)
6	(6829)
6:1	(3331)
7	(6830)

Volume XI¹ A

1	(6853)
2	(3648)
3	(4804)
4	(1924)
5	(1436)
6	(6856)
7	(4906)

Volume XI¹ A

8	(4704)
9	(4705)
11	(3463)
13	(363)
14	(1619)
15	(4296)
16	(2968)
17	(4223)
18	(4224)
19	(3532)
20	(4805)
21	(2134)
22	(1925)
23	(1274)
24	(1275)
25	(2172)
26	(2901)
27	(1926)
28	(711)
29	(4907)
30	(4225)
31	(3236)
33	(3663)
34	(4347)
35	(1437)
36	(2047)
37	(2563)
38	(696)
39	(545)
40	(2674)
41	(1927)
42	(2048)
43	(1801)
45	(364)
47	(6857)
49	(6858)
51	(3219)
52	(2615)
53	(3171)
54	(4226)
55	(3582)
56	(6859)
57	(4883)
59	(697)
60	(2049)
61	(2546)
62	(3560)
63	(4495)
64	(2969)
65	(2564)
66	(4706)
67	(3649)
68	(3172)
69	(6860)
70	(546)
71	(6861)

Volume XI[1] A	Volume XI[1] A	Volume XI[1] A	Volume XI[1] A	Volume XI[1] A
72 (6862)	132 (2231)	195 (3065)	263 (2764)	327 (4952)
73 (2902)	133 (6871)	196 (3066)	264 (551)	329 (4806)
74 (4496)	134 (2762)	197 (1804)	265 (552)	330 (4231)
75 (3872)	136 (6872)	198 (2763)	266 (4528)	332 (555)
76 (6863)	137 (6873)	199 (3620)	267 (3632)	333 (556)
77 (2547)	138 (2905)	201 (4569)	268 (2096)	334 (4298)
78 (3873)	139 (2224)	202 (3585)	269 (4732)	335 (1963)
79 (3775)	140 (3876)	203 (3586)	270 (733)	336 (1805)
80 (2329)	141 (4998)	204 (3041)	271 (3834)	337 (1806)
81 (2050)	142 (6874)	205 (2330)	272 (2059)	338 (1931)
82 (2051)	143 (3777)	206 (6880)	274 (3237)	339 (3023)
83 (3958)	144 (3877)	208 (4707)	275 (6888)	340 (4709)
84 (5024)	146 (4884)	209 (6881)	276 (6889)	341 (3221)
85 (2761)	148 (2053)	210 (6882)	277 (6890)	342 (2174)
86 (3173)	149 (6876)	211 (4348)	278 (733)	343 (1765)
87 (3618)	150 (2617)	212 (4527)	279 (2443)	344 (3178)
88 (3174)	151 (2225)	213 (3621)	280 (365)	345 (2731)
89 (3533)	152 (2226)	214 (6883)	281 (5003)	346 (2975)
90 (6864)	153 (6877)	215 (6884)	282 (5004)	347 (216)
91 (547)	154 (2906)	216 (6885)	283 (3778)	348 (4499)
92 (6865)	155 (2907)	217 (2805)	284 (200)	349 (557)
93 (4227)	156 (3336)	219 (3966)	285 (3903)	350 (4710)
94 (2824)	157 (2908)	220 (3967)	286 (5027)	351 (4909)
95 (4908)	158 (1929)	221 (3968)	287 (2973)	352 (4885)
96 (2052)	159 (3833)	222 (550)	288 (1832)	353 (1066)
97 (3220)	160 (2107)	224 (3622)	289 (3643)	354 (3222)
98 (4228)	161 (3337)	225 (81)	291 (5028)	355 (4886)
99 (4229)	162 (3338)	226 (5000)	292 (4733)	356 (2444)
100 (3583)	164 (4999)	227 (2970)	293 (553)	357 (4711)
101 (3584)	165 (3878)	228 (3175)	294 (6891)	358 (83)
102 (4497)	167 (4526)	229 (3176)	295 (2620)	359 (1439)
103 (4979)	168 (2054)	230 (3177)	296 (4922)	360 (3039)
104 (1928)	169 (2618)	231 (5001)	297 (2551)	361 (2331)
105 (4498)	171 (6878)	232 (2173)	298 (2552)	362 (698)
106 (3619)	172 (3534)	233 (5002)	299 (3098)	363 (4349)
107 (2903)	173 (111)	234 (2971)	300 (6892)	364 (3602)
108 (2548)	175 (2055)	235 (2972)	301 (5029)	366 (4232)
110 (2904)	176 (1518)	236 (82)	302 (5030)	367 (3361)
111 (3874)	177 (6879)	237 (180)	306 (1930)	368 (2063)
112 (3875)	178 (3879)	242 (6886)	307 (19)	369 (2064)
113 (3601)	179 (3880)	243 (5025)	308 (405)	370 (2065)
114 (2664)	180 (1620)	245 (404)	309 (406)	371 (4299)
115 (4980)	181 (3881)	246 (3208)	310 (2060)	372 (2976)
116 (3776)	182 (3882)	247 (3623)	311 (4708)	373 (2977)
118 (4230)	183 (1621)	248 (5044)	313 (2621)	374 (2232)
120 (1301)	184 (2227)	250 (2676)	315 (6893)	375 (3238)
121 (6866)	185 (4981)	251 (5045)	316 (2909)	376 (3779)
123 (548)	186 (2724)	252 (1003)	318 (4297)	377 (4712)
124 (549)	187 (2725)	253 (2619)	319 (2061)	378 (6894)
125 (6867)	188 (1438)	254 (5026)	320 (2062)	380 (4570)
126 (3133)	189 (2056)	255 (2135)	321 (2097)	381 (1440)
127 (2549)	190 (2057)	257 (5046)	322 (2108)	382 (6895)
128 (6868)	191 (4982)	258 (6887)	323 (2109)	383 (6896)
129 (2616)	192 (1149)	259 (3969)	324 (554)	384 (2066)
130 (1802)	193 (2550)	260 (2058)	325 (2974)	385 (84)
131 (6870)	194 (1803)	261 (4921)	326 (845)	386 (85)

Volume XI¹ A	Volume XI¹ A	Volume XI¹ A	Volume XI¹ A	Volume XI² A
387 (2978)	445 (6902)	505 (6908)	564 (4486)	29 (4489)
388 (1647)	446 (1648)	506 (2073)	565 (728)	30 (4382)
389 (3179)	447 (1811)	507 (4233)	566 (5033)	31 (6919)
390 (3180)	448 (4302)	508 (4888)	567 (5034)	32 (6920)
391 (1932)	449 (4303)	510 (6909)	568 (4914)	33 (4383)
392 (2910)	450 (3587)	511 (2666)	569 (2693)	35 (5048)
393 (3223)	451 (1004)	512 (2980)	570 (827)	36 (6921)
394 (826)	452 (2912)	513 (2981)	571 (2913)	37 (2333)
395 (2911)	453 (4941)	514 (2982)	572 (2554)	38 (3210)
396 (1933)	454 (2979)	515 (1813)	573 (1936)	39 (2379)
397 (4529)	455 (2070)	516 (4911)	574 (4487)	40 (6922)
398 (4530)	456 (4480)	517 (4912)	575 (4488)	41 (4355)
399 (4807)	457 (4481)	518 (2074)	576 (2076)	42 (4490)
400 (2098)	458 (4942)	519 (5031)	577 (1955)	43 (2569)
402 (1807)	459 (2449)	520 (2332)	578 (3464)	44 (6923)
403 (1808)	460 (6903)	521 (4944)	579 (4722)	45 (6924)
404 (4713)	461 (3865)	522 (1176)	580 (4723)	46 (3561)
405 (2445)	462 (2665)	523 (3024)	581 (3590)	47 (559)
406 (2446)	463 (1953)	524 (4352)	582 (2983)	48 (828)
407 (86)	464 (1441)	525 (3736)	583 (3868)	49 (560)
408 (87)	465 (3866)	526 (4913)	584 (3184)	50 (5049)
409 (1091)	466 (3603)	527 (4304)	585 (3043)	51 (3099)
410 (794)	467 (3588)	528 (1005)	586 (6914)	52 (3100)
411 (2447)	468 (4810)	529 (408)	587 (2077)	53 (1444)
412 (6897)	469 (6904)	532 (3182)	588 (1937)	54 (2570)
413 (4714)	472 (4482)	533 (2075)	589 (2567)	55 (2571)
414 (2448)	473 (3589)	534 (4500)	590 (2568)	56 (2572)
415 (2067)	474 (6905)	535 (4811)	591 (1443)	57 (4986)
417 (3181)	475 (4483)	536 (4234)	592 (88)	58 (3885)
418 (4892)	476 (1812)	537 (3883)	593 (6915)	59 (3886)
419 (4808)	477 (3535)	538 (4353) Volume XI² A	Volume XI² A	60 (4916)
420 (4809)	478 (4484)	539 (1814)	1 (2678)	61 (6925)
421 (2068)	479 (727)	540 (1815)	2 (4915)	62 (4356)
422 (4715)	480 (3604)	541 (4719)	3 (1224)	63 (1067)
423 (6898)	481 (4485)	542 (4720)	4 (1537)	64 (2104)
424 (6899)	482 (3042)	543 (6910)	5 (1538)	65 (3664)
425 (6900)	483 (366)	544 (4983)	6 (4049)	66 (4724)
426 (5005)	484 (6906)	545 (5032)	7 (3362)	67 (4725)
427 (4910)	485 (2071)	546 (602)	8 (2450)	68 (2667)
428 (4300)	486 (2566)	547 (1954)	9 (2451)	69 (2078)
429 (1809)	487 (4350)	548 (3183)	10 (3836)	70 (5006)
430 (4301)	488 (2136)	549 (2677)	11 (6916)	71 (3538)
431 (4531)	489 (2732)	550 (1935)	14 (4050)	72 (4726)
432 (1810)	490 (2072)	551 (6911)	15 (367)	73 (4491)
433 (4716)	491 (2099)	552 (3209)	16 (3040)	75 (6926)
434 (1092)	492 (1934)	553 (1442)	17 (2984)	76 (4813)
435 (2565)	493 (4717)	554 (4812)	18 (1150)	77 (1816)
436 (191)	494 (4718)	555 (4984)	19 (6917)	78 (6927)
437 (3624)	495 (3650)	556 (5047)	20 (3884)	79 (6928)
438 (4887)	497 (6907)	557 (3867)	21 (6918)	80 (614)
439 (6901)	498 (4351)	558 (4354)	22 (2772)	81 (3101)
440 (3835)	500 (2103)	559 (6912)	23 (4235)	82 (4727)
441 (2069)	501 (1562)	560 (6913)	24 (4236)	84 (1151)
442 (2553)	502 (4943)	561 (4721)	25 (368)	85 (4237)
443 (2765)	503 (407)	562 (4055)	26 (2985)	86 (4953)
444 (558)	504 (3536)	563 (4985)	27 (3537)	88 (2986)

Volume XI² A	Volume XI² A	Volume XI² A	Volume XI² A	Volume XI² A
89 (2987)	150 (2622)	213 (6933)	275 (2084)	348 (3781)
90 (2988)	151 (2995)	214 (3005)	278 (2684)	349 (409)
91 (2679)	152 (2575)	215 (3006)	279 (4360)	352 (4240)
92 (2989)	153 (2623)	216 (3592)	280 (829)	353 (4362)
93 (2990)	154 (2624)	217 (3227)	281 (3540)	354 (4573)
94 (3869)	155 (2996)	218 (3593)	282 (4978)	355 (3738)
95 (369)	156 (2997)	219 (5036)	283 (6844)	356 (4241)
96 (3644)	159 (2998)	220 (3007)	284 (1497)	358 (1939)
97 (4571)	160 (2625)	221 (563)	285 (1498)	360 (2085)
98 (1445)	161 (4057)	222 (2337)	286 (1499)	361 (2086)
99 (1446)	162 (3625)	223 (5037)	288 (6845)	362 (3871)
100 (1500)	163 (3044)	224 (1519)	289 (3541)	363 (2773)
101 (6929)	164 (370)	225 (4492)	291 (4222)	364 (2917)
102 (561)	166 (2576)	226 (1502)	292 (4239)	366 (4574)
103 (2359)	167 (2999)	227 (4889)	294 (1800)	367 (1504)
104 (4945)	168 (3000)	228 (4358)	295 (3581)	368 (3596)
105 (2452)	169 (3001)	229 (603)	296 (6846)	370 (6948)
106 (4056)	170 (1450)	230 (3008)	297 (4703)	371 (6949)
107 (3224)	171 (1451)	231 (2628)	298 (3780)	372 (2631)
108 (4238)	172 (2626)	232 (4493)	301 (2543)	373 (4503)
109 (2991)	174 (2914)	233 (3594)	302 (11)	374 (6950)
110 (562)	175 (1452)	234 (1649)	303 (2544)	375 (565)
111 (4501)	176 (2627)	235 (1650)	304 (2545)	376 (3597)
112 (4502)	177 (3225)	237 (1956)	305 (3617)	377 (6951)
113 (1006)	178 (3226)	238 (2629)	311 (6847)	378 (4363)
114 (2205)	179 (1453)	239 (5032)	312 (6848)	379 (6952)
115 (1152)	180 (1454)	241 (2630)	313 (1820)	380 (1154)
116 (2992)	181 (2915)	242 (4051)	314 (6849)	381 (1007)
117 (3870)	182 (1501)	243 (3009)	315 (564)	382 (4816)
118 (2573)	183 (1766)	244 (6934)	316 (2916)	383 (6953)
119 (1276)	184 (3002)	245 (1520)	317 (4361)	385 (2683)
121 (6930)	185 (3003)	246 (4359)	318 (4815)	386 (2918)
122 (1018)	187 (3211)	247 (1093)	319 (4058)	387 (2919)
123 (4814)	189 (1767)	248 (6935)	320 (4919)	390 (2453)
124 (2079)	190 (1768)	249 (3539)	321 (6850)	395 (2920)
125 (2080)	191 (2303)	250 (6936)	323 (2681)	396 (4730)
127 (2993)	192 (5007)	251 (6937)	324 (3010)	397 (2733)
128 (2334)	193 (5008)	252 (6938)	325 (3212)	398 (2626)
129 (2335)	194 (2555)	253 (6939)	326 (2682)	399 (6958)
130 (1447)	195 (1817)	254 (6940)	327 (3124)	400 (3186)
131 (1448)	196 (4572)	255 (1769)	328 (181)	401 (3187)
132 (4384)	197 (1938)	256 (6941)	330 (256)	402 (3228)
133 (1449)	198 (4357)	257 (6942)	331 (830)	403 (2921)
134 (6931)	199 (729)	259 (2083)	332 (3696)	404 (192)
135 (2081)	200 (730)	260 (688)	334 (6851)	405 (2744)
136 (4728)	201 (1818)	261 (1277)	335 (6852)	406 (6955)
138 (2680)	202 (3970)	262 (2668)	336 (1153)	407 (6956)
139 (89)	203 (5035)	263 (615)	338 (3616)	409 (6959)
140 (90)	204 (4917)	264 (1819)	339 (2726)	410 (4504)
142 (3987)	205 (4918)	266 (2556)	340 (3720)	411 (6964)
143 (3988)	206 (6932)	267 (1822)	341 (616)	416 (4505)
144 (2574)	208 (4729)	270 (3595)	342 (1503)	421 (2454)
146 (2994)	209 (3591)	271 (1823)	343 (4059)	422 (731)
147 (2336)	210 (3067)	272 (1824)	344 (1821)	424 (1278)
148 (3185)	211 (3004)	273 (3718)	346 (3737)	426 (2455)
149 (2082)	212 (3102)	274 (3719)	347 (3339)	427 (2685)

Volume XI² A	Volume XI³ B	Volume XI³ B	Letters	Letters
431 (3229)	57 (6947)	260:8 (2577)	68 (5551)	155 (note 1652)
434 (1940)	93 (6954)	291:4 (6965)	69 (5552)	156 (6047)
435 (2687)	109 (3069)	Letters	71 (5527)	157 (6048)
436 (6966)	115 (2774)	2 (5051)	80 (5655)	161 (6057)
437 (6967)	120 (6957)	4 (note 109)	82 (5665)	166 (6090)
438 (6968)	124 (846)	15 (5477)	83 (5679)	167 (6091)
439 (6969)	125:8 (847)	17 (5478)	101 (5711)	180 (6197)
Volume XI³ B	126 (4242)	18 (5479)	107 (5727)	192 (6267)
13 (6869)	128 (6960)	21 (5480)	113 (5757)	195 (6294)
15 (6854)	129 (6961)	23 (5481)	119 (5806)	196 (6295)
28 (6855)	131 (6962)	27 (5482)	120a (5852)	213 (6434)
43 (3068)	132 (6963)	29 (5483)	134 (5910)	239 (6537)
45 (3837)	146 (4533)	42 (5505)	136 (5911)	240 (6560)
47 (4532)	148 (4494)	49 (5513)	149 (6003)	243 (6381)
49 (6875)	175 (3213)	54 (5542)	150 (6063)	257 (6606)
53 (6943)	177 (2686)	55 (5543)	152 (6030)	262 (note 2648)
54 (6944)	197 (3188)	56 (5544)	153 (note 1650)	265 (note 2733)
55 (6945)	199 (1825)	62 (5548)	154 (6046)	276 (6799)
56 (6946)				